G·L·O·B·A·L S·T·U·D·I·E·S

CHINA

EIGHTH EDITION

Dr. Suzanne Ogden

Northeastern University

OTHER BOOKS IN THE GLOBAL STUDIES SERIES

- Africa
- India and South Asia
- Japan and the Pacific Rim
- Latin America
- The Middle East
- Russia, the Eurasian Republics, and Central/Eastern Europe
- Western Europe

Dushkin/McGraw-Hill
Sluice Dock, Guilford, Connecticut 06437
Visit us on the Internet—http://www.dushkin.com

STAFF

Ian A. Nielsen	Publisher
Brenda S. Filley	Production Manager
Lisa M. Clyde	Developmental Editor
Roberta Monaco	Editor
Charles Vitelli	Designer
Cheryl Greenleaf	Permissions Coordinator
Lisa Holmes-Doebrick	Administrative Coordinator
Lara M. Johnson	Design/Advertising Coordinator
Laura Levine	Graphics
Michael Campbell	Graphics
Tom Goddard	Graphics
Juliana Arbo	Typesetting Supervisor

Cataloging in Publication Data
Main Entry under title: Global Studies: China. 8th ed.
     1. China—History—1976–. 2. Taiwan—History—1945–. I. Title: China. II. Ogden, Suzanne, *comp.*
ISBN 0–07–024969–5

Eighth Edition

We would like to thank Digital Wisdom Inc. for allowing us to use their Mountain High Maps cartography software. This software was used to create the relief maps in this edition.

Printed in the United States of America   1234567890BAHBAH5432109   Printed on Recycled Paper

China

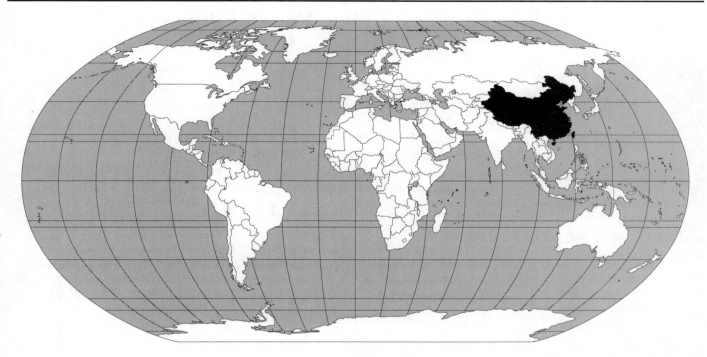

AUTHOR/EDITOR
Dr. Suzanne Ogden

Dr. Suzanne Ogden is professor of the Political Science Department at Northeastern University and research associate at the Fairbank Center for East Asian Research, Harvard University. She has lived in both Taiwan and Hong Kong and has traveled frequently to the People's Republic of China. Dr. Ogden is the author of *China's Unresolved Issues: Politics, Development, and Culture* (Prentice Hall, 1989, 1992, 1995), and chief editor and project director of *China's Search for Democracy: The Student and Mass Movement of 1989* (M. E. Sharpe, 1992). Dr. Ogden's current research is focused on democratization in the P.R.C.

SERIES CONSULTANT
H. Thomas Collins
PROJECT LINKS
George Washington University

Contents

Global Studies: China, Eighth Edition

People's Republic of China   Page 24

Taiwan   Page 60

Hong Kong   Page 82

Using Global Studies: China

THE GLOBAL STUDIES SERIES

The Global Studies series was created to help readers acquire a basic knowledge and understanding of the regions and countries in the world. Each volume provides a foundation of information—geographic, cultural, economic, political, historical, artistic, and religious—that will allow readers to better assess the current and future problems within these countries and regions and to comprehend how events there might affect their own well-being. In short, these volumes present the background information necessary to respond to the realities of our global age.

Each of the volumes in the Global Studies series is crafted under the careful direction of an author/editor—an expert in the area under study. The author/editors teach and conduct research and have traveled extensively through the regions about which they are writing.

MAJOR FEATURES OF
GLOBAL STUDIES: CHINA

The Global Studies volumes are organized to provide concise information on the regions and countries within those areas under study. The major sections and features of this volume are described here.

Country Reports

Concise reports are written for each of the countries within the region under study. These reports are the heart of each Global Studies volume. *Global Studies: China, Eighth Edition,* contains three "country" reports: People's Republic of China, Taiwan (Republic of China), and Hong Kong (China Special Administrative Region).

Each report contains a detailed map visually positioning the country among its neighboring states; a summary of statistical information; and a current essay providing important historical, geographical, political, cultural, and economic information. A timeline is also provided in the report on the People's Republic of China.

A Note on the Statistical Reports

The statistical information has been drawn from a wide range of sources. (The most frequently referenced are listed on page 202.) Every effort has been made to provide the most current and accurate information available. However, sometimes the information cited by these sources differs to some extent; and sometimes the information available for some countries is dated. Aside from these occasional difficulties, the statistical summaries are generally up to date. Care should be taken, however, in using these statistics (or, for that matter, any published statistics) in making hard comparisons among countries. We have also provided comparable statistics for the United States and Canada, which can be found on pages viii and ix.

World Press Articles

Within each Global Studies volume is reprinted a number of articles carefully selected by our editorial staff and the author/editor from a broad range of international periodicals and newspapers. The articles have been chosen for currency, interest, and their differing perspectives on the subject countries. There are 28 articles in *Global Studies: China, Eighth Edition.*

The articles section is preceded by an annotated table of contents as well as a topic guide. The annotated table of contents offers a brief summary of each article, while the topic guide indicates the main theme(s) of each article. Thus, readers desiring to focus on articles dealing with a particular theme, say, the environment, may refer to the topic guide to find those articles.

WWW Sites

An extensive annotated list of selected World Wide Web sites can be found on the facing page (vii) in this edition of *Global Studies: China.* In addition, the URL addresses for country-specific Web sites are provided on the statistics page of most countries. All of the Web site addresses were correct and operational at press time. Instructors and students alike are urged to refer to those sites often to enhance their understanding of the region and to keep up with current events.

Glossary, Bibliography, Index

At the back of each Global Studies volume, readers will find a glossary of terms and abbreviations, which provides a quick reference to the specialized vocabulary of the area under study and to the standard abbreviations used throughout the volume.

Following the glossary is a bibliography, which lists general works, national histories, and current-events publications and periodicals that provide regular coverage on the People's Republic of China, Taiwan and Hong Kong.

The index at the end of the volume is an accurate reference to the contents of the volume. Readers seeking specific information and citations should consult this standard index.

Currency and Usefulness

Global Studies: China, like the other Global Studies volumes, is intended to provide the most current and useful information available necessary to understand the events that are shaping the cultures of the region today.

This volume is revised on a regular basis. The statistics are updated, regional essays and country reports revised, and world press articles replaced. In order to accomplish this task, we turn to our author/editor, our advisory boards, and—hopefully—to you, the users of this volume. Your comments are more than welcome. If you have an idea that you think will make the next edition more useful, an article or bit of information that will make it more current, or a general comment on its organization, content, or features that you would like to share with us, please send it in for serious consideration.

Selected World Wide Web Sites for *Global Studies: China*

(Some Web sites continually change their structure and content, so the information listed here may not always be available.—Ed.)

GENERAL SITES

BBC World Service—**http://www.bbc.co.uk/worldservice/index. htm**—The BBC, one of the world's most successful radio networks, provides the latest news from around the world, including China, Taiwan, and Hong Kong. It is possible to access the news in several languages.

CNN Online Page—**http://www.cnn.com**—U.S. 24-hour video news channel. News, updated every few hours, includes text, pictures, and film. Good external links.

C-SPAN ONLINE—**http://www.c-span.org**—See C-SPAN International on the Web for International Programming Highlights and archived C-SPAN programs.

International Network Information Center at University of Texas—**http://inic.utexas.edu**—Gateway has pointers to international sites, including China, Hong Kong, and Taiwan.

I-Trade International Trade Resources & Data Exchange—**http://www.i-trade.com**—Find monthly exchange-rate data, U.S. Document Export Market Information (GEMS), U.S. Global Trade Outlook, and recent World Factbook statistical demographic and geographic data for over 180 countries.

Penn Library: Resources by Subject—**http://www.library. upenn. edu/resources/subject/subject.html**—This vast site is rich in links to information about Asian studies, including population and demography.

Political Science RESOURCES—**http://www.psr.keele.ac.uk**—Dynamic gateway to country sources available via European addresses. Included are official government pages, documents, speeches, elections, and political events.

ReliefWeb—**http://wwwnotes.reliefweb.int**—UN's Department of Humanitarian Affairs clearinghouse for international humanitarian emergencies. Has daily updates, including Reuters, VOA, PANA.

Social Science Information Gateway (SOSIG)—**http://sosig. esrc.bris.ac.uk**—Project of the Economic and Social Research Council (ESRC). It catalogs 22 subjects and lists developing countries' URL addresses.

Speech and Transcript Center—**http://gwis2.circ.gwu.edu/~ gprice/speech.htm**—This unusual site is the repository of transcripts of every kind, from radio and television, to speeches by world government leaders, and the proceedings of groups such as the United Nations, NATO, and the World Bank.

United Nations System—**http://www.unsystem.org**—This is the official Web site for the UN system of organizations.

UN Development Programme (UNDP)—**http://www.undp. org**—Publications and current information on world poverty, Mission Statement, UN Development Fund for Women, and more. Be sure to see Poverty Clock.

UN Environmental Programme (UNEP)—**http://www.unchs. unon.org**—Official site of UNEP. Available are information on UN environmental programs, products, services, events, and a search engine.

U.S. Agency for International Development (USAID)—**http://www.info.usaid.gov**—U.S. trade statistics with China, Hong Kong, and Taiwan in graphic form are available at this site.

U.S. Central Intelligence Agency Home Page—**http://www. odci.gov/cia**—This site includes publications of the CIA, such as the World Factbook, Factbook on Intelligence, Handbook of International Economic Statistics, and CIA Maps.

U.S. Department of State Home Page—**http://www.state.gov/ index. html**—Organized by categories: Hot Topics (i.e. Latest Country Reports on Human Rights Practices), International Policy, Business Services.

World Bank Group—**http://www.worldbank.org/html/Welcome. html**—News (i.e. press releases, summary of new projects, speeches), publications, topics in development, countries and regions. Links to other financial organizations, including IBRD, IDA, IFC, MIGA.

World Health Organization (WHO)—**http://www.who.ch**—Maintained by WHO's headquarters in Geneva, Switzerland, this site uses Excite search engine to conduct keyword searches.

World Trade Organization—**http://www.wto.org**—Topics include the foundation of world trade systems, data on textiles, intellectual property rights, legal frameworks, trade and environmental policies, recent agreements, etc.

GENERAL CHINA, TAIWAN, AND HONG KONG SITES

Asia Web Watch—**http://www.ciolek.com/Asia-Web-Watch/ main-page.html**—Here is a register of statistical data that can be accessed alphabetically. Data includes Asian Online Materials statistics and Appendices about Asian cyberspace.

Asian Arts—**http://asianart.com**—This online journal provides for the study and exhibition of Asian arts.

Asian Studies WWW Virtual Library—**http://coombs.anu. edu.au/WWWVL-AsianStudies.html**—Australia National University maintains these sites, which link to many other Web sources, and are available at each country's location.

PEOPLE'S REPUBLIC OF CHINA

Information Office of State Council of People's Republic of China—**http://www.cityu.edu.hk/HumanRights/index.htm**—Official site of China's government. It contains policy statements that are related to human rights.

Inside China Today—**http://www.insidechina.com**—This Web site is part of the European Information Network, and contains Headline News, Government, and Related Sites, as well as Mainland China, Hong Kong, Macao, and Taiwan.

TAIWAN

Taiwan Government Information Office—**http://www.roc-taiwan. org**—This is a good starting place for all kinds of information about Taiwan. It includes Web sites and search engines.

HONG KONG

Hong Kong Internet & Gateway Services—**http://www. hk.net**—This gateway has up-to-date information about Hong Kong, past and present, and also contains a search engine.

Hong Kong News Stand—**http://www.asiadragons.com/hong_ kong/news/**—This site leads to many additional Hong Kong news sites and to Hong Kong Online. It also includes Hong Kong NetSearch.

Hong Kong SAR Government Information Centre—**http:// info.gov.hk/frame1886851.html**—Access government information, budget data, news, basic law, and much more here.

See individual statistics pages for additional Web sites.

The United States (United States of America)

GEOGRAPHY

Area in Square Miles (Kilometers):
3,618,770 (9,578,626) (slightly larger than China)

Capital (Population): Washington, D.C. (567,100)

Environmental Concerns: air pollution resulting in acid rain; water pollution from runoff of pesticides and fertilizers; desertification; habitat loss; other concerns

Geographical Features: vast central plain, mountains in the west; hills and low mountains in the east; rugged mountains and broad river valleys in Alaska; volcanic topography in Hawaii

Climate: mostly temperate; wide regional variations

PEOPLE

Population

Total: 270,312,000

Annual Growth Rate: 0.87%

Rural/Urban Population Ratio: 24/76

Major Languages: predominantly English; a sizable Spanish-speaking minority; many others

Ethnic Makeup: 83% white; 12% black; 5% Asian, Amerindian, and others

Religions: 56% Protestant; 28% Roman Catholic; 2% Jewish; 14% others or no affiliation

Health

Life Expectancy at Birth: 73 years (male); 80 years (female)

Infant Mortality Rate (Ratio): 6.44/1,000

Average Caloric Intake: 138% of FAO minimum

Physicians Available (Ratio): 1/381

Education

Adult Literacy Rate: 97.9% (official) (estimates vary widely)

Compulsory (Ages): 7–16; free

COMMUNICATION

Telephones: 1 per 1.6 people

Daily Newspaper Circulation: 228 per 1,000 people; approximately 63,000,000 circulation

Televisions: 1 per 1.2 people

TRANSPORTATION

Highways in Miles (Kilometers): 3,906,960 (6,261,154)

Railroads in Miles (Kilometers): 149,161 (240,000)

Usable Airfields: 13,387

Motor Vehicles in Use: 200,500,000

GOVERNMENT

Type: federal republic

Independence Date: July 4, 1776 (from United Kingdom)

Head of State: President William ("Bill") Jefferson Clinton

Political Parties: Democratic Party; Republican Party; others of minor political significance

Suffrage: universal at 18

MILITARY

Military Expenditures (% of GDP): 3.8%

Current Disputes: none

ECONOMY

Per Capita Income/GDP: $30,200/$8.08 trillion

GDP Growth Rate: 3.8%

Inflation Rate: 2%

Unemployment Rate: 4.9%

Labor Force: 136,300,000

Natural Resources: metallic and non-metallic minerals; petroleum; natural gas; timber

Agriculture: food grains; feed crops; oil-bearing crops; livestock; dairy products

Industry: diversified in both capital- and consumer-goods industries

Exports: $625.1 billion (primary partners Canada, Western Europe, Japan, Mexico)

Imports: $822 billion (primary partners Canada, Western Europe, Japan, Mexico)

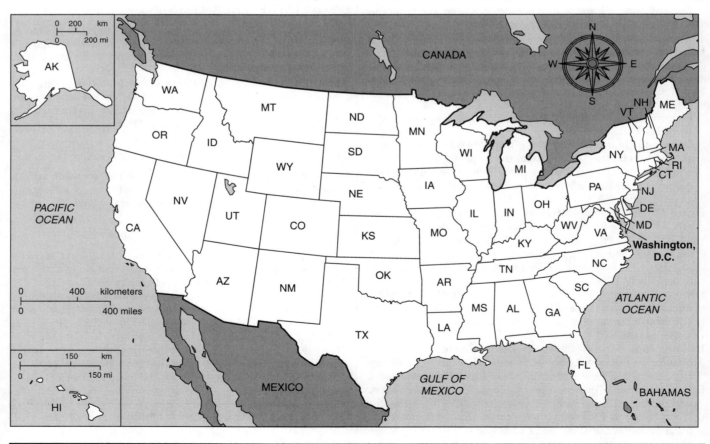

Canada*

GEOGRAPHY

Area in Square Miles (Kilometers):
3,850,790 (9,976,140) (slightly larger than the United States)

Capital (Population): Ottawa (1,000,000)

Environmental Concerns: air pollution and resulting acid rain severely affecting lakes and damaging forests; water pollution

Geographical Features: permafrost in the north; mountains in the west; central plains

Climate: from temperate in south to subarctic and arctic in north

PEOPLE

Population

Total: 30,676,000

Annual Growth Rate: 1.09%

Rural/Urban Population Ratio: 23/77

Major Languages: both English and French are official

Ethnic Makeup: 40% British Isles origin; 27% French origin; 20% other European; 1.5% indigenous Indian and Eskimo; 11.5% others, mostly Asian

Religions: 46% Roman Catholic; 16% United Church; 10% Anglican; 28% others

Health

Life Expectancy at Birth: 76 years (male); 83 years (female)

Infant Mortality Rate (Ratio): 5.59/1,000

Average Caloric Intake: 127% of FAO minimum

Physicians Available (Ratio): 1/464

Education

Adult Literacy Rate: 97%

Compulsory (Ages): primary school

COMMUNICATION

Telephones: 1 per 1.7 people

Daily Newspaper Circulation: 189 per 1,000 people

Televisions: 1 per 1.5 people

TRANSPORTATION

Highways in Miles (Kilometers): 637,104 (1,021,000)

Railroads in Miles (Kilometers): 48,764 (78,148)

Usable Airfields: 1,139

Motor Vehicles in Use: 16,700,000

GOVERNMENT

Type: confederation with parliamentary democracy

Independence Date: July 1, 1867 (from United Kingdom)

Head of State/Government: Queen Elizabeth II; Prime Minister Jean Chrétien

Political Parties: Progressive Conservative Party; Liberal Party; New Democratic Party; Reform Party; Bloc Québécois

Suffrage: universal at 18

MILITARY

Military Expenditures (% of GDP): 1.53%

Current Disputes: none

ECONOMY

Currency ($U.S. Equivalent): 1.53 Canadian dollars = $1

Per Capita Income/GDP: $21,700/$658 billion

GDP Growth Rate: 3.5%

Inflation Rate: 1.8%

Unemployment Rate: 8.6%

Labor Force: 15,300,000

Natural Resources: petroleum; coal; natural gas; fish and other wildlife; minerals; cement; forestry products

Agriculture: grains; livestock; dairy products; potatoes; hogs; poultry and eggs; tobacco

Industry: oil production and refining; natural-gas development; fish products; wood and paper products; chemicals; transportation equipment

Exports: $208.6 billion (primary partners United States, Japan, United Kingdom)

Imports: $194.4 billion (primary partners United States, Japan, United Kingdom)

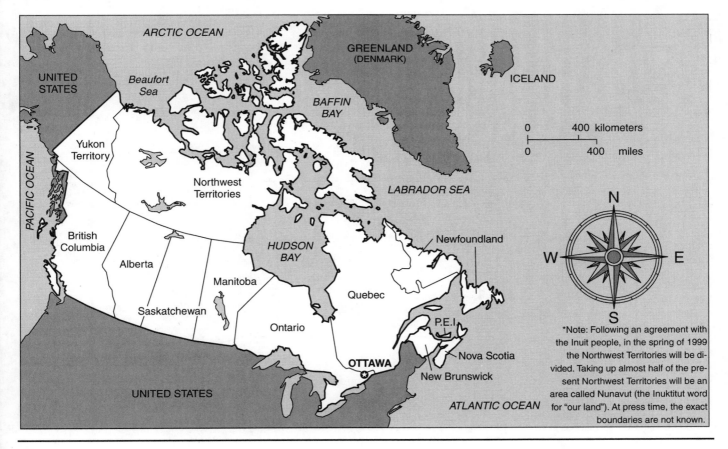

*Note: Following an agreement with the Inuit people, in the spring of 1999 the Northwest Territories will be divided. Taking up almost half of the present Northwest Territories will be an area called Nunavut (the Inuktitut word for "our land"). At press time, the exact boundaries are not known.

GLOBAL STUDIES

This map is provided to give you a graphic picture of where the countries of the world are located, the relationships they have with their region and neighbors, and their positions relative to the superpowers and power blocs. We have focused on certain areas to illustrate these crowded regions more clearly.

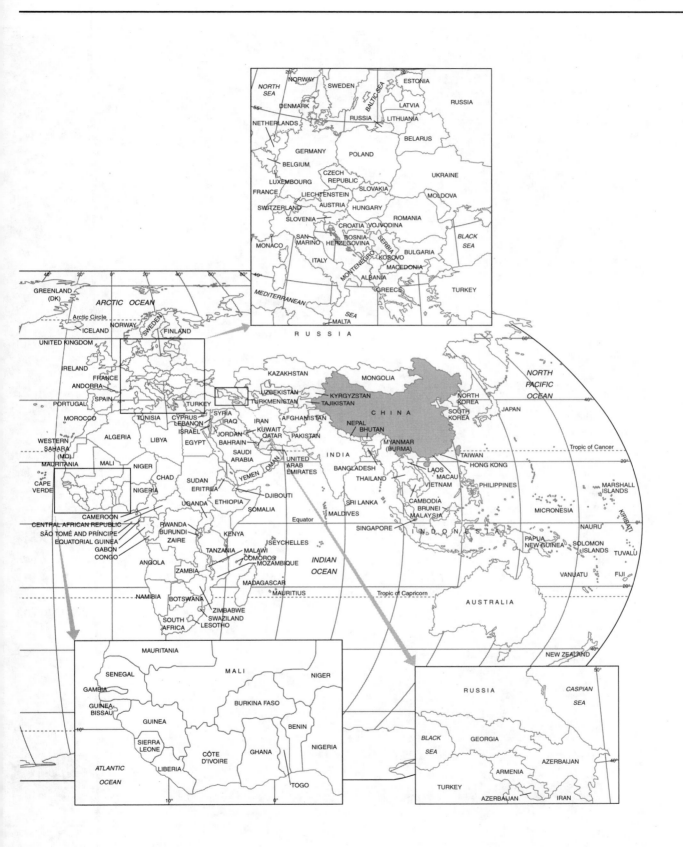

China

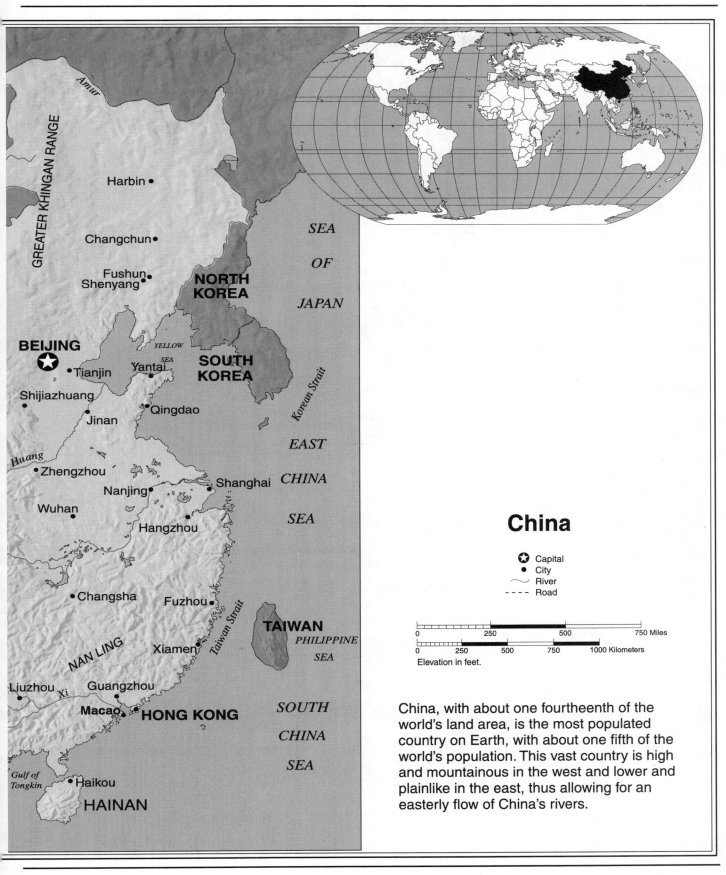

China

⭐ Capital
● City
〜 River
---- Road

0 — 250 — 500 — 750 Miles
0 — 250 — 500 — 750 — 1000 Kilometers
Elevation in feet.

China, with about one fourteenth of the world's land area, is the most populated country on Earth, with about one fifth of the world's population. This vast country is high and mountainous in the west and lower and plainlike in the east, thus allowing for an easterly flow of China's rivers.

China (People's Republic of China)

GEOGRAPHY
Area in Square Miles (Kilometers):
3,723,000 (9,596,960) (slightly smaller than the United States)
Capital (Population): Beijing (11,299,000)
Environmental Concerns: air and water pollution; water shortages; desertification; trade in endangered species; acid rain; loss of agricultural land to soil erosion and economic development
Geographical Features: mostly mountains, high plateaus, deserts in the west; plains, deltas, and hills in the east
Climate: extremely diverse; tropical to subarctic

PEOPLE

Population
Total: 1.3 billion
Annual Growth Rate: 0.93%
Rural/Urban Population Ratio: 71/29
Major Languages: Standard Chinese (Putonghua) or Mandarin; Yue (Cantonese); Wu (Shanghainese); Minbei (Fuzhou); Minuan (Hokkien-Taiwanese); Xiang; Gan; Hahka
Ethnic Makeup: 92% Han Chinese; 8% minority groups (the largest being Chuang, Hui, Uighur, Yi, and Miao)
Religions: officially atheist; but Taoism, Buddhism, Islam, Christianity, ancestor worship, and animism practiced

Health
Life Expectancy at Birth: 69 years (male); 71 years (female)
Infant Mortality Rate (Ratio): 37.9/1,000
Average Caloric Intake: 104% of FAO minimum
Physicians Available (Ratio): 1/630

Education
Adult Literacy Rate: 81.5%
Compulsory (Ages): 7–16

COMMUNICATION
Telephones: 1 per 30 people
Daily Newspaper Circulation: 23 per 1,000 people
Televisions: 1 per 5.3 people

TRANSPORTATION
Highways in Miles (Kilometers): 670,200 (1,117,000)
Railroads in Miles (Kilometers): 37,500 (62,500)
Usable Airfields: 206
Motor Vehicles in Use: 7,900,000

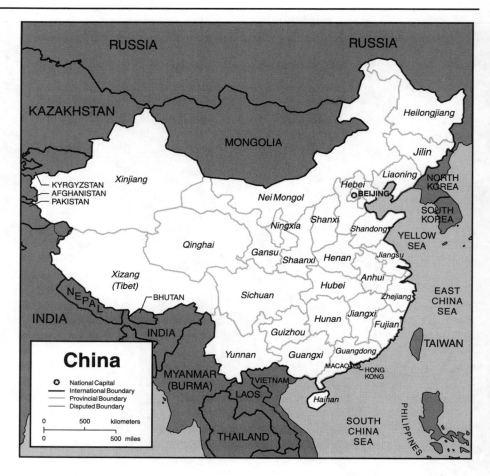

GOVERNMENT
Type: one-party Communist state
Independence Date: October 1, 1949
Head of State/Government: President Jiang Zemin; Premier Zhu Rongji
Political Parties: Chinese Communist Party; eight registered small parties controlled by the CCP
Suffrage: universal at 18 (but only in lower-level elections)

MILITARY
Military Expenditures (% of GDP): na
Current Disputes: boundary disputes with India

ECONOMY
Currency ($ U.S. Equivalent): 8.28 yuan = $1
Per Capita Income/GDP: $2,500/$2.97 trillion
GDP Growth Rate: 8.8%
Inflation Rate: 10%
Unemployment Rate: officially 3% in urban areas; probably 8%–10%

Labor Force: 614,700,000
Natural Resources: coal; petroleum; iron ore; tin; tungsten; antimony; lead; zinc; vanadium; magnetite; uranium
Agriculture: food grains; cotton; oil seeds; pork; fish; tea; potatoes; peanuts
Industry: iron and steel; coal; machinery; light industry; textiles and apparel; food processing; consumer durables and electronics; telecommunications; armaments
Exports: $151 billion (primary partners Hong Kong, Japan, United States)
Imports: $138.8 billion (primary partners Japan, United States, Taiwan)

http://www.chinaexpo.com/main.html
http://www.odci.gov/cia/publication/factbook/country-frame.html

People's Republic of China

Tensions between Modernization and Ideology

HISTORY

Chinese civilization originated in the Neolithic Period, which began around 5000 B.C., but scholars know little about it until the Shang Dynasty, which dates from about 2000 B.C. By that time, the Chinese had already developed the technology and art of bronze casting to a high standard; and they had a sophisticated system of writing with ideographs, in which words are portrayed as picturelike characters. From the fifth to the third centuries B.C., the level of literature and the arts was comparable to that of Greece in the Classical Period, which occurred at the same time. Science flourished, and the philosopher Confucius developed a highly sophisticated system of ethics for government and moral codes for society. Confucian values were dominant until the collapse of the Chinese imperial system in 1911, but even today they influence Chinese thought and behavior in China and Taiwan and in Chinese communities throughout the world.

The Chinese Empire

By 221 B.C., the many feudal states ruled by independent princes had been conquered by Qin (Ch'in) Shi Huang Di, the first ruler of a unified Chinese Empire. He established a system of governmental institutions and a concept of empire that continued in China until A.D. 1911. Although China was unified from the Qin Dynasty on, it was far less concrete than the term *empire* might indicate. China's borders really reached only as far as its cultural influence did. Thus China contracted and expanded according to whether or not other groups of people accepted the Chinese ruler and culture as their own.

Those peoples outside "China" who refused to acknowledge the Chinese ruler as the "Son of Heaven" or pay tribute to him were called "barbarians." In part, the Great Wall, which stretches more than 2,000 miles across north China and was built in stages between the third century B.C. and the seventeenth century A.D., was constructed in order to keep marauding "barbarians" out of China. Nevertheless, they frequently invaded China and occasionally even succeeded in subduing the Chinese—as in the Yuan (Mongol) Dynasty (1279–1368) and, later, the Qing (Ch'ing, or Manchu) Dynasty (1644–1911).

However, the customs and institutions of the invaders eventually yielded to the powerful cultural influence of the Chinese. Indeed, in the case of the Manchus, who seized control of the Chinese Empire in 1644 and ruled until 1911, their success in holding onto the throne for so long may be due in part to their willingness to assimilate Chinese ways and to rule through existing Chinese institutions, such as the Confucian-ordered bureaucracy. By the time of their overthrow, the Manchu rulers were hardly distinguishable from the pure (Han) Chinese in their customs, habits, and beliefs. When considering today's policies toward the numerous minorities who inhabit such a large expanse of the People's Republic of China, it should be remembered that the central Chinese government's ability to absorb minorities was the key to its success in maintaining a unified entity called *China* for more than 2,000 years.

The Imperial Bureaucracy

A distinguishing feature of the political system of imperial China was the civil-service examinations through which government officials were chosen. These examinations tested knowledge of the moral principles embodied in the classical Confucian texts. Although the exams were, in theory, open to all males in the Chinese Empire, the lengthy and rigorous preparation required meant that, in practice, the sons of the wealthy and powerful with access to a good education had an enormous advantage. Only a small percentage of those who began the process actually passed the examinations and received an appointment in the imperial bureaucracy. Those who were successful were sent as the emperor's agents to govern throughout the far-flung realm.

The Decline of the Manchus

The vitality of Chinese institutions and their ability to respond creatively to new problems came to an end during the Manchu Dynasty (1644–1911). This was due in part to internal rebellions, caused by a stagnant agriculture incapable of supporting the growing population and by increasing exploitation of the poor peasants who made up the vast majority of Chinese society. As the imperial bureaucracy and the emperor's court itself became increasingly corrupt and incompetent, they gradually lost the ability to govern the empire effectively. Furthermore, the social-class structure rewarded those who could pass the archaic, morality-based civil-service examination rather than scientists and others who could make contributions to China's material advancement.

China's decline in the nineteenth century was exacerbated by cultural "blinders" that prevented the Chinese from understanding the dynamism of the Industrial Revolution then taking place in the West. Gradually the barriers erected by the Manchu rulers to prevent Western culture and technology from polluting the ancient beauty of Chinese civilization were knocked down.

The Opium War

The British began importing opium into China in the nineteenth century. Eventually they used the Chinese attack on British ships carrying opium as an excuse for declaring war on the decaying and decrepit Chinese Empire. The Opium War (1839–1842) ended with defeat for the Chinese and the forcible entry of European merchants and missionaries into China.

Other wars brought further concessions—the most important of which was the Chinese granting of "treaty ports" to Europeans. These ports inevitably led to the spread of Western values that challenged the stagnant, and by then morally impotent, Chinese Empire. As the West and Japan nibbled away at China, the Manchu rulers made a last-ditch effort at reform, so as to strengthen and enrich China. But the combination of internal decay, provincialism, revolution, and foreign imperialism finally toppled the Manchu Dynasty. Thus ended more than 2,000 years of imperial rule in China.

REPUBLICAN CHINA

The 1911 Revolution, which derived its greatest inspiration from Sun Yat-sen (even though he was on a political fundraising trip in the United States when it happened), led to the establishment of the Republic of China (R.O.C.)—in name, if not in fact. China was briefly united under the control of the dominant warlord of the time, Yuan Shih-kai. But with his death in 1916, China was again torn apart by the resurgence of contending warlords, internal political decay, and further attempts at territorial expansion, especially by the militant Japanese, who were searching for an East Asian empire of their own. Attempts at reform failed because China was so divided and weak.

Chinese intellectuals searched for new ideas from abroad to strengthen their nation in the vibrant May Fourth period, spanning from roughly 1917 through the early 1920s. In the process, influential foreigners such as English mathematician and philosopher Bertrand Russell, American philosopher and educator John Dewey, and Indian poet Rabindranath Tagore came to lecture in China. Thousands of Chinese students traveled and studied abroad. Ideas such as liberal democracy, syndicalism, guild socialism, and communism were contemplated as possible solutions to China's many problems.

The Founding of the Chinese Communist Party

In 1921, a small Marxist study group founded the Chinese Communist Party (CCP). The Moscow-based Comintern (Communist International) advised this highly intellectual but politically impotent group to link up with the more promising and militarily powerful Kuomintang (KMT, or Nationalist Party, led first by Sun Yat-sen and, after his death in 1925, by Chiang Kai-shek), in order to reunify China under one central government. Without adequate support from the Soviets or from forces within China—because there were so few capitalists in China, there was no urban proletariat, and there-

(New York Public Library)

CONFUCIUS: CHINA'S FIRST "TEACHER"

Confucius (551–479 B.C.), whose efforts to teach the various central governments of China how to govern well were spurned, spent most of his life teaching his own disciples. Yet 300 years later, Confucianism, as taught by descendants of his own disciples, was adopted as the official state philosophy. The basic principles of Confucianism include hierarchical principles of obedience and loyalty to one's superiors, respect for one's elders, and filial piety; principles and practices for maintaining social order and harmony; and the responsibility of rulers to exercise their power benevolently.

fore the Marxist aim of "overthrowing the capitalist class" was irrelevant—the Chinese Communists agreed to form a united front with the KMT. They hoped that once they had built up their own organization while cooperating with the KMT, they could break away to establish themselves as an independent political party. Thus, it was with Communist support that Chiang Kai-shek successfully united China under his control during the Northern Expedition. Chiang Kai-shek understood the Communist Party's ambitions to gain political power, however, so in 1927, he brutally quashed the Communist Party.

The Long March

The Chinese Communist Party's ranks were decimated two more times by the KMT's superior police and military forces,

THE OPIUM WAR: NARCOTICS SMUGGLING JUST A PRETEXT FOR WAR

Although the opium poppy is native to China, large amounts of opium were shipped to China by the English-owned East India Company from the British colony of India. Eventually India exported so much opium to China that 5 to 10 percent of its revenues derived from its sale.

By the late 1700s, the Chinese government had officially prohibited first the smoking and selling of opium, and later its importation or domestic production. But because the sale of opium was so profitable—and also because so many Chinese officials were addicted to it—the Chinese officials themselves illegally engaged in the opium trade. As the number of addicts grew and the Chinese government became more corrupted by its own unacknowledged participation in opium smuggling, so grew the interest of enterprising Englishmen in smuggling it into China for financial gain.

The British government was primarily interested in establishing an equal diplomatic and trade relationship with the Chinese to supplant the existing one, in which the Chinese court demanded that the English kowtow to the Chinese emperor. Britain was interested in expanded trade with China. But it also wanted to secure legal jurisdiction over its nationals residing in China to protect them against Chinese practices of torture

(New York Public Library)

of those suspected of having committed a crime.

China's efforts to curb the smuggling of opium and the Chinese refusal to recognize the British as equals reached a climax in 1839, when the Chinese destroyed thousands of chests of opium aboard a British ship. This served as an ideal pretext for the British to attack China with their sophisticated gunboats

(pictured above destroying a junk in Canton's harbor). Ultimately their superior firepower gave victory to the British.

Thus the so-called Opium War (1839–1842) ended with defeat for the Chinese and the signing of the Treaty of Nanking, which ceded the island of Hong Kong to the British and allowed them to establish trading posts on the Chinese mainland.

---

largely because the CCP had obeyed Moscow's advice to organize an orthodox Marxist urban-based movement in the cities. The cities, however, were completely controlled by the KMT. It is a testimony to the strength of the appeal of Communist ideas in that era that the CCP managed to recover its strength each time. Indeed, the growing power of the CCP was such that Chiang considered it, even more than the invading Japanese, the main threat to his complete control of China. Eventually the Chinese Communist leaders agreed that an urban strategy was doomed, yet they lacked adequate military power to confront the KMT head-on. They retreated in what became known as the Long March (1934–1935), traveling 6,000 miles from the southeast, through the rugged interior, to the windswept plains of Yanan in northern China.

It was during this retreat, in which as many as 100,000 people perished, that Mao Zedong (Mao Tse-tung) staged his contest for power within the CCP. With his victory, the Chi-

nese Communist Party reoriented itself toward a rural strategy and attempted to capture the loyalty of the peasants, then comprising some 85 percent of China's total population. Mao saw the peasants as the major source of support for revolution. In most areas of China, the peasants were suffering from an oppressive and brutal system of landlord control; they were the discontented masses who had "nothing to lose but [their] chains." Appealing to the peasants' desire to own their own land as well as to their disillusionment with KMT rule, the CCP slowly started to gain control over the countryside.

"United" against the Japanese

In 1937, Japan invaded China and occupied China's coastal provinces and Manchuria in the northeast. Although the CCP and KMT were determined to destroy each other, Japan's threat to China caused the CCP and KMT to agree again to a unified front to halt the Japanese advance. Both the KMT and

MAO ZEDONG: CHINA'S REVOLUTIONARY LEADER

(New York Public Library)

Mao Zedong (1893–1976) came from a moderately well-to-do peasant family and, as a result, received a very good education, as compared to the vast majority of the Chinese. Mao was one of the founders of the Chinese Communist Party in 1921, but his views on the need to switch from an orthodox Marxist strategy, which called for the party to seek roots among the urban working class, to a rural strategy centered on the exploited peasants were spurned by the leadership of the CCP and its sponsors in Moscow.

Later, it became evident that the CCP could not flourish in the Nationalist-controlled cities, as time and again the KMT quashed the idealistic but militarily weak CCP. Mao appeared to be right: "Political power grows out of the barrel of a gun."

The Communists' retreat to Yanan on the Long March was not only for the purpose of survival but also for re-grouping and forming a stronger "Red Army." There the followers of the Chinese Communist Party were taught Mao's ideas about guerrilla warfare, the importance of winning the support of the people, principles of party leadership, and socialist values. Mao consolidated his control over the leadership of the CCP during the Yanan period and led it to victory over the Nationalists in 1949.

From that time onward, Mao became a symbol of the new Chinese government, of national unity, and of the strength of China against foreign humiliation. In later years, although his real power was eclipsed, the party maintained the illusion that Mao was the undisputed leader of China.

In his declining years, Mao waged a struggle, in the form of the "Cultural Revolution," against those who followed policies antagonistic to his own, a struggle that brought the country to the brink of civil war and turned the Chinese against one another. The symbol of Mao as China's "great leader" and "great teacher" was used by those who hoped to seize power after him: first the minister of defense, Lin Biao, and then the "Gang of Four," which included Mao's wife.

Mao's death in 1976 ended the control of policy by the Gang of Four. Within a few years, questions were being raised about the legacy that Mao had left China. By the 1980s, it was broadly accepted throughout China that Mao had been responsible for a full 20 years of misguided policies. Since the Tiananmen protests of 1989, however, there has been a resurgence of nostalgia for Mao. This nostalgia is captured in such aspects of popular culture as a tape of songs about Mao entitled "The Red Sun"—an all-time best-selling tape in China, at 5 million copies—that encapsulates the Mao cult and Mao mania of the Cultural Revolution; and in a small portrait of Mao that virtually all car owners and taxi drivers hang over their rear-view mirrors for "good luck." Many Chinese long for the "good old days" of Mao's rule, when crime and corruption were at far lower levels than today and when there was a sense of collective commitment to China's future. But they do not long for a return to the mass terror of the Cultural Revolution, for which Mao also bears responsibility.

the CCP had ulterior motives, but, according to most accounts, the Communists contributed more to the national wartime efforts. The Communists organized guerrilla efforts to peck away at the fringes of Japanese-controlled areas while Chiang Kai-shek, head of the KMT, retreated to the wartime capital of Zhongjing (Chungking). His elite corps of troops and officers kept the best of the newly arriving American supplies for themselves, leaving the rank-and-file Chinese to fight bootless and with inferior equipment against the Japanese. The unstinting efforts of the self-sacrificing Chinese people and the American victory over Japan helped bring

World War II to an end in 1945. Once again, Chiang Kai-shek was free to focus on defeating the Communists.

The Communists Oust the KMT

It seemed as if the Communists' Red Army had actually been strengthened through its hard fighting during World War II, leaving it a formidable force for the KMT to confront. Meanwhile, the relatively soft life of the KMT military elite during the war did not leave them well prepared for the hardships of the civil war that they now faced. Moving quickly to annihilate the Communists, Chiang Kai-shek relied on his old strategy of trying to capture China's cities. By contrast, the Communists, who had gained control over the countryside by winning the support of the vast peasantry, surrounded China's cities. Like besieged fortresses, the cities eventually fell to Communist control. By October 1949, the Chinese Communist Party could claim control over all of China except for the island of Taiwan. It was to Taiwan that the KMT's political, economic, and military elite, with American support, had fled.

Scholars still dispute why the Red Army ultimately defeated the KMT Army, citing as probable reasons the CCP's appeal to the Chinese people, the Communists' more virtuous behavior in comparison to that of the KMT soldiers, the CCP's more successful appeal to the Chinese sense of nationalism, and Chiang's unwillingness to undertake reforms that would bring about economic development and control corruption. Even had the KMT made greater efforts to bring about reform, however, any wartime government confronted with the demoralization of a population ravaged by war, inflation, economic destruction, and the humiliation of a foreign occupation would have found it difficult to maintain the loyal support of its people. Even the Chinese middle class eventually deserted the KMT. Indeed, many of those industrial and commercial capitalists who had supported the KMT stayed behind in the cities in order to join in a patriotic effort with the CCP to rebuild China. Others, however, stayed behind only because they were unable to flee to Hong Kong or Taiwan.

In any event, one thing is clear: The Communists did not gain victory because of support from the Soviet Union; for the Soviets, who were anxious to be on the winning side in China, chose to give aid to the KMT until it was clear that the Communists would win. Furthermore, the Communists' victory was due not to superior weapons but, rather, to a superior strategy, support from the Chinese people, and (as Mao Zedong believed) a superior political "consciousness." It was because of the Communist victory over a technologically superior army that Mao thereafter believed in the superiority of "man over weapons" and that the support of the people was essential to an army's victory. The relationship of the soldiers to the people is, Mao said, like the relationship of fish to water—without the water, the fish will die.

THE PEOPLE'S REPUBLIC OF CHINA

The Red Army's final victory came rapidly—far faster than anticipated. Suddenly China's large cities fell to the Communists, who now found themselves in charge of a nation of more than 600 million people. They had to make critical decisions about how to unify and rebuild the country. They were obligated, of course, to fulfill their promise to redistribute land to the poor and landless peasants in return for the peasants' support of the Communists. The CCP leaders were, however, largely recruited from among the peasantry; and while they knew how to make a revolution, they had little

experience with governance. Rejected by the Western democratic-capitalist countries because of their embrace of communism and desperate for aid and advice, the Communists turned to the Soviet Union for direction and support.

The Soviet Model
In the early years of CCP rule, China's leaders "leaned to one side" and followed the Soviet model of development in education, the legal system, the economic system, and elsewhere. The Soviet economic model favored capital-intensive industrialization, which required a reliance on Soviet experts and well-educated Chinese, whom the Communists were not sure they could trust. Without Soviet support in the beginning, however, it is questionable whether the CCP would have been as successful as it was in developing China in the 1950s.

The Maoist Model
China soon grew exasperated with the limitations of Soviet aid—which did not come without price or obligation—and the inapplicability of the Soviet model to Chinese circumstances. Thus, China's preeminent Communist leader, Mao Zedong, proposed a model of development more appropriate to Chinese circumstances. What came to be known as the Maoist model took account of China's low level of development, poverty, and large population. Instead of expensive capital equipment, Mao hoped to utilize China's enormous manpower for development by organizing people into ever larger working units.

In 1958, in what became known as the Great Leap Forward, Mao Zedong launched his Chinese model of development. It was a bold scheme to sharply accelerate the pace of industrialization so that China could catch up with the industrialized states of the West. Land was merged into large communes, untested and controversial planting techniques were introduced, and peasant women were engaged fully in the fields in order to increase agricultural production. The communes became the basis for industrializing the countryside through a program of peasants building their own "backyard furnaces." The Maoist model assumed that those people possessing a proper revolutionary, or "red," consciousness would be able to produce more than those who were "expert" but lacked revolutionary consciousness—that is, a commitment to achieving communism.

The Maoist model was a rejection of the Soviet model of development, which Mao came to see as an effort to hold the Chinese back from more rapid industrialization. In particular, the Soviets' refusal to give the Chinese the most advanced industrial plant equipment and machinery, or to share nuclear technology with them, made Mao suspicious of their intentions.

Sino-Soviet Relations Sour
For their part, the Soviets believed that the Maoist model was doomed to failure. The Soviet leader, Nikita Khrushchev, denounced the Great Leap Forward as "irrational"; but he was

(New York Public Library)

RED GUARDS: ROOTING OUT THOSE "ON THE CAPITALIST ROAD"

During the Cultural Revolution, Mao Zedong called upon the country's young people to "make revolution." Called Mao's Red Guards, these youngsters' ages varied, but for the most part they were teenagers.

Within each class and school, various youths would band together in a Red Guard group that would take on a revolutionary-sounding name and would then carry out the objective of challenging people in authority. But the people in authority—especially schoolteachers, school principals, bureaucrats, and local leaders of the Communist Party—initially ignored the demands of the Red Guards that they reform their "reactionary thoughts" or eliminate their "feudal" habits.

The Red Guards initially had no real weapons and could only threaten. Since they were considered just misdirected children by those under attack, their initial assaults had little effect. But soon the frustrated Red Guards took to physically beating and publicly humiliating those who stubbornly refused to obey them. Since Mao had not clearly defined precisely what should be their objectives or methods, the Red Guards were free to believe that the ends justified extreme and often violent means. Moreover, many Red Guards took the opportunity to take revenge against authorities, such as teachers who had given them bad grades. Others (like those pictured above wearing masks to guard against the influenza virus while simultaneously concealing their identities) would harangue crowds on the benefits of Maoism and the evils of foreign influence.

Mao eventually called on the army to support the Red Guards in their effort to challenge "those in authority taking the capitalist road." This created even more confusion, as many of the Red Guard groups actually supported the people they were supposed to be attacking. But their revolutionary-sounding names and their pretenses at being "Red" (Communist) confused the army. Moreover, the army was divided within itself and did not particularly wish to overthrow the Chinese Communist Party authorities, the main supporters of the military in their respective areas of jurisdiction.

The Red Guards began to go on rampages throughout the country, breaking into people's houses and stealing or destroying their property, harassing people in their homes in the middle of the night, stopping girls with long hair and cutting it off on the spot, destroying the files of ministries and industrial enterprises, and clogging up the transportation system by their travels throughout the country to "make revolution." Different Red Guard factions began to fight with one another, each claiming to be the most revolutionary.

Since the schools had been closed, the youth of China were not receiving any formal education during this period. Finally, in 1969, Mao called a halt to the excesses of the Red Guards. They were disbanded and sent home or out to the countryside to labor in the fields with the peasants. But the chaos set in motion during the Cultural Revolution did not come to a halt until the arrest of the Gang of Four, some 10 years after the Cultural Revolution had begun.

Children of school age during the "10 bad years," when schools were either closed or operating with a minimal program, received virtually no formal education beyond an elementary-school level. Although this meant that China's development of an educated elite in most fields came to a halt, nevertheless it resulted in well over a 90 percent basic literacy rate among the Chinese raised in that generation.

equally distressed at what seemed a risky scheme by Mao Zedong to bring the Soviets and Americans into direct conflict over the Nationalist-controlled Offshore Islands in the Taiwan Strait. Unwilling to risk war with the Americans, the thousands of Soviet experts residing in China in 1959 abruptly packed up their bags—as well as spare parts for machinery and blueprints for unfinished factories—and left the country.

The Soviets' action, combined with the disastrous decline in production resulting from the policies of the Great Leap Forward and several years of bad weather, set China's economic development back many years. Population figures now available indicate that somewhere between 20 million and 30 million people died in the years from 1959 to 1962, mostly from starvation and diseases caused by malnutrition. Within the CCP, Mao Zedong's ideas were paid mere lip service. The Chinese people were not told that Mao Zedong bore blame for their problems, but the Maoist model was abandoned for the time being. More pragmatic leaders took over the direction of the economy, but without further support from the Soviets. Not until 1962 did the Chinese start to recover their productivity gains of the 1950s.

By 1963, the Sino–Soviet split had become public, as the two Communist powers found themselves in profound disagreement over a wide range of issues: whether socialist countries could use capitalist methods, such as free markets, to advance economic development; appropriate policies toward the United States; and whether China or the Soviet Union could claim to follow Marxism-Leninism more faithfully, entitling it to lead the Communist world. The Sino–Soviet split was not healed until the late 1980s. But by then, neither country was interested in claiming Communist orthodoxy.

The Cultural Revolution

In 1966, whether Mao Zedong hoped to provoke an internal party struggle and regain control over policy, or (as he alleged) to re-educate China's exploitive, corrupt, and oppressive officials in order to restore a revolutionary spirit to the Chinese people and to prevent China from abandoning socialism, Mao launched what he termed the "Great Proletarian Cultural Revolution." He called on China's youth to "challenge authority," particularly "those revisionists in authority who are taking the capitalist road." If China continued along its "revisionist" course, he said, the achievements of the Chinese revolution would be undone. China's youth were therefore urged to "make revolution."

Such vague objectives invited abuse, including personal feuds and retribution for alleged past wrongs. Determining just who was "Red" (Communist) and who was "reactionary" itself generated chaos, as people tried to protect themselves by attacking others—including friends and relatives.

During that period, people's cruelty was profound. People were psychologically, and sometimes physically, tortured until they "admitted" to their "rightist" or "reactionary" behav-

ior. Murders, suicides, ruined careers, and broken families were the debris left behind by this effort to "re-educate" those who had strayed from the revolutionary path. It is estimated that approximately 10 percent of the population—that is, nearly *100 million people*—became targets of the Cultural Revolution and that tens of thousands lost their lives during the decade of political chaos.

The Cultural Revolution attacked Chinese traditions and cultural practices as being feudal and outmoded. It also destroyed the authority of the Chinese Communist Party, through attacks on many of its most respected leaders. Policies changed frequently in those "10 bad years" from 1966 to 1976, as first one faction and then another gained the political upper hand. Few leaders escaped unscathed. Ultimately, the Chinese Communist Party and Marxist-Leninist ideology were themselves the victims of the Cultural Revolution. By the time the smoke cleared, the legitimacy of the CCP had been destroyed, and the people could no longer accept the idea that the party leaders were infallible. Both traditional Chinese morality and Marxist-Leninist values had suffered a near total breakdown.

Reforms and Liberalization

With the death of Mao Zedong and the subsequent arrest of the politically radical "Gang of Four" (which included Mao's wife) in 1976, the Cultural Revolution came to an end. Deng Xiaoping, a veteran leader of the CCP who had been purged twice during the "10 bad years," was "rehabilitated" in 1977.

By 1979, China once again set off down the road of construction and put an end to the radical Maoist policies of "continuous revolution" and the idea that it was more important to be "Red" than "expert." Saying that he did not care whether the cat was black or white, as long as it caught mice, Deng Xiaoping pursued more pragmatic, flexible policies in order to modernize China. He thus deserves credit for opening up China to the outside world and to reforms that led to the liberalization of both the economic and the political spheres. When he died in 1997, Deng left behind a country that, despite some setbacks and reversals, had already traveled a significant distance down the road to liberalization and modernization.

In spite of the fact that Deng Xiaoping followed policies that were more pragmatic than revolutionary, and more "expert" than "Red," and in spite of Mao Zedong's clear responsibility for precipitating policies that were devastating to the Chinese people, Mao has never been defrocked; for to do so would raise serious questions about the CCP's right to rule. China's leaders have admitted that, beginning with the "Anti-Rightest Campaign" of 1957 and the "Great Leap Forward" of 1958, Mao made "serious mistakes"; but the CCP insists that these errors must be seen within the context of his many accomplishments and his commitment, even if sometimes misdirected, to Marxism-Leninism.

(China Pictorial)

The radical leaders of China's Cultural Revolution, who came to be known as the Gang of Four, were brought to trial in late 1980. Here they are pictured (along with another radical who was not part of the Gang) in a Beijing courtroom, listening to the judge pass sentence. The Gang of Four are the first four (from right to left) standing in the prisoners' dock: Jiang Qing, Yao Wenyuan, Wang Hongwen, and Zhang Chunqiao.

THE GANG OF FOUR

The current leadership of the Chinese Communist Party views the Cultural Revolution of 1966–1976 as having been a period of total chaos that brought the People's Republic of China to the brink of political and economic ruin. While Mao Zedong is criticized for having begun the Cultural Revolution with his mistaken ideas about the danger of China turning "capitalist," the major blame for the turmoil of those years is placed on a group of extreme radicals labeled the Gang of Four.

The Gang of Four consisted of Jiang Qing, Mao's wife, who began playing a key role in China's cultural affairs during the early 1960s; Zhang Chunqiao, a veteran party leader in Shanghai; Yao Wenyuan, a literary critic and ideologue; and Wang Hongwen, a factory worker catapulted into national prominence by his leadership of rebel workers during the Cultural Revolution. By the late 1960s, these four individuals were among the most powerful leaders in China. Drawn together by common political interests and a shared belief that the Communist Party should be relentless in ridding China of suspected "capitalist roaders," they worked together to keep the Cultural Revolution on a radical course. One of their arch enemies was Deng Xiaoping, who emerged as China's paramount leader in 1978, after the members of the Gang of Four were arrested.

Although they had close political and personal ties to Mao and derived many of their ideas from him, Mao became quite disenchanted with the radicals in the last few years of his life. He was particularly displeased with the unscrupulous and secretive way in which they behaved as a faction within the top levels of the party. Indeed, it was Mao who coined the name Gang of Four, as part of a written warning to the radicals to cease their conspiracies and obey established party procedures.

The Gang of Four hoped to be able to take over supreme power in China following Mao's death on September 9, 1976. However, their plans were upset less than a month later, when other party and army leaders had them arrested—an event that is now said to mark the formal end of the Cultural Revolution. By removing from power the party's most influential radicals, the arrest of the Gang of Four set the stage for the dramatic reforms that have become the hallmark of the post-Mao era in China.

In November 1980, the Gang of Four were put on trial in Beijing. They were charged with having committed serious crimes against the Chinese people and accused of having had a hand in "persecuting to death" tens of thousands of officials and intellectuals whom they perceived as their political enemies. All four were convicted and sentenced to long terms in prison.

The Challenge of Reform

The erosion of traditional Chinese values, then of Marxist-Leninist values and faith in the Chinese Communist Party's leadership, and finally of "Mao Thought" (the Chinese adaptation of Marxism-Leninism to Chinese conditions) left China without any strong belief system. Such Western values as materialism, capitalism, individualism, and freedom swarmed into this vacuum to undermine both Communist ideology and the traditional Chinese values that had provided the glue of society. Deng Xiaoping's prognosis had proven correct: The "screen door" through which Western science and technology (and foreign investments) could flow into

(United Nations photo/John Isaac)

The Chinese government has made great efforts to curb the country's population growth by promoting the merits of the one-child family. Today, China has an average annual population growth rate of 0.93 percent.

China was unable to keep out the annoying "insects" of Western values. The screen door appeared to have holes that were too large to prevent this invasion.

The less "pragmatic," more ideologically oriented "conservative" or "hard-line" leadership (who in the new context of reforms could be viewed as hard-line ideologues of a Maoist vintage) challenged the introduction of economic reforms precisely because they threatened to undo China's earlier socialist achievements and erode Chinese culture. To combat the negative side effects from the introduction of free-market values and institutions, China's leadership therefore launched a number of "mass campaigns": the campaign in the 1980s against "spiritual pollution";[1] a repressive campaign following the crackdown against those challenging the leadership of the CCP in Tiananmen Square in 1989; ongoing campaigns against corruption; and campaigns to "strike hard" against crime and "get civilized" in the late 1990s.[2]

Since 1979, in spite of setbacks and campaigns that have attempted to address some of the unintended consequences of reforms, China's leadership has been able to keep the country on the path of liberalization. As a result, the economy has been growing at double-digit rates for much of the last 2 decades. China has dramatically reformed the legal and political system as well, even though much work remains to be done. When Deng Xiaoping died in 1997, he was succeeded in a peaceful transition by Jiang Zemin, another committed reformer. Jiang is, however, just one leader—although a very effective one—within what is now a collective, well-institutionalized leadership. The problems that the leadership faces as a consequence of China's rapid modernization and liberalization since 1979 are formidable: massive, and growing, unemployment; increasing crime, corruption, and social dislocation; a lack of social cohesion; and challenges to the CCP's monopoly on power. These problems are discussed below.

THE PEOPLE OF CHINA

Population Control

By 1999, China's population was close to 1.3 billion. In the 1950s, Mao had encouraged population growth, as he considered a large population to be a major source of strength. No sustained attempts to limit Chinese population occurred until the mid-1970s. Even then, population-control programs were only marginally successful, because there were no penalties for those Chinese who ignored them.

In 1979, the government launched a serious birth-control campaign, rewarding families giving birth to only one child with work bonuses and priority in housing. The only child was later to receive preferential treatment in university admissions and job assignments (a policy later abandoned). Families that had more than one child, on the other hand, were to be penalized by a 10 percent decrease in their annual wages, and their children would not be eligible for free education and health-care benefits.

The one-child policy in China's major cities has been rigorously enforced, to the point where it is almost impossible for a woman to get away with a second pregnancy. Who is allowed to have a child, as well as when she may give birth, is rigidly controlled by the woman's work unit. Furthermore, with so many state-owned enterprises now paying close to half of their entire annual wages as "bonuses," authorities have come up with further sanctions to ensure compliance: Workers are usually organized in groups of 10 to 30 individuals. If any woman in the group gives birth to more than one child, *the entire group* will lose its annual bonus. With such overwhelming penalties for the group as a whole, pressures not to give birth to a second child are enormous.

To ensure that any unauthorized pregnancy does not occur, women who have already given birth are required to stand in front of x-ray machines to verify that their IUDs (birth-control devices) are still in place. Abortions can and will be performed throughout the period of a woman's unsanctioned pregnancy. (The moral issues that surround abortions for some Christians concerning the rights of the unborn fetus are not concerns for the Chinese.)

The effectiveness of China's birth-control policy in the cities is not merely attributable to the surveillance by state-owned work units, neighborhood committees, and the "granny police" who watch over the families in their locale. Changed social attitudes also play a critical role, and urban Chinese now accept the absolute necessity of population control in their overcrowded cities.

The one-child policy in China's cities has led, however, to the problem of spoiled children. Known as "little emperors," these only children are the center of attention of six anxious adults (two sets of grandparents and the parents), who carefully scrutinize their every movement. It has led to the overuse of medical services by these parents and grandparents, who rush their only child/grandchild to the doctor at the first signs of a sniffle or sore throat. It has also led to overfed, even obese, children. Being overweight used to be considered a hedge against bad times, and the Chinese were initially pleased that their children were becoming heavier. A common greeting showing admiration had long been, "You have become fat!" But as contemporary urban Chinese adopt many of the values associated in the developed world with becoming wealthier, they are changing their perspectives and no longer are quite so enthusiastic about extra weight. Nevertheless, salad bars and diet programs do not loom on the immediate horizon, and the major purpose of people exercising still is to keep China a strong nation, not to look attractive.

The one-child policy has resulted in other, more serious concerns. One is the demographic issue of too few young people to support the large number of elderly people in future years. The other is the aborting of female fetuses.[3] In spite of governmental efforts to stop it, this practice continues. And, although female infanticide is illegal, it sometimes happens, especially in rural areas. The decline in the ratio of women to men is in turn leading to another demographic crisis: an insufficient number of brides. Apart from societal unhappiness, this has led to a sharp increase in the kidnapping of young women and the practice of selling girls as brides in rural marketplaces as they have come of marriageable age in the 1990s.[4]

In the vast rural areas of China, where some three quarters of the population still live, efforts to enforce the one-child policy have met with less success than in the cities, because the benefits and punishments are not as relevant for peasants. Since the communes have been disbanded and families have been given their own land to till, peasants want sons to do the heavy farm labor. As a result, the government's policy in the countryside has become more flexible. In some villages, if a woman gives birth to a girl and decides to have another child in hopes of having a boy, she may pay the government a substantial fee (usually an amount more than the entire annual income of the family) in order to do so.

It is estimated that at least several million peasants have taken steps to ensure that their female offspring are not counted toward their one-child (and now, in some places two-child) limit: A pregnant woman will simply move to another village to have her child. Since the local village leaders are not responsible for women's reproduction when they are not from their own village, women are not harassed into getting an abortion in other villages. If the child is a boy, she can simply return to her native village and register him; if a girl, she can return and not register her. Thus a whole generation of young girls is growing up in the countryside without ever having been registered. Since, except for schooling, peasants have few claims to state-supplied benefits anyway, they may consider this official nonexistence of their daughters a small price to pay for having as many children as necessary until giving birth to a boy. And if this practice is as common as some think, it may mean that China will not face quite such a large demographic crisis in the ratio between males and females as believed.

One important reason why males continue to be more valued in Chinese culture is because only sons are permitted to perform traditional Chinese family rituals and ancestor worship. This is unbearably painful—in fact, unacceptable—for families without sons, who feel that their entire ancestral history, often recorded for over several hundred years on village-temple tablets, is coming to an end. As a result, a few villages have changed the very foundations of ancestral worship: They permit daughters to continue the family lineage down the female line. The government itself is encouraging this practice, and it is also changing certain other family-re-

(United Nations photo/John Isaac)

This one-child family lives in a commune in Inner Mongolia. China's central government has long attempted to undermine distinctive national identities on and around its borders.

lated policies, such as who is responsible under the law for taking care of their parents. It used to be the son, meaning that parents of a daughter could not expect to be supported in their old age. Now both sons and daughters are deemed responsible. Furthermore, through instituting a new system of social security and pensions for the retired, the responsibility for caring for the elderly is gradually being absorbed by the state and employers.

China's strict population-control policies have been effective: Since 1977, the population has grown at an average annual rate of 1.1 percent, one of the lowest rates in the developing world. Unfortunately, even this low rate means an average annual increase of China's population of more than 12 million people. This is an ever-growing drain on limited resources and poses a challenge, and perhaps a threat, to future economic development.

Women

It is hardly surprising that overlaying (but never eradicating) China's traditional culture with a Communist ideology in which men and women are supposed to be equal has generated a bundle of contradictions. Under Chinese Communist Party rule, women have long had more rights and opportunities than women in almost any other developing country; in certain respects, they have even outpaced the rights of women in some of the developed countries.[5] Although Chinese women have rarely broken through the "glass ceiling" to the highest levels of the CCP or management, and although they have often been given traditional "women's work," they have received pay fairly equal to that of men. This is in an economy where the gap between the highest and lowest paid, whether male or female, was small as well. Furthermore, an ideological morality that insists on respect for women as equals (with both men and women being addressed as "comrades" during the Maoist period), combined with a de-emphasis on the importance of sexuality, has resulted in at least a superficial respect for women that was rare before the Communist period.

The economic reforms that began in 1979 have, however, precipitated changes in the manner in which women are treated and how women act. While many women entrepreneurs and workers are benefiting as much as the men from economic reforms, there have also been certain throwbacks to earlier times that have undercut women's equality. Women are now treated much more as sex objects than they used to be; and, while some women revel in their new freedom to beautify themselves, some companies will hire only women who are attractive, and many enterprises are now using women as "window dressing." For example, women dressed in *qipao*—the traditional, slim-fitting Chinese dress slit high on the thigh—stand outside restaurants and other establishments to entice customers. At business meetings, many have become mere tea-pourers. In newspapers, many job ads for Chinese enterprises state in so many words that only young and good-looking women need apply.

The emphasis on profits and efficiency since the reforms have also made state-run enterprises reluctant to hire women because of the costs in maternity benefits (including 3 to 12 months of maternity leave at partial or even full pay) and because mothers are still more likely than fathers to be in charge of sick children and the household. Under the socialist system, where the purpose of an enterprise was not necessarily to make profits but to fulfill such socialist objectives as the equality of women and full employment, women fared better. Economic reforms have provided enterprise managers with the excuse they need not to hire women. Whatever the real reason, they can always claim that their refusal to hire more women or to promote them is justified: They are more costly, or less competent, or less reliable.

National Minorities

Ninety-four percent of the population are Han Chinese. Although only 6 percent are "national minorities," they occupy more than 60 percent of China's geographical expanse. These minorities inhabit almost all the border areas, including Tibet, Inner Mongolia, and Xinjiang, the stability of which is important for China's national security. Furthermore, China's borders with many countries are poorly defined, and members of the same minority usually live on both sides of the borders.

To address this issue, China's central government has pursued policies designed to get the minorities on the Chinese side of the borders to identify with the Han Chinese majority. Rather than admitting to this objective of undermining distinctive national identities, the CCP leaders have phrased the policies in terms of getting rid of the minorities' "feudal" customs, such as religious practices, which are contrary to the "scientific" values of socialism. At times these policies have been brutal and have caused extreme bitterness among the minorities, particularly the Tibetans and the large number of minority peoples who practice Islam.

In the 1980s, the Deng Xiaoping leadership conceded that Beijing's harsh assimilation policies had been ill conceived, and it tried to gain the loyalty of the national minorities through more sensitive policies. By the end of the decade, however, the loosening of controls had led to further challenges to Beijing's control, so the central government tightened up security in Xinjiang (China's far northwestern province) and reimposed martial law in Tibet in an effort to quell protests and riots against Beijing's discriminatory policies. Martial law was lifted in 1990, but security has remained tight ever since.

Tibet

In recent years, there has been a surge of demonstrations for a more autonomous, and even independent, Tibet. The Dalai Lama is the most important spiritual leader of the Tibetans, but he lives in exile in India, where he fled after a Chinese crackdown on Tibetans in 1959. He has stepped up his efforts to reach some form of accommodation with Beijing. He insists that as long as he is in charge, Tibetans will use only nonviolent methods to gain greater autonomy for Tibet. The Dalai Lama also asserts that he wants greater autonomy for Tibet, but not independence; and that more control over their own affairs is necessary to protect Tibetan culture from extinction.

The threat to Tibetan culture at this point comes not from efforts by China's government to assimilate Tibetans into Han culture but, rather, from highly successful Chinese entrepreneurs who, under economic-liberalization policies, have taken over many of the commercial and entrepreneurial activities of Tibet. Ironically, the Tibetan feelings about the Chinese mirror the feelings of the Chinese toward the West: They want their technology and commercial goods but not the values that come with the people bringing those goods and technology. And among Tibetans as among the Chinese, the young are more likely to want to join the world, to be modern and hip, and to leave behind traditional culture and values.

Not all Tibetans accept the path of nonviolence that the Dalai Lama insists upon. Many even challenge the Dalai Lama's leadership. In 1996, for the first time in decades, Beijing admitted that there were isolated bombing incidents and violent clashes between anti-Chinese Tibetans (reportedly armed) and Chinese authorities. The government in response sealed off most monastaries in Lhasa, the capital of Tibet.[6] Nevertheless, thus far, most actions have been confined to peaceful demonstrations against China's control over Tibet.

Much of the anger in Tibet against China's central government arose from Beijing's decision in 1995 not to accept the Tibetan Buddhists' choice of a young boy as the reincarnation of the former Panchen Lama,[7] the second-most important spiritual leader of the Tibetans. Instead of accepting the Tibetans' recommendation, chosen according to traditional Tibetan Buddhist ritual to be their next Panchen Lama, Beijing substituted its own 6-year-old candidate. The Tibetans' choice, meanwhile, is living in seclusion somewhere in Beijing, under the watchful eye of the Chinese. China's concern is that any new spiritual leader could become a focus for a new push for Tibetan independence, an eventuality it wishes to avoid.

Muslim Minorities

In the far northwest, the predominantly Muslim population of Xinjiang province continues to challenge the authority of China's central leadership. The loosening of policies aimed at assimilating the minority populations into the Han (Chinese) culture has given a rebirth to Islamic culture and practices, including prayer five times a day, architecture in the Islamic style, traditional Islamic medicine, and teaching Islam in the schools. With the dissolution of the Soviet Union into 15 independent states, the ties between the Islamic states on China's borders (Kazakhstan, Kyrgyzstan, and Tajikistan, as well as Afghanistan and Pakistan) are accelerating rapidly.

Beijing is certainly concerned that China's Islamic minorities may find that they have more in common with these neighboring Islamic nations than with the Chinese Han majority and may attempt to secede from China. Beijing's concern was heightened in late 1992, when Turkey held a summit conference at which it announced that the next century would be the "century of Islam." Subsequent signs of a growing worldwide Islamic movement have exacerbated Beijing's anxieties about controlling China's Islamic minority.

As in Tibet, there has been a growing number of demonstrations for greater autonomy, and even independence in Xinjiang. Several thousand people were arrested for separatist activities in the 1996–1997 "Strike Hard" campaign against crime. Officials in Xinjiang have also banned at least temporarily the construction of new mosques, tightened existing controls on religious practices, and intensified the search for weapons hidden in goods arriving in Xinjiang.[8] In spite of these efforts, occasional bombs planted by Xinjiang separatists have exploded in recent years in Beijing and Xinjiang.

Inner Mongolia

Events in (Outer) Mongolia have also led China's central leadership to keep a watchful eye on Inner Mongolia, an autonomous region under Beijing's control. In 1989, Mongolia's government—theoretically independent but in fact under Moscow's tutelage—decided to permit multiparty rule at the expense of the Communist Party's complete control; and in democratic elections held in 1996, the Mongolian Communist Party was ousted from power.

Beijing has grown increasingly anxious that these democratic leanings might spread to their neighboring cousins in Inner Mongolia, with a resulting challenge to one-party CCP rule. As with the Islamic minorities, China's leadership is concerned that the Mongols in Inner Mongolia may try to secede from China and join with the independent state of Mongolia, because of their shared culture. So far, however, those Inner Mongolians who have traveled to Mongolia have been surprised by the relative lack of development there and have remained fairly quiet about seceding in order to become part of Mongolia.

Religion

Confucianism is the "religion" most closely associated with China. It is not, however, a religion in Western terms, as there is no place for gods, the afterlife, or most other beliefs associated with formal religions. But, like most religions, it does have a system of ethics for governing human relationships; and it adds to this what most religions do not have, namely, ethics and principles for good governance.

The Chinese Communists rejected Confucianism until the 1980s, but not because they saw it as an "opiate of the masses." (That was Karl Marx's description of religion, which he viewed as a way of trapping people in a web of superstitions, robbing them of their money and causing them to passively endure their miserable lives on Earth.) Instead, they denounced Confucianism for providing the ethical rationale for a system of patriarchy that allowed officials to insist on obedience from subordinates. During the years in which "leftists" set the agenda, moreover, the CCP rejected Confucianism for its emphasis on education as a criterion for joining the ruling elite. Instead, the CCP favored ideological commitment as the primary criterion for ruling. The series of reforms that began in 1979, however, have generally supported an emphasis on an educated elite, and Confucian values of hard work and the importance of the family are frequently referred to.

Buddhism and Islam have remained important among some of the largest of the national minorities, notably the Tibetans (for Buddhism) and the Uygars and Mongols (for Islam). The CCP's efforts to eradicate these religious influences have been interpreted by the minorities as national oppression by the Han Chinese. As a result, the revival of Islam and Buddhism in the 1980s was associated with efforts by the national minorities to assert their national identities and to gain greater autonomy in formulating their own policies.

For most Chinese, however, folk religions are far more important than any organized religion.[9] The CCP's best efforts to eradicate folk religions and to impart in their place an educated "scientific" viewpoint have failed. Animism—the belief that nonliving things have spirits that should be respected through worship—continues to be practiced by China's vast peasantry. Ancestor worship—based on the belief that the living can communicate with the dead and that the dead spirits to whom sacrifices are ritually made have the ability to bring a better (or worse) life to the living—absorbs much of the excess income of China's peasants. The costs of offerings, burning paper money, and using shamans and priests to perform rituals that will heal the sick, appease the ancestors, and exorcise ghosts (who are often those poorly treated ancestors, returned to haunt their descendants) at times of birth, marriage, and death can be financially burdensome. But peasants are once again spending money on traditional religious folk practices, thereby contributing to the reconstruction of practices prohibited in earlier decades of Communist rule.

DENG XIAOPING = TENG HSIAO-P'ING. WHAT IS PINYIN?

Chinese is the oldest of the world's active languages and is now spoken and written by more people than any other modern language. Chinese is written in the form of characters, which have evolved over several thousand years from picture symbols (like ancient Egyptian hieroglyphics) to the more abstract forms now in use. Although spoken Chinese varies greatly from dialect to dialect (for example, Mandarin, Cantonese, Shanghai-ese), the characters used to represent the language remain the same throughout China. Dialects are really just different ways of pronouncing the same characters.

There are more than 50,000 different Chinese characters. A well-educated person may be able to recognize as many as 25,000 characters, but basic literacy requires familiarity with only a few thousand.

Since Chinese is written in the form of characters rather than by a phonetic alphabet, Chinese words must be transliterated so that foreigners can pronounce them. This means that the sound of the character must be put into an alphabetic approximation.

Since English uses the Roman alphabet, Chinese characters are Romanized. (We do the same thing with other languages that are based on non-Roman alphabets, such as Russian, Greek, Hebrew, and Arabic.) Over the years, a number of methods have been developed to Romanize the Chinese language. Each method presents what the linguists who developed it believe to be the best way of approximating the sound of Chinese characters. Pinyin (literally, "spell sounds"), the system developed in the People's Republic of China, has gradually become the most commonly accepted system of Romanizing Chinese.

Chinese characters are the symbols used to write Chinese. Modern Chinese characters fall into two categories: one with a phonetic component, the other without it. Most of those without a phonetic component developed from pictographs. From ancient writing on archaeological relics we can see their evolution, as in the examples shown (from left to right) above.

However, other systems are still used in areas such as Taiwan. This can cause some confusion, since the differences between Romanization systems can be quite significant. For example, in pinyin, the name of China's dominant leader is spelled Deng Xiaoping. But the Wade-Giles system, which was until recently the Romanization method most widely used by Westerners, transliterates his name as Teng Hsiao-p'ing. Same person, same characters, but a difference in how to spell his name in Roman letters.

Taoism, which requires its disciples to renounce the secular world, has had few adherents in China since the early twentieth century. But during the repression that followed the crackdown on Tiananmen Square's prodemocracy movement in 1989, many Chinese who felt unable to speak freely turned to mysticism and Taoism. *Qigong,* the ancient Taoist art of deep breathing, had by 1990 become a national pastime. Some 30 Taoist priests in China took on the role of national soothsayers, portending the future of everything from the weather to China's political leadership. What these priests said—or were believed to have said—quickly spread through a vast rumor network in the cities. Meanwhile, on Chinese Communist Party–controlled television, *qigong* experts swallow needles and thread, only to have the needles subsequently come out of their noses perfectly threaded. It is widely believed that, with a sufficient concentration of *qi* (vital energy or breath), a practitioner may literally knock a person to the ground.[10] The revival of Taoist mysticism and meditation, folk religion, and formal religions may reflect a need to find meaning from religion to fill the moral and ideological vacuum created by the near-collapse of Communist values.

In the 1980s, under the influence of the more moderate policies of the Deng Xiaoping reformist leadership, the CCP reconsidered its efforts to eliminate religion. The 1982 State Constitution permits religious freedom, whereas previously, only atheism was allowed. The state has actually encouraged the restoration of Buddhist temples and Islamic mosques, in part because of Beijing's awareness of the continuing tensions caused by its efforts to deny minorities their respective religious practices, and in part because of a desire to attract both tourists and money to the minority areas.

Christianity, which was introduced in the nineteenth and early twentieth centuries by European missionaries, has several million known adherents; and its churches, which were often used as warehouses or public offices after the Communist victory in 1949, have been reopened for religious practice. Today, a steady stream of Christian proselytizers flow to China in search of new converts. Churches are now attended as much by the curious as by the devout. As with eating Western food in places such as McDonald's and Kentucky Fried Chicken, attending Christian churches is a way that some Chinese feel they can participate in Western culture.

The government generally permits mainstream Christian churches to practice in China, but it continues to exercise one major control over Roman Catholics: Their loyalty must be declared to the state, not to the pope. The Vatican is not permitted to be involved in China's practice of Catholicism; and Beijing does not recognize the Vatican's appointment of bishops and cardinals for China as valid.

Since the mid-1990s, the government has tried to clamp down on nonmainstream Christian churches and religious sects, arresting and even jailing some of their leaders. They have justified their actions on the grounds that, as in the West, some of them are involved in practices that endanger their adherents; some are actually involved in seditious activities against the state; and some are set up as fronts for illegal activities, including gambling, prostitution, and drugs. Some sort of religious practice often provides the foundation for illegal or "black" societies. Now that rural elections take place in villages all over China, religious sects and black societies often provide the basis of power for candidates for office. They are known to be involved in pressuring villagers to vote for their candidates in many villages.

Marxism-Leninism-Mao Zedong Thought

In general, Marxists are atheists. They believe that religions hinder the development of "rational" behavior and values that are so important to modernization. Yet societies seem to need some sort of spiritual, moral, and ethical guidance. For Communist party–led states, Marxism is believed adequate to fill the role of moral, if not spiritual, guidance. In China, however, Marxism-Leninism was reshaped by Mao Zedong Thought to account for Chinese conditions, and it was called Marxism-Leninism-Mao Zedong Thought. The Chinese leadership believed that it provided the ethical values necessary to guide China toward communism; and it was considered an integrated, rational thought system.

Nevertheless, this core of China's Communist political ideology exhibited many of the trappings of religions. It included scriptures (the works of Marx, Lenin, and Mao, as well as party doctrine); a spiritual head (Mao); and ritual observances (particularly during the Cultural Revolution, when Chinese were forced to participate in the political equivalent of Bible study each day). Largely thanks to the shaping of this ideology by Maoism, it included moral axioms that embodied traditional Chinese—and, some would say, Confucian—values that resemble teachings in other religions. Thus the moral of the story of "The Foolish Old Man Who Wanted to Remove a Mountain" is essentially identical to the Christian principle "If you have faith you can walk on water," based on a story in the New Testament. Like this moral, the essence of Mao Thought concerned the importance of a correct political (moral) consciousness.

In the 1980s, the more pragmatic leadership focused on liberalizing reforms; it encouraged the people to "seek truth from facts" rather than from Marxism-Leninism-Mao Zedong Thought. As a result, the role of this political ideology declined, in spite of efforts by more conservative elements in the political leadership to keep it as a guiding moral and political force. The required weekly "political study" sessions in most urban work units abandoned any pretense of interest in politics. Instead, they focused on such issues as "how to do our work better" (*i.e.,* how to become more efficient and make a profit) that were in line with the more pragmatic approach to the workplace. Nevertheless, campaigns like the "get civilized" and anticorruption ones do have a strong moralistic tone to them.

Ideology has not, therefore, been entirely abandoned. In the context of modernizing the economy and raising the standard of living, the current leadership is still committed to building "socialism with Chinese characteristics." Marxist-Leninist ideology is still being reformulated in China; but it is increasingly evident that few true believers in communism remain. Rarely does a Chinese leader even mention Marxism-Leninism in a speech. Leaders instead focus on modernization and becoming more efficient; they are more likely to discuss interest rates and trade balances than ideology.

Fully aware that they need something to replace these guiding ideological principles, however, and fearing that pure materialism and consumerism have already taken their place, China's leaders seem to be relying on patriotism and nationalism as the key components of a new ideology whose primary purpose is very simple: economic modernization and support of the leadership of the Chinese Communist Party. To oppose the CCP or its objective of modernization is unpatriotic. China's nationalism, on the other hand, is fired, as it almost always has been, by antiforeign sentiments. These sentiments derive from the belief that foreign countries are, either militarily, economically, or through insidious cultural invasion, attempting to hurt China or to intervene in China's sovereign affairs by telling China's rulers how to govern properly. This is most notably the case whenever the Western countries condemn China for its human-rights record. Undergirding China's nationalism is a fierce pride in China's history, civilization, and people. Insult, snub, slight, or challenge the Chinese, and the result is certain to be a country united behind its leadership against the offender.

Language

The Chinese had a written language by the time of the Shang Dynasty, which ruled in the second millennium B.C. It has evolved through 4,000 years into its present-day form, which is still ideographic. Each Chinese character, or *ideograph,* originally represented both a picture and/or a sound of a word. Before the May Fourth Movement of the 1920s, only a tiny elite of highly educated men could read these ideographs in the difficult grammar of the classical style, a style that in no way reflected the spoken language. All this changed with language reform in the 1920s: The classical style was abandoned, and the written language became almost identical in its structure to the spoken language.

Increasing Literacy

When the Chinese Communists came to power in 1949, they decided to facilitate the process of becoming literate by allowing only a few thousand of the more than 50,000 Chinese characters in existence to be used in printing newspapers, official documents, and educational materials. However, since a word usually comprises a combination of two characters, these few thousand characters form the basis of a very rich vocabulary: Any single character may be used in numerous combinations in order to form many different words. The Chinese Communists have gone even further in facilitating literacy by simplifying thousands of characters, often reducing a character from more than 20 strokes to 10 or even fewer.

In 1979, China adopted a new system, *pinyin,* for spelling Chinese words and names. This system, which uses the Latin alphabet of 26 letters, is still largely for foreign consumption and is not widely used within China. Because so many characters have the same Romanization (and pronunciation), and because of cultural resistance, ideographs have thus far remained the basis for Chinese writing. There are, as an example, at least 70 different Chinese ideographs that are pronounced *zhu,* but each means something different. Usually the context is adequate to indicate which word is being used, but Chinese often use their fingers to draw a particular character in the air so that those talking to them will know which of the homonyms is meant.

Spoken Chinese

Finally, to facilitate national unity, the government decided that all Chinese would speak the same dialect. Although the Chinese have shared the same written language over the last 2,000 years, regardless of which dialect of Chinese they spoke (the same written characters were simply pronounced in different ways, depending on the dialect), a sense of national unity was difficult when people needed interpreters to speak with someone even a few miles away. After the Communist victory in 1949, a majority of the delegates to the National People's Congress voted to adopt the northern dialect, Mandarin, as the national language and required all schools to teach in Mandarin (standard Chinese).

But the reality in the countryside was that it was difficult to find teachers capable of speaking Mandarin; and at home, whether in the countryside or the cities, the people continued to speak their local dialects. The liberalization policies of the 1980s and 1990s have had as their by-product a discernible trend back to speaking local dialects even in the workplace and on the streets. Whereas a decade ago a traveler could count on the national language being spoken in China's major cities, this is no longer the case. As a unified language is an important factor in maintaining national cohesion, the re-emergence of local dialects at the expense of standard Chinese threatens China's fragile unity.

One force that is slowing this disintegration is television, for it is broadcast almost entirely in standard Chinese. As there is now a wide variety of interesting programming available on Chinese television, it may be that most Chinese will make an effort to acquire at least the ability to understand, if not speak, standard Chinese.

Education

The People's Republic of China can be proud of its success in educating its people. Before 1949, less than 20 percent of the population could read and write. Today, 9 years of schooling are compulsory, and close to 90 percent of those children living in rural areas attend at least primary school. Village schools often lack even such rudimentary equipment as chairs and desks, however. Rural education also suffers from a lack of qualified teachers, as any person educated enough to teach can probably get a better-paying job in the industrial or commercial sector. In the larger cities, 12 years of schooling is becoming the norm, with children attending either a vocational middle school or a college-preparatory school; but in the countryside, few children receive an education beyond the primary level. Not only are they needed to help in the fields, but even the very low school tuition is too expensive for many peasant families.

Overeducated Students

As in the West, in China there is concern that too many students are now preparing to go on to a university; but China's reason for concern is different. In the United States, for example, *college graduates* who lack vocational training often find themselves poorly prepared to get a good job. In China, only about 5 percent of the senior middle-school graduates will pass the university entrance examinations and be admitted; but far more people than that pursue a college-oriented curriculum. Thus, in China it is *high school graduates* who find themselves inappropriately educated for the workplace. As a result, the government is attempting to augment vocational training at the high school level. At the same time, China is increasing the number of slots available in colleges and universities. Private high schools and colleges are becoming increasingly popular as parents try to optimize the chances for their only child to succeed.

The freewheeling, small-enterprise capitalist economy that has thrived since the early 1980s has made many Chinese cynical about the value of a college education. Apart from those working for foreign-run joint ventures, those making the most money have generally not been those with a college education but, rather, those who are good at entrepreneurship. A college graduate, who is usually assigned to the low-paying state-run sector, still makes a mere $60 to $200 per month. An uneducated individual selling noodle soup out of the family home can often make at least that much in just a week. And workers in the state industrial sector have always earned far more money than have China's "intellectuals." At a time when moonlighting is permitted, ordinary workers often move on to a second job at the end of the day. Few such opportunities are available, however, to those with a "liberal arts" college education.

Political Education

Until the reforms that began in 1979, the content of Chinese education was suffused with political values and objectives.

(United Nations photo)

Communes were disbanded by the early 1980s. In some areas, however, farmers have continued to work their land as a single unit in order to benefit from the economies of scale of large tracts of land.

A considerable amount of school time—as much as 100 percent during political campaigns—was devoted to political education. Often this amounted to nothing more than learning by rote the favorite axioms and policies of the leading faction in power. When that faction lost power, the students' political thought had to be reoriented in the direction of the new policies and values. History, philosophy, literature, and even foreign languages and science were laced with a political vocabulary.

The prevailing political line has affected the balance in the curriculum between political study and the learning of skills and scientific knowledge. Beginning in the 1960s, the political content of education increased dramatically until, during the Cultural Revolution, schools were shut down. When they reopened in the early 1970s, politics dominated the curriculum. When Deng Xiaoping and the "modernizers" consolidated their power in the late 1970s, this tendency was reversed. During the 1980s, in fact, schools jettisoned the study of political theory because both administrators and teachers wanted their students to do well on college-entrance

examinations, which by then focused on academic subjects. As a result, students refused to clog their schedules with the study of political theory and the CCP's history. The study of Marxism and party history was revived in the wake of the events of Tiananmen Square in 1989, with students entering many universities required to spend the first year in political study and indoctrination, sometimes under military supervision; but this practice was abandoned after 2 years. Today, political study is again confined to a narrow part of the curriculum, in the interest of giving students an education that will help advance China's modernization.

Study Abroad

Since 1979, when China began to promote an "open door" policy, more than 100,000 P.R.C. students have been sent for a university education to the United States, and tens of thousands more have gone to Europe and Japan; for although China does have universities, only a tiny percentage of all high school graduates will be able to attend them. Furthermore, until the late 1980s, Chinese universities were unable to offer graduate training. Unlike Americans, Chinese students take 2 to 3 months to study for the Graduate Record Exams (GREs), required for entrance to American graduate programs. Those taking the GREs are, moreover, already among the brightest students in China, as only some 1 to 2 percent of all Chinese high school graduates (compared to more than 40 percent of Americans) ever gain admission to China's undergraduate colleges and universities. Thus, Chinese generally outperform Americans in their GRE scores and are welcomed into American programs.

Those trained abroad are expected to return to China to establish graduate education in Chinese universities. But the fate of P.R.C. students educated abroad who return to China has not always been a happy one. The elite educated in Western universities who were in China in 1949, or who returned to China thereafter, were not permitted to hold leadership positions within their fields. Ultimately, they were the targets of class-struggle campaigns and purges in the 1950s, 1960s, and 1970s, precisely because of their Western education. For the most part, those students who returned to China in the 1980s after studying abroad were given the same positions they occupied before they received advanced education abroad. This was largely because their less-well-educated seniors who had not been able to study abroad held a jealous regard for their own positions. These individuals still had the power to make arbitrary decisions about their subordinates, and they ignored the mandate from the central authorities to promote the returned students to positions appropriate to their advanced education.

Since 1992, however, when Deng Xiaoping announced a major shift in government economic and commercial policy to support just about anything that would help China become rich and powerful, much has changed. The result is that the government is offering students significant incentives to return to China, including excellent jobs, good salaries, and

(United Nations photo)

COMMUNES: PEASANTS WORK OVERTIME DURING THE GREAT LEAP FORWARD

In the socialist scheme of things, communes are considered ideal forms of organization for agriculture. They are supposed to increase productivity and equality, reduce inefficiencies of small-scale individual farming, and bring modern benefits to the countryside more rapidly through rural industrialization.

These objectives are attained largely through the economies of scale of communes; that is, it is presumed that things done on a large scale are more efficient and cost-effective than when done on a small scale. Thus, using tractors, harvesters, trucks, and other agricultural machinery makes sense when large tracts of land can be planted with the same crops and plowed at one time. Similarly, small-scale industries may be based on the communal unit of 30,000 to 70,000 people, since, in such a large work unit, some people can take care of agricultural needs for the entire commune, leaving others to work in commune-based industries.

Because of its size, a commune may also support other types of organizations that smaller work units would find impossible to support, both financially and otherwise. A commune, for example, can support a hospital, a high school, an agricultural-research organization, and, if the commune is wealthy enough, even a "sports palace" and a cultural center for movies and entertainment.

During the Great Leap Forward, launched in 1958, peasants were—much against their will—forced into these larger agricultural and administrative units. They were particularly distressed that their remaining private plots were taken away from them. Communal kitchens, run by women, were to prepare food for everyone while workers went about their other productive work. Peasants were told that they had to eat in the communal mess halls rather than in the privacy of their own homes.

When the combination of bad policies and bad weather led to a severe famine, widespread peasant resistance forced the government to retreat from the Great Leap Forward policy and abandon the communes. But a modified commune system remained intact in much of China until the late 1970s, when the government ordered communes to be dissolved. A commune's collective property was then distributed to the peasants belonging to it, and a system of contract responsibility was launched. Today, with the exception of a few communes that refused to be dissolved, agricultural production is no longer collectivized. Individual households are again, as before 1953, engaged in small-scale agricultural production on private plots of land.

even the chance to start up new companies. Chinese students who have graduated from foreign universities are also recruited, for both their expertise and their understanding of the outside world, by the rapidly multiplying number of joint ventures in China, and by universities attempting to develop their own graduate programs.

The Chinese government also now realizes that those Chinese who do stay abroad and become citizens of other countries are forming critical links for China to the rest of the world. They have become the bridges over which contracts, loans, and trade flow to China. The fact that many remain abroad after their education is complete is now viewed as an asset in China. Finally, like immigrants elsewhere, Chinese who settle in the developed world tend to send remittances back to their families in China. These remittances amount to hundreds of millions of dollars in foreign currency each year. They are valuable not just to the family recipients but also to the government's bank reserves.

Chinese studying abroad also learn much about liberal democratic societies. When they return to China—and to date, only a small percentage of students have—they bring with them the values at the heart of liberal democratic societies. The more conservative central CCP leadership faction placed the blame for massive street demonstrations for political reform in China in 1986 and 1989 on the liberalization policies that permitted an opening to the West, including the education of Chinese students abroad. For a few years after

the crackdown on demonstrations in Beijing's Tiananmen Square, Chinese students found it very difficult to get permission to study abroad. As noted above, however, all this changed in 1992, with the result that more Chinese students than ever now study abroad.

THE ECONOMIC SYSTEM

A Command Economy

Until 1979, the Chinese had a centrally controlled command economy. That is, the central leadership determined the economic policies to be followed and allocated all of the country's resources—labor, capital, and raw materials. It also determined how much each enterprise, and even each individual, would be allocated for production and consumption. Once the Chinese Communist Party leadership determined the country's political goals and the correct ideology, the State Planning Commission and the State Economic Commission would then decide how to implement these objectives through specific policies for agriculture and industry and the allocation of resources. This is in striking contrast to a capitalist laissez-faire economy, in which government control over both consumers and producers is minimal and market forces of supply and demand play the primary role in determining what is produced and how goods are distributed.

The CCP leadership adopted the model of a centralized planned economy from the Soviet Union. Such a system was

(Hsin-Hua News Agency)

DENG XIAOPING: TAKING A "PRACTICAL" APPROACH TO CHINA'S PROBLEMS

Deng Xiaoping, a controversial figure throughout his political career, was twice purged from power. Deng became the dominant figure in Chinese politics after he returned to power in 1978. Under Deng's leadership, China implemented policies of economic liberalization, including the market system of supply and demand for distributing goods, services, and resources. These policies replaced many of China's centrally planned economic policies. Deng's statement that "I don't care whether the cat is black or white as long as it catches mice" illustrates his practical, nonideological approach to modernizing China. In other words, Deng did not care if he used capitalist methods as long as they helped modernize China faster than socialist methods.

Deng's economic liberalization policies frequently were blamed when problems such as inflation and corruption occurred in the 1980s and 1990s. Those opposing his policies used this as their rationale for retreating from economic liberalization twice during the 1980s. Since 1992, however, when Deng reasserted the need to move ahead with economic liberalization, the leadership has fairly steadily implemented Deng's policies.

Deng did not hold any official post in his final years of life; but, from 1992 until he died in February 1997, his policies were not successfully challenged. By 1997, the liberalizing reforms he had introduced had enjoyed such remarkable success that it is unlikely they will be undone any time soon, regardless of who leads China.

not only in accord with the Leninist model of centralized state governance; it also made sense for a government desperate to unify China after more than 100 years of internal division, instability, and economic collapse. Historically, China suffered from large regions evading the grasp of central control over such matters as currency and the payment of taxes. The inability of the Kuomintang government to gain control over the country's economy in the 1930s and early 1940s undercut its power and contributed to its failure to win control over China. Thus, the Chinese Communist Party's decision to centralize economic decision making after 1949 contributed to the state functioning as an integrated whole.

Over time, however, China's highly centralized economy became inefficient and inadequately flexible to address the complexity of the country's needs. Although China possesses a large and diverse economy, with a broad range of resources, topography, and climate, its economic planners made policy as if it were a uniform, homogeneous whole. Merely increasing production was itself considered a contribution to development, regardless of whether a market for the products existed or whether the products actually helped advance modernization.

State planning agencies, without the benefit of market research, determined whether or not a product should be manufactured, and in what quantity. For example, the central government might set a goal for a factory to manufacture 5 million springs per year—without knowing if there was even a market for them. The factory management did not care, as the state was responsible for marketing the products and paid the factory's bills. If the state had no buyer for the springs, they would pile up in warehouses; but rarely would production be cut back, much less a factory be closed, because this would create a problem for employing the workers cut from the payroll. Economic inefficiencies of this sort were often justified because socialist political objectives such as full employment were being met. Even today the state worries about shutting down a state-owned factory that is losing money, because it creates unemployment. In turn, unemployment leads to popular anger and provides a volatile, unstable environment, ripe for public political protest.

Quality control was similarly not as important an issue as it should have been for state-run industries in a centrally planned economy. Until market reforms occurred after 1979, the state itself allocated all finished products to other industries that needed them. If a state-controlled factory made defective parts, the industry using them had no recourse against the supplier, because each factory had a contract with the state, not with other factories. It was the state that would pay the costs to have additional parts made, so the enterprises did not need to worry about the exorbitant costs involved.

As a result, China's economic development under the centralized political leadership of the CCP occurred by fits and starts. Much waste resulted from planning that did not take into account market factors of supply and demand. Centrally set production quotas took the place of profit-and-loss issues

(Xinhua News Agency)

Under the economic liberalization program, shops such as this one in Sichuan were allowed to prosper.

in the allocation of resources. Although China's command economy was able to meet the country's most important industrial needs, problems like these took their toll over time. Enterprises had little incentive to raise productivity, quality, or efficiency when doing so did not affect their budgets, wages, or funds for expansion.

Disastrous Agricultural Programs

By the late 1950s, central planning was causing significant damage to the agricultural sector. Regardless of geography or climate, China's economic planners repeatedly ordered the peasants to restructure their economic production units according to one centralized plan. China's peasants, who had supported the CCP in its rise to power before 1949 in order to acquire their own land, had enthusiastically embraced the CCP's fulfillment of its pledge of "land to the tillers" after the Communists took over in 1949. But in 1953, the leadership, motivated by a belief that small-scale agricultural production could not meet the production goals of socialist development,

With the highly centralized or command economy in place until the 1980s, China's manufacturing energy was focused on production, with little regard to need or markets. These women in Shanghai were producing mechanical toys for no defined market.

ordered all but 15 percent of the arable land to be pooled into "lower-level agricultural producer cooperatives" of between 300 and 700 workers. The remaining 15 percent of land was to be set aside as private plots for the peasants, and they could market the produce from these plots in private markets throughout the countryside. Then, in 1956, the peasants throughout the country were ordered into "higher-level agricultural producer cooperatives" of 10 times that size, and the size of the private plots allotted to them was reduced to 5 percent of the cooperatives' total land.

Many peasants felt cheated by these wholesale collectivization policies. When in 1958 the central leadership ordered them to move into communes 10 times larger still than the cooperatives they had just joined, they were irate. Mao Zedong's "Great Leap Forward" policy of 1958 forced all peasants in China to become members of large communes: enormous economic and administrative units consisting of between 30,000 and 70,000 peasants. With communization, all of the peasants' private plots and private utensils, as well as their household chickens, pigs, and ducks, were to be turned over to the commune. Resisting this mandate, many peasants killed and ate their livestock. Since private enterprise was no longer permitted, home handicraft industries ground to a halt.

CCP chairman Mao Zedong's vision for catching up with the West was to industrialize the vast countryside. Peasants were therefore ordered to build "backyard furnaces" to smelt steel. Lacking iron ore, much less any knowledge of how to make steel, and under the guidance of party cadres who themselves were ignorant of steelmaking, the peasants tore out metal radiators, pipes, and fences. Together with pots and pans, they were dumped into their furnaces. Almost none of the final smelted product was usable. Finally, the central economic leadership ordered all peasants to eat in large, communal mess halls. This was reportedly the last straw for a people who valued family above all else. Being deprived of time alone with their families for meals, the peasants refused to cooperate further in agricultural collectivization.

When the catastrophic results of the Great Leap Forward policy poured in, the CCP retreated—but it was too late. Three subsequent years of bad weather, combined with the devastation wreaked by these policies and the Soviet withdrawal of all assistance, brought economic catastrophe. Demographic data indicate that in the "three bad years" from 1959 to 1962, some 20 million to 30 million Chinese died from starvation and malnutrition-related diseases.

By 1962, central planners had condoned peasants returning to production and accounting units the size of the higher- and lower-level cooperatives. Furthermore, peasants were again allowed to farm a small percentage of the total land as private plots, to raise domestic animals for their own use, and to engage in household handicrafts. Free markets, at which the peasantry could trade goods from private production, were reopened. The commune structure was retained throughout

CHINA'S SPECIAL ECONOMIC ZONES

In 1979, China opened four Special Economic Zones (SEZs) within the territory of the People's Republic of China as part of its program of far-reaching reform of the socialist economy. The SEZs were allowed a great deal of leeway in experimenting with new economic policies. For example, Western management methods, including the right to fire unsatisfactory workers (something unknown under the Soviet-style centrally planned economy), were introduced into SEZ factories. Laws and regulations on foreign investment were greatly eased in the SEZs in order to attract capital from abroad. Export-oriented industries were established with the goal of earning large amounts of foreign exchange in order to help China pay for the imported technology needed to hasten modernization. To many people, the SEZs looked like pockets of capitalism inside the socialist economy of the P.R.C.; indeed, they are often referred to as "mini-Hong Kongs."

The largest of the Special Economic Zones is Shenzhen, which is located just across the border from the Hong Kong New Territories. The transformation of Shenzhen over the last 2 decades from a sleepy little rural town to a large, modern urban center and one of China's major industrial cities has been phenomenal. The city now boasts broad avenues and China's tallest skyscrapers, and the standard of living is the highest in the country.

But with growth and prosperity have come numerous problems. The pace of construction has gotten out of hand, outstripping the ability of the city to provide adequate services to the growing population. Speculation and corruption have been rampant, and crime is a more serious problem in Shenzhen than it is elsewhere in China. Strict controls on immigration have been implemented to stem the flood of people who are attracted to Shenzhen in the hopes of making their fortune.

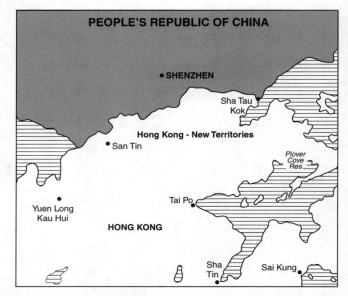

Shenzhen is the largest of China's SEZs. It is located close to the Hong Kong New Territories.

Nevertheless, the success of Shenzhen and other Special Economic Zones has led the leadership to expand the concept of SEZs throughout the country. The special privileges, such as lower taxes, that foreign businesses and joint ventures could originally enjoy only in these zones were expanded first along the coast and then to the interior, so that it too could benefit from foreign investment. Eventually, all of these special privileges will be eradicated.

---

the countryside, however, and until the CCP leadership introduced the "contract responsibility system" in 1979, it provided the infrastructure of rural secondary school education, hospitals, and agricultural research.

Other centrally determined policies, seemingly oblivious to reality, have compounded the P.R.C.'s difficulties in agriculture. These include attempts to plant three crops per year in areas that for climatic reasons can support only two (as the Chinese put it, "Three times three is not as good as two times five"); and to plant twice as much grain as was normal in a field, with the result that all of it grew to less than full size or simply wilted for lack of adequate sunshine and nutrients. Such policies were carried out during both the Great Leap Forward and the Cultural Revolution.

A final example of centrally determined agricultural policy bringing catastrophe was the decision during the Cultural Revolution that "the whole country should grow grain." The purpose was to establish China's self-sufficiency in grain. Considering China's immense size and diverse climates, soil types, and topography, a policy ordering everyone to grow the

same thing was doomed to failure. Peasants plowed under fields of cotton and cut down rubber plantations and fruit orchards, planting grain in their place. China's planners—largely CCP cadres, not economic experts—ignored overwhelming evidence that grain would not grow well in all areas and that China would have to import everything that it had replaced with grain, at far greater costs than it would have paid for importing just grain. Peasant protests were futile in the face of local-level Communist Party leaders who hoped to advance their careers by implementing central policy. The policy of self-sufficiency in grain was abandoned only with the arrest of the Gang of Four in 1976.

Economic Reforms:
Decentralization and Liberalization
In 1979, the Deng Xiaoping government began to implement a program of economic reform and liberalization in order to increase productivity and speed up modernization. In brief, although the program tried to maintain centralized state control of the direction of policy and the distribution and pricing

of strategic and energy resources, it actually decentralized decision making, down to the level of local enterprises. Decentralization was meant to facilitate more rational decision making, based on local conditions, needs, and efficiency criteria. Although the state retained the right to set overall economic priorities, local factories and enterprises were now encouraged to respond to local market forces of supply and demand. Centrally determined quotas and pricing were gradually phased out, and enterprises now contracted directly with each other rather than the state. Thus, after 1979, the government gradually phased out its role as the go-between in commercial transactions and as the central planner and allocator of everything in the economy.

Today, most collective and individual enterprises, instead of fulfilling centrally determined production quotas, meet contractual obligations that they themselves set. After they have fulfilled their contracts and paid their taxes, enterprises are permitted to use any remaining profits to expand production facilities, improve equipment, and award bonuses. These are effectively private enterprises. Some 70 percent of China's gross national product (GNP) is now produced by these nonstate enterprises. They compete with state-run enterprises to supply goods and services; and if they are not profitable, they go bankrupt.

On the other hand, although the government has threatened to shut down state-run enterprises if they operate at a loss, fear of the political instability that might result from a high level of unemployment has left the government in a difficult position: It believes that it has to continue to subsidize the heavy losses in the state-controlled sector. This, in turn, consumes a significant portion of the state's budget and contributes to China's inflation.

The state has, however, reached a crisis point. Under a very carefully managed scheme, it has started to spin off some state-run industries to the collective and private sectors. Whoever buys these state industries usually must guarantee some sort of livelihood, even if not full employment, to the former employees of the state-run enterprises; but the owners have far more freedom to make a profit than did the state-run enterprises. Recently, in the face of competititon from collective enterprises and under the threat of bankruptcy, some state-run enterprises have themselves become more efficient, to the point where they are no longer generating significant losses. The state is also slowly introducing state-run pension and unemployment funds to take care of those workers who lose their jobs when state-owned enterprises are shut down.

In agriculture, the collectivized economy is almost completely gone. Under the contract responsibility system, individual households to whom the formerly collective lands and production tools have been distributed are responsible for planning and carrying out production on their own land. The "10,000 yuan" household (about $2,000), a measure of extraordinary wealth in China, has now become a realizable goal for many peasants. Free markets are booming in China,

and peasants who used to produce only what the centralized state bureaucracy ordered now produce whatever they can get the best price for in the market. Today, wealthy rural towns are springing up throughout the agriculturally rich and densely populated east coast as well as along China's major transportation lines.

Theoretically, the collectives still own the land that they have "leased" to the peasants, but in practice the land is treated as if it is owned by the peasants. Those who choose to leave their land may contract it out to others, so that some peasants have amassed large amounts of land once again suitable for large-scale farm machinery. To encourage development, the government has permitted land to be leased for as long as 30 years, and it allows leased rights to be inherited. Furthermore, peasants have built houses on what they consider their own land—itself a problem, because it is usually arable land. Nevertheless, the village councils also have some ability to reallocate land, so that soldiers and others who settle in the villages can receive adequate land to farm.

With the growth of free enterprise in the rural towns since 1979, some 60 million to 100 million peasants have left the land to work for far better pay in small-scale rural industry, or to search for jobs in China's large cities. Many roam the country searching for work. For some, especially those able to find employment in the construction industry, which is booming in many of China's cities, this new system has meant vast personal enrichment; but tens of millions of unemployed peasants clog city streets, parks, and railroad stations. By 1999, they had been joined by tens of millions of workers displaced by the more vigorous efforts of the government to shut down bankrupt enterprises. Together, they have contributed to a vast increase in criminality and social instability.

Problems Created by Economic Reforms

Economic Crime

In the last 20 years, problems have inevitably arisen from new economic policies that created a mixed socialist and capitalist economy. For example, with decentralization, industrial enterprises have tried to hide their profits but "socialize" their losses. That is, if they make a profit, they try to hide them to avoid paying taxes to the state; but if they are state-owned enterprises and *losing* money, they ask the state to subsidize them to keep them in business. In spite of the dramatic increase in the value of industrial output since 1979, therefore, the profits turned over to the state have actually declined.

Another problem resulting from China's mixed economy is that some localities and enterprises withhold materials normally allocated by the state, such as rolled steel, glass, cement, and timber. They either hoard them as a safeguard against future shortages or resell them at unauthorized higher prices. Not only do these enterprises make illegal profits for themselves; they also deprive the state of access to building materials for its key construction projects. This reflects the problem of China's mixed economy: With the state controlling the pricing and allocation of some resources and the free market determining the rest, there are many opportunities for corruption and abuse of the system.

The needs of the centralized state economy remain in tension with the interests of provinces, counties, towns, and individuals, most of which now operate under the dual rules of a part-market, part-command economy. Thus, even as enterprises are determining whether they will expand production facilities based on the demands of a market economy, the state continues to allocate resources centrally, based on a national plan. A clothing factory that expands its production, for instance, requires more energy (coal, oil, water) and more cotton. The state, already faced with inadequate energy resources to keep most industries operating at more than 70 percent capacity, continues to allocate the same amount to the now-expanded factory. Profitable enterprises want a greater share of centrally allocated scarce resources, but find they cannot acquire them without the help of "middlemen" and a significant amount of under-the-table dealing. Corruption has, therefore, become rampant at the nexus where the capitalist and socialist economies meet.

Widespread corruption in the economic sector has led the Chinese government to wage a series of campaigns against economic crimes such as embezzlement and graft. An increasing number of economic criminals are going to prison, and serious offenders are frequently executed. Until energy and transportation bottlenecks and the scarcity of key resources are dealt with, however, it will be extremely difficult to halt the bribery, smuggling, stealing, and extortion now pervasive in China. The relaxation of central controls, the mandate for the Chinese people to "get rich," and a mixed economy have exacerbated what was already a problem under the socialist system. In a system suffering from serious scarcities but controlled by bureaucrats, political power, not the market, determines who gets what—not only goods, but also opportunities, licenses, permits, and approvals.

Although the Chinese may now purchase in the market many essential products previously distributed solely through bureaucratically controlled channels, there are still many goods that they can acquire only through the "back door"— that is, through people they know and for whom they have done favors. Scarcity, combined with bureaucratic control, has led to "collective corruption": Individuals engage in corrupt practices, even cheat the state, in order to benefit the enterprise for which they work. Since today's non-state-owned "collectives" survive or perish on the basis of profits and losses, the motivation for corrupt activities is stronger than under the previous system.

Liberalization of the economy is, then, providing a massive number and variety of goods for the marketplace. The Chinese people may buy almost any basic consumer goods in stores or the open markets. But the nexus between continued state control and the free economy still fuels a rampant corruption that threatens the strength of China's economy.

Unequal Benefits

Not all Chinese have benefited equally from the last 20 years of economic reforms. Those who inhabit cities in the interior, and peasants living far from cities and transportation lines or tilling less arable land, have reaped far fewer benefits. Nevertheless, the vast majority of Chinese have seen some improvement in their lives. At the same time, short-term gains in income will be threatened in the long term by the deterioration of education and medical care in large parts of China's hinterland. This deterioration is due to the elimination of the commune as the underlying structure for education and health care. On the other hand, the wealthier peasants send their children into the larger towns and cities for schooling, and their family members can travel to the more comprehensive health clinics and hospitals farther away. In some areas, however, the wealthier peasants have actually built local schools and private hospitals. Furthermore, in a remarkable move away from dependency on the state for benefits, the Chinese now support Project Hope, an international charity whose purpose is to improve health care for China's poorest children.

In the cities, employees of state-run enterprises suffer from being on fixed state salaries that are barely adequate to buy goods whose prices are no longer state-controlled. By the mid-1990s, however, the state managed to bring inflation under greater control. China's annual inflation rate is now in the single digits, but many urban workers feel that they must have two jobs in order to make ends meet. In such an environment, there is also a greater temptation to engage in corruption in order to lead a better life. With the withering away of state control over the economy, but an inadequate system of regulations and laws to replace it, white-collar crime is surging in China.

The visible polarization of wealth, which had been virtually eradicated in the first 30 years of Communist rule, has returned to China with the return of the free market. The creation of a crassly ostentatious wealthy class and simply ostentatious middle class, in the context of high unemployment, poverty, and a mobile population, is breeding the very class conflict that the Chinese Communists fought a revolution to eliminate. When reforms began some 20 years ago, street crime was almost unheard of in China's cities. Now it is a serious problem, one that the government fears may lead to the overthrow of CCP rule if it is not brought under control.

Mortgaging the Future

One of the most damaging aspects of the capitalist "get-rich" atmosphere prevailing in China is the willingness to sacrifice the future for profits today. The environment is literally being destroyed by uncontrolled pollution, the rampant growth of new towns, cities, and highways, the building of houses on arable land, and the destruction of forests. Some middle schools have turned their basketball courts into parking lots in China's crowded cities, which are unable to provide parking facilities for the huge number of newly owned private cars. And they have used state funds allocated to the schools for education to build shops all along the outside walls of the schools. Teachers and administrators deal themselves the profits; but in the meantime, classroom materials and facilities are deteriorating.

Overall, however, the tensions among the central state, the provinces, the cities, the towns, and the enterprises that have been generated by decentralization of economic power have been beneficial to economic growth. Greater economic autonomy at each level has led to a concomitant growth in the political autonomy at that level. Thus, provinces—especially those that are producing significant revenues—can now challenge central economic policy, and even refuse to carry it out. For example, the wealthier eastern coastal provinces have successfully challenged the central government's right to collect more taxes on provincial revenues. Similarly, cities now have greater autonomy vis-à-vis the former all-encompassing power of the provinces over them. In short, this sort of economic power, won through the free market, has brought with it the political power necessary to challenge China's leaders. Indeed, some commentators wonder whether the unwillingness of the provinces to dutifully obey Beijing will lead to the breakup of China in the twenty-first century. In this

sense also, the Chinese must be wondering whether they are mortgaging the future for profits now.

SOCIALIST LEGALITY

China's legal system must be viewed within the particular Chinese cultural context for law as well as the goals of law in a socialist system. Reforms in China's legal system since 1979 have, however, brought a remarkable transformation in Chinese attitudes toward the law; and China's laws and legal procedures look increasingly like those used in the West. This is particularly true for laws that relate to the economy, including contract, investment, property, and commercial laws. The Chinese have discovered that the legal system has developed into a powerful protector of their rights in economic transactions. Criminal law and procedure have also undergone a rapid transformation. In civil law (when it relates to disputes with neighbors and family members), however, the Chinese are still more likely to rely on mediation to settle their disputes.

Ethical Basis of Law

In imperial China, the Confucian system provided the basis for the social and political order. Confucianism posited that

(UN photo by John Isaac)

Settling civil disputes in China today still usually involves neighborhood mediation committees, family members, and friends.

ethics were based on maintaining correct personal relationships among people, not based on laws. A legal system did exist, but the Chinese resorted to it in civil cases only in desperation, for the inability to resolve one's problems oneself, or through a mediator, usually resulted in considerable loss of "face," or dignity and pride. (In criminal cases, the state normally became involved in determining guilt and punishment.)

This perspective on law carried over into the period of Communist rule. Until legal reforms began in the 1980s, most Chinese preferred to call in CCP officials, local neighborhood or factory mediation committees, family members, and friends, not lawyers or judicial personnel, to settle disputes. Only when mediation failed did the Chinese resort to the courts. By contrast, the West lacks both this strong support for the institution of mediation and the concept of face. So Westerners have difficulty understanding why China has had so few lawyers and why the Chinese lack faith in the law.

Like Confucianism, Marxism-Leninism is an ideology that embodies a set of ethical standards for behavior. After 1949, it easily built on China's cultural predisposition toward ruling by ethics instead of law. Although Marxism-Leninism did not completely replace the Confucian ethical system, it did establish new standards of behavior based on socialist morality. These ethical standards emerge in the works of Marx and Lenin, in the writings of Mao Zedong, and in the CCP's policies.

Law and Politics

From 1949 until the legal reforms that began in 1979, Chinese universities trained very few lawyers. Legal training consisted of learning law and politics as an integrated whole; for according to Marxism, law is meant to reflect the values of the "ruling class" and to serve as an instrument of "class struggle." The Chinese Communist regime viewed law as a branch of the social sciences, not as a professional field of study. For this reason, China's citizens tended to view law as a mere propaganda tool, not as a means for protecting their rights. They have never really experienced a law-based society. Not only were China's laws and legal education highly politicized, but politics also pervaded the judicial system. With few lawyers available, few legally trained judges in the courts, and even fewer laws to refer to for standards of behavior, inevitably China's legal system has been subject to abuse. China has been ruled by people, not by law; by politics, not by legal standards; and by party policy, not by a constitution. Interference in the judicial process by party officials has been all too common.

After 1979, however, the government moved quickly to write new laws. Fewer than 300 lawyers, most of them trained before 1949 in Western legal institutions, undertook the immense task of writing a civil code, a criminal code, contract law, economic law, law governing foreign investment in China, tax law, and environmental and forestry laws. One

strong motivation for the Chinese Communist leadership to formalize the legal system was its growing realization, after years of a disappointingly low level of foreign investment, that the international business community was reluctant to invest further in China without substantial legal guarantees.

Even China's own potential entrepreneurs wanted legal protection against the *state* before they would assume the risks of developing new businesses. Enterprises, for example, want a legal guarantee that, if the state should fail to supply resources contracted for, it can be sued for losses issuing from its nonfulfillment of contractual obligations. Since the objective of economic reform is to encourage investment, the leadership has necessarily had to supplement economic reforms with legal reforms. Formalization of the legal system has fostered a stronger basis for modernization. New laws have, moreover, helped limit abuse of the people's rights by the government and the CCP.

Criminal Law

Procedures followed in Chinese criminal courts have differed significantly from those in, for example, the United States. Until 1996—when the concept of "innocent until proven guilty" was first introduced in China—it was presumed that people brought to trial in criminal cases were guilty. Not only was there a presumption of guilt, but the judicial process itself confirmed this guilt. That is, after the suspect was arrested by the police, the procuracy (the investigative branch of the judiciary system) would spend considerable time and effort finding out the facts and establishing whether the suspect was indeed guilty. This is important to understand when assessing the fact that 99 percent of all the accused who were brought to trial in China were judged guilty. Theoretically, had the facts not substantiated their guilt, the procuracy would have dismissed their cases before going to trial.

In short, those adjudged to be innocent were never brought to trial in the first place. For this reason, court appearances of the guilty functioned mainly to present the evidence upon which the guilty verdict was based—not to weigh the evidence to see if it indicated guilt—and to remind the public that criminals are punished. A trial was a "morality play" of sorts: the villain was punished, justice was done, the people's interests were protected. In addition, the trial process emphasized the importance of confessing one's crimes, for those who confessed and appeared repentant in court would usually be dealt more lenient sentences. Criminals were encouraged to turn themselves in, on the promise that their punishment would be less severe than if they were caught. Those accused of crimes were encouraged to confess rather than deny their guilt or appeal to the next level, all in hopes of gaining a more lenient sentence from the judge.

From the Western perspective, the real problem with this system was that once the procuracy established "the facts," they were not open to question by the lawyer or representative of the accused. (In China, a person may be represented by a

CONSUMER PROTECTION: COPYRIGHTS, TRADEMARKS, AND FAKE PRODUCTS

In the area of intellectual property rights (IPR)—a source of much controversy between China and the West—the Chinese government is increasingly concerned, for its own domestic reasons, that copyrights and trademarks be respected. China is awash with false labels and fake products. From hair tonics and soaps to appliances and fruit juices, the Chinese people are being duped daily because of inadequate state controls over labeling, trademarks, and copyrights. Fakes have had serious consequences. Fertilizers have destroyed crops, and medicines have made people sick. Low-quality liquor, clothing, compact discs, and other consumer goods are often falsely marketed under famous labels—and in any event are the patented or copyrighted property of someone else. Scores of people have died in China after drinking "white liquor" made from ethylene. Beer bottles falsely labeled with the name of well-known breweries explode and harm people. And people buy expensive home remedies, such as ankle massagers, that do not function, or that even do harm.

In an effort to crack down on those producing goods under false labels, the government set up an "Anti-Fake Bureau." The government allows legitimate enterprises to use a special hologram on their products to indicate authenticity—but already the hologram is being sold on the black market to anyone who wishes to stick it on their own products.

Consumer protection has become an important issue, and many large companies and department stores urge consumers to report products that are defective or are suspected fakes. In most countries, consumer protection is still a "luxury" right, a right that is ignored until the country is much further along in development than is China. It is strikingly paradoxical that just when the government is trying to decentralize control over social and economic policy and to privatize state property, the Chinese people are actually demanding that their government play a larger role in protecting the people—*from one another.* The area of consumer protection is a good example of the continuance of the traditional Chinese view that the state should act as the "parents" of the people, who are the "children" and need to be taken care of.

family member, friend, or colleague, largely because there are simply not enough lawyers to fulfill the guarantee of a person's "right to a defense.") The lawyer for the accused was not allowed to introduce new evidence, make arguments to dismiss the case based on technicalities or improper procedures (such as wire tapping), or make insanity pleas for the client. Instead, the lawyer's role in a criminal case was simply to represent the person in court and to bargain with the court for a reduced sentence for the repentant client. The 1996 legal reforms are supposed to have improved the rights of the accused by giving them access to a lawyer within several days of being formally arrested. So far, however, it appears that many suspects (including some well-known democratic dissidents) have not been accorded this right.

Although the accused have the right to a defense, it has always been presumed that a lawyer will not defend someone who is guilty. The lawyer is, in fact, an employee of the state and is paid by the state. As such, a lawyer's obligation is first and foremost to protect the state's interests, not the individual's interests at the expense of the state. When lawyers have done otherwise, they have risked being condemned as "counterrevolutionaries" or traitors. Small wonder that after 1949, the study of law did not attract China's most talented students.

The Need for Lawyers

In the areas of civil and commercial law, however, the role of the lawyer has become increasingly important since the opening of China's closed door to the outside world. Now that the leadership views trade with other countries and foreign investment as crucial to China's development, its goal is to train at least one lawyer for every state, collective, or private organization and enterprise. Increasingly, the Chinese recognize that upholding the law is not merely a question of correctly understanding the party "line" and then following it in legal disputes but, rather, of interpreting the meaning of law according to the concrete circumstances of a case. Yet even in economic disputes, lawyers who have vigorously defended their clients' interests against the state's interests have occasionally been condemned for being "anti-socialist."

Since China has had so little experience in dealing with civil conflicts and economic disputes in the courts, and since Western investors insist that Chinese courts be prepared to address such issues, the leadership has been forced to train lawyers in Western law and to draft literally thousands of new laws. To protect themselves against what is difficult to understand in the abstract, however, the Chinese used to refuse to publish their newly written laws. Claiming a shortage of paper or the need to protect "state secrets," they withheld publication of many laws until their actual impact on China's state interests could be determined. This practice frustrated potential investors, who dared not risk capital investment in China until they knew exactly what the relevant laws were. As relations with foreign investors as well as the entrepreneurial activities of their own citizens have grown increasingly complex, however, the Chinese government now feels obligated to publish most of its laws as quickly as possible.

THE POLITICAL SYSTEM

The Party and the State

In China, the Chinese Communist Party is the fountainhead of power and policy. But not all Chinese people are party

CENTRAL GOVERNMENT ORGANIZATION OF THE PEOPLE'S REPUBLIC OF CHINA

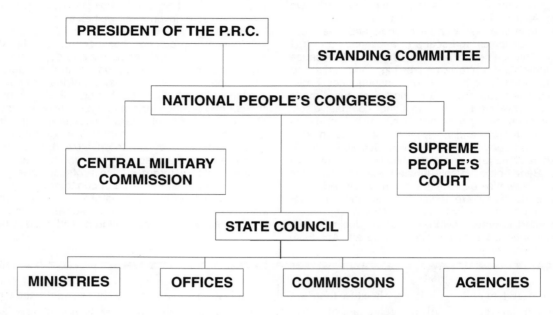

This central government organization chart represents the structure of the government of the People's Republic of China as it appears on paper. However, since all of the actions and overall doctrine of the central government must be reviewed and approved by the Chinese Communist Party, political power ultimately lies with the party. To ensure this control, virtually all top state positions are held by party members.

THE CHINESE COMMUNIST PARTY (CCP)

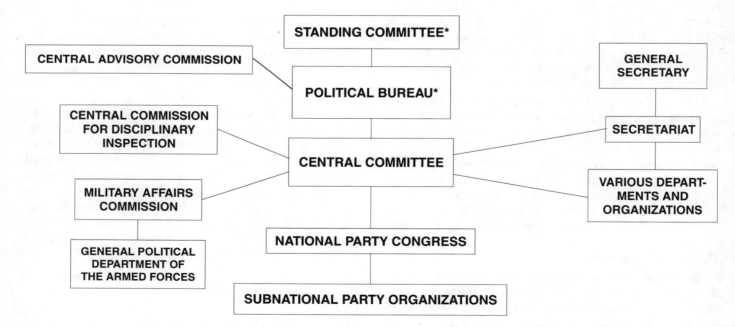

*This Political Bureau and its Standing Committee are the most powerful organizations within the Chinese Communist Party and are therefore the real centers of power in the P.R.C.

(Chinese News Service photo)

Although the Chinese Communist Party (shown here at its 11th National Congress) has hand-picked one candidate for each public office in the past, it is now allowing more than one person to run for the same post.

members. Although the CCP has some 50 million members, this represents less than 5 percent of the population.

Joining the CCP is a competitive, selective, rigorous process. Some have wanted to join out of a commitment to Communist ideals, others in hopes of climbing the ladder of opportunity, still others to gain access to limited goods and opportunities. By the late 1980s, however, so many students and educated individuals had grown cynical about the CCP that they refused to join. The motives of many of those who do join are considered suspect by ordinary people, as being a party member is likely to open more doors for advancement—and corruption—than are available to non-party members. Still, those who travel to China today are likely to find that many of the most talented people they meet are party members.

The CCP is the ultimate institutional authority and determines the "general line"—that is, the ideological justification of policy. All state policies must conform to the "general line." Although in theory the state is distinct from the party, in practice the two overlapped almost completely from the late 1950s to the early 1990s. By then, efforts by the reformers to get the party out of the day-to-day work of the government had started to take effect.

The state apparatus consists of a State Council, headed by the premier. Under the State Council are the ministries and agencies and "people's congresses" responsible for the formulation of policy. The CCP, however, exercises firm control over these state bodies through interlocking organizations. For example, CCP branches exist within all government organizations, and all key state personnel are also party members.

China's socialist system is subject to enormous abuses of power. The lines of authority within both the CCP and the state system are poorly defined, as are the rules for succession to the top leadership positions. This has allowed individuals like Mao Zedong and the Gang of Four to usurp power and rule arbitrarily. By the late 1980s, China's bureaucracy appeared to have become more corrupt than at any time since 1949. Anger at the massive scale of official corruption was, in fact, the major factor unifying ordinary citizens and workers with students during the antigovernment protests in the spring of 1989.

Campaigns to control official corruption continue. Individuals are encouraged to write letters to the editors of the country's daily newspapers to expose corruption or to suggest how corruption might be ferreted out. Some cases are investigated by journalists, thereby focusing public attention on official abuse. Television has a daily program running in prime time that records the successes of China's public-security system in cracking down on corruption and crime.

Reform of the political system has been another avenue that the government has pursued in its effort to curb corruption. The Chinese have tried to separate the party from the functions of the state bureaucracy and economic enterprises. For some leadership positions, there are now limits on tenure in office. There are also strict prohibitions on a leader developing a personality cult, such as that which reached fanatical proportions around CCP chairman Mao Zedong during the Cultural Revolution. Reforms have also encouraged, if not demanded, that the Chinese state bureaucracy reward merit more than mere seniority, and expertise more than political activism. And, in 1996, the government's practice since 1949 of leading officials staying in one ministry during their entire career was replaced by new regulations requiring officials from divisional chiefs up to ministers and provincial governors to be rotated every 5 years. In addition, no high official may work in the same office as his or her spouse or direct blood relative. It is hoped that such regulations will curtail the building of power bases that foster corruption within ministries.

So far, most efforts to control official corruption have had little effect. Officials continue to use their power to achieve personal gain, trading official favors for others' services (such as better housing, jobs for their children, admission to the right schools, and access to goods in short supply). Getting things done in a system that requires layers of bureaucratic approval still depends heavily upon a complex set of personal connections and relationships, all reinforced through under-the-table gift giving. This stems in part from the still heavily centralized aspect of Chinese governance, and in part from the overstaffing of a bureaucracy that is plagued by red tape. Countless offices must sign off on requests for anything from buying a typewriter to getting a telephone. This gives enormous power to individual officials who are willing to take charge of processing an individual's or work unit's request for something, such as a license or a building permit. In today's more market-oriented China, for example, anyone with adequate funds may buy an air conditioner. But because all electrical service is controlled by the government, people who do purchase air conditioners must pay off an official to allow the electrical service to their living units to be upgraded so that they can actually use an air conditioner. Similarly, brothels can be run in the open, virtually without interference from the police, because they are bribed to look the other way.

An example of the difficulty in controlling corruption is this: To cut down on the abuse of official privilege, the government issued a new regulation stipulating that governmental officials doing business could order only four dishes and one soup. But as most Chinese like to eat well, especially at the government's expense, the restaurants accommodated them by simply giving them much *larger* plates on which they put many different dishes, and wrote it up as one dish! Another example concerns middlemen who are paid for arranging business transactions. They used to be considered corrupt. Now a government regulation says it is all right for a middleman to keep 5 percent of the total value of the transaction as a "fee," and it is no longer called corruption. The Chinese have also adopted the custom in other countries of permitting tour guides who take tourists to a shop to receive a percentage of the total sales, behavior that previously was considered corrupt.

ENVIRONMENT FOR DEMOCRACY
When assessing the Chinese political system's level of freedom, democracy, and individual rights, it is important to remember that the Chinese do not share the values and traditions of the West's Greco–Roman political heritage. For millennia, Chinese thought has run along different lines, with far less emphasis on such ideals as individual rights, privacy, and limits on state power. The Chinese political tradition is one of authoritarianism and moral indoctrination. For more than 2,000 years, China's rulers have shown greater concerns for establishing their authority and maintaining unity in the vast territory and populations they controlled than in Western concepts of democratic liberalism. Apart from China's intellectuals in the twentieth century, the vast majority of the Chinese people have appeared to be more afraid of chaos than rule by an authoritarian despot. As a result, even today the Chinese people seem more concerned that their rulers have enough power to control China than that the rights of the citizens vis-à-vis their rulers be protected.

Cultural and Historical Authoritarianism
The heavy weight of more than 2,000 years of Chinese history helped shape the development of today's political system. The Chinese inherited a patriarchal culture, in which the hierarchical values of superior–inferior and subordination, loyalty, and obedience prevailed over those of equality; a historical predisposition toward official secrecy; a fear of officials and official power; a traditional repugnance for courts, lawyers, and formal laws that resulted in a legal system inadequately developed to defend democratic rights; and a legacy of authoritarianism. These cultural factors provided the context for the introduction of Western democratic values and institutions into China from the nineteenth century onward. As a result, the Chinese people have not embraced Western democratic values with fervor.

China's limited experience with democracy in the twentieth century has been bitter. Virtually the entire period from the fall of China's imperial monarchy in 1911 to the Communist victory in 1949 (the period of the "Republic of China" on the mainland) was marred by warlordism, chaos, war, and a government masking brutality, greed, and incompetence under the label of "democracy." Although it is hardly fair to blame this period of societal collapse and externally imposed war on China's efforts to practice "democracy" under the "tutelage of the Kuomintang," the Chinese people's experience of democracy was nevertheless negative.

China's experience of democracy from 1912 until 1949, together with its political culture, helps explain the people's reluctance to pursue democracy aggressively. During that period, the existence of both democratic political institutions and a complete legal system (on paper) proved inadequate to guarantee the protection of individual rights. Under Communist rule after 1949, the period described as "democratic mass rule" (the "10 bad years" or "Cultural Revolution" from 1966 to 1976) was in fact a period of mass tyranny. For the Chinese, the experience of relinquishing power to "the masses" turned into the most horrific period of unleashed terrorism and cruelty that they had experienced since the Communist takeover.[11]

Socialist Democracy

When the CCP came to power in 1949, it inherited a country that had been torn by civil war, internal rebellion, and foreign invasions for more than 100 years. The population was overwhelmingly illiterate and desperately poor, the economy in shambles. The most urgent need was for order. Despite some serious setbacks and mistakes, Mao Zedong and his colleagues made great strides in securing China's borders, establishing the institutions of government, and enhancing the material well-being of the Chinese people. But they also severely limited the development of "democracy" as the liberal democratic West would understand it, in the name of order and stability.

The Chinese people are accustomed to "eating bitterness," not to standing up to authority. The traditional Confucian emphasis on the group rather than the individual and an emphasis on respect for authority, although now being undercut by the effects of modernization and disenchantment with the CCP leadership, continue to this Day.

An atmosphere of greater freedom is pervasive in China as it nears the millennium, but all will admit that a gnawing fear persists as to what *could* happen. As one faculty member in a university remarked, although he doesn't think the atrocities of the Cultural Revolution could happen again, he still writes his diary in code. As he put it, when you feel you have been watched every day of your life for 43 years, it is difficult to rid yourself of deeply ingrained fears when no one is watching any longer. Furthermore, many would admit that, although those scholars and students studying abroad who protested the Chinese government's brutal suppression of the 1989 Tiananmen demonstrations need not fear being jailed or persecuted if they return to China (unless, of course, like Shen Tong, an actual leader of those demonstrations, they are brazen enough to publicly advocate democratization on their return), they might well be punished in other ways—such as by the state offering them jobs inappropriate for the level of education they received abroad. Thus, the government continues to decide which rights individuals will receive—and when to withdraw them.

The Chinese people lack interest in political participation in part because it appears "ineffective in getting what they want for themselves. For that purpose, they have found that under-the-table gift giving to, and entertainment of local officials, together with developing a 'web of connections,' are far more effective. Chinese peasants and workers seem inclined to believe that policies change only when high-level officials mandate it, not in response to popular pressure."[12] This helps explain the pervasive gift giving and outright bribery in China.

As the impersonal market forces of supply and demand undercut the power of officials to control the distribution of resources and opportunities in the society, these patterns are changing. Participation in the political process at the local level is already reaping significant results, with some officials eagerly seeking out advice for improving the economic conditions in their localities, and with incompetent officials unable to gain reelection. Nevertheless, many Chinese continue to believe that voicing their opinions in some situations is useless and can even be dangerous; and memories of forced participation in the many campaigns and movements in China since 1949 "continue to give political participation a negative connotation. The result is that an active political participant is often regarded with deep suspicion."[13]

To the extent that the unwillingness of Chinese to challenge the political institutions and rulers of the CCP regime may be labeled as passive or submissive behavior, not to mention "collusion" with their oppressors, is it in any sense unique to China? One could argue that Central/Eastern Europeans also participated in their own political oppression simply by complying with the demands of the system. Vaclav Havel, president of Czechoslovakia and subsequently of the Czech Republic, once stated: "All of us have become accustomed to the totalitarian system, accepted it as an unalterable fact and therefore kept it running. . . . None of us is merely a victim of it, because all of us helped to create it together."[14] Can we say that the Chinese, any more than the Czechs, passively *accepted* totalitarianism if they did not go into exile outside of their country or did not refuse to work? Is anyone who does not actively revolt against an oppressive system necessarily in collusion with it?

> The danger of losing jobs and the threats to survival make many people fearful. Fear also comes from the policy of implication, the personal dossiers. . . . The people, therefore, can only try to cope with the situation by burying anger deep in their hearts.[15]

In short, those who do not challenge the system out of fear of the consequences cannot be said to be supportive of the system; but one cannot assume that the major reason why people are not challenging the Communist system is out of fear of punitive consequences.

Were the CCP to step back from its state policies of punishment for political crimes, then, there is nothing in an abstract Chinese culture that would necessarily cause Chinese to remain submissive to an authoritarian regime. Rather, it is the political system that has reinforced the authoritarian qualities of Chinese culture. Nor should a lack of rules and institutions be considered an insurmountable object, as "democratic" behavioral skills can be acquired through practice.[16] In short, as the political system becomes more liberal, the political culture is likely to evolve—indeed, it *is* evolving—in a more liberal direction.

Limited Popular Demands for Greater Democracy

So far, China has experienced only limited popular demand for democracy. When the student-led demonstrations in Beijing began in 1989, the demands for democratic reforms were confined largely to the small realm of the elite—students and well-educated individuals as well as some members of the political and economic ruling elite. The workers and farmers of China remained more concerned about bread-and-butter issues—inflation, economic growth, and their own personal enrichment—not democratic ideals.

By the mid-1990s, many Chinese had discovered that they could get exactly what they wanted through channels other than mass demonstrations, because of the development of numerous alternative groups, institutions, and processes. Many of these groups are not political in origin, but the process by which they are pressing for policy changes in the government is highly political. Literally hundreds of thousands of interest groups and associations have sprung up in the last decades. While many of these interest groups are organized and controlled by the state (such as the Women's Association and the Communist Party Youth League), others are not. It is perhaps ironic that the Chinese Communist Party's penchant for organizing people resulted in teaching them organizational skills that they now use in the non-government-directed sphere—and sometimes for the purpose of pressuring the government to change policy.[17] They work through these organizations to advance and protect their members' interests within the framework of existing laws and regulations.

Even those Chinese not working through officially organized associations ban together to petition local officials in the style they learned through socialization by the CCP. For example, urban neighborhoods join forces to stop local noise pollution emanating from stereos blasting on the street where thousands of Chinese couples learn ballroom dancing, or from the cymbals, tambourines, gongs, and drums of old ladies doing "fan dancing" on the city streets.[18] In turn, the fan dancers and the ballroom dancers petition the local officials to maintain their "right" to express themselves through dance in the streets, some of the few public spaces available to them in a crowded urban environment.

The tendency to organize around issues and interests in China today is more than a reflection of the decline of the role of Communist ideology in shaping policy. It also reflects the government's assertion of highly pragmatic concerns in policy making, and the desire of distinct constituencies to fall in line with, or take advantage of, this approach to issues and policy. Although China has never been homogeneous and uncomplicated, it is certainly a far more complicated economy, society, and polity today than it was before 1980. Today's China has far more diverse needs and interests to be represented than previously, and specialized associations and interest groups serve the need of articulating these interests.

Lack of an Alternative Leadership

One of the critical problems for democratization in China has been the people's inability to envision an alternative to CCP rule: It has been *unthinkable*. What form would it take? How would it get organized? Wouldn't the organizers be jailed? And if the CCP were overthrown, who would lead a new system? These questions are still far from being answered even today.

So far, no dissident leadership capable of offering an alternative to CCP leadership and laying claim to popular support has formed. Even the mass demonstrations in 1989 were not led by either a worker, or a peasant, or by an intellectual with whom the common people could identify:

[C]ompared with the intellectuals of Poland and Czechoslovakia, for example, Chinese intellectuals have little contact with workers and peasants and are not sensitive to their country's worsening social crisis; they were caught unawares by the democratic upsurge of 1989, and proved unable to provide the people with either the theoretical or practical guidance they needed.[19]

In fact, during the Tiananmen protests in 1989, students were actually annoyed with the workers' participation in the demonstrations. They wanted to press their own political demands, not the workers' more concrete work-related issues. Some Chinese have commented that the students' real interest in demanding respect for their own goals from China's leadership was because they wanted to enhance their own power vis-à-vis the regime: The students' major demands were for a "dialogue" with the government as "equals," and for free speech—issues of primary interest to them, but of secondary interest to the workers of China.

Many Chinese believe that the leaders of the 1989 demonstrations would have differed little from the CCP elite had they suddenly been catapulted to power. The student movement itself admitted to being authoritarian, of kowtowing to its own leaders, and of expecting others to obey rather than to discuss decisions. As one Beijing University student wrote during the 1989 Tiananmen Square protests:

The autonomous student unions have gradually cut themselves off from many students and become a machine kept constantly on the run in issuing orders. No set of organizational rules widely accepted by the students has emerged, and the democratic mechanism is even more vague.[20]

STOCK MARKETS, GAMBLING, AND LOTTERIES

China has had two stock markets since just before the Tiananmen Square demonstrations of 1989. One is in the Special Economic Zone of Shenzhen; the other is in Shanghai. With only seven industries originally registered on them, strict rules about how much daily profit or loss (1.2 percent for the Shanghai exchange until July 1992) a stock could undergo, and deep public suspicion that these original issues of stocks were worthless, these markets got off to a slow start. But when these same stocks were worth five times their original value just a year later, the public took notice. Rumors—as important in China as actual news—took over and exaggerated the likelihood of success in picking a winning stock. The idea of investors actually losing money, much less a stock-market crash, did not seem to be an idea whose time had come.

Soon there were so many Chinese dollars chasing so few stocks that the government began a lottery system: Anyone who wanted to buy a stock had first to buy a coupon, which was then put into a national lottery. The supply/demand ratio for stocks was so out of proportion that an individual had only a 1 in 100 chance of having a coupon chosen from the lottery. The coupon would, in turn, enable its bearer to buy a mere five shares of a stock that might or might not make a profit. Today, thanks to the rapid increase in stocks registered on the two stock exchanges, there is now a 70 in 100 chance of getting the right to buy a stock.

As communications remain poor in China, and as it is still largely a cash economy, making a stock-market transaction does not resemble what happens in a Western country. Instead of simply telephoning a stockbroker and giving an order, with a simple bank transfer or check to follow shortly, most Chinese must still appear in person, stand in line, and pay cash on the spot. Taiwan has added its own angle to the stockmania by selling to the Mainlanders small radios that are tuned in to only one frequency—stock-market news.

Issuing, buying, and selling stocks has become a near-national obsession. Not only do ordinary companies selling commercial goods, such as computers and clothing, issue stocks. So do taxicab companies and even universities. Thus far, few such stocks are actually listed on the national stock exchanges; but employees of these work units are eager to purchase the stocks. In most cases, the original issues are sold at far higher prices than their face value, as employees (and even nonemployees) eagerly buy up fellow employees' rights to purchase stocks, at grossly inflated prices. Presumably, the right of employees to own stock in their own work unit will make them eager to have it do well, and thus increase efficiency and profits.

Companies that are owned and run by state agencies and ministries, such as the Ministry of Defense, have used state funds to invest in stocks and real estate, including international stock markets and real estate abroad. Regrettably, they have sometimes lost millions of yuan in the process. As a result, the government has now prohibited state-run units from investing state money in stocks and real estate. Some still do it, however, through the companies which they control, especially those with foreign connections.

Learning from Western practices and catering to a national penchant for gambling (illegal, but indulged in nevertheless, in mahjong and cards), the Chinese have also begun a number of lotteries. Thus far, most of these have been for the purpose of raising money for specific charities or causes, such as for victims of floods and for the disabled. Recently, because the items offered, such as brand-new cars, have been so desirable, the lotteries have generated billions of yuan in revenue. The government has found these government-controlled lotteries to be an excellent way of addressing the Chinese penchant for gambling while simultaneously generating revenues to compensate for those it seems unable to collect through taxes.

Finally, following Western marketing gimmicks for increasing sales, some companies put Chinese characters on the inside of packages or bottle caps to indicate whether the purchaser has won a prize. With a little Chinese ingenuity, the world could witness never-before-imaged realms of betting and competitive business practices that appeal to people's desire to get something for nothing.

In any event, few of those who participated in the demonstrations in 1989 are interested in politics or political leadership today. Most have thrown themselves into business and making money.

Apart from students and intellectuals, the major proponents of democratic reform today hail from China's newly emerging business circles; but these two groups have not united to achieve reform, as they neither like nor trust each other. Intellectuals view venture capitalists "as uncultured, and business people as driven only by crass material interests." They in turn regard intellectuals and students as "well-meaning but out of touch with reality and always all too willing and eager to serve the state" when it suits their needs.[21]

One thing seems clear: Those dissidents who left China and remain abroad have lost their political influence with the Chinese people. Apart from everything else, dissidents abroad still have no way to make themselves heard in China, where their articles cannot be published. Although e-mail and fax machines keep them in touch with other dissidents in China, their influence is largely limited to their ability to supply funds to the dissident movement in China. Doing so, however, often gets the recipients in China in considerable trouble, including lengthy prison sentences.

The Impact of Global Interdependency on Democratization

Since the late 1970s, the cultural context for democracy in China has shifted. Growing awareness of global interdependency, with the expansion of the global capitalist economy to include China, has brought with it a social and economic transformation of China. For the first time in Chinese history, a significant challenge to the "we–they" dichotomy—of China on the one hand, against the rest of the world on the other—is occurring. This in turn has led many Chinese to question the heretofore assumed superiority of Chinese civilization to all other civilizations.

Such an idea does not come easily for a people long accustomed to believing in their own superiority. Hence the fuss caused by "River Elegy," a television series first shown on Chinese national television in 1988. In this series, the producers argued that the Chinese people must embrace the idea of global interdependency—technological, economic, and cultural. To insist at this time in history on the superiority of Chinese civilization, with the isolation of China from the world of ideas that this implies, would only contribute to China's continued stagnation. The series suggested that the Chinese must see themselves as equal, not superior, to others; and as interdependent with, not as victims of, others. Such concepts of equality, and opening up China to ideas from outside of China, implicitly challenge the CCP's authoritarian rule and are still resisted by the more conservative reformers remaining in China's top leadership today.

The Press and Mass Media

When the student-led demonstrations for democracy began in the spring of 1989, China's press had witnessed remarkable growth in its diversity and liberalization of its content. With some 1,500 newspapers, 5,000 magazines, and 500 publishing houses, the Chinese were able to express a wider variety of viewpoints and ideas than at any time since the CCP came to power in 1949. The importation and domestic production of millions of television sets, radios, short-wave radios, cassette recorders, players, and VCRs also facilitated the growth of the mass media in China. They have been accompanied by a wide array of "un-Chinese" and "non-Communist" audio and video materials. The programs of the British Broadcasting Corporation (BBC) and the Voice of America, the diversification of domestic television and radio programs (a choice made by the Chinese government and facilitated by international satellite communications), and the importation and translation of foreign books and magazines—all contributed to a more pluralistic press in China. In fact, by 1989, the stream of publications had so overwhelmed the CCP Propaganda Department that it was simply no longer able to monitor their content.

During the demonstrations in Tiananmen Square in 1989, the Chinese press, under pressure from students and from the international press in Beijing (which, unlike the Chinese press, freely filmed and filed reports on the demonstrations), took a leap into complete press freedom. With cameramen and microphones in hand, reporters covered a student hunger strike that began on May 13 in its entirety. But with the imposition of martial law in Beijing on May 20, press freedom came to a crashing halt.

In the immediate aftermath of the crackdown on Tiananmen Square in June 1989, the CCP imposed a ban on a variety of books, journals, and magazines. Vice Premier Wang Zhen

ordered the "cleansing" of media organizations, with "bad elements" removed and not permitted to leave Beijing for reporting. All press and magazine articles written during the prodemocracy movement, all television and radio programs shown during that period, were analyzed to see if they conformed to the party line. Those individuals responsible for editing during that time were dismissed. And, as had been the practice in the past, press and magazine articles once again had to be on topics specified by the editors, who were under the control of the CCP. In short, press freedom in China suffered a significant setback because of the prodemocracy demonstrations in the spring of 1989.

In the new climate of experimentation launched by Deng Xiaoping in 1992, however, the diversity of television and radio programs soared. China's major cities now have multiple television and radio channels, carrying a broad range of programs from Hong Kong, Taiwan, Japan, and the West. These programs—whether soap operas about daily life for Chinese people living in Hong Kong and Taiwan, or art programs exposing the Chinese to the world of Western religious art through a visual art-history tour of the Vatican, or in news about protests and problems faced by other nations in the world—are both subtly and blatantly exposing the Chinese to values, ideas, and standards of living previously unknown to them. The Chinese are even learning about the American legal process through China's rebroadcasting of American television dramas that focus on police and the judicial system. Chinese are fascinated that American police, as soon as they arrest suspects, inform them that they have "the right to remain silent" and "the right to a lawyer." Such programs may do more to bring reform to the Criminal Procedure Code than all the efforts of the human-rights groups have achieved.

Today, ownership of television sets is widespread. China even has 50 million cable-television subscribers, with 5 million new subscribers being added each year. And virtually all families have radios. Round-the-clock, all-news radio stations broadcast the latest political, economic, and cultural news and conduct live radio and television interviews; and radio talk shows take phone calls from anonymous listeners about everything from sex to political corruption. There are even blatant critiques of corruption in the leadership, police brutality,[22] and the failure of government policies on everything from trade policy to health care and unemployment. There is also far better coverage of social and economic news in all the media than previously, and there is serious investigative reporting on corruption and crime.

To paint the picture in quantitative terms, about 5,000 books were published annually around 1970. By 1990, the total was close to 90,000 annually; by 1995, it was about 104,000. In 1970, there were fewer than 50 newspapers. By 1990, the number had grown to 1,444, and by 1995, to 2,202—an overall increase of more than 4,000 percent in 25 years. Similarly, in 1970, virtually no journals were published.

(Photo by Liu Li)

Students from the University of Law and Politics staged a sit-in during the Tiananmen Square demonstrations in 1989.

By 1990, there were more than 6,000 *registered* journals and magazines; by 1995, there were 8,135—an official number that excludes the large number of nonregistered magazines and illegal publications.[23] The number of radio stations increased from 635 in 1990 to 1,210 in 1995; the number of television stations, from 509 to 980. By 1995, there were also 1,200 cable-television stations and 54,084 ground satellite stations. Today, close to 90 percent of the population have access to television.[24] In fact, print and electronic media are so prolific and diverse that much of it escapes any monitoring whatsoever, especially newspapers, magazines, and books.

The sheer quantity of output on television, radio, books, and the press allows the Chinese people to make choices among the types of news, programs, and perspectives that they find most appealing. The choice is not necessarily for the most informative or the highest quality, but for the most entertaining. As a result, the media have become market-driven, and consumers' preferences, not government regulations or ideological values, shape programming and publishing decisions. This market orientation is due to economic reforms: By the 1990s, the government had cut subsi-

dies to the media, thereby requiring that even the state-controlled media had to make money or be shut down; and this in turn meant that the news stories it presented had to be more newsworthy in order to sell advertising and subscriptions. Similarly, television programs, which now lack adequate state subsidies, must be appealing to viewers in order to attract advertising. In short: "Even though China's media can hardly be called free, the emergence of divergent voices means the center's ability to control people's minds has vanished."[25]

The end of government subsidies to the media has spurred publication. Thinking that there is money to be made, township and village enterprises in the countryside, and even private entrepreneurs, have set up thousands of printing facilities over the last 10 to 15 years. Similarly, "China's 500 state presses and 6000 registered journals and magazines have . . . turned themselves into profit maximizers."[26] All of the media now respond to consumers' tastes.

The printed press has regained substantial freedom since the crackdown on dissidents in 1989. "Week-end editions" print just about any story that will sell. Often about the seamier side of Chinese life, all are undercutting the puritannical aspect of CCP rule and expanding the range of topics available for discussion in the public domain. And China's official newspapers, which now must make money because the state no longer subsidizes them, cater to readers' interests so that they can solicit more advertising fees. So many publishing houses have sprung up that the CCP no longer has the resources to monitor the content of their publications. And even China's movies, plays, and fine arts have been able to provide commentary on heretofore prohibited topics.[27]

The Student and Mass Movement of 1989

Symbolism is very important in Chinese culture; the death of a key leader is a particularly significant moment. In the case of the former head of the CCP, Hu Yaobang, his sudden death in April 1989 became symbolic of the death of liberalizing forces in China. The students used Hu's death as an excuse to place his values and policies in juxtaposition with those of the then increasingly conservative leadership. The deceased leader's career and its meaning were touted as symbols of liberalization, even though his life was hardly a monument to liberal thought. More conservative leaders in the CCP had removed him from his position as the CCP's general secretary in part because he had offended their cultural sensibilities. Apart from everything else, Hu's suggestions that the Chinese turn in their chopsticks for knives and forks and not eat food out of a common dish because it spread disease were culturally offensive to them.

The students' reassessment of Hu Yaobang's career in a way that rejected the party's evaluation was in itself a challenge to the authority of the CCP's right to rule China. A student hunger strike during the visit of then–Soviet president Mikhail Gorbachev to China was, even in the eyes of ordinary Chinese people, an insult to the Chinese leadership. Many Chinese later contended that the students went too far—that by humiliating the leadership, they humiliated *all* Chinese.

Part of the difficulty in reaching an agreement between the students and China's leaders was that the students' demands changed over time. At first they merely wanted a reassessment of Hu Yaobang's career. But quickly the students added new demands: An end to official corruption, exposure of the financial and business dealings of the central leadership, a free press, dialogue between the government and the students (with the students to be treated as equals with top CCP leaders), retraction of an offensive *People's Daily* editorial, the removal of the top CCP leadership, and still other actions that challenged continued CCP rule.

The students' hunger strike, which lasted for one week in May, was the final straw that brought down the wrath of the central leadership. Martial law was imposed in Beijing; and when the citizens of Beijing resisted its enforcement and blocked the army's efforts to reach Tiananmen Square to clear out the hunger-strikers, both students and CCP leaders dug in; but both were deeply fractured bodies. Indeed, divisions within the student-led movement caused it to lose its direction; and divisions within the central CCP leadership incapacitated the leadership. For 2 weeks, the central leadership wrangled over who was right and what to do. On June 4, the "hard-liners" won out, and they chose to use military power over a negotiated solution with the students.

Did the students make significant or well-thought-out statements about "democracy" or realistic demands on China's leaders? The short and preliminary answer is no; but then, is this really the appropriate question to be asking in the first place? One could argue that what the students *said* was less important than what they *did:* They mobilized the population of China's capital and other major cities to support a profound challenge to the legitimacy of the CCP's leadership. Even if workers believed that "You can't eat democracy," and even if they participated in the demonstrations for their own reasons (such as gripes about inflation and corruption), they did support the students' demand that the CCP carry out further political reforms. This was because the students successfully promoted the idea that if China had had a different sort of system—a democratic system rather than authoritarian rule—the leadership would have been more responsive to the workers' bread-and-butter issues and to corruption.

Repression within China Following the Crackdown

By August 1989, the CCP leadership had established quotas of "bad elements" for work units and identified 20 categories of people to be targeted for punishment. But people were more reluctant than in the past to follow orders to expose their friends, colleagues, and family members—not only because such verdicts had often been reversed at a later time, but also because few believed the CCP's version of what happened in Beijing on June 4. Although many people worried about informers,[28] there seemed to be complicity from top to bottom, whether inside or outside the ranks of the CCP, in refusing to go along with efforts to ferret out demonstrators and sympathizers with the prodemocracy, antiparty movement. Party leaders below the central level appeared to believe that the central-government's leadership was doomed; for this reason, they dared not carry out its orders. Inevitably, there would be a reversal of verdicts, and they did not want to be caught in that reversal.

As party leaders in work units droned on in mandatory political study sessions about Deng Xiaoping's important writings, workers wondered how long it would be before the June 4 military crackdown was condemned as a "counterrevolutionary crime against the people." Individuals in work units had to fill out lengthy questionnaires. A standard one had 24 questions aimed at "identifying the enemy." Among them were such questions as, "What did you think when Hu Yaobang died?" "When Zhao Ziyang went to Tiananmen Square, what did you think? Where were you?" At one university, each questionnaire had to be verified by two people (other than one's own family), or else the individual involved would not be allowed to teach.[29]

As part of the repression that followed the military crackdown in June 1989, the government carried out announced and unannounced arrests of hundreds of "liberal" intellectuals, students, workers, and others supporting the democracy movement. Some were summarily executed, although available information indicates that almost all of those executed were workers involved in the formation of labor unions. During the world's absorption with the Persian Gulf War in 1991, the Chinese government announced the trials and verdicts on some of China's most famous dissident leaders of the 1989 demonstrations.

All of the known 1989 student and intellectual dissidents leaders have been released since then, although several of the best known have been deported to the West as a condition of their release. The government has also occasionally re-arrested some dissidents for other activities. In 1998, for example, several of those who participated in the 1989 demonstrations made bold attempts to form a new party to challenge Chinese Communist Party rule. Although their efforts to register this new party were at first tolerated, they were later arrested, tried, and sentenced to prison.

As with the mass media, many repressive controls in Chinese society have slowly disappeared. Chinese people are free to criticize the government, though they cannot take political action that would threaten CCP rule. In any event, in spite of the government's best efforts, the Internet is virtually uncontrollable. China's students, intellectuals, businesspeople, and ordinary citizens know what is going on in the world and can spend their time chatting to dissidents abroad on e-mail if they so choose. As a result, although there are occasional arrests of dissidents who are blatantly challenging CCP rule, the leadership is more focused on harnessing the talents of its best and brightest for China's modernization than it is on controlling dissent.

INTERNATIONAL RELATIONS

From the 1830s onward, foreign imperialists nibbled away at China, subjecting it to one national humiliation after another. As early as the 1920s, both the KMT and the CCP were committed to unifying and strengthening China in order to rid it of foreigners and resist further foreign incursions. When the Communists achieved victory over the KMT in 1949, they vowed that foreigners would never again be permitted to tell China what to do. This historical background is essential to understanding China's foreign policy in the period of Chinese Communist rule.

From Isolation to Openness

The Communists had forced all but a handful of foreigners to leave China by the early 1950s. China charted an independent, and eventually an isolationist, foreign policy. After the end of the Cultural Revolution in 1976, and the return to power of more pragmatic "reformers" in 1978, China re-opened its door to the outside world. By the 1980s, it was hosting several million tourists annually, inviting foreign investors and foreign experts to help with China's modernization, and allowing Chinese to study and travel abroad. Nevertheless, inside China, contacts between Chinese and foreigners were still affected by the suspicion on the part of ordinary Chinese that ideological and cultural contamination comes from abroad and that association with foreigners might bring trouble.

Today, these attitudes have moderated considerably, to the point where some Chinese are more willing to make friends with foreigners, invite them to their homes, and even date and marry them; but this greater openness to things foreign sits uncomfortably together with a sort of neo-nationalism that has crept into the picture. The broad masses of Chinese people remain suspicious, even disdainful, of foreigners. Sensitivity to any suggestion of foreign control and a strong xenophobia (dislike and fear of foreigners) mean that the Chinese are likely to rail at any effort by other countries to tell them what to do. The Chinese continued to exhibit this sensitivity on a wide variety of issues, from human rights to China's policy toward Tibet and Taiwan; from intellectual property rights to working conditions in factories.

The Chinese people appear, moreover, to be just as nationalistic in their individual responses to foreign criticism of China as is the government. In addition to concurring with the government on its position on Taiwan, Tibet, Tiananmen, the U.S. threat of economic sanctions to challenge China's human-rights policies, and so on, the Chinese people exhibited extraordinary anger at losing the Olympics-site bid for the year 2000. They believe that China lost the bid only because of American manipulation of the decision to punish China for its human-rights abuses. The Chinese people were also enraged at the American broadcasters' suggestion on television during the 1996 Summer Olympics that China's swimmers had won medals only by using performance-enhancing drugs.

China's xenophobia continues to show up in its efforts to keep foreigners isolated in certain living compounds; to limit social contacts between foreigners and Chinese; to control the importation of foreign literature, films, and periodicals; and to keep foreign ideas—and diseases—out of China. In some respects, it has been a losing battle, with growing numbers of foreigners in China socializing with Chinese; television swamped with foreign programs; Kentucky Fried Chicken, McDonald's, and pizza parlors proliferating; "Avon calling" at several million homes;[30] body building and disco becoming part of the culture; and AIDS cases rocketing skyward. In 1996, in an effort to protect China's culture, the government ordered television stations to broadcast only Chinese-made programs during prime time. The pride of the Chinese in their culture and country has been enhanced in recent years by their economic success and by China's outstanding performance in international events, such as the Olympics and Asian Games, music competitions, and film festivals.

By any measure, China is today a much more open country than at any time since 1949. This is in spite of the concern of the more conservative wing of the CCP about the impact of

China's "open door" policy on the political system (the influx of ideas about democracy and individual rights), on economic development (a market economy, corruption, and foreign control and ownership), and on Chinese culture ("pollution" from foreign literature and pornography). Although a large number of foreign businesses left in the wake of the crushing of the student-led protests in June 1989, they were soon back. The favorable investment climate created by Deng's 1992 "experiment" (try-anything-that-works) speech accelerated the return of foreign capital. Since then, China has seemed less worried about the invasion of foreign values than anxious to attract foreign investments. The government's view now seems to be: If it takes night clubs, discos, exciting stories in the media, stock markets, rock concerts, the Internet, and consumerism to make the Chinese people content and the economy flourish under CCP rule, then so be it.

THE SINO–SOVIET RELATIONSHIP

While forcing most other foreigners to leave China in the 1950s, the Chinese Communist regime invited experts from the Soviet Union to China to give much-needed advice, technical assistance, and aid. This convinced the United States (already certain that Moscow controlled communism wherever it appeared) that the Chinese were Soviet puppets. Indeed, for most of the 1950s, the Chinese Communist regime had to accept Soviet tenets of domestic and foreign policy along with Soviet aid. But China's leaders soon grew concerned about the limits of Soviet aid and the relevance of Soviet policies to China's conditions—especially the costly industrialization favored by the Soviet Union. Ultimately, the Chinese questioned their Soviet "big brother" and turned, in the form of the Great Leap Forward policy, to a Chinese model of development. Khrushchev warned the Chinese of the dangers to China's economy in undertaking the Great Leap Forward; but Mao Zedong interpreted this as evidence that the Soviet Union wanted to hold back China's development.

The Soviets' refusal to use their military power in support of China's foreign-policy objectives further strained the Sino–Soviet relationship. First in the case of China's confrontation with the United States and the forces of the "Republic of China" over the Offshore Islands in the Taiwan Strait in 1958, and then in the Sino–Indian Border War of 1962, the Soviet Union backed down from its promise to support China.

The final blow to the by-then fragile relationship came with the Soviet Union's signing of the 1963 Nuclear Test Ban Treaty. The Chinese denounced this as a Soviet plot to exclude China from the "nuclear club" of Great Britain, France, the United States, and the Soviet Union. Subsequently, Beijing publicly broke Communist Party relations with Moscow.

The Sino–Soviet relationship, already in shambles, took on an added dimension of fear during the Vietnam War, when the Chinese grew concerned that the Soviets (and Americans) might use the war as an excuse to attack China. China's distrust of Soviet intentions was heightened in 1968, when the Soviets invaded Czechoslovakia in the name of the "greater interests of the socialist community," which, they contended, "override the interests of any single country within that community." Soviet skirmishes with Chinese soldiers on China's northern borders soon followed.

Ultimately, it was the Chinese leadership's concern about the Soviet threat to China's national security that, in 1971, caused it to reassess its relationship with the United States. The Sino–American ties that ensued made the Soviets anxious about their own security. The alleged threat of "Soviet hegemony" to world peace became the main theme of almost every public Chinese foreign-policy statement.

The Sino–Soviet relationship did not really improve until close to the end of the cold war. The Soviets began making peaceful overtures in 1987: They reduced troops on China's borders, and they withdrew support for Vietnam's puppet government in neighboring Cambodia. Moscow's withdrawal from Vietnam provided Beijing with further evidence of the Soviets' desire for reconciliation. Beijing responded positively to the *glasnost* ("open door") policy of Soviet Communist Party general secretary Mikhail Gorbachev. Ideological conflict between the two Communist giants abated; for with the Chinese themselves abandoning much of Marxist dogma in their economic policies, they could hardly continue to denounce the Soviet Union's "revisionist" policies and make self-righteous claims to ideological orthodoxy. With both the Soviet Union and China abandoning their earlier battle over who should lead the Communist camp, they shifted away from ideological and security issues toward economic issues.

The End of the Cold War and the Chinese Military

With the collapse of Communist Party rule, first in the Central/Eastern European states in 1989, and subsequently in the Soviet Union, the dynamics of China's foreign policy changed dramatically. Apart from fear that its own reforms might lead to the collapse of CCP rule in China, the disintegration of the Soviet Union into 15 independent states removed China's ability to play off the two superpowers against each other: The formidable Soviet Union simply no longer existed. Yet its fragmented remains had to be treated seriously. The state of Russia still shares a common border of several thousand miles with China, and Kazakhstan shares a common border of nearly 1,000 miles.

The question of what type of war the Chinese military might have to fight has affected its military modernization. China's military leaders have been in conflict for decades over whether China would have to fight a high-tech war or a "people's war" in which China's huge army would draw in the enemy on the ground and destroy it. In 1979, the military modernizers won out and jettisoned the idea that a large army, motivated by ideological fervor but armed with hopelessly outdated equipment, could win a war against a highly modernized military such as that of Japan or even the Soviet Union. The People's Liberation Army (PLA) began by shedding a few million soldiers and putting its funds into better armaments. A significant catalyst to modernizing the military still further came with the Gulf War of 1991, during which CNN vividly conveyed the power of high technology weaponry to China's leaders.[31]

China's military believed that it was allocated an inadequate budget for modernization, so it struck out on its own along the capitalist road to raise money. By the late 1990s, the PLA had become one of the most powerful actors in the Chinese economy. It had purchased considerable property in Special Economic Zones near Hong Kong; taken over ownership of major tourist hotels and industrial enterprises; and invested in everything from golf courses, brothels, and publishing companies to CD factories and the computer industry as means for funding military modernization. In 1998, however, President Jiang Zemin demanded that the military relinquish its economic enterprises and return to its primary task of building a modern military and protecting China. The promised payoff is that China's government will allocate more funding to the PLA, making it unnecessary for it to rely on its own economic activities.

In recent years, China's military has purchased weaponry and military technology from Russia as Moscow has scaled back its own military, in what sometimes resembles a going-out-of-business sale; but in doing so, China's military may have simply bought into a higher level of obsolescence, since Russia's weaponry lags years behind the technology of the West. China possesses nuclear weapons and long-distance bombing capability, but its ability to fight a war beyond its own borders is quite limited. Today, however, China's military power at least counterbalances that of Asia's most feared potential enemy, Japan. Perhaps for this reason, China's neighbors (many of whom are themselves building considerable military power) seem willing to tolerate China's military modernization.[32]

Furthermore, long before the cold war came to an end in the late 1980s, China's leadership was primarily concerned with economic development. Although ever-alert to threats to its national security (including sovereignty over Taiwan), there are no indications that China is preparing for a major war with any country. Instead, China is working to become an integral part of the international economic, commercial, and monetary systems. It is negotiating to join the World Trade Organization and has rapidly expanded trade with the international community and its potential enemies across the Russian and Kazakhstani borders. China has also won praise from the international community for not devaluing the Chinese yuan in response to the Asian financial and economic crisis that raged from 1997 to 1999. And, by late 1998, the Chinese had also agreed to negotiate again with the government in Taiwan as well as with the several governments involved in competing claims to the Spratley Islands. In short, Beijing seems far more interested in economic and diplomatic gains than in military gains; but the country's leadership would be acting

irresponsibly if it did not continue to modernize China's military capabilities.

THE SINO–AMERICAN RELATIONSHIP

China's relationship with the United States has historically been an emotionally turbulent one.[33] It has never been characterized by indifference. During World War II, the United States gave significant help to the Chinese, who at that time were fighting under the leadership of the Nationalist Party (KMT) head, General Chiang Kai-shek. The Chinese Communists were fighting together with the Nationalists in a "united front" against the Japanese, so American aid was not seen as directed against communism.

After the defeat of Japan at the end of World War II, the Japanese military, which had occupied much of the north and east of China, was demobilized and sent back to Japan. Subsequently, civil war broke out between the Communists and Nationalists. The United States attempted to reconcile the two sides, but to no avail. As the Communists moved toward victory in 1949, the KMT leadership fled to Taiwan. Thereafter, the two rival governments each claimed to be the true rulers of China. The United States, already in the throes of the cold war because of the "iron curtain" falling over Central/Eastern Europe, viewed communism in China as a major threat to the world.

Korea, Taiwan, and Vietnam

The outbreak of the Korean War in 1950 helped the United States to rationalize its decision to support the Nationalists, who had already lost power on the mainland and fled to Taiwan. The Korean War began when the Communists in northern Korea attacked the non-Communist south. When United Nations troops (mostly Americans) led by American general Douglas MacArthur successfully pushed Communist troops back almost to the Chinese border and showed no signs of stopping their advance, the Chinese—who had been sending the Americans anxious messages about their concern for China's own security—entered the war. China's participation resulted in the UN troops being pushed back to what is today still the demarcation line between North and South Korea. Thereafter, China became a target of America's cold war isolation and containment policies.

With the People's Republic of China condemned as an international "aggressor" for its action in Korea, the United States felt free to recognize the KMT government in Taiwan as the legitimate government of all of China. The United States supported the Nationalists' claim that the people on the Chinese mainland actually wanted the KMT to return to the mainland and defeat the Chinese Communists. As the years passed, however, it became clear that the Chinese Communists controlled the mainland and that the Chinese people were not about to rebel against Communist rule.

Sino–American relations steadily worsened as the United States continued to build up a formidable anti-Communist military bastion in the tiny Offshore Islands under KMT control, just off China's coast. Tensions were exacerbated when the U.S. military involvement in Vietnam steadily escalated in the 1960s and early 1970s. China, fearful that the United States was really using the war in Vietnam as the first step toward attacking China, concentrated on civil-defense measures: Chinese citizens used shovels and even spoons to dig air-raid shelters in major cities such as Shanghai and Beijing, with tunnels connecting them to the suburbs. Some industrial enterprises were moved out of China's major cities in order to make them less vulnerable in the event of a massive attack on concentrated urban areas. The Chinese received a steady barrage of what we would call propaganda about the United States "imperialist" as China's number-one enemy; but it is important to realize that the Chinese leadership actually *believed* what it told the people, especially in the context of the continuing escalation of the war in Vietnam toward the Chinese border, and the repeated "mistaken" overflights of southern China by American planes bombing Vietnam. Apart from everything else, it is unlikely that China's leaders would have made such an immense expenditure of manpower and resources on civil-defense measures had they not truly believed that the United States was preparing to attack China.

Diplomatic Relations

By the late 1960s, China was completely isolated from the world community, including the Communist bloc. In the throes of the Cultural Revolution, it had withdrawn its diplomatic staff from all but one of its embassies. It saw itself as surrounded on all sides by enemies—the Soviets to the north and west, the United States to the south in Vietnam as well as in South Korea and Japan, and the Nationalists to the east in Taiwan. Internally, China was in such turmoil from the Cultural Revolution that it appeared to be on the verge of complete collapse.

In this context, it was the Soviet invasion of Czechoslovakia in 1968 and Soviet military incursions on China's northern borders, combined perhaps with an assessment of which country could offer China the most profitable economic relationship, that led China to consider the United States as the lesser of two evil giants and to respond positively to American overtures. In 1972, U.S. president Richard Nixon visited China, the first official American contact with China since breaking diplomatic relations in 1950. With the signing of the Shanghai Communique, the initial steps in reversing more than 2 decades of hostile relations were taken.

A new era of Sino–American friendship had begun, but it fell short of full diplomatic relations until January 1, 1979. This long delay in bringing the two states into full diplomatic relations reflected not only each country's domestic political problems but also mutual disillusionment with the nature of the relationship. Although both sides had entered the relationship with the understanding of its strategic importance as a bulwark against the Soviet threat, the Americans had assumed that the 1972 opening of partial diplomatic relations would lead to a huge new economic market for American products; the Chinese assumed that the new ties would quickly bring the United States to end its diplomatic relations with Taiwan. Both were disappointed. Nevertheless, pressure from both sides eventually led to full diplomatic relations between the United States and the People's Republic of China.

The Taiwan Issue in U.S.–China Relations

Because the People's Republic of China and the Republic of China both claimed to be the legitimate government of the Chinese people, the establishment of diplomatic relations with the former necessarily entailed breaking them with the latter.[34] Nevertheless, the United States continued to maintain extensive informal economic and cultural ties with Taiwan. It also continued the sale of military equipment to Taiwan. Although these military sales are still a serious issue, American ties with Taiwan have diminished, while China's own ties with Taiwan have grown steadily closer since 1988. Taiwan's entrepreneurs (by way of Hong Kong front companies, as certain laws still prohibit their investment in China) have become one of the largest groups of investors in China's economy. Although Taiwan used to have one of the cheapest labor forces in the world, its workers now demand wages too high to remain competitive in international trade. Consequently, Taiwanese entrepreneurs have dismantled many of Taiwan's older industries and reassembled them on the mainland. With China's cheap labor, these same industries are now profitable, and both China and Taiwan's entrepreneurs are the beneficiaries.

Ties between Taiwan and the mainland have also been enhanced by the millions of tourists, most of them with relatives in China, who have traveled to the mainland since the late 1980s. They bring with them both presents and goodwill. Families that have not seen each other for 40 years have reestablished contact, and "the enemy" now seems less threatening. Furthermore, as China continues to liberalize its economic system and to raise the standard of living, the Chinese leadership hopes that reunification will become more attractive to Taiwan. This very positive context has been disturbed at various times: by the military crackdown on the demonstrators in Tiananmen Square in 1989; by Taiwan president Lee Teng-hui's visit to the United States in 1995; and by threats in 1996 of Taiwan declaring independence. The latter was serious, however, and China responded by "testing" missiles in the waters around Taiwan. High-level talks to discuss eventual reunification were broken off and did not resume until late 1998. Nevertheless, it is in the interests of both sides to maintain the status quo—a peaceful and profitable relationship in which Taiwan continues to act as an independent state but does not declare its independence.

In short, without firing a single shot, Taipei and Beijing are coming closer together. This does not mean that the two will soon be fully reunified in law; but whether or not this happens

SHANGHAI: THE HONG KONG THAT MIGHT HAVE BEEN

Situated on China's eastern coast, Shanghai (pictured above) was China's major port before 1949. Various groups of foreigners lived there in areas called concessions, and, together with the Chinese, they built Shanghai into a bustling world port in the nineteenth and twentieth centuries. It was also a city of crime and vice, and large numbers of its citizens lived in terrible poverty.

After 1949, both because China's former major trading partners joined the American embargo against trade with the People's Republic of China and because China itself at times pursued isolationist policies, Shanghai's role in international trade was eclipsed. The situation was aggravated by socialist policies that took trade out of the hands of independent trading corporations and placed it in the hands of a single state-run trading corporation. The state determined what was bought and sold, thus eliminating competition among Chinese companies. Some observers fear that Chinese control of Hong Kong may rob it of its economic dynamism.

The reforms in China in the 1980s and the opening of China to world trade did much to revive Shanghai's economy. Earlier in their rule, the Chinese Communists took steps to rid the city of notorious problems, like prostitution and drug dealing, and to establish a basic standard of welfare for most of its residents. Unfortunately, the return of the capitalist style to Shanghai in recent years has brought with it many of the problems that before 1949 had made it a "city of sin."

matters far less as their two economies become more and more intertwined. There remains, however, the black cloud of Beijing possibly using military force against Taiwan, as it threatened to do in 1996, if Taiwan makes efforts to become an independent state. Beijing refuses to pledge that it will never use military force to reunify Taiwan with the mainland, on the grounds that what it does with Taiwan is China's internal affair and, hence, no other country has a right to tell China what to do about Taiwan.[35]

Human Rights in U.S.–China Relations
The election of Bill Clinton as president of the United States in 1992 caused considerable consternation to China's leadership and to its people. The Chinese people were confused and distraught at the prospect of the punitive economic measures that the new Clinton administration threatened to take in response to China's human-rights abuses. They saw their government as having taken economic measures to bring in foreign investment, integrate China into the international economy, and enhance development; and many saw their government's law-and-order campaigns, which sometimes involved jailing dissidents, as necessary to China's continued economic growth and political stability. China's phenomenal growth in the 1980s and 1990s had improved the daily lives of hundreds of millions of ordinary Chinese people. They were far more interested in the prospect of a higher standard of living than in the rights of dissidents. Even China's intellectuals no longer seemed interested in politics. They did not "love the party," but they accepted the status quo. They just wanted a promotion and to make money. As one university

| The Treaty of Nanking cedes Hong Kong to Great Britain **1842** | China cedes the Kowloon Peninsula to Great Britain **1860** | The Sino–Japanese War **1894–1895** | Taiwan is under Japanese colonial control **1895–1945** | China leases Northern Kowloon and the New Territories (Hong Kong) to Great Britain for 99 years **1898** | The Boxer Rebellion **1900–1901** | Revolution and the overthrow of the Qin Dynasty **1911** | The Republic of China **1912–1949** |

(UPI/Bettmann Newsphotos)

In 1971, U.S. secretary of state Henry Kissinger made the first overtures toward reversing the hostile Sino–American relationship. In 1972, President Richard Nixon visited China, and a new era of cooperation began. Nixon is pictured above with Vice Premier Li Xiannian on the Great Wall of China during this historic visit.

professor put it, it is easy to be idealistic in one's heart; but to be idealistic in action is a sign of a true idealist, and there haven't been many of those in China since 1989. Today in China, it is difficult to find any student who demonstrated in Tiananmen Square in 1989 still doing anything remotely political. Most have gone into business or government.

It is not just the number of democratic idealists that is limited; so are the number of idealists committed to communism. Few Chinese want to discuss Marxism or communism. Even government officials rarely mention communism. They prefer to talk about development. In doing so, they are appealing to the strong nationalism in China, which has seemingly almost replaced communism as the glue holding the country together.

The Chinese perspective is this: They only know what their government tells them; they assume it lies to them, but they nevertheless know no more than what they are told. Why should they risk their careers to fight for the rights of jailed dissidents when they really know very little about what they have done? They then argue that the American government has also brutalized its population, pointing to such matters as the Kent State killings by the National Guard during the Vietnam War, and the brutality of the Los Angeles police against Rodney King. They also mention the many deaths at the hands of the British in Northern Ireland. They have heard about the abominable behavior of several student leaders of the Tiananmen Square demonstrations in 1989, both during the movement and after it. They wonder aloud if, upon examination, any of them were more virtuous than their own corrupt and brutal government leaders.

Some Chinese intellectuals argue that the recent difficulties in the United States and in other Western democracies indicate that their citizens frequently elect the wrong leaders, leaders who not only make bad policies but are increasingly being prosecuted in courts for corruption. This, they argue, indicates that democracy does not necessarily work any better than socialism. Many also support the view that the Chinese people are inadequately prepared for democracy because of a low level of education. The proceedings of the Kenneth Starr investigation, the House of Representatives' Judicial Committee, and the impeachment hearings in the House moved President Jiang Zemin to say that China would *never* have a democracy that looked like America's democracy.

China's intellectuals do not see the point in punishing hundreds of millions of Chinese for human-rights abuses committed not by the people, but by their leadership. Not infrequently, moreover, it is the Chinese people themselves who demand the harshest penalties for common criminals, if not political dissidents. For example, urban residents in Beijing have repeatedly demanded that the government remove the squatters and shantytowns that have sprung up, on the grounds that they are breeding grounds for criminality in the city. And many ordinary people now seem to believe the government's overall assessment of the events of the spring of 1989, which is that they posed a threat to the stability and order of China. To the Chinese people, no less than to their government, stability and order are critical to the continued economic development of China.

President Clinton quickly abandoned his 1992 campaign platform in favor of breaking the linkage between most-fa-

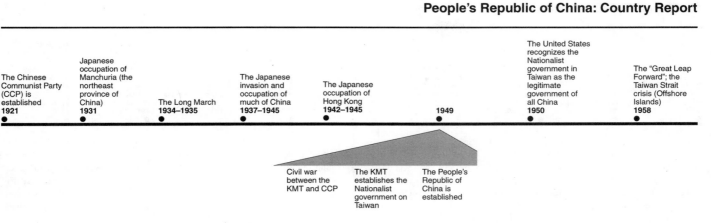

The Chinese Communist Party (CCP) is established
1921

Japanese occupation of Manchuria (the northeast province of China)
1931

The Long March
1934–1935

The Japanese invasion and occupation of much of China
1937–1945

The Japanese occupation of Hong Kong
1942–1945

1949

The United States recognizes the Nationalist government in Taiwan as the legitimate government of all China
1950

The "Great Leap Forward"; the Taiwan Strait crisis (Offshore Islands)
1958

Civil war between the KMT and CCP

The KMT establishes the Nationalist government on Taiwan

The People's Republic of China is established

vored-nation trade status for China and its human-rights record. This was due in part to his conviction—a conviction President George Bush had had before him—that the United States dare not risk jeopardizing its relations with an increasingly powerful state containing one quarter of the world's population through measures that would simply give Japan and other countries a better trading position while undercutting the opportunity for Americans to do business with China.

Clinton's China policy was also shaped by a new strategy of "agreeing to disagree" on certain issues such as human rights while efforts continued to be made to bring the two sides closer together. This strategy came out of a belief that China and the United States had so many common interests that neither side could afford to endanger the relationship on the basis of a single issue.

Today, the United States follows a policy of "engagement" with China, a policy based on the belief that isolating China has proven counterproductive and that "engagement" allows the two countries to work together toward shared objectives. Among these are security arrangements in northeast Asia and fewer restraints on trade. The belief is that human-rights issues can be more fruitfully addressed in a relationship that is in its broader aspects more positive. In the context of the Asian financial and economic crisis that began in 1997, China's willingness to cooperate with the United States and the International Monetary Fund, and not to devalue its currency, has been critical to efforts to keep the economies of the Asian countries afloat. It is a good example of what a relationship that is positive can achieve.

THE FUTURE

In 2 decades, China has moved from being a relatively closed and isolated country to one that is fully engaged in the world. China's agenda for the future is daunting: It must avoid war; maintain internal political stability in the context of international pressures to democratize; continue to carry out major economic, legal, and political reforms without endangering CCP control; sustain economic growth while limiting environmental destruction; and limit population growth. Since 1980, the Chinese Communist Party leadership has, with the

exception of limiting environmental damage, succeeded in all these efforts.

After the death of Deng Xiaoping in 1997, China also carried out a smooth leadership transition. Although President Jiang Zemin is not yet as powerful as Deng was, he does not need to be, in the new context of a collective leadership. The speculation about civil war or a military coup d'etat occurring after Deng's death has now abated, and the leadership's position seems secure for the moment. As long as economic growth continues, it is unlikely that the CCP leadership of China will be overthrown.

Nevertheless, massive unemployment, corruption, and common criminality continue to provide the fuel that could one day explode politically and bring down Chinese Communist Party rule. This would not, however, be in anyone's interests—neither that of the Chinese people, nor of any other country. An unstable and insecure China would be a more dangerous China, and it would be one in which the Chinese people would suffer immeasurably.

Finally, the integration of China into the international economic and political networks has made China's leaders at least slightly more sensitive to pressures from the international system on specific issues: human rights, environmental protection, intellectual property rights, prison labor, and legal codes. But it is still likely that China's leadership will insist on moving at its own pace, and in a way that takes into account China's culture, history, and institutions.

In the meantime, as is the case in so many other developing countries, China must worry about the increasing polarization of the population into the rich and the poor, high levels of inflation and unemployment, uncontrolled economic growth, environmental degradation, corruption, and the strident resistance by whole regions within China to follow economic and monetary policies formulated at the center. These would be formidable tasks for any country. How much more so for a leadership responsible for feeding, educating, and controlling the world's largest population.

NOTES

1. A concern about "spiritual pollution" is not unique to China. It refers to the contamination or destruction of one's own spiritual and cultural values by other values. Europeans are as concerned about it as the Chinese and have, in an

Soviet withdrawal of aid to the P.R.C. 1959	The public Sino–Soviet split 1963	The "Great Proletarian Cultural Revolution" 1966–1976	The United Nations votes to seat the P.R.C. in place of the R.O.C. 1971	U.S. president Richard Nixon visits the P.R.C.; the Shanghai Communique 1972	Mao Zedong dies; removal of the Gang of Four 1976	Deng Xiaoping is restored to power 1977	The Democracy Wall movement 1978–1979	The United States recognizes the P.R.C. and withdraws recognition of the R.O.C.; the Sino–Vietnamese War 1979
●	●	●	●	●	●	●	●	●

effort to combat spiritual pollution, limited the number of television programs made abroad (*i.e.*, in the United States) that can be broadcast in European countries.

2. The essence of the "get civilized" campaign was an effort to revive a value that had seemingly been lost: respect for others and common human decency. Thus, drivers were told to drive in a "civilized" way—that is, courteously. Ordinary citizens were told to act in a "civilized" way by not spitting or throwing garbage on the ground. Students were told to be "civilized" by not stealing books or cheating.

3. The sex of fetuses is usually known through the widespread use of sonarscan machines. To reveal the sex of the child is now illegal, but for a very small bribe, doctors will usually let the mother know the sex.

4. Most of these young women are likely to be sold as brides to men who live in remote villages where there are not enough women.

5. For example, Chinese women (at least in the cities) have had paid maternity leave, a child-care support system, the right to divorce, and the right to choose their own marriage partner.

6. Reuters, as reported in *China News Digest* (online) (May 19, 1996).

7. That Panchen Lama died in 1989.

8. Report from Xinjiang Television, as reported in *Hong Kong Standard* (June 4, 1996), excerpted in *China News Digest* (online), (June 5, 1996).

9. For excellent detail on Chinese religious practices, see Robert Weller, *Taiping Rebels, Taiwanese Ghosts, and Tiananmen* (Seattle: University of Washington Press, 1994 and Alan Hunter and Kim-Kwong Chan, *Protestanism in Contemporary China* (Cambridge: Cambridge University Press, 1993). The latter notes that Chinese judge gods "on performance rather than theological criteria" (p. 144). That is, if the contributors to the temple in which certain gods were being worshipped were doing well financially and their families were healthy, then those gods were judged well. Furthermore, Chinese pray as individuals rather than as congregations. Thus, before the Chinese government closed most temples, they were full of individuals praying randomly, children playing inside, and general noise and confusion. Western missionaries have found this style too casual for their own more structured religions (p. 145).

10. Professor Rudolf G. Wagner (Heidelberg University). Information based on his stay in China in 1990.

11. Of course, the Chinese people were really manipulated by power-hungry members of China's elite, an ever-shifting nouveau elite, who were in a desperate competition with other pretenders to power.

12. Suzanne Ogden, *China's Unresolved Issues: Politics, Development and Culture,* 3rd ed. (Englewood Cliffs: Prentice Hall, 1995), p. 136.

13. *Ibid.*

14. Vaclav Havel, as quoted by Timothy Garton Ash, "Eastern Europe: The Year of Truth," *New York Review of Books* (February 15, 1990), p. 18, referenced in Giuseppe De Palma, "After Leninism: Why Democracy Can Work in Eastern Europe," *Journal of Democracy,* Vol. 2, No. 1 (Winter 1991), p. 25, note 3.

15. Anonymous, "Letter to Friends from a County-Level Party Official" (June 4, 1992), Document 200, in Suzanne Ogden, Kathleen Hartford, Lawrence R. Sullivan, and David Zweig, eds., *China's Search for Democracy: The Student and Mass Movement of 1989,* p. 439.

16. De Palma, p. 26.

17. For an excellent analysis of how the "patterns of protest" in China have replicated the "patterns of daily life," see Jeffrey N. Wasserstrom and Liu Xinyong, "Student Associations and Mass Movements," in Deborah S. Davis, Richard Kraus, Barry Naughton, Elizabeth J. Perry, eds., *Urban Spaces in Contemporary China: The Potential for Autonomy and Community in Post-Mao China* (Cambridge: Cambridge University Press and Woodrow Wilson Center Press, 1995), pp. 362–366, 383–386. The authors make the point that students

learned how to organize, lead, and follow in school. This prepared them for organizing so masterfully in Tiananmen Square. The same was true for the workers who participated in the 1989 protests "not as individuals or members of 'autonomous' unions but as members of *danwei* delegations, which were usually organized with either the direct support or the passive approval of work-group leaders, and which were generally led onto the streets by people carrying flags emblazoned with the name of the unit." p. 383.

18. In 1996–1997, the citizens of Beijing who were unable to sleep through the racket finally forced the government to pass a noise ordinance that lowered the decible level allowed on streets by public performers, such as the fan dancers and ballroom dancers.

19. Liu Binyan, "China and the Lessons of Eastern Europe," *Journal of Democracy,* Vol. 2, No. 2 (Spring 1991), p. 8.

20. Beijing University student, "My Innermost Thoughts—To the Students of Beijing Universities," May 1989, Document 68, in Ogden, et al., eds., *China's Search for Democracy,* pp. 172–173.

21. Vivienne Shue in a speech to a USIA conference of diplomats and scholars, as quoted and summarized in "Democracy Rating Low in Mainland," *The Free China Journal* (January 24, 1992), p. 7.

22. Joyce Barnathan, et al., "China: Is Prosperity Creating a Freer Society?" *Business Week* (June 6, 1994), p. 98.

23. These figures are a composite of figures from Information Office of the State Council of the People's Republic of China, "The Progress of Human Rights in China" (December 1995), *Beijing Review,* Special Issue (1996), pp. 11–12; and Shaoguang Wang, "The Politics of Private Time: Changing Leisure Patterns in Urban China," in Deborah S. Davis, Richard Kraus, Barry Naughton, Elizabeth J. Perry, eds., *Urban Spaces in Contemporary China: The Potential for Autonomy and Community in Post-Mao China* (Cambridge: Cambridge University Press and Woodrow Wilson Center Press, 1995), from charts on pp. 162–163.

24. Information Office of the State Council of the People's Republic of China, "The Progress of Human Rights in China" (December 1995), *Beijing Review,* Special Issue (1996), pp. 11–12.

25. Barnathan, et al., pp. 98–99.

26. Shaoguang Wang, "The Politics of Private Time...," pp. 170–171.

27. Because there are relatively few films, however, censorship of them is likely to be greater than for the print media. Furthermore, all films are shot in a small number of film studios, making control easier. Finally, a film is likely to have a much larger audience than most books, and so the censors are concerned that it be carefully reviewed before being screened. Wang Meng (former minister of culture and a leading novelist in China), speech at Cambridge University (May 23, 1996). An example of a movie banned in China is the famous movie producer Chen Kaige's *Temptress Moon.* This movie, which won the Golden Palm award at the Cannes film festival in 1993, is, however, allowed to be distributed abroad. The government has adopted a similar policy of censorship at home but distribution abroad for a number of films by China's most famous film directors—including *Farewell My Concubine.*

28. "Campaign to Crush Dissent Intensifies," *South China Morning Post* (August 9, 1989).

29. Chinese student (anonymous) in the United States, conversation (summer 1990).

30. In 1998, Avon was, at least temporarily, banned from China, as were other companies that used similar sales and marketing techniques. Too many Chinese found themselves bankrupted when they could not sell the products that they had purchased to sell.

31. It is rumored today that China has acquired Patriot missiles, used in the Gulf War with such vaunted success (which has subsequently been seriously questioned), from Israel.

1980s–1990s	Resumption of arms sales to Taiwan ●	Beijing announces its intention to restore Chinese sovereignty over Hong Kong ●	A short-lived campaign against "spiritual pollution" from the West and capitalism ●	Sino–Soviet relations begin to thaw ●	The Special Party Conference removes many aged and infirm leaders; conservative opposition to Deng's reforms grows ●	Student demonstrations for democracy are widespread in China's cities; political liberalization is condemned ●	China sells Silkworm missiles to Iran and Saudi Arabia ●	Student demonstrations in Tiananmen Square; military crackdown; political repression follows ●
	The Shanghai Communique II: the United States agrees to phase out arms sales to Taiwan	The P.R.C. and United States reach agreement on textile quotas and the selling of technology	China and Great Britain sign an agreement on Hong Kong's future		Deng is named *Time* magazine's "Man of the Year"	CCP general secretary Hu Yaobang is removed; ties with Taiwan expand rapidly	Premier Li Peng reasserts centralized economic control	Deng encourages "experimentation" and the economy booms
							Criminal laws are reformed ●	Den Xiaoping dies; Jiang Zemin assumes power ●

32. Gregor Benton and Alan Hunter, "Chinese Nationalism and the Western Agenda," unpublished paper (Spring 1996).

33. For excellent analyses of the Sino–American relationship from the nineteenth century to the present, see Warren Cohen, *America's Response to China: A History of Sino–American Relations,* 3rd ed. (New York: Columbia University Press, 1990); Richard Madsen, *China and the American Dream: A Moral Inquiry* (Berkeley: University of California Press, 1995); Michael Schaller, *The United States and China in the Twentieth Century,* 2nd ed. (New York: Oxford University Press, 1990); David Shambaugh, ed., *American Studies of Contemporary China* (Armonk, NY: M.E. Sharpe, 1993); and David Shambaugh, *Beautiful Imperialist: China Perceives America, 1972–1990* (Princeton: Princeton University Press, 1991).

34. For more detail on the Taiwan issue, see the Taiwan Country Report, "Taiwan: A Dynamo in East Asia," in this book.

35. *Ibid.*

Taiwan

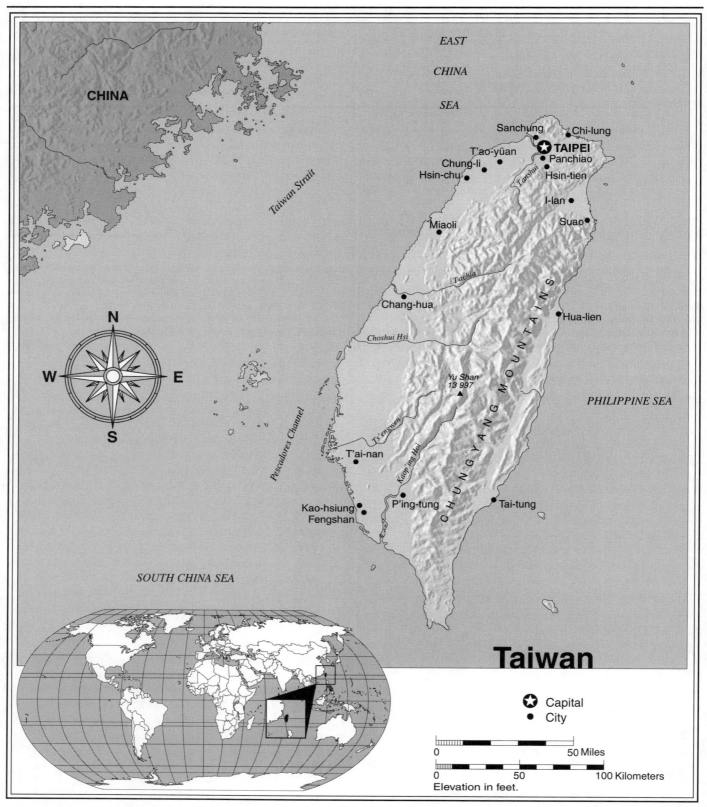

CHINA

EAST CHINA SEA

Taiwan Strait

Tanshui

Sanchung • Chi-lung
T'ao-yüan
Chung-li ⭐ **TAIPEI**
Hsin-chu • Panchiao
Hsin-tien

Tachia

Miaoli • I-lan •
Suao •

Chang-hua •

Choshui Hsi

Hua-lien •

Yu Shan
13 997 ▲

CHUNGYANG MOUNTAINS

Ts'engwen

PHILIPPINE SEA

Kaop'ing Hsi

Pescadores Channel

T'ai-nan •

Kao-hsiung •
Fengshan

P'ing-tung •

Tai-tung •

SOUTH CHINA SEA

Taiwan

⭐ Capital
● City

0 ——————— 50 Miles

0 ——— 50 ——— 100 Kilometers
Elevation in feet.

Taiwan has been considered the center of the government of the Republic of China (Nationalist China) since 1949. The province of Taiwan consists of the main island, 15 islands in the Offshore Islands group, and 64 islands in the Pescadores Archipelago. While the Pescadores are close to Taiwan, the Offshore Islands are only a few miles off the coast of mainland China.

Taiwan (Republic of China)

GEOGRAPHY

Area in Square Miles (Kilometers): 22,320 (36,002) (slightly smaller than Maryland and Delaware combined)

Capital (Population): Taipei (2,626,000)

Environmental Concerns: water and air pollution; poaching; radioactive-waste disposal

Geographical Features: rugged mountains in east to gently rolling plains in west

Climate: tropical; marine

PEOPLE

Population

Total: 21,701,000

Annual Growth Rate: 0.95%

Rural/Urban Population Ratio: 25/75

Major Languages: Taiwanese; Mandarin Chinese

Ethnic Makeup: 84% Taiwanese; 14% Mainlander (Standard) Chinese; 2% aborigine

Religions: 93% mixture of Buddhism, Confucianism, and Taoism; 4% Christian; 3% others

Health

Life Expectancy at Birth: 72 years (male); 79 years (female)

Infant Mortality Rate (Ratio): 7/1,000

Physicians Available (Ratio): 1/804

Education

Adult Literacy Rate: 92%

Compulsory (Ages): 6–15; free

COMMUNICATION

Telephones: 1 per 2.3 people

Televisions: 1 per 3 people

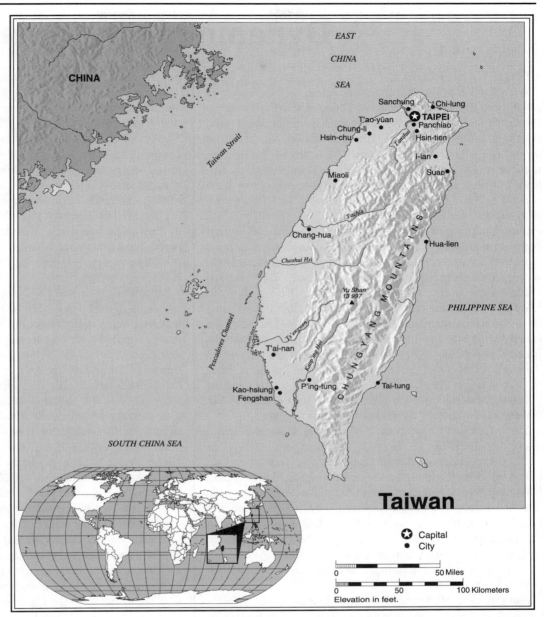

Taiwan

★ Capital
● City

0 ——— 50 Miles
0 —— 50 —— 100 Kilometers
Elevation in feet.

TRANSPORTATION

Highways in Miles (Kilometers): 11,750 (19,584)

Railroads in Miles (Kilometers): 2,760 (4,600)

Usable Airfields: 38

Motor Vehicles in Use: 4,950,000

GOVERNMENT

Type: multiparty democratic regime

Head of State: President Lee Teng-hui

Political Parties: Nationalist Party (Kuomintang); Democratic Progressive Party; Chinese New Democratic Party; Labour Party; New Party; Taiwan Independence Party

Suffrage: universal at 20

MILITARY

Military Expenditures (% of GDP): 3.6%

Current Disputes: officially (but not actually) in a state of war with the People's Republic of China; territorial disputes

ECONOMY

Currency ($ U.S. Equivalent): 32.14 New Taiwan dollars = $1

Per Capita Income/GDP: $14,700/$315 billion

GDP Growth Rate: 4%–5%

Inflation Rate: 3.1%

Unemployment Rate: 2.6%

Labor Force: 9,310,000

Natural Resources: coal; natural gas; limestone; marble; asbestos

Agriculture: rice; tea; bananas; pineapples; sugarcane; sweet potatoes; wheat; soybeans; peanuts

Industry: steel; pig iron; aluminum; shipbuilding; cement; fertilizer; paper; cotton; fabrics

Exports: $116 billion (primary partners United States, Hong Kong, European Union countries)

Imports: $102.4 billion (primary partners Japan, United States, European Union countries)

http://www.taiwaninformation.org
http://www.yam.com.tw/en/yam

Taiwan

A Dynamo in East Asia

HISTORY AND PEOPLE

Taiwan,* today a powerful economic center in Asia, was once an obscure island off the coast of China, just 90 miles away. It was originally inhabited by aborigines from Southeast Asia. By the seventh century A.D., Chinese settlers had begun to arrive. The island was subsequently "discovered" by the Portuguese in 1590, and Dutch as well as Spanish settlers followed. Today, the aborigines' descendants, who have been pushed into the remote mountain areas by the Chinese settlers, number fewer than 400,000, a small fraction of the 21.7 million people now living in Taiwan. Most of the current population are descended from those Chinese who emigrated from the Chinese mainland's southern provinces before 1885, when Taiwan officially became a province of China. Although these people originally came from China, they are known as *Taiwanese,* as distinct from the Chinese who came from the China mainland from 1947 to 1949. The latter are called *Mainlanders* and represent fewer than 20 percent of the island's population. After 1949, the Mainlanders dominated Taiwan's political elite; but the "Taiwanization" of the political realm that began after Chiang Kai-shek's death in 1975 and the political liberalization since 1988 have allowed the native Taiwanese to take up their rightful place within the elite.

The Manchus, "barbarians" who came from the north, overthrew the Chinese rulers on the mainland in 1644. In 1683, they conquered Taiwan; but because Taiwan was an island 90 miles distant from the mainland, the Manchus paid less attention to it and exercised minimal sovereignty over the Taiwanese people. With their defeat in the Sino–Japanese War (1894–1895), the Manchus were forced to cede Taiwan to the Japanese. The Taiwanese people refused to accept Japanese rule, however, and proclaimed Taiwan a republic. As a result, the Japanese had to use military force to gain actual control over Taiwan.

For the next 50 years, Taiwan remained under Japan's colonial administration. Taiwan's economy flourished under Japanese rule. Japan helped to develop Taiwan's agricultural sector, a modern transportation network, and an economic structure favorable to later industrial development. Furthermore, by creating an advanced educational system, the Japanese developed an educated workforce, which proved critical to Taiwan's economic growth.

With Japan's defeat at the end of World War II in 1945, Taiwan reverted to China's sovereignty. By that point, the Chinese had overthrown the Manchu Dynasty (in 1911) and established a republican form of government. Beginning in 1912, China was known as the Republic of China (R.O.C.). Thus it was Chiang Kai-shek who, as head of the R.O.C.

*Taiwan has also been known as Formosa, Free China, the Republic of China, and Nationalist China. Today, the government in Taiwan calls the island "Taiwan" and the government the "Republic of China."

government, accepted the return of the island province of Taiwan to R.O.C. rule in 1945. Relations between Taiwanese and Mainlanders were, however, full of tension: The ragtag, undisciplined military forces of the KMT (Kuomintang or Nationalist Party) who arrived in Taiwan met with hatred and contempt from the local people, who had grown accustomed to the orderliness and professionalism of the Japanese occupation forces. Angered by the incompetence and corruption of KMT officials, demonstrations against rule by Mainlanders occurred in February 1947. KMT troops killed thousands of Taiwanese opposed to mainland rule. Among those murdered were many members of the island's political elite. Needless to say, relations between the Taiwanese and the KMT were badly scarred.

Meanwhile, the KMT's focus remained on the mainland, where, under the leadership of General Chiang Kai-shek, it was continuing to fight the Chinese Communists in a civil war that had ended their fragile truce during World War II. Civil war raged from 1945 to 1949 and diverted the KMT's attention away from Taiwan. As a result, Taiwan continued, as it had under Manchu rule, to function fairly independently of Beijing. In 1949, when it became clear that the Chinese Communists would defeat the KMT, General Chiang and some 2 million members of his loyal military, political, and commercial elite fled to Taiwan to establish what they claimed to be the true government (in exile) of the Republic of China. This declaration reflected Chiang's determination to regain control over the mainland and his conviction that the then more than 600 million people living on the mainland would welcome the return of the KMT to power.

During the McCarthy period of the "Red scare" in the 1950s (a period during which Americans believed to be Communists or Communist sympathizers were persecuted by the government), the U.S. government supported Chiang Kai-shek. In response to the Chinese Communists' entry into the Korean War in 1950, the United States applied its cold-war policies of support for any Asian government that was anti-Communist, regardless of how dictatorial and ruthless that government might be, in order to "isolate and contain" the Chinese Communists. It was within this context that the United States committed itself to the military defense of Taiwan and the offshore islands in the Taiwan Strait, by ordering the U.S. Seventh Fleet to the Strait (in 1950) and by giving large amounts of military and economic aid to Taiwan. General Chiang Kai-shek continued to lead the government of the Republic of China on Taiwan until his death in 1975, at which time his son, Chiang Ching-kuo, succeeded him.

Two Governments, One China

Taiwan's position in the international community and its relationship to the government in Beijing have been determined by perceptions and values as much as by actions. In 1949, when the R.O.C. government fled to Taiwan, the Chinese Communists renamed China the People's Republic of China (P.R.C.), and they proclaimed the R.O.C. government illegitimate. Mao Zedong, the P.R.C.'s preeminent leader until his death in 1976, was later to say that adopting the new name instead of keeping the name Republic of China was the biggest mistake he ever made, for it laid the groundwork for future claims of "two Chinas." Beijing claimed that the P.R.C. was the legitimate government of all of China, including Taiwan. Beijing's attempt to regain de facto control over Taiwan was, however, forestalled first by the outbreak of the Korean War and later by the presence of the U.S. Seventh Fleet in the Taiwan Strait. Nevertheless, Beijing has always insisted that the Taiwan issue is an "internal" Chinese affair, that international law is therefore irrelevant, and that other countries have no right to interfere. For its part, the government of Taiwan agreed until 1995 that there was only one China and that Taiwan was a province of China. The KMT still claims that this "one China" must be the Republic of China, but there are hints that calling the unified country simply "China" would allow both sides to get over this hurdle.

Although the Chinese Communists' control over the mainland was long evident to the world, the United States managed to keep the R.O.C. in the China seat at the United Nations by insisting that the issue of China's representation in the United Nations was an "important question." This meant that a two-thirds affirmative vote of the UN General Assembly, rather than a simple majority, was required. With support from its allies, the United States was able to block the P.R.C. from winning this two-thirds vote until 1971.

At that critical moment, when the R.O.C.'s right to represent "China" in the United Nations was withdrawn, the R.O.C. could have put forward the claim that Taiwan had the right to be recognized as an independent state, or at least to be granted observer status. Instead, it steadfastly maintained that there was but one China and that Taiwan was merely a province of China. As a result, today the Republic of China has no representation in any international organization under the name of the R.O.C.; and it has representation only as "Taipei" in organizations in which the P.R.C. is a member—that is, if the P.R.C. allows it any representation at all.

International Acceptance of the People's Republic of China

The seating of the P.R.C. in the United Nations in 1971 thus led to a serious erosion of the R.O.C.'s position in international affairs. Not wanting to anger China, which has a huge and growing economy and significant military power, the state members of international organizations have given in to Beijing's unrelenting pressure to exclude Taiwan. Furthermore, Beijing insists that in bilateral state-to-state relations, any state wishing to maintain diplomatic relations with it must accept China's "principled stand" on Taiwan—notably,

New York Public Library

McCARTHYISM: ISOLATING AND CONTAINING COMMUNISM

The McCarthy period in the United States was an era of rabid anticommunism. McCarthyism was based in part on the belief that the United States was responsible for losing China to the Communists in 1949 and that the reason for this loss was the infiltration of the U.S. government by Communists. As a result, Senator Joseph McCarthy (pictured above) spearheaded a "witch-hunt" to ferret out those who allegedly were selling out American interests to the Communists. McCarthyism took advantage of the national mood in the cold war era that had begun in 1947, in which the world was seen as being divided into two opposing camps: Communists and capitalists.

The major strategy of the cold war, as outlined by President Harry Truman in 1947, was the "containment" of communism. This strategy was based on the belief that if the United States attempted—as it had done with Adolf Hitler's aggression against Czechoslovakia (the first step toward World War II)—to appease communism, it would spread beyond its borders and threaten other free countries.

The purpose of the cold war strategy, then, was to contain the Communists within their national boundaries and to isolate them by hindering their participation in the international economic system and in international organizations. Hence, in the case of China, there was an American-led boycott against all Chinese goods, and the United States refused to recognize the People's Republic of China as the legitimate representative of the Chinese people within international organizations.

CHIANG KAI-SHEK: DETERMINED TO RETAKE THE MAINLAND

Until his dying day, Chiang Kai-shek (1887–1975), pictured here with his wife, maintained that the military, led by the KMT (Kuomintang, or Nationalist Party), would one day invade the mainland and, with the support of the Chinese people living there, defeat the Communist government. During the years of Chiang's presidency, banner headlines proclaimed daily that the Communist "bandits" would soon be turned out by internal rebellion and that the KMT would return to control on the mainland. In the last years of Chiang Kai-shek's life, when he was generally confined to his residence and incapable of directing the government, his son, Chiang Ching-kuo, always had two copies of the newspaper made that proclaimed such unlikely feats, so that his father would continue to believe these were the primary goals of the KMT government in Taiwan. In fact, a realistic appraisal of the situation had been made long before Chiang's death, and most of the members of the KMT only pretended to believe that an invasion of the mainland was imminent.

Chiang Ching-kuo, although continuing to strengthen Taiwan's defenses, turned his efforts to building Taiwan into an economic showcase in Asia. Taiwan's remarkable growth and a certain degree of political liberalization were the hallmarks of Chiang Ching-kuo's leadership. A man of the people, he shunned many of the elitist practices of his father and the KMT ruling elite, and he helped to bring about the Taiwanization of both the KMT party and the government. The "Chiang dynasty" in Taiwan came to an end with Chiang Ching-kuo's death in 1988. It was, in fact, Chiang Ching-kuo who made certain of this, by barring his own sons from succeeding him and by grooming his own successor, a native Taiwanese.

that Taiwan is a province of China and that the People's Republic of China is the sole representative of the Chinese people.

Commercial ventures, foreign investment in Taiwan, and Taiwan's investments abroad have not suffered as a result of other countries' ending diplomatic relations with Taipei. After being forced to close all but a handful of their embassies as one state after another switched recognition from the R.O.C. to the P.R.C., Taipei has simply substituted offices that function as if they are actually embassies. They handle all commercial, cultural, and official business for people from the various countries, including the issuance of visas to those traveling to Taiwan.

To adjust to its loss of official international recognition, in the 1990s, the KMT adopted a new approach. Entitled "flexible diplomacy," it essentially allows Taiwan to justify its own decision to join international organizations to which China already belongs by calling itself "China Taipei." But, with only a few exceptions, such as the Olympics, Beijing has been adamant about not letting this happen.

This has led to increasing frustration and a sense of humiliation in Taiwan. It came to a head in early 1996. Under increasing pressure to respond to demands from its people that Taiwan get the international recognition that it deserved for its remarkable accomplishments, Taiwan's president, Lee Teng-hui, engaged in a series of maneuvers to get the international community to confer de facto recognition of its statehood. Not the least of these bold forays was President Lee's offer of $1 billion to the United Nations in return for a seat for Taiwan—an offer rejected by the UN secretary general. President Lee's campaign for election in the spring of 1996 proved to be the final straw for Beijing: Lee had as one of his central themes the demand for greater international recognition of Taiwan as an independent state. Beijing responded with a military buildup of some 200,000 soldiers in Fujian Province and the "testing" of missiles in the waters around Taiwan. Under pressure from the United States not to provoke a war with the mainland, and after a refusal on the part of the United States to say exactly what it would do if a war occurred, President Lee toned down his campaign rhetoric. A military conflict was averted, but it was not until late 1998 that Taipei and Beijing agreed to move forward with their temporarily shelved plans to further link Taiwan with the mainland.

THE OFFSHORE ISLANDS

Crises of serious dimensions erupted between China and the United States in 1954–1955, 1958, 1960, and 1962 over the blockading of supplies to the Taiwan-controlled Offshore Islands in the Taiwan Strait. Thus, the perceived importance of these tiny islands grew out of all proportion to their intrinsic worth. The two major island groups, Quemoy (about 2 miles from the Chinese mainland) and Matsu (about 8 miles from the mainland) are located almost 90 miles from Taiwan. As a consequence, Taiwan's control of them has made them strategically valuable for pursuing the government's professed goal of retaking the mainland—and valuable for psychologically linking Taiwan to the mainland.

The lack of industry and manufacturing on the islands has led to a steady emigration of their natives to Southeast Asia for better jobs. The civilian population is about 50,000 (mostly farmers) in Quemoy and about 6,000 (mostly fishermen) in Matsu. The small civilian population in Quemoy is significantly augmented by an estimated 10,000 to 100,000 soldiers. The heavily fortified islands appear to be somewhat deserted, however, since the soldiers live mostly underground: hospitals, kitchens, sleeping quarters—everything is located in tunnels blasted out of granite, including two-lane highways that can accommodate trucks and tanks. Heavily camouflaged anti-artillery aircraft dot the landscape, and all roads are reinforced to carry tanks.

In the first years after their victory on the mainland, the Chinese Communists fairly steadily shelled the Offshore Islands. When there was not a crisis, their shells were filled with pro-Communist propaganda materials, which littered the islands. When the Chinese Communists wanted to test the American commitment to the Nationalists in Taiwan and the Soviet commitment to their own objectives, they shelled the islands heavily and intercepted supplies to the islands. In the end, China always backed down; but in 1958 and 1962, it did so only after going to the brink of war with the United States. After 1979, Deng Xiaoping's "peace initiatives" toward Taiwan moved the confrontation over the Offshore Islands to the level of an exchange of gifts by balloons and packages floated across the channel:

> The Nationalists load their balloons and seaborne packages with underwear, children's shoes, soap, toys, blankets, transistor radios and tape recorders, as well as cookies emblazoned with Chiang Ching-kuo's picture and audio tapes of Taiwan's top popular singer, Theresa Teng, a mainland favorite.
>
> The Communists send back beef jerky, tea, herbal medicines, mao-tai and cigarettes, as well as their own varieties of soap and toys.
>
> [There is] confirmation from the mainland of the balloons' reaching as far as Tibet. . . . Unpredictable winds make the job harder for the Communists, but enough of the packages reach Quemoy and Taiwan for the authorities to have passed a law requiring people to hand over all pamphlets and gifts.[1]

Although the brutal suppression of the Tiananmen Square demonstrators in Beijing in the spring of 1989 temporarily led to increased tensions in the Taiwan Strait and a military emergency alert, by 1992 the political situation in China had stabilized enough to make an attack unlikely. A sign of the diminished sense of threat came in November 1992, when Taiwan's military administration of Quemoy and Matsu ended. By the mid-1990s, however, an acrimonious debate had broken out over the future of these Offshore Islands. The opposition Democratic Progressive Party (DPP) argues that, given today's military technology, these islands just off the China coast could easily be taken as "hostages" by the Chinese Communists. The DPP has therefore proposed that the Quemoy and Matsu be made into an international monetary zone. As such, they would attract foreign investment while simultaneously making it less likely that China would invade. As an international monetary zone, they could also compete with Hong Kong's role as the financial center in Asia. The ruling KMT considers this proposal treasonous and argues that the islands are still vital to the defense of Taiwan.[2]

CULTURE AND SOCIETY

Taiwan is a bundle of contradictions: "great tradition, small island; conservative state, drastic change; cultural imperialism, committed Nationalism; localist sentiment, cosmopolitan sophistication."[3] Over time, Taiwan's culture has been shaped by various cultural elements—Japanese, Chinese, and American culture; localism, nationalism, cosmopolitanism, materialism; and even Chinese mainland culture (in the form of "mainland mania"). At any one time, several of these forces have coexisted and battled for dominance. As Taiwan has become tightly integrated into the international system, the power of the central government to control cultural development has declined. This has unleashed not just global cultural forces but also local *Taiwanese* culture.[4]

The Taiwanese people were originally immigrants from the Chinese mainland; but their culture, which developed in isolation from that of the mainland, is not the same as the "Chinese" culture of the so-called Mainlanders who arrived from 1947 to 1949. Although the KMT saw Taiwan largely in terms of security and as a bastion from which to fight against and defeat the Chinese Communist regime on the mainland, "it also cultivated Taiwan as the last outpost of traditional Chinese high culture. Taiwanese folk arts, in particular opera and festivals, did thrive, but as low culture."[5]

The Taiwanese have continued to speak their own dialect of Chinese, distinct from the standard Chinese spoken by the Mainlanders, and almost all Taiwanese engage in local folk-religion practices. However, the Mainlander-controlled central government has dictated a cultural policy that emphasizes Chinese cultural values via education and the mass media. As a result, the distinctions institutionalized in a political system that discriminated against the Taiwanese have been culturally reinforced.

In recent years, the Taiwanese have grown increasingly resistant to efforts by the KMT Mainlanders to "Sinify" them—to force them to speak standard Chinese and to adopt the values of the dominant Chinese Mainlander elite. State-controlled television now offers programs in the Taiwanese dialect, and many more radio programs are conducted in Taiwanese. Taiwanese must still fight to maintain their cultural identity, but they may be winning the battle. Taiwanese legislators (the vast majority of legislators from *all* political parties) are refusing to use Chinese during the Legislature's proceedings, so now the Mainlanders in the Legislative Yuan and National Assembly must learn Taiwanese![6]

Generally speaking, however, Taiwanese and Mainlander culture need not be viewed as two cultures in conflict, for they share many commonalities. As Taiwanese move into leadership positions in what used to be exclusively Mainlander institutions and intermarriage between the two groups grows more common, an amalgamation of Taiwanese and traditional Chinese practices is becoming evident throughout the society. As is discussed later in this essay, the real source of conflict is the desire of the Taiwanese not to have their culture or political system controlled by Chinese from the mainland of China, whether they be KMT Nationalists or Communists.

On the other hand, rampant materialism as well as the importation of foreign ideas and values are eroding both Taiwanese *and* Chinese values. The Big Mac culture affects more than waistlines. Although the KMT government has engaged in a massive campaign to reassert Chinese values, the point seems lost in its larger message, which asks all to contribute to making Taiwan an Asian showplace. The government's emphasis on hard work and economic prosperity has seemingly undercut its focus on traditional Chinese values of politeness, the sanctity of the family, and the teaching of culturally based ethics (such as filial piety) throughout the school system. Materialism and an individualism that focuses on personal needs and pleasure seeking are slowly undermining collectively oriented values.[7] The "I can do whatever I want" attitude is, in the view of many, leading to a breakdown in social order.[8]

While playing a part in Taiwan's economic boom of the past decade, the emphasis on materialism has contributed to a variety of problems, not the least of which are the alienation of youth, juvenile crime, the loosening of family ties, and the general decline of community values. The pervasive spread of illicit sexual activities through such phony fronts as dance halls, bars, saunas, "barber shops," and movies-on-video and music-video establishments, as well as hotels and brothels, grew so scandalous and detrimental to social morals and social order that the government has even suggested cutting off their electricity.[9] Another major activity that goes virtually uncontrolled is gambling. Part of the problem in clamping down on either illicit sexual activities or gambling (both of which are often combined with drinking in clubs) is that organized crime is involved; and part of the problem is that, in exchange for bribes, the police look the other way.[10]

THE ENVIRONMENT

The pursuit of individual material benefit without a concomitant concern for the public good has led to uncontrolled growth and a rapid deterioration in the quality of life, even as the people in Taiwan become richer. Although recycling and efforts to prevent environmental degradation throughout the island have begun, individuals continue to do such things as dump and burn refuse in public places; and purchase cars at the rate of 300,000 per year, even though the expansion of the island's roads has not kept pace and even though vast num-

bers of cars are parked illegally, to the detriment of both traffic and pedestrians. They continue to build illegal structures that similarly obstruct sidewalks; and spit bright red betel-nut juice on the pavement.

As Taiwan struggles to catch up with its own success, the infrastructure has faltered. During the hot, humid summers in Taipei, both electricity and water are frequently shut off; roads are clogged from 7:00 A.M. until 10:00 P.M.; and the city's air is so dense with pollution that eyes water, hair falls out, and many people suffer from respiratory illness. Inadequate recreational facilities leave urban residents with few options but to join the long parade of cars out of the city on weekends. Taiwan's citizens have begun forming public-interest groups to address such problems, and public protests about the government's neglect of quality-of-life issues have grown increasingly frequent in recent years. Environmental groups have burgeoned, addressing such issues as building more nuclear plants in Taiwan, wildlife conservation, industrial pollution, and waste disposal; but environmental campaigns and legislation have hardly kept pace with the rapid growth of Taiwan's material culture.

RELIGION

A remarkable mixture of religions thrives in Taiwan. The people feel comfortable with placing Buddhist, Taoist, and local deities—and even occasionally a Christian saint—in their family altars and local temples. Restaurants, motorcycle-repair shops, businesses small and large—all maintain altars. The major concern in prayers is for the good health and fortune of the family. The focus is on life in this world, not on an afterlife. People pray for prosperity, for luck in the stock market, and even more specifically for the winning lottery number. If the major deity in one temple fails to answer prayers, people will seek out another temple where other deities have brought better luck. Alternatively, they will demote the head deity of a temple and promote others to his or her place. The gods are thought about and organized in much the same way as the Chinese bureaucracy is; in fact, they are often given official clerical titles to indicate their rank within the deified bureaucracy.

Offerings of food and money are important in making sure that the gods answer one's prayers. It is equally important to appease one's deceased relatives, for if they are neglected or offered inadequate amounts of food, money, and respect, they will cause endless problems for their living descendants by coming back to haunt them as ghosts. Thus, those who cannot get their computer programs to work or those with car trouble will take time to go to the temple to pray to the gods and ancestors.

The Chinese designate the seventh month of the lunar calendar as "Ghost Month." For the entire month, most Chinese do whatever is necessary "to live in harmony with the omnipotent spirits that emerge to roam the world of the living." This includes:

preparing doorway altars full of meat, rice, fruit, flowers and beverages as offerings to placate the anxious visitors. Temples [hang] out red lanterns to guide the way for the roving spirits. . . . Ghost money and miniature luxury items made of paper are burned ritualistically for ghosts to utilize along their desperate journey. . . . The influence of Ghost Month is widespread in society, with Chinese heeding a long list of taboos that have a strong impact on business activity during this cautious time.

The real estate industry feels the negative forces more so than any other business sector. Buying or moving into new houses is the last thing citizens would dare do, fearing that homeless ghosts might become permanent guests. . . . [M]any customers do not want their new cars delivered until after Ghost Month.

Traditionally, the number of newlyweds drops drastically. According to folk belief, a man who marries during the period could discover before long that his bride is actually a ghost. . . . Some pregnant women, after realizing they will most likely undergo childbirth during Ghost Month, [ask] that Caesarean sections be performed prior to the beginning of the month.

Busy lawyers on the island know they can take a breather in Ghost Month. Legal suits traditionally decrease due to the common belief that ghosts do not appreciate those who sue.[11]

Finally, there continues to be a preference for seeking medical cures from local temple priests over help from either traditional Chinese or modern Western medicine. The concern of local religion is, then, a concern with this life, not with salvation in the afterlife. The attention to deceased ancestors, spirits, and ghosts is quite different from attention to one's own fate in the afterlife.

What is unusual in the case of Taiwanese religious practices is that, as the island has become increasingly "modern" and wealthy, it has not become less religious. Technological modernization has seemingly not brought secularization with it. In fact, aspiring capitalists often build temples in hopes of getting rich. People bring offerings of food, burn incense and bundles of paper money to honor the temple gods, and burn expensive paper reproductions of houses, cars, and whatever other material possessions they think their ancestors might like to have in their ethereal state. They also pay real money to the owner of their preferred temple to make sure that the gods are well taken care of. Since money goes directly to the temple owner, not to a religious organization, the owner of a temple whose constituents prosper will become wealthy. Given the rapid growth in per capita income in Taiwan in the last 20 years, then, temples to local deities have proliferated, as a builder of a temple was almost guaranteed to get rich if its constituents' wealth grew steadily.

Although the vast majority of Taiwan's citizens follow folk religions, Christianity is not left out of the melange of religions. About 4 percent of the population are Christian; but even Christianity does not escape local adaptations, such as setting off firecrackers inside a church during a wedding ceremony to ward off ghosts, and flashing neon lights around the Virgin Mary. The Presbyterian Church, established in Taiwan by missionaries in 1865, has frequently been harassed by the KMT because of its activist stance on social and human-rights issues and because it has generally supported the Taiwan independence viewpoint.[12]

As for Confucianism, it is more a philosophy than a religion. Confucianism is about self-cultivation, proper relationships among people, ritual, and proper governance. Although Confucianism accepts ancestor worship as legitimate, it has never been concerned directly with gods, ghosts, or the afterlife. In imperial China, if drought brought famine, or if a woman gave birth to a cow, the problem was the lack of morality on the part of the emperor—not the lack of prayer—and required revolt.

In the KMT's efforts to restore Chinese traditional values, it has tried to reinstitute the formal study of Confucianism in the schools in Taiwan, but its plea has largely fallen on deaf ears. Nevertheless, Confucian values suffuse the culture. Streets, restaurants, corporations, and stores are named after major Confucian virtues; advertisements appeal to Confucian values of loyalty, friendship, and family to sell everything from toothpaste to computers; children's stories focus on Confucian sages in history; and the vocabulary that the government and party officials use to conceptualize issues is the vocabulary of Confucianism—moral government, proper relationships between officials and the people, loyalty, harmony, and obedience.

EDUCATION

The Japanese are credited with establishing a modern school system in Taiwan in the early twentieth century. Under KMT rule since 1949, Taiwan's educational system has developed steadily. Today, Taiwan offers 9 years of free, compulsory education. Almost all school-age children are enrolled in elementary schools, and most go on to junior high schools. More than 70 percent continue on to senior high school. Illiteracy has been reduced to about 8 percent and is still declining. Night schools that cater to those students anxious to test well and make the cut for the best senior high schools and colleges flourish. Such extra efforts attest to the great desire of Taiwan's students to get ahead through education.

Taiwan has one of the best-educated populations in the world, a major factor in its dramatic economic development. Its educational system is, however, criticized for its insistence on uniformity through a unified national curriculum, a lecture format that does not allow for student participation, the high school and university entrance examinations, tracking, rote memorization, heavy homework assignments, and humiliating punishments. Its critics say that the system inhibits creativity.[13] Reforms in recent years have tried to modify some of these practices.

The island has more than 100 colleges and universities, but the demand for higher education still outstrips the ability of the system to provide spaces for all qualified students. As a result, many students go abroad for study—and of those, many never return to Taiwan. From 1950 to 1978, only 12 percent of the some 50,000 students who studied abroad returned, a reflection both of the lack of opportunity in Taiwan and the oppressive nature of government in that period. This outward flood of human talent, or "brain drain," was stemmed in the 1980s and 1990s as Taiwan grew more prosperous and the political system more open.

WOMEN

The societal position of women in Taiwan reflects an important ingredient of Confucianism. "Women in classical Chinese society were expected to obey their fathers before marriage, their husbands after, and their sons when widowed. Furthermore, women were expected to cultivate the "Four Virtues": morality, skills in handicrafts, feminine appearance, and appropriate language."[14] In Taiwan, as elsewhere throughout the world, women have received lower wages than men and have rarely made it into the top ranks of government and business—this in spite of the fact that it was women who managed the tens of thousands of small businesses and industries that fueled Taiwan's economic boom. In the workplace, women are treated differently than men. "For example, all female civil servants, regardless of rank, are expected to spend half a day each month making pants for soldiers, or to pay a substitute to do this."[15]

Today, there are countervailing values and new trends toward greater opportunities and respect for women. Women are more visible in politics and the media than before. The fact that women may now receive an education the equal of a man's has helped promote their social and economic mobility, as has the advocacy by Taiwan's feminists of equal rights for women. It has also eroded the typical marriage pattern, in which a man is expected to marry a woman with an education inferior to his own.

THE ECONOMY

The rapid growth of Taiwan's economy and foreign trade has enriched Taiwan's population. A newly industrialized economy (NIE), Taiwan has shed its "Third World," underdeveloped image. With a gross domestic product per capita income that has risen from $100 in 1951 to about $14,700, and a highly developed industrial infrastructure and service industry, Taiwan has entered the ranks of some of the most developed economies in the world. As with the leading industrial nations, however, the increasing costs of manufacturing in an economy where labor demands ever higher wages has meant that the percentage of the economy in the industrial sector is steadily declining. Manufacturing jobs are being relocated to other countries, those with cheaper raw materials and lower wages.

Taiwan's economic growth rate over the last 3 decades has been phenomenal, averaging more than 8 percent per year. Although Taiwan has not been able to insulate itself from the effects of the Asian financial and economic crisis that began in 1997, its growth has continued, even if at lower rates. Even in 1998, its growth rate of between 4 and 5 percent means that it still has one of the highest growth rates in the world.[16] Its high per capita income does not, however, bring with it a lifestyle comparable to that in the most developed Western states: Taiwan's cities are crowded and badly polluted; housing is too expensive for most urbanites to afford more than a small apartment; and the overall infrastructure is inadequate to handle traffic, parking, sewage, electricity, and provide other services expected in a more advanced society.

Most of the critical reforms that helped Taiwan's economy grow were initiated by the KMT government elite's state-regulating policies. These have included land redistribution, currency controls, central banking, and the establishment of government corporations.[17] Today, however, Taiwan is moving toward privatization of those same government corporations that have had complete control over many strategic materials, and sectors such as transportation and telecommunications. Much like mainland China, the workforce is resisting the loss of the "iron rice bowl" of permanent employment in state enterprises. Also similar is the government's concern that social instability may result if organized labor, instead of accepting the "global trend" toward privatization, resists it through street protests.[18] Under such circumstances, Taiwan's government may be just as inclined as the mainland's government to use force to maintain social order.

Taiwan's economic success thus far may also be attributed to a largely free-enterprise economy in which businesspeople have developed international markets for their products and promoted an export-led economy, and in which Taiwan's labor force has contributed through its high productivity. Workers have tended to lack class consciousness, because they progress so rapidly from being members of the "proletariat" to becoming capitalists and entrepreneurs. Even factory workers are often involved in small businesses.[19]

Sometimes called "Silicon Island," Taiwan has some 1.2 million small and medium-size enterprises, and only a handful of megagiants. Most of these smaller enterprises are not internationally recognized names, but they provide the heart and even the backbone of technological products worldwide. They make components, or entire products, according to specifications set by other, often well-known, large firms, whose names go on the final product. Furthermore, because Taiwan's firms tend to be small, they are flexible and can respond quickly to changes in technology. This is particularly true in the computer industry, where, thanks to the many students who have gone to the United States to study and then stayed to work in the computer industry's Silicon Valley, there are strong ties with, and dependency on, Taiwan's entrepreneurs.[20]

A stable political environment has facilitated Taiwan's rapid growth. So has a protected market, which has brought protests over unfair trade policies from those suffering from an imbalance in their trade with Taiwan. Slowly Taiwan has shed most of the regulations that have protected its industries, including agriculture, from international trade competition. But the Asian financial crisis has made the government pause, as it was precisely because of some of the tight controls over investments, banks, credit, and currency flows that Taiwan has weathered the crisis better than most of its (non-Chinese) Asian brethren.

From 1990 to 1998, Taiwan businesspeople invested some $80 billion abroad. The largest share was invested in the China mainland, where Taiwanese enterprises run what amounts to a parallel economy that is completely entangled with China's own. "By some estimates, up to a third of consumer goods for export marked 'Made in China' are actually made by Taiwanese-owned firms. Analysts attribute more than 70% of the growth in America's trade deficit with China to the exports of Taiwanese firms."[21] Taiwanese firms and the government itself have also established nonprofit foundations in the United States and helped fund U.S. university research centers that study Taiwan. Such investments abroad have helped shrink the trade imbalance (as does the purchase of F16s from the United States), but Taiwan still holds billions of U.S. dollars in its central reserve bank.

Agriculture and Natural Resources

After arriving in Taiwan, the KMT government carried out a sweeping land-reform program: The government bought out the landlords and sold the land to their tenant farmers. The result was equalization of land distribution, an important step in promoting income equalization among the farmers of Taiwan.

The land-reform program was premised upon one of Sun Yat-sen's famous Three Principles, the "people's livelihood." One of the corollaries of this principle was that any profits from the increase in land value attributable to factors not related to the real value of farmland—such as through urbanization, which makes nearby agricultural land more valuable—would be turned over to the government when the land was sold. Thus today, although the price of land has skyrocketed around Taiwan's major cities, and although many farmers feel that they are being squeezed by low prices for their produce, they would get almost nothing for their land if they sold it to developers. As a result, many farmers have felt trapped in agriculture. Evidence of the high productivity of Taiwan's farmers is that Taiwan is almost self-sufficient in agriculture, an impressive performance for a small island where only 25 percent of the land is arable.

Natural resources, including land, are quite limited in Taiwan. Taiwan's rapid industrialization and urbanization have put a strain on what few resources exist. Taiwan's energy resources, such as coal, gas, and oil, are particularly limited. The result is that the government has had to invest in the building of a number of nuclear-power plants to provide sufficient energy to fuel Taiwan's rapidly modernizing society and economy. (Popular protest against further nuclear-

power plants, however, brought an energy crisis in the 1990s.) Investment in developing China's vast natural resources, as well as moving industries to other countries where resources, energy, land, and labor are cheaper, allows Taiwan to postpone its energy and resource crisis. In doing so, "Taiwan Inc is becoming a virtual company. A small headquarters in Taipei now supports vast manufacturing and distribution facilities around the world."[22]

Taiwan as a Model of Economic Development

Taiwan is often cited as a potential model for other developing countries seeking to lift themselves out of poverty. They could learn some useful lessons from certain aspects of Taiwan's experience, such as the encouragement of private investment and labor productivity, an emphasis on basic health care and welfare needs, and policies to limit gross extremes of inequality. But Taiwan's special advantages during its development have made it hard to emulate. These advantages include its small size, the benefits of improvements to the island's economic infrastructure and educational system made under the Japanese occupation, massive American financial and technical assistance, and a highly favorable international economic environment during Taiwan's early stages of growth.

What has made Taiwan extraordinary among the rapidly developing economies of the world is the government's ability—and commitment—to achieve and maintain income equality. Although there are beggars in Taiwan, it is difficult to find them. Government programs to help the disabled and a thriving economy that offers employment to almost everyone certainly helps, as does a tight-knit family system that supports family members facing difficult times. The KMT's commitment to Sun Yat-sen's principle of the "people's livelihood," or what in the West might be called a "welfare state," is still an important consideration in policy formation.

The growth of Taiwan's stock market—a market built on the thin air of gossip and rumor—has created (and destroyed) substantial wealth almost overnight. Nevertheless, Taiwan's economic wealth is still fairly evenly distributed, contributing to a strongly cohesive social system and political stability.

Taiwan's economy is not without growing pains. The government has so far been unable to solve many of the problems arising from its breathtakingly fast modernization: massive pollution; an inadequate urban infrastructure for housing, transportation, electricity, and water; and rampant corruption as everyone tries to get ahead in a now relatively open economy. In the cities, the rapid acquisition of air conditioners and automobiles has made the environment unbearable and transportation a nightmare. In spite of—and in some cases because of—Taiwan's astounding economic growth, the quality of life has deteriorated greatly. Complaints of oily rain, ignitable tap water, stunted crops due to polluted air and land, and increased cancer rates abound. "Garbage wars" over the "not-in-my-back-yard" issue of sanitary landfill placement have led to huge quantities of uncollected garbage.[23] Numerous

(United Nations photo/Chen)

The Chinese Communists have said that Taiwan may maintain its free-market economy after reunification with the mainland, but many Taiwanese fear that the island's textile and other industries would falter under Communist control.

public-interest groups have emerged to pressure the government to take action. Antinuclear activists even tried to use the recall vote to remove legislators who favored building Taiwan's fourth nuclear-power plant.[24]

Inflation, although still low, has been fueled by labor's demand for higher wages. Higher wages have, in turn, priced Taiwan's labor-intensive products out of the international market. Foreign investors have begun to look elsewhere as Taiwan has lost its competitive advantage. Even Taiwan's own entrepreneurs have set up shop outside of Taiwan, notably in Thailand, the Philippines, and China, where labor is far cheaper.

To encourage Taiwan's manufacturers to keep their plants in Taiwan instead of moving overseas for cheaper labor, since 1988 the government has allowed businesses to import an increasing number of laborers from Southeast Asia to do work at wages too low, hours too long, and conditions too dangerous for their own citizens. Numbering 143,000 by the

mid-1990s, they introduce their own invisible "costs" to Taiwan: Lonely and isolated within a society where they are considered socially inferior and where they rarely speak the language, they tend to engage in heavy drinking, gambling, and other socially dysfunctional behaviors.[25]

Despite these problems, Taiwan has continued to run a trade and international-currency surplus. Internationalization of its economy is also part of Taiwan's strategy to thwart China's efforts to cut off Taiwan's relationships with the rest of the world. With Taiwan an increasingly important actor in the international economy, it is virtually impossible for its trade, commercial, and financial partners to ignore it. And this, in turn, saves Taiwan from the international diplomatic isolation that it might otherwise face in light of its current "non-state" status. In the meantime, its economy is also becoming increasingly integrated with that of the China mainland, to the mutual benefit of both Taiwan and the P.R.C.

SUN YAT-SEN: THE FATHER OF THE
CHINESE REVOLUTION

New York Public Library

Sun Yat-sen (1866–1925) was a charismatic Chinese nationalist who, in the declining years of the foreign-ruled Manchu Dynasty, played upon Chinese-nationalist hostility to both foreign colonial powers and to the Manchu rulers themselves.

Sun (pictured at the left) drew his inspiration from a variety of sources, usually Western, and combined them to provide an appealing program for the Chinese. This program was called the Three People's Principles, which translates the American tenet "of the people, by the people, and for the people" into "nationalism," "democracy," and "the people's livelihood."

This last principle, the people's livelihood, is the source of dispute between the Chinese Communists and the Chinese Nationalists, both of whom claim Sun Yat-sen as their own. The Chinese Communists believe that the term means socialism, while the Nationalists in Taiwan prefer to interpret the term to mean the people's welfare in a broader sense.

Sun Yat-sen is, in any event, considered by all Chinese to be the father of the Chinese Revolution of 1911, which overthrew the feeble Manchus. He thereupon declared China to be a republic and named himself president. However, he had to relinquish control immediately to the warlord Yuan Shih-K'ai, who was the only person in China powerful enough to maintain control over all other contending military warlords in China.

When Sun died, in 1925, Chiang Kai-shek assumed the mantle of leadership of the Kuomintang, the Chinese Nationalist Party. After the defeat of the KMT in 1949, Sun's widow chose to remain in the People's Republic of China and held high honorary positions until her death in 1982.

THE POLITICAL SYSTEM

From 1949 to 1988, the KMT justified the unusual nature of Taiwan's political system with three extraordinary propositions. First, the government of the Republic of China, formerly located on the mainland of China, was merely "in exile" on China's island province of Taiwan.[26] Second, the KMT was the legitimate government not just for Taiwan but also for the hundreds of millions of people living on the Chinese mainland, under the control of the Chinese Communist Party. Third, the people living under the control of the Communist "bandits" would rush to support the KMT if it invaded the mainland to overthrow the Chinese Communist Party regime. Taiwan's political and legal institutions flowed from these three unrealistic propositions. Underlying all of them was the KMT's acceptance, in common with the Chinese Communist Party, that there was only one China and that Taiwan was a province of that one China. Indeed, until the early 1990s, it was a *crime* in Taiwan to advocate independence.[27]

The Constitution

In 1946, while the KMT was still the ruling party on the mainland, it promulgated a Constitution for the Republic of China. This Constitution took as its foundation the same political philosophy as the newly founded R.O.C. adopted in 1911 when it overthrew China's Manchu rulers on the mainland: Sun Yat-sen's Three People's Principles (nationalism, democracy, and "the people's livelihood"). Democracy, however, was to be instituted only after an initial period of "party tutelage." During this period, the KMT would exercise virtually dictatorial control while preparing China's population for democratic political participation.

The Constitution provided for the election of a National Assembly, with the responsibility of electing a president and vice president; a Legislative Yuan ("branch") to pass new laws, decide on budgetary matters, declare war, and conclude treaties; an Executive Yuan to interpret the Constitution and all other laws and to settle lawsuits; a Control Yuan, the highest supervisory organ, to supervise officials through its powers of censure, impeachment, and auditing; and an Examination Yuan (a sort of personnel office) to conduct civil-service examinations. The Examination Yuan and Control Yuan were holdovers from Chinese imperial traditions dating back thousands of years.

Because this Constitution went into effect in 1947 while the KMT, as the governing party of the Republic of China, still held power in the mainland, it was meant to be applicable to all of China, including Taiwan. The KMT government called nationwide elections to select delegates for the National Assembly. Then, in 1948, it held elections for representatives to the Legislative Yuan and indirect elections for members of the Control Yuan. Later in 1948, as the Civil War between Communists and Nationalists on the mainland raged on, the KMT government amended the Constitution to allow for the declaration of martial law and a suspension of regular elections; for by that time, the Communists were taking control of vast geographical areas of China. Soon afterward, the Nationalist government, under Chiang Kai-shek, fled to Taiwan. With emergency powers in hand, it was able to suspend elections and all other democratic rights afforded by the Constitution.

By October 1949, the Communists controlled the entire Chinese mainland. As a result, the KMT, in what it thought was only temporary exile in Taiwan, could not hold truly "national" elections for the National Assembly or for the Legislative and Control Yuans, as mandated by the 1946 Constitution. But to foster its claim to be the legitimate government of all of China, the KMT retained the 1946 Constitution and governmental structure, as if the KMT alone could indeed represent all of China. With "national" elections suspended, those individuals elected in 1947 from all of China's mainland provinces (534 out of a total 760 elected had fled with General Chiang to Taiwan) continued to hold their seats in the National Assembly, the Legislative Yuan, and the Control Yuan—usually until death—without standing for reelection. Thus began some 40 years of a charade in which the "National" Assembly and Legislative Yuan in Taiwan pretended to represent all of China. In turn, the government of the island of Taiwan was considered a mere provincial government under the "national" government run by the KMT.

Although the commitment to retaking the China mainland was quietly abandoned by the KMT government even before President Chiang Kai-shek's death in 1975, the 1946 Constitution and governmental structure remained in force. Over those many years, of course, numerous members of the three elected bodies died. Special elections were held to fill their vacant seats. The continuation of this atavistic system raised serious questions about the government's legitimacy. The Taiwanese, who comprised more than 80 percent of the population, accused the KMT Mainlanders of keeping a stranglehold on the political system and pressured them for greater representation. Because the holdovers from the pre-1949 period were of advanced age and often too feeble to attend meetings of the Legislative Yuan (and some of them no longer even lived in Taiwan), it was virtually impossible to muster a quorum. Thus, in 1982, the KMT was forced to "reinterpret" parliamentary rules in order to allow the Legislative Yuan to get on with its work.

By the time a Taiwanese, Lee Teng-hui, succeeded President Chiang Ching-kuo in 1988 as the new KMT party leader and president of the "Republic of China," 70 percent of the KMT were Taiwanese. Pressures therefore built for party and governmental reforms that would undercut the power of the old KMT Mainlanders. In July 1988, behind the scenes at the 13th KMT Party Congress, the leadership requested the "voluntary" resignation of the remaining pre-1949 holdovers: Allegedly as much as $1 million was offered for some of them to resign, but few accepted. Finally, the Council of Grand Justices forced all those Chinese mainland legislators who had gained their seats in the 1946 elections to resign by the end of 1991.

Under the Constitution, the Legislative, Judicial, Control, and Examination Yuans hold certain specific powers. Theoretically, this should result in a separation of powers, preventing any one person or institution from the arbitrary abuse of power. In fact, however, until after the first completely democratic legislative elections of December 1992, none of these branches of government exercised much, if any, power independent of the president (himself chosen by the KMT instead of by a democratic election until 1996) or the KMT.

A final consequence of the three propositions upon which political institutions in Taiwan were created is that, since 1949, Taiwan has maintained two levels of government. One is the so-called national government of the "Republic of China," which rules Taiwan as just one province of all of China. The other is the actual provincial government of Taiwan, which, as on the Chinese mainland, reports to the "national" government that pretends to control all of China. In this provincial-level government, native Taiwanese have always had considerable control over the actual functioning of Taiwan province in all matters not directly related to the R.O.C.'s relationship with the Chinese mainland. Taiwan's provincial government thus became the training ground for native Taiwanese to ascend the political ladder once the KMT reformed the political system after 1988.

Martial Law

The imposition of martial law in Taiwan from 1949 to 1988 was a critical period in Taiwan's politics. Concerned with the security of Taiwan against subversion or an invasion by the Chinese Communists, the KMT declared a state of martial law on Taiwan in 1949. Martial law allowed the government to suspend civil liberties and to limit political activity, such as organizing political parties or mass demonstrations. Thus it was a convenient weapon for the KMT Mainlanders to control potential Taiwanese resistance. In particular, the KMT invoked martial law to quash any efforts to organize a "Taiwan independence" movement. Police powers were widely abused, press freedoms were sharply restricted, and dissidents were jailed. As a result, the Taiwan Independence Movement was forced to organize abroad, mostly in Japan and the United States. Taiwan was run as a one-party dictatorship supported by the secret police. Beginning in 1977, however, non-KMT candidates were eventually permitted to run for office under the informal banner of *tangwai* (literally, "outside the party"); but they had to run as individuals, not as members of new political parties, which were forbidden until 1989.

The combination of international pressures for democratization, the growing confidence of the KMT, a more stable situation on the China mainland, and diminished threats from Beijing led the KMT to lift martial law in July 1987. Thus ended the state of "Emergency" under which almost any governmental use of coercion against Taiwan's citizens had been justified.

Civil Rights

Until the late 1980s, the rights of citizens in Taiwan did not receive much more protection than they did on the Chinese mainland. The R.O.C. Constitution has a "bill of rights," but most of these civil rights never really existed until martial law was lifted. Civil rights have been suspended when their invocation by the citizenry has challenged KMT power or policies. Because the "Emergency" regulations provided the rationale for the restriction of civil liberties, the KMT used military courts (which do not use normal judicial procedure) to try what were actually civil cases.[28] The KMT also arrested political dissidents and used police repression, such as in the brutal suppression of the 1980 Kaohsiung Incident.[29] Even today, individuals may be imprisoned for political crimes—but this is far less likely than before.

Political Reform in Taiwan

Taiwan's economic growth and rapidly rising standard of living over several decades gave the KMT regime much of the legitimacy that it needed. The government's success in developing the economy meant at the least that economic issues did not provide fuel for political grievances. Thus, with the end of martial law in 1987, the KMT could undertake political reform with a certain amount of confidence. Its gradual introduction of democratic processes and values undercut much of its former authoritarian style of rule. Reform generated considerable tensions, but by the 1990s, the KMT realized that street demonstrations would not bring down the government and that it was unnecessary to use harsh measures to suppress the opposition. This being the case, the KMT liberalized the political realm still further. Today, Taiwan is functioning as a democracy in most respects.

Taiwan has an important condition for political liberalization: a large middle class, with increasingly diverse and complex social and economic interests of its own that arise from ownership of and concern for private property. Moreover, because of the generally egalitarian distribution of wealth and the lack of a large underclass, economic discontent is low.[30] Thus, the KMT regime has gradually modified its authoritarian rule and become responsive to demands from an ever more politically aware and active citizenry.

One way in which the KMT has maintained dominance while reforming is by opening up its membership to a broader segment of the population. Social diversity and political pluralism may now be expressed within the KMT. The "Taiwanization" of both the KMT and governmental institutions after Chiang Kai-shek's death actually permitted the KMT not to respond to the demands of the Taiwanese for an independent opposition party until the late 1980s. By "Taiwanization" and, subsequently by *co-opting* the most appealing platforms of the Democratic Progressive Party (DPP),[31] Taiwan's political system has been able to institutionalize channels for conflict within a party-government system still under the KMT's control.[32] In short, as Taiwan has become more socially and politically diverse, the KMT has been willing to move away from authoritarian methods and toward persuasion, conciliation, and open debate as the means to maintain control.

External pressures have played a significant role in the democratization of Taiwan's institutions. Substantial American aid, for instance, was accompanied by considerable American pressure for liberalizing Taiwan's economy and political institutions. Taiwan's dependence on foreign trade has made it anxious to become accepted into membership in the World Trade Organization. To gain acceptance, Taiwan must open up its domestic market to foreign imports through such measures as cutting tariffs, lifting trade barriers, and reducing government subsidies on agricultural products.[33] Taiwanese businesspeople have added their own pressures to these.

The KMT government's efforts to bolster the integration of Taiwan into the global economy have allowed it to reap the benefits of internationalization. The KMT has also responded positively to demands from its citizens for greater economic and cultural contact with China, and for reform of the party and government. As a result, the KMT can continue to claim responsibility for Taiwan's prosperity and political liberalization.

With the KMT moving quickly to claim key elements of the most popular opposition-party policies as its own, the opposition has had to struggle to provide a clear alternative to the KMT. Without making a point of pushing Taiwan independence, an issue that could inflame Beijing's sensitivities as much as those of the KMT elite, the DPP has taken on the KMT. Its demands for more rapid political reforms and its criticism of KMT corrupt practices have resonated with the people. The public has been outraged and has demanded that, in addition to institutional reforms that end the KMT's monopolistic control of government, the KMT divest itself of corporate holdings that involve conflicts of interest. (The KMT *as a political party, not as the government,* owns a sizable percentage of corporate wealth in Taiwan.)[34]

By the time of the first democratic elections for the president of Taiwan in March 1996[35] (which the KMT candidate President Lee Teng-hui won handily), much had changed in the platforms of both the KMT and the DPP. The KMT, which had by then developed a powerful internal faction that demanded greater international recognition of Taiwan as an independent state, adopted what amounted to an "independent Taiwan" position. Although President Lee Teng-hui said that this was a "misinterpretation" by Beijing and the international community, and that Taiwan merely wanted more international "breathing space," his offer of $1 billion to the United Nations if it would give Taiwan a seat was hardly open to interpretation.

In the weeks leading up to Taiwan's first truly democratic elections for president, in March 1996, China began missile "tests" in the waters close to Taiwan. Fortunately, none of the missiles hit Taiwan. President Lee insisted that the missiles did not have warheads and were meant only to intimidate the Taiwanese people. But clearly Taiwan's people were anxious. Many stockpiled rice, and so many Taiwanese swapped their savings in local currency for hard currency that some of the banks ran out of U.S. dollars.[36] The KMT was, as a result of Beijing's response and pressures from the United States, forced to back down from efforts to gain greater recognition of Taiwan as an independent state. Since the March 1996 elections, both sides have made serious efforts to end the tensions and to return to mutually cooperative endeavors. And, in an effort to rationalize his having to back down from a position of confrontation with Beijing, President Lee adopted a different slant on the issue: Since the Republic of China was Taiwan, which already was a sovereign state, it was not necessary to declare sovereignty. Taiwan was already independent and sovereign.[37]

Political Parties

Not until 1989 did the KMT pass new laws legalizing opposition political parties. This decision was made in the context of a growing resistance to KMT rule because of the continued restriction of democratic rights, and in the favorable environment created by widespread prosperity and economic growth. The DPP, a largely Taiwanese-based opposition party, was officially recognized as a legal party. Even after 1989, however, the KMT continued to regulate political parties strictly, in the name of maintaining political and social stability, which the KMT believed might be jeopardized by a truly competitive political system.[38]

The first real elections, for 101 of the total seats in the Legislative Yuan (Parliament), occurred in December 1989. The results indicated the DPP's appeal as an opposition party. However, in both these and subsequent elections, internal differences marred the ability of the DPP to project a unified electoral strategy; but the KMT was similarly hurt by its own factionalism. Progressive reformers in the KMT have pushed for further liberalization of the economic and political systems, but more conservative elements have resisted it. Factionalism has become even more serious over the issue of whether Taiwan should press for greater international recognition as a state.

In the 1996 and 1998 elections, the most divisive issue for all parties was whether or not to press for an independent Taiwan. While most of the Taiwanese people would very much like to have an independent state, they considered it risky for its political leaders to advocate it as policy in the face of Beijing's clear threats to use military force, if necessary, to stop any movement toward an independent Taiwan. The re-

sults of the December 1998 elections favored those candidates in all parties who promised a continuation of the status quo—a Taiwan that agreed it was a province of China but continued to act as an independent state.

What is important to remember, however, is that the DPP has *never* accepted the view that there is only one China and that Taiwan should become reunified with China. Everyone in Taiwan understands it, but the DPP dares not say it. What the DPP resents is that the Taiwanese people have never been permitted to voice their objections to KMT declarations that Taiwan is part of China and that Taiwan *will be reunited* with the mainland, as was so unequivocably stated by KMT leaders in talks with China's leaders in late 1998.[39] Were the DPP to gain political power in Taiwan, however, many DPP legislators say that they would *not* pay lip service to the "one China" policy.[40] In any event, there is a consensus that the strategy of President Lee Teng-hui, who is both the head of the KMT and a Taiwanese, is to agree with Beijing that Taiwan will eventually unify with China, but at the same time "to assure Taiwan's citizens that this is not a possibility in the foreseeable future."[41]

In their first years in the Legislature, DPP legislators, no doubt frustrated by their role as a minority party that could not get through any of its own policies, sometimes engaged in physical brawls on the floor of the Legislature, ripping out microphones and throwing furniture. As the DPP steadily gained more power and influence over the legislative agenda, its behavior became more subdued. Still, policy gridlock has continued to plague the Legislature.[42] Taiwan's December 1998 elections, in which the KMT scored a stunning reversal against what had been a steady rise in power by the DPP, will do little to ameliorate the legislative gridlock issue. The election results do not mean that the DPP has been knocked out of the ring, but its inability to move forward was deeply hurt by its infighting.[43]

Today, then, the DPP's major problems are similar to those of the KMT and the New Party: internal disunity and corruption. Infighting became so serious that it led to the formation of three new parties—breakaway parties from the KMT and DPP that competed for the first time in the 1998 elections.[44] The more radical faction within the DPP broke off in 1998 to form the Taiwan Independence Party. Unlike the DPP, it refuses to be intimidated by Beijing's possible military response and is willing to support Taiwan's independence openly. On the other hand, one wing of the KMT, angry that the KMT was not moving more actively to bring about reunification with the mainland of China, broke off to form the New Party, which first ran candidates in the 1994 elections. Overall, the New Party's policy position is more radical than that of the KMT: It favors unification with the mainland (and on a stepped-up timetable). The New Party still has only 7 percent of the vote (clearly lacking support for its party platform—unification with the mainland), and its bitter disputes with its former colleagues in the KMT continue to make consensus difficult. Money politics, vote-buying practices, and general dishonesty, which have plagued all of Taiwan's parties since elections were first held, have burgeoned over the years. This stems in part from the growing importance of elections.[45] Candidates throw lavish feasts, make deals with businesspeople, and spread money around in order to get the vote. Equally disturbing to the Taiwanese people is the growing amount of election-related violence and the influence of the "underworld" on the elections.[46]

Because the KMT and the DPP have moved toward each other's positions on the issue of Taiwan independence, and because they are in basic agreement on most social and economic issues, there is not a major ideological rift between the two parties. Both are committed to democracy, both vehemently oppose communism and advocate capitalism, both believe it is important to maintain good relations with the P.R.C., and both support an equitable distribution of wealth, even though this requires governmental intervention. As a result, the growing power of the DPP and other opposition parties does not significantly threaten policies that the KMT has so carefully laid out during its many decades in power.

Finally, although Mainlanders are almost all within the KMT or the new party, the KMT has become so thoroughly "Taiwanized" that the earlier clear divide between the DPP and KMT based on Mainlander or Taiwanese identity has eroded considerably. Indeed, in today's Taiwan, it pays to have a Taiwanese identity. Even those who strongly favor reunification with the mainland, such as the new KMT mayor of Taipei, identify themselves not as Mainlanders but as "new Taiwanese." They are, in short, "born-again Taiwanese."[47]

Interest Groups

As Taiwan has become more socially, economically, and politically complex, alternative sources of power have developed that are independent of the KMT. Economic-interest groups comprised largely of Taiwanese, whose power arises from private property and wealth, are the most important; but there are also public-interest groups that challenge the KMT's policies in areas such as civil rights, the environment, women's rights, consumer protection, agricultural policy, aborigine rights, and nuclear power. Even before the lifting of martial law in 1988, these and other groups were organizing hundreds of demonstrations each year to protest government policy.

The thousands of interest groups have been spawned by political liberalization and economic growth, and they have added to the social pluralism in Taiwan. They have also increased the pressures for a still greater institutionalization of democratic procedures and are important instruments for democratic change.

The Future of Political Reform in Taiwan

The KMT has, then, been able to harness popular pressure, in part by allowing dissent to have an outlet through interest groups and opposition parties. At this point, should the KMT

THE U.S. SEVENTH FLEET HALTS INVASION

In 1950, in response to China's involvement in the Korean War, the United States sent its Seventh Fleet to the Taiwan Straight to protect Taiwan and the Offshore Islands of Quemoy and Matsu from an invasion by China. Because of improved Sino–American relations in the 1970s, the enhanced Chinese Nationalist capabilities to defend Taiwan and the Offshore Islands, and problems in the Middle East, the Seventh Fleet was eventually moved out of the area. In 1996, however, part of the Seventh Fleet briefly returned to the Taiwan Strait when China threatened to use military force against Taiwan if its leaders sought independent statehood. The aircraft carrier *Enterprise,* a part of the Seventh Fleet, is shown above.

feel its power threatened, it would be difficult to remove the many democratic rights that it has bestowed on the Taiwanese people in the last decade. Undoing them would be easier, of course, if Taiwan's security were threatened—either because of internal political turmoil or an external political threat from China. Were internal pressures to threaten KMT control, it might try to revert to authoritarian measures—and it is even plausible that the majority of the population would accept this as necessary. The KMT has, however, benefited from the legitimization of its right to rule by the gradual introduction of a more democratic system.

Finally, the ability of the KMT to keep the lid on the expression of political discontent is aided by the politically conservative value system of the majority of people in Taiwan who fear the consequences for stability of too many different ideas. Much like the perspective of the Chinese living on the mainland, people in Taiwan fear instability more than they treasure freedom.

MASS MEDIA

With the official end to martial law in July 1987, the police powers of the state were radically curtailed. The media abandoned former taboos and grew more willing to openly address social and political problems, including the "abuse of authority and unwarranted special privilege."[48] A free press, strongly critical of the government and KMT, now flourishes. Taiwan, with only 21.7 million people, boasts close to 4,000 magazines; about 100 newspapers, with a total daily circulation of 5 million; 150 news agencies; three domestic television channels; and more than 30 radio stations, which now include foreign broadcasts such as CNN, NHK (from Japan), and the BBC. Thus, although television and radio are still controlled by the government, they have become far more independent since 1988; and 1.2 million households receive 20 to 30 channels through a satellite "dish."[49] Television stations show programs from all over the world, exposing people to alternative ideas, values, and lifestyles, and contributing to social pluralism.[50]

Political magazines, which are privately financed and therefore not constrained by governmental financial controls, have played an important role in undercutting state censorship of the media and developing alternative perspectives regarding issues of public concern. New technology that defies national boundaries (including satellite broadcasts from Japan and mainland China), cable television, and VCRs are diminishing the relevance of the state monopoly of television.[51]

THE TAIWAN–P.R.C.–U.S. TRIANGLE

From 1949 until the 1960s, Taiwan received significant economic, political, and military support from the United States. Even after it became abundantly clear that the Communists effectively controlled the China mainland and had the support of the people, the United States never wavered in its support of President Chiang Kai-shek's position that the R.O.C. was the legitimate government of all China. U.S. secretary of state Henry Kissinger's secret trip to China in 1971, followed by President Richard M. Nixon's historic visit in 1972, led to an abrupt change in the American position and to the gradual erosion of the R.O.C.'s diplomatic status.

Allies of the United States, most of whom had loyally supported its diplomatic stance on China, soon severed diplomatic ties with Taipei, a necessary step before they could, in turn, establish diplomatic relations with Beijing. Only one government could claim to represent the Chinese people; and with the KMT in complete agreement with the Chinese Communist regime that there was no such thing as "two Chinas"

or "one Taiwan and one China," the diplomatic community had to make a choice between the two contending governments. Given the reality of the Chinese Communist Party's control over 1 billion Chinese people and the vast continent of China, and, more cynically, given the desire of the business community throughout the world to have ties to China, Taipei found itself increasingly isolated diplomatically.

The United States found it painful to desert its long-time Asian ally. The R.O.C. had, after all, been a loyal ally in Asia and a bastion against communism, if not a democratic oasis. The United States had, moreover, heavily invested in Taiwan's economy. But on January 1, 1979, President Jimmy Carter announced the severing of diplomatic relations with Taipei and the establishment of full diplomatic relations with Beijing.

Taiwan's disappointment and anger at the time cannot be overstated, but the relationship between the United States and what became known as simply the "Taiwan government" has continued. American interests in Taiwan are overseen by a huge, quasi-official "American Institute in Taiwan," while Taiwan is represented in the United States by multiple branches of the "Taipei Economic and Cultural Office." In fact, the personnel in these offices continue to be treated in most respects as if they were diplomatic personnel. Except for the handful of countries that officially recognize the R.O.C., Taiwan's commercial, cultural, and political interests are represented abroad by these unofficial offices.

Once the United States agreed to the Chinese Communists' "principled stand" that Taiwan is a province of China and that the People's Republic of China is the sole legal government of all of China, it could hardly continue to maintain a military alliance with one of China's provinces. Recognition of Beijing, therefore, required the United States to give the mandated 1-year termination notice to its mutual defense treaty with the R.O.C. In the Taiwan Relations Act of 1979, however, the United States stated its concern for the island's future security, its hope for a peaceful resolution of the conflict between the KMT government and Beijing, and its decision to put a moratorium on the sale of new weapons to Taiwan.

Renewal of Arms Sales

In spite of this agreement, by 1981, the newly ensconced Reagan administration had announced its intention to resume arms sales to Taiwan. It argued that Taiwan needed its weapons upgraded in order to defend itself. Irate, Beijing demanded that, in accordance with American agreements and implicit promises to China, the U.S. phase out the sale of military arms over a specified period. The issue of U.S. arms sales to Taiwan has plagued relations with China ever since.[52] China's conflicts with the United States over its own sales of military equipment—such as the sale of medium-range missiles to Saudi Arabia, Silkworm missiles to Iran (eventually used against American ships), nuclear technology to Pakistan, and massive sales of semiautomatic assault weapons to the United States (one of which was used to attack the White House in 1994)—have put it in a weak position for protesting U.S. sales of military equipment to Taiwan.

Countries such as the Netherlands and France, which have proposed selling military equipment to Taiwan, have been forced to back down in the face of Beijing's threatened punitive measures, so Taiwan has taken further steps to develop its own defense industry.[53] In the 1980s, the United States intervened to stop Taiwan's efforts to develop nuclear weapons; but Taiwan's scientists continue to do research on nuclear weapons and missiles. They are hoping to follow the Israeli approach of doing computer simulations rather than actual tests to develop nuclear weapons.[54]

The United States wants Beijing to agree to the "peaceful resolution of the Taiwan issue," but "on principle," China refuses to make any such commitment. China insists that Taiwan is an "internal" affair, not an international matter over which other states might have some authority. From China's perspective, then, it has the right as a sovereign state to choose to use force to settle the Taiwan issue. In fact, apart from a mild statement from Japan protesting China's "testing" of missiles over Taiwan in 1996, no Asian country questioned China's right to use force when Taiwan pressed for independent statehood.

CHINA'S "PEACE OFFENSIVE"

Since the early 1980s, the People's Republic of China has combined its threats and warnings about Taiwan's seeking independence with a "peace offensive" in an effort to get the KMT leaders to negotiate a future reunification of Taiwan with the mainland. Beijing has invited the people of Taiwan to visit their friends and relatives on the mainland and to witness the progress made under Communist rule. In the first year (1987–1988) since 1949 that Taiwan's government agreed to allow visits to the mainland, more than 170,000 people seized the opportunity. Since then, more than one third of Taiwan's adult population have traveled to the mainland. In turn, less than 0.1 percent of Chinese from the mainland have been permitted by the KMT government to visit Taiwan (although more may have entered through a third area, such as Hong Kong or the United States).[55] The KMT government has, however, arranged for mainland Chinese students studying abroad to come for "study tours" of Taiwan. The KMT has treated them as if they were visiting dignitaries, and the students have usually returned to their universities full of praise for Taiwan.

China's "peace offensive" is based on a nine-point proposal originally made in 1981. Its major points include Beijing's willingness to negotiate a mutually agreeable reintegration of Taiwan under the mainland's government; encouragement of trade, cultural exchanges, travel, and communications between Taiwan and the mainland; the offer to give Taiwan "a high degree of autonomy as a special administrative region"

of China after reunification (the same status that it offered to Hong Kong when it came under Beijing's rule in 1997); and the promise that Taiwan could keep its own armed forces, continue its socioeconomic systems, maintain political control over local affairs, and allow Taiwan's leaders to participate in the national leadership of a unified China. This is far more than China offered to Hong Kong.

The KMT's original official response to Beijing's "peace offensive" was negative. The KMT's bitter history of war with the Chinese Communists and what the KMT sees as a pattern of Communist duplicity explain much of the government's hesitation. Since 1992, however, Taiwan has engaged in "unofficial" discussions on topics of mutual interest, such as the protection of Taiwan's investments in the mainland, tourism, cross-Strait communication and transportation links, and the dumping of Taiwan's nuclear waste on the mainland. Taipei remains sensitive, however, to the Taiwanese people's concern about the unification of Taiwan with the mainland implicit in Beijing's "peace offensive." The Taiwanese have asserted that they will never accede to rule by yet another mainland Chinese government, especially a Communist one. And they have insisted that no deals between the KMT Mainlander leadership and the Chinese Communist regime be struck. The Taiwanese are afraid that the KMT Mainlander elite could join in an agreement with the Beijing leadership, at the expense of the Taiwanese. But the fact that Taiwanese are among the most powerful leaders of the KMT has done much to diminish the concerns of the Taiwanese.

With only a handful of countries recognizing the R.O.C. instead of the P.R.C., and with Beijing blocking membership for the R.O.C. in most international organizations, the KMT has to be able to show some positive results in its evolving relationship with Beijing. Thus, it has been eager to promote links between Taiwan and the mainland. "Indirect" trade between China and Taiwan, by way of Hong Kong, has continued to soar. China is Taiwan's third largest trading partner after the United States and Japan. Meanwhile, "illegal" trade between mainland fishermen and Taiwanese continues at a brisk pace (as much as an estimated $2 billion a year by the mid-1990s), with fishermen trading much-coveted traditional Chinese medicines for made-in-Taiwan VCRs, televisions, and videotapes. Originally, the KMT permitted such aspects of its relationship with China to develop in part to let some of the steam out of the Taiwan Independence Movement. Now, it is more concerned with countering the DPP's arguments that, under KMT policies, Taiwan has essentially been removed from international diplomatic circles.

To keep up at least the pretense of moving toward unification with the mainland, Taiwan's government-controlled television presents travelogues about China as if it were just another place that any ordinary citizen in Taiwan could visit (no longer a land occupied by Communist "bandits"). Taiwan's radio and television programs feature news about

China, including weather forecasts, under the topic of "national news," symbolizing the fact that Taiwan is indeed a part of China.

On the other hand, the KMT's policy on mainland spouses is particularly stringent and clearly indicates that China's citizens are viewed as potential enemies, not compatriots. Few Taiwanese residents who marry individuals from the mainland are permitted to actually live with them in Taiwan. This is in startling contrast to Beijing's policy, which welcomes Taiwan spouses to come live on the mainland. After 1992, the KMT government formulated slightly more humane policies, permitting several hundred Mainlanders each year to come to reside with their respective spouses in Taiwan; but thousands are still prohibited from doing so. The government's argument is that the mainland spouses could be spies—a possibility that the Beijing government seemingly discounts.

In the meantime, China continues to deepen and widen harbors to receive ships from Taiwan; wine and dine influential Taiwanese; give preferential treatment to Taiwan's entrepreneurs in trade and investment on the mainland; open direct telephone lines from Taiwan to the mainland; rebuild some of the most important temples to local deities in Fujian Province, favorite places for Taiwanese to visit; establish special tourist organizations to care solely for people from Taiwan; and refurbish the birthplace of Chiang Kai-shek, the greatest enemy of the Chinese Communists in their history.

Various segments of the Taiwan population view the relationship differently. Businesspeople and scholars want direct trade and personal contacts. They do not believe that there is much to fear, and they think that political concerns should be separated from economic interests and international scientific exchanges. Those in the economic sector are particularly concerned with penetrating and, if possible, controlling the China market. Otherwise, they argue, businesspeople from other countries will do so.

For Taiwanese faced with Taiwan's ever-higher labor costs and the need for cheap raw materials unavailable in Taiwan, investing in China offers definite advantages: They can move Taiwan's now outdated labor-intensive factories and machinery to the mainland. There, significantly cheaper labor allows these same factories to continue to make a profit. Since the factories are not profitable if left in Taiwan, not much can be lost by moving them to the mainland.

Many are concerned, however, that Taiwan, which already has put 15 percent of its total foreign investment in the mainland, could become "hostage" to Beijing. That is, if China were to refuse to release Taiwan's assets or repay investors for their assets on the mainland in case of a political conflict between Taipei and Beijing, Taiwan's enterprises would form a pressure point that would give the advantage to Beijing. Furthermore, without diplomatic recognition in China, Taiwan's businesses on the mainland are at risk in case of a conflict with local businesses or the government. Yet so

far, affairs have turned out quite the opposite: China has actually *favored* Taiwan's businesses over all others. As for Taiwan's investors, they have in general managed to make such a quick profit—and to put in so many safeguards—that their losses from any possible seizure of assets would be negligible.

PROSPECTS FOR THE REUNIFICATION OF TAIWAN WITH THE MAINLAND

Many of those opposed to reunification would nevertheless agree that the KMT government's policy toward China should be progressive, assertive, and forward-looking; and that lacking a long-term plan and simply reacting to Beijing's initiatives puts the real power to determine the future relationship in the hand of the Chinese Communist Party. Reform-minded individuals in the KMT have insisted that the government abandon its head-in-the-sand behavior and actively structure how that relationship evolves. In 1990, the KMT set up a National Unification Council for the purpose of accelerating the process of "unification of all China as a free, democratic nation."[56] Taiwan's former premier proposed a "one country, two regions" model "as a means for handling legal and other disputes arising from unofficial contact."[57]

Whether this model or Beijing's model for Hong Kong as a "Special Administrative Region" (SAR) would be used were reunification to occur is debatable. Indeed, President Lee made a remarkably unambiguous statement: "Our 'One China' is the Republic of China which will for the first time become the true 'One China' after reunification [with mainland China]." He added that Beijing's perspective of a "One China" ruled by Beijing, with Taiwan as a province, would be unacceptable to Taipei; and he repeated his hope that Taiwan would be admitted to the United Nations.[58]

This view does not, however, necessarily challenge the agreement that Taipei and Beijing reached in 1992: " . . . [E]ach would maintain its own interpretation of the one-China concept. [Beijing] equates China with the present People's Republic of China government and ignores the existence of the R.O.C. Taipei holds that Taiwan and the mainland are separate and politically equivalent parts of one China. . . ."[59] In short, President Lee is not necessarily rejecting the concept of "One China"—if Taipei is in charge. He is rejecting the idea that it would be called the People's Republic of China, or that Beijing would be in charge of the new unified government. He did not indicate why he thought that the government of the "Republic of China" would—even were free and democratic elections for all of the mainland and Taiwan to be held—come out the winner. There is certainly no evidence to suggest that most people on the mainland would welcome the return to power of the KMT government, which was so unsuccessful in resolving China's problems before 1949.

In spite of rhetoric such as this, changes in Taipei's policies toward the P.R.C. have been critical to an improvement to cross-Strait ties. For example, the KMT ended its 40-year-old policy of stamping "Communist bandit" on all printed materials from China and prohibiting ordinary people from reading them; Taiwan's government officials and others formerly prohibited from visiting relatives in China are now permitted to go; scholars from Taiwan may now attend some international conferences in the P.R.C., and Taipei now permits a few P.R.C. scholars to attend conferences in Taiwan; and KMT retired veterans, who fought against the Communists and retreated to Taiwan in 1949, are actually encouraged to return to the mainland to live out their lives, because their limited KMT government pensions would buy them a better life there! Certainly some members of Taiwan's upper class are acting as if the relationship will eventually be a harmonious one when they purchase large mansions in Shanghai.

Other circumstances also encourage Taiwan to expand its ties, if not yet reunify with the mainland. For example, both Taiwan and China would prefer the establishment of a Chinese trading zone to a Japan-dominated East Asian trading zone. A "Chinese common market" would incorporate China, Taiwan, Hong Kong, Macau, and perhaps other places with large ethnic Chinese communities, such as Singapore and Malaysia. Economically integrating these Chinese areas would strengthen them against the Japanese powerhouse, particularly against a Japan community that incorporates Taiwan, Hong Kong, and South Korea. Adopting common policies on taxes, trade, and currencies would be an important step toward eventual reunification of Taiwan with the mainland.[60]

In addition, China's leaders have over the last few years stopped referring to China as "the People's Republic of China." Now they just call it "China." This is clearly an effort to repackage China in the eyes of Taiwan, and the world. Removing the "people's republic" nameplate is meant to suggest that Taiwan would not be integrated into a Communist people's republic, which it would find utterly unacceptable but, rather, into a cultural and national entity called China. And it symbolically eliminates the issue of two different governments claiming to represent China, and whether that China would be called a "people's republic" or a "republic." It would be called neither.

Growing ties between Taiwan and the mainland do not, however, add up to a desire on Taipei's part for reunification. And, with an ever-smaller number of first-generation Mainlanders in top positions in the KMT and Taiwan's government, few are keen to push for reunification. Indeed, the majority of people in Taiwan still oppose reunification, under current conditions. They are particularly concerned about two issues. The first is the gap in living standards. Taiwan is fully aware of the high price that West Germany paid to reunify with East Germany. Obviously, the price tag to close the gap with mammoth China would be prohibitive for tiny Taiwan. The second issue is democracy. Whether Mainlander or Taiwanese, KMT or DPP, the Chinese Communist Party's crackdown on Tiananmen Square demonstrators in June 1989 and

subsequent arrests of dissidents have continued to dampen enthusiasm for formal reunification. Combined with a fear of loss of certain political freedoms and control over their own institutions, such as they perceive as certain to happen in Hong Kong, Taiwanese generally wonder what benefits would accrue to them from reunification.

Finally, whether or not "one country, two systems" succeeds in protecting Hong Kong from Beijing's intervention and repression, they reject a parallel being drawn between Hong Kong and Taiwan. Hong Kong was, after all, a British colony, whereas Taiwan, even if only in the last decade, is a fledgling democracy. When the KMT returned to the negotiating table with mainland China in late 1998, then, it made further development and greater democracy the conditions for reunification. What was most remarkable about the talks was, however, that the KMT clearly stated that once these conditions were fulfilled, *mainland China and Taiwan would be reunified.* Cynics interpret this as a "non-event," however, because it allows Taiwan's government to decide when, if ever, those conditions are fulfilled.

Thus, the KMT has been caught in a dilemma. Its efforts to move more quickly toward reunification were not fast enough to avoid alienating both the military and the conservatives within the KMT, who broke off to form the New Party; and they were *too* fast to avoid giving the DPP more appeal in its platform that encourages greater independence for Taiwan. Over the years, many have pushed the KMT to propose a new model for reunification. Germany's reunification and the possibility of reunification between North and South Korea increase the pressure on Taiwan to reunify with the mainland.

There are encouraging signs on both sides. Taiwan's government intends to create a Special Economic Zone for direct trade with the China mainland.[61] For its part, mainland China makes access and investment by Taiwanese easy. Its government has been remarkably stable, and it has made significant progress in development and democratization in the last 20 years. Greater contacts and exchanges between the two sides should in themselves help lay the basis for mutual trust and understanding. Already they have led to a greater appreciation on the mainland of an alternative to communism in a Chinese society.

The Chinese Communist regime has been watching closely to see if political and economic liberalization in Taiwan will lead to the sort of chaos that followed on the heels of political and economic liberalization in Central/Eastern Europe and the former Soviet Union. So far, in spite of both the growing economic polarization of Taiwan into rich and poor and the increasing number of protests and demonstrations that challenge government policies, the KMT government has had few problems in controlling the effects of liberalization and rapid growth. On the other hand, Taiwan's democratization has been accompanied by increasing corruption. Neither the positive nor the negative aspects of political liberalization in Taiwan have gone unnoticed in Beijing.

Although China had by 1999 moved many of its missiles to positions facing Taiwan, there is no sense of an imminent threat of attack by China, as long as Taiwan does not again push seriously for recognition as an independent state. An attack for any other reason seems increasingly improbable, as the mainland continues to benefit from Taiwan's trade and billions of dollars of Taiwanese investment as well as from remittances and tourism from Taiwan (more than 8 million visitors since 1987). China's leadership, committed to rapid economic development, would also have to consider the risks involved in draining its limited resources into a war that it might not win. They would not know in advance, moreover, whether an attack on Taiwan would cause the United States to intervene on behalf of Taiwan; but Beijing could well worry that it might.

Taiwan's high labor costs and lack of natural resources, and China's abundance of both natural resources and cheap labor, mean that closer ties with China offer Taiwan a chance to continue its rapid growth into the twenty-first century. Combined with Taiwan's heavy dependence on trade, Taipei must at least talk as if it is interested in unification, even if it simultaneously pursues "a policy which, if effective would create the basis for both *de facto* and *de jure* independence." It is, in short, a strategy aimed at using "the unification *process* to set up conditions advantageous for the emergence of some form of *de jure* independent Taiwan with no commitment to unification with China."[62]

Thus, it seems to be in Taiwan's best interests for the relationship with China to develop in a careful and controlled manner—and to avoid public statements on the issue of reunification versus an independent Taiwan, even as that issue haunts every hour of the day in Taiwan. It is also in Taiwan's interest to wait and see how China integrates Hong Kong under its formula of "one country, two systems." In the meantime, Taiwan's international strategy—acting like an independent state, while insisting that it is not attempting to become independent, and conducting business and diplomacy with other states as usual—has proved remarkably successful. It has allowed Taiwan to get on with its own economic development without too many concerns about military security.

Beijing's leadership knows that Taiwan acts as a de facto independent state, but it is willing to turn a blind eye as long as Taipei does not push too openly for recognition. The reality does not matter to Beijing as long as the symbolism of Taiwan being a province of China is recognized. Beijing's leadership is far more interested in putting its resources into China's economic development than fighting a war with no known outcome. But because China's sovereignty over Taiwan has been an emotional patriotic, even nationalistic, issue for the Chinese people ever since 1949, Beijing will not make a "rational" cost–benefit analysis of the costs of using force against a rebellious Taiwan.

As Taiwan's relationship with China deepens and broadens, it is possible that more arrangements could be made for the representation of both Taiwan and China in international organizations, without Beijing putting up countless roadblocks. In any event, the concrete results of Taiwan declaring independence would be virtually nil. Already Beijing refuses to have diplomatic relations with any country that officially recognizes the Republic of China as the legitimate government of China. Those countries that do recognize the R.O.C. cannot trade with the P.R.C. Given the size of the China market, this is an unacceptable price for most countries to pay. Beijing would no doubt use this trump card to punish those who would dare to recognize an independent state of Taiwan, just as it does now.

NOTES

1. John F. Burns, "Quemoy (Remember?) Bristles with Readiness," *The New York Times* (April 5, 1986), p. 2.

2. Susan Yu, "Lien Vows Defense Outposts to Stay," *The Free China Journal* (November 4, 1994), p. 1.

3. Edwin A. Winckler, "Cultural Policy on Postwar Taiwan," in Stevan Harrell and Chun-chieh Huang, eds., *Cultural Change in Postwar Taiwan* (Boulder, CO: Westview Press, 1994), p. 22.

4. *Ibid.*, p. 29.

5. Thomas B. Gold, "Civil Society and Taiwan's Quest for Identity," in Harrell and Huang, p. 60.

6. Parris Chang, "The Impact of the 1996 Missile Crisis on US–China–Taiwan Relations," seminar at Harvard University (November 13, 1998). Chang is a DPP legislator in the Legislative Yuan.

7. Thomas A. Shaw, "Are the Taiwanese Becoming More Individualistic as They Become More Modern?" Taiwan Studies Workshop, *Fairbank Center Working Papers*, No. 7 (August 1994), pp. 1–25.

8. David Chen, "From Presidential Hopeful, Frank Words on Democracy," *The Free China Journal* (September 9, 1994), p. 6.

9. "Premier Hau Bristling about Crime in Taiwan," *The Free China Journal* (September 13, 1990), p. 1.

10. Winckler, in Harrell and Huang, p. 41.

11. Lee Fan-fang, "Ghosts' Arrival Bad for Business," *The Free China Journal* (August 7, 1992), p. 4.

12. Marc J. Cohen, *Taiwan at the Crossroads* (Washington, D.C.: Asian Resource Center, 1988), pp. 186–190. For further detail, see his chapter on "Religion and Religious Freedom," pp. 185–215. Also, see Gold, in Harrell and Huang, p. 53.

13. See *Free China Review*, Vol. 44, No. 9 (September 1994), which has a series of articles on educational reform, pp. 1–37.

14. Cohen, p. 107.

15. *Ibid.*, p. 108. For more on women, see the chapter on "Women and Indigenous People," pp. 106–126.

16. "Taiwan: In Praise of Paranoia" (a special "Taiwan Survey"), *The Economist* (November 7, 1998), p. 3.

17. James A. Robinson, "The Value of Taiwan's Experience," *The Free China Journal* (November 6, 1992), p. 7.

18. Kelly Her, "Not-So-Iron Rice Bowl," *Free China Review* (October 1998), pp. 28–35.

19. In addition, Taiwan's workers could not get higher wages through strikes, which were forbidden under martial law. The alternative was to try starting up one's own business. Gold, in Harrell and Huang, pp. 50, 53.

20. "Taiwan: In Praise of Paranoia," pp. 8–15.

21. *Ibid.*, p. 17.

22. *Ibid.*, p. 16.

23. Robert P. Weller, "Environmental Protest in Taiwan: A Preliminary Sketch," Taiwan Studies Workshop, *Fairbank Center Working Papers,* No. 2 (1993), pp. 1, 4.

24. Susan Yu, "Legislature Acts to Protect Lawmakers from Recall Movements," *The Free China Journal* (October 14, 1994), p. 2.

25. Dianna Lin, "Alien Workers Face Problems in New Life," *The Free China Journal* (September 9, 1994), pp. 7–8.

26. Actually, since both sides agreed that Taiwan was a part of China, the KMT government was not really "in exile," just relocated.

27. The maps of China in Taiwan's schools still include not just Taiwan and all of China proper but also Tibet, Inner Mongolia, and even Outer Mongolia, which is an independent state.

28. From 1950 to 1986, military courts tried more than 10,000 cases involving civilians. These were in violation of the Constitution's provision (Article 9) that prohibited civilians from being tried in a military court. Hung-mao Tien, *The Great Transition: Political and Social Change in the Republic of China* (Palo Alto, CA: Hoover Institution, Stanford University, 1989), p. 111.

29. The Kaohsiung rally, which was followed by street confrontations between the demonstrators and the police, is an instance of KMT repression of *dangwai* activities, activities that were seen as a challenge to the KMT's absolute power. The KMT interpreted the Kaohsiung Incident "an illegal challenge to public security." For this reason, those arrested were given only semi-open hearings in a military, not civil, tribunal; and torture may have been used to extract confessions from the defendants. Tien, p. 97.

30. In recent years, however, Taiwan has had to cope with the effect of a growing disparity in income distribution. By 1994, the wealthiest 20 percent of the population possessed 54 percent of the total wealth of Taiwan. See Philip Liu, "Discontent with a Growing Wealth Gap," *Free China Review* (June 1994), pp. 36–41.

31. For example, the DPP's demand for more flexibility in relations with the P.R.C.; ecology and environmental issues; including DPP in discussions; and permitting greater freedom of the press. By the time of the 1996 elections, the dominant wing of the KMT had even co-opted the DPP's platform for a more independent Taiwan.

32. Tien, p. 72.

33. Philip Liu, "Revving Up for the GATT Shock," *Free China Review* (September 1994), pp. 47–53.

34. "Taiwan: In Praise of Paranoia," p. 12.

35. Prior to this, the head of the KMT, chosen by the KMT itself, was the president of Taiwan.

36. *South China Morning Post* (March 7, 1996), as excerpted in *China News Digest* on the Internet (March 8, 1996).

37. Charles Freeman, "Same Straits, Different Dreams: The Taiwan Dilemma," seminar at Harvard University (January 30, 1998).

38. Jiang Ping-lun, "Competition Mixed with Consensus," *Free China Review* (October 1989), p. 36.

39. The conditions for reunification are, however, not ones likely to be met easily: democratization at a level acceptable to Taiwan; and substantial economic development, which would close the developmental gap between Taiwan and the mainland.

40. Parris Chang, "The Impact of the 1996 Missile Crisis on US-China-Taiwan Relations," seminar at Harvard University, November 13, 1998. Parris Chang is a DPP legislator in the Legislative Yuan.

41. Cal Clark, "Taiwan in the 1990s: Moving Ahead or Back to the Future?" in William Joseph, *China Briefing: The Contradictions of Change* (Armonk, NY: M. E. Sharpe, 1997), p. 213.

42. Clark, in Joseph, p. 206.

43. The KMT regained the mayorship of Taipei, which is considered the key political position in Taiwan (outside the presidency itself). It also established a solid majority in the Parliament and won 44 percent of Taipei's city council seats. It won 52 percent of city council seats in Kaohsiung, Taiwan's second largest city. In the Legislature, the DPP lost both seats and popular support: Its share of the popular vote dropped from nearly 36 to 29.5 percent, the worst showing for the DPP since 1992. On the other hand, the DPP scored an upset victory against the KMT incumbent of the Kaohsiung mayorship. For more detail, see Deborah A. Brown, James A. Robinson, and Eric P. Moon, "Taiwan's December Elections: Implications for Beijing," e-notes, distributed by Foreign Policy Research Institute (fpri@aol.com) (December 11, 1998).

44. Myra Lu and Frank Chang, "Election Trends Indicate Future of Taiwan Politics," *Free China Journal* (November 27, 1998), p. 7. The breakaway parties include the Taiwan Independence Party and the New Nation Alliance, which split off from the DPP, and the Green Party.

45. Clark, p. 206.

46. Lu and Chang, p. 7.

47. Deborah A. Brown, James A. Robinson, and Eric P. Moon, "In Taiwan's December Elections: Implications for Beijing" (fpri@aol.com), December 11, 1998.

48. Lee Changkuei, "High-Speed Social Dynamics," *Free China Review* (Taipei), Vol. 39, No. 10 (October 1989), p. 6.

49. Yu-ming Shaw, "Problems and Prospects of the Democratization of the Republic of China on Taiwan," Taiwan Studies Workshop, *Fairbank Center Working Papers,* Harvard University, No. 2 (October 1993), pp. 1–2.

50. For more detail on television programming, see Minh-ha Nguyen, "Telecommunications: Business Is Beaming," *Free China Review* (September 1994), pp. 54–59.

51. Chin-chuan Lee, "Sparking a Fire: The Press and the Ferment of Democratic Change in Taiwan," in Chin-chuan Lee, ed., *China's Media, Media China* (Boulder, CO: Westview Press, 1994), pp. 188–192.

52. The Chinese government continues to protest against the appropriations by the U.S. Congress for Taiwan. "The Omnibus Appropriation Act and the 1999 Fiscal Year Department of Defence Authorization Act serve to interfere in China's internal affairs by supporting Tibetan separatist elements, putting Taiwan into the Theatre Missile Defence (TMD) system and allowing the sale of arms to Taiwan. . . ." Ma Chenguang, "Resentment Expressed on Anti-China US Bills," *China Daily* (October 30, 1998), p. 1.

53. By 1994, Taiwan had produced its own squadron of 20 jet fighters, armed with Taiwan-made air-to-air missiles. Peter Chen, "Taiwan-made Fighters Go into Active Service," *The Free China Journal* (December 30, 1994), pp. 1, 2.

54. Change, November 13, 1998.

55. As excerpted in *China News Daily,* on Internet (May 5, 1996). A different perspective is offered by these figures: 12 million visits by 3 million people from Taiwan to Mainland since 1988, but only 10,000 per year from China to Taiwan since 1988. Ninety percent of the visits are family visits, not pure tourism. From "The Koo-Wang Talks: Constructive Dialogue," seminar at Harvard University, October 30, 1998.

56. "NUC's Charter Approval May Hasten Unification," *The Free China Journal* (September 17, 1990), p. 1.

57. "One China, Two Regions," *The Free China Journal* (September 6, 1990), p. 1.

58. Japan Economic Newswire, as excerpted on Internet by *China News Daily* (June 21, 1996).

59. Virginia Sheng, "Lee Restates Offer to Visit Mainland for Talks, " *The Free China Journal* (July 12, 1996), p. 1.

60. Willy Wo-lap Lam, "Beijing 'Reconsidering' 'Chinese Common Market,' " *Foreign Broadcasts Information Service* (FBIS-China-89-043) (March 7, 1989), pp. 58–59.

61. "Lien Chan Proposed Plan to Sign 'Peace Accord' with the Mainland," *China News Daily* (May 6, 1996).

62. Alastair I. Johnston, "Independence through Unification: On the Correct Handling of Contradictions Across the Taiwan Strait," *Contemporary Issues,* no. 2, Fairbank Center for East Asian Research, Harvard University (September 1993), pp. 5–6.

Hong Kong

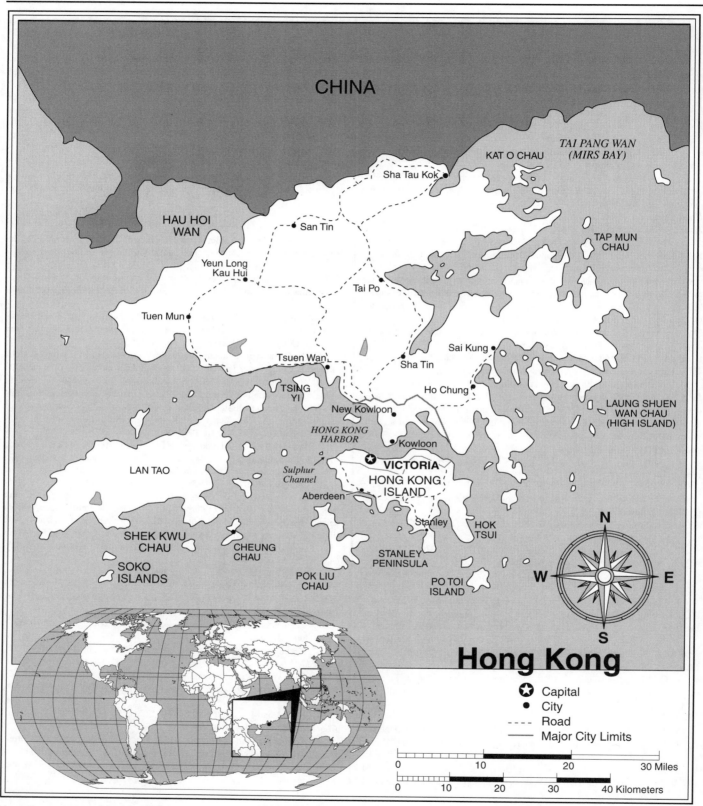

Hong Kong consists of the island of Hong Kong, adjacent islets, the Kowloon Peninsula, and the New Territories. More than 230 islands make up Hong Kong. Since land is constantly being reclaimed from the sea, the total land area of Hong Kong is continually increasing by small amounts. All of Hong Kong reverted to Chinese sovereignty on July 1, 1997.

Hong Kong (China Special Administrative Region)

GEOGRAPHY

Area in Square Miles (Kilometers): 671 (1,054) (about 6 times the size of Washington, D.C.)
Capital: Victoria
Environmental Concerns: air and water pollution
Geographical Features: hilly to mountainous, with steep slopes; lowlands in the north
Climate: tropical monsoon

PEOPLE

Population

Total: 6,547,000
Annual Growth Rate: 2.59%
Rural/Urban Population Ratio: 9/91
Major Languages: Chinese (Cantonese); English
Ethnic Makeup: 98% Chinese (mostly Cantonese); 2% others
Religions: 90% a combination of Buddhism and Taoism; 10% Christian

Health

Life Expectancy at Birth: 76 years (male); 82 years (female)
Infant Mortality Rate (Ratio): 5.3/1,000
Physicians Available (Ratio): 1/1,000

Education

Adult Literacy Rate: 92%

TRANSPORTATION

Highways in Miles (Kilometers): 1,030 (1,717)
Railroads in Miles (Kilometers): 22 (34)
Usable Airfields: 2

GOVERNMENT

Type: special administrative region (SAR) of the People's Republic of China; Chinese sovereignty reestablished on July 1, 1997
Chief Executive: Tung Chee-hwa
Political Parties: United Democrats of Hong Kong; Liberal Democratic Federation; Hong Kong Democratic Federation; Association for Democracy and People's Livelihood; Progressive Hong Kong Society
Suffrage: residents over age 21 who have lived in Hong Kong for at least 7 years

MILITARY

Military Expenditures (% of GDP): defense is the responsibility of China

ECONOMY

Currency ($ U.S. Equivalent): 7.74 Hong Kong dollars = $1
Per Capita Income/GDP: $26,000/$163.6 billion
GDP Growth Rate: 4.7%
Inflation Rate: 6.5%
Unemployment Rate: 3.1%
Labor Force: 3,251,000

Natural Resources: outstanding deepwater harbor; feldspar
Agriculture: vegetables; poultry
Industry: tourism; electronics; service
Exports: $197.2 billion (primary partners China, United States, Japan)
Imports: $217.2 billion (primary partners China, Japan, Taiwan)

http://www.info.gov.hk/sitemap.htm
http://www.hkstandard.com/online/news/001/asia/asia.htm
http://www.asiawind.com/hkwwwvl/

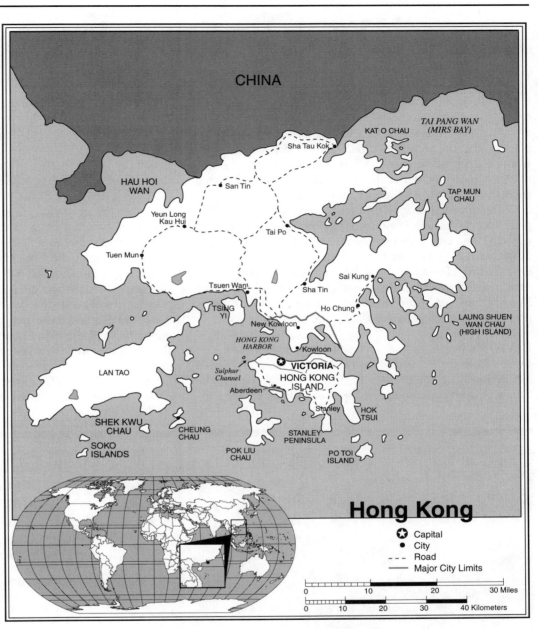

CHINA

KAT O CHAU

TAI PANG WAN (MIRS BAY)

Sha Tau Kok

TAP MUN CHAU

HAU HOI WAN

San Tin

Yeun Long Kau Hui

Tai Po

Tuen Mun

Sai Kung

Tsuen Wan

Sha Tin

Ho Chung

LAUNG SHUEN WAN CHAU (HIGH ISLAND)

TSING YI

New Kowloon

HONG KONG HARBOR

Kowloon

Sulphur Channel

VICTORIA
HONG KONG ISLAND

LAN TAO

Aberdeen

Stanley

HOK TSUI

SHEK KWU CHAU

CHEUNG CHAU

STANLEY PENINSULA

SOKO ISLANDS

POK LIU CHAU

PO TOI ISLAND

Hong Kong

⊛ Capital
● City
- - - Road
— Major City Limits

| 0 | 10 | 20 | 30 Miles |
| 0 | 10 | 20 | 30 | 40 Kilometers |

Hong Kong

From British Colony to Chinese Rule

Hong Kong, the "fragrant harbor" situated on the southeastern edge of China, has been characterized by such epithets as a "capitalist paradise," "the pearl of the Orient," a "borrowed place living on borrowed time," and a "den of iniquity." Under a British colonial administration committed to a laissez-faire economy, but in the context of a highly structured and tightly controlled political system, Hong Kong's dynamic and vibrant people shaped the colony into one of the world's great success stories. The history of Hong Kong's formation and development, its achievements, and its handling of the difficult issues emanating from a "one country, two systems" formula provide one of the most fascinating stories of cultural, economic, and political transition in the world. Hong Kong's "borrowed time" has ended; but its efforts to shape itself into the "Manhattan of China" are in full swing.

HISTORY

In the 1830s, the British sale of opium to China was creating a nation of drug addicts. Alarmed by this development, the Chinese imperial government banned opium; but private British "country traders," sailing armed clipper ships, continued to sell opium to the Chinese by smuggling it (with the help of Chinese pirates) up the coast and rivers. In an effort to enforce the ban, the Chinese imperial commissioner, Lin Zexu, detained the British in their warehouses in Canton and forced them to surrender their opium. Eventually, Commissioner Lin took the more than 21,000 chests that he had seized and destroyed them in public.[1] The British, desperate to establish outposts for trade with an unwilling China, used this siege of British warehouses as an excuse to declare war on the Chinese. Later called the Opium War (1839–1842), the conflict ended with China's defeat and the Treaty of Nanking.

In truth, Great Britain did not wage war against the Chinese in order to sell a drug that was addictive and debilitating, that destroyed people's lives, and that was banned by the Chinese government. Rather, the Chinese government's attack on the British opium traders, whose status as British citizens suddenly proved convenient to the British government, provided the necessary excuse for its getting what it really wanted: free trade with a government that restricted trade with the British

New York Public Library

THE SECOND ANGLO/CHINESE CONVENTION CEDES THE KOWLOON PENINSULA TO THE BRITISH

The second Anglo/Chinese Convention, signed in 1860, was the result of a string of incidents and hostilities among the Chinese, the British, and the French. Although the French were involved in the outbreak of war, they were not included in the treaty that resulted from conflict.

The catalyst for the war was that, during a truce, the Chinese seized the chief British negotiator and executed 20 of his men. In reprisal, the English destroyed nearly 200 buildings of the emperor's summer palace and forced the new treaty on the Chinese. This called for increased payments ("indemnities") by the Chinese to the English for war-inflicted damages as well as the cession of Kowloon Peninsula to the British.

to one port, Canton (Guangzhou). It also allowed London to assert Great Britain's diplomatic and judicial equality with China, which considered itself the "Central Kingdom" and superior to all other countries. In addition, the Chinese imperial government's demand that all "barbarians," including the British, kowtow to the Chinese emperor, incensed the British and gave them further cause to set the record straight.

Just as important to London was its concern that the China trade was draining the British treasury of its gold and silver species; for the British purchased large quantities of Chinese porcelain, silk, tea, and spices, while the Chinese, smug in their belief that their cultural and moral superiority was sufficient to withstand any military challenge from a "barbarian" country, refused to purchase the products of Great Britain's nineteenth-century Industrial Revolution. An amusing example of the thought process involved in "Sinocentrism"—the Chinese belief that China was the center of the world and superior to all other countries—was Imperial Commissioner Lin's letter to Queen Victoria. Here he noted "Britain's dependence on Chinese rhubarb, without which the English would die of constipation."[2] China's narrow world view blinded it to the growing power of the West and resulted in China's losing the opportunity to benefit from the Industrial Revolution at an early stage. The Opium War turned out to be only the first step in a century of humiliation for China—the step that led to a British foothold on the edge of China.

For their part, the British public did not generally understand that the Chinese might have a problem with addiction, and they largely ignored moral considerations. Opium was available for self-medication in Britain, "was even administered by working mothers as a tranquilliser for their infants," and was not considered toxic by the British medical community at that time.[3]

The Treaty of Nanking gave the British the right to trade with the Chinese from five Chinese ports; and Hong Kong, a tiny island off the southern coast of China, was ceded to them "in perpetuity." In short, according to the practices of the colonizing powers of the nineteenth century, Hong Kong became a British colony forever. The Western imperialists were still in the acquisition phase of their history. They were not contemplating that one day the whole process of colonization might be reversed. As a result, Great Britain did not foresee that it might one day have to relinquish the colony of Hong Kong, either to independence or to Chinese rule.

Hong Kong island's total population of Chinese villagers and people living on boats then numbered fewer than 6,000. From 1842 onward, however, Hong Kong became the primary magnet for Chinese immigrants fleeing the poverty, chaos, and cruelty of China in favor of the relatively peaceful environment of Hong Kong under British rule. Then, in 1860, again as a result of a British victory in battle, the Chinese ceded to the British "in perpetuity" Cutter Island and a small ($3\frac{1}{2}$ square miles) but significant piece of land facing the island of Hong Kong: Kowloon Peninsula. Just a few minutes by ferry (and, since the 1970s, by tunnel) from Hong Kong Island, it became an important part of the residential, commercial, and business sector of Hong Kong. The New Territories, the third and largest part (89 percent of the total area) of what is now known as "Hong Kong," were not granted "in perpetuity" but were merely leased to the British for 99 years under the second Anglo–Chinese Convention of Peking in 1898. The New Territories, which are an extension of the Chinese mainland, comprise the major agricultural area supporting Hong Kong.

The distinction between those areas that became a British colony (Hong Kong Island and Kowloon) and the area merely "leased" for 99 years (the New Territories) is crucial to understanding why, by the early 1980s, the British felt compelled to negotiate with the Chinese about the future of "Hong Kong"; for although colonies are theoretically colonies "in perpetuity," the New Territories were merely leased and would automatically revert to Chinese sovereignty in 1997. Without that large agricultural area, the rest of Hong Kong could not survive; the leased territories have, moreover, become tightly integrated into the life and business of Hong Kong Island and Kowloon.

With the exception of the period of Japanese occupation (1942–1945) during World War II, Hong Kong was administered as a British Crown colony from the nineteenth century onward. After the defeat of Japan in 1945, however, Britain almost did not regain control over Hong Kong because of the United States, which insisted that it did not fight World War II in order to return colonies to its allies.

At the end of the Civil War that raged in China from 1945 to 1949, the Communists' Red Army stopped its advance just short of Hong Kong. Beijing never offered an official explanation. Perhaps it did not want to get in a war with Great Britain (even though the Red Army would probably have won it); or perhaps the Communists thought that Hong Kong would be of more value to it if left in British hands. Indeed, at no time did the Chinese Communists attempt to force Great Britain out of Hong Kong, even when Sino–British relations were greatly strained, as during China's "Cultural Revolution."[4]

This did not mean that Beijing accepted the legitimacy of British rule. It did not. After coming to power on the mainland in 1949, the Chinese Communist Party held that Hong Kong was a part of China stolen by British imperialists and that it was merely "occupied" by Great Britain. The People's Republic of China insisted that Hong Kong *not* be treated like other colonies; for the process of decolonization has in practice meant sovereignty and freedom for a former colony's people.[5] China was not about to allow Hong Kong to become independent. After the People's Republic of China gained the China seat in the United Nations (UN) in 1971, it protested Hong Kong and Macau (a Portuguese colony) being listed as colonies by the UN General Assembly's Special Committee on Colonialism. In a letter to the Committee, Beijing insisted they were merely:

(United Nations photo)

Hong Kong's economy is supported by a hardworking and dynamic population. The people at this outdoor market typify the intense entrepreneurial tendency of Hong Kong's citizens.

part of Chinese territory occupied by the British and Portuguese authorities. The settlement of the questions of Hong Kong and Macao is entirely within China's sovereign right and does not at all fall under the ordinary category of colonial territories. Consequently they should not be included in the list of colonial territories covered by the declaration on the granting of independence to colonial countries and peoples. . . . The United Nations has no right to discuss these questions.[6]

No doubt the Chinese Communists were ideologically uncomfortable in proclaiming China's sovereign rights and spouting Communist principles while at the same time tolerating the continued existence of a capitalist and British-controlled Hong Kong on its very borders. China could have acquired control within 24 hours simply by shutting off Hong Kong's water supply from the mainland. But China profited from the British presence there and, except for occasional flare-ups, did little to challenge it.

Unlike other colonies, however, Hong Kong's colonial subjects did not have the option of declaring independence, for overthrowing British colonial rule would have led directly to

the reimposition of China's control. And, although there is for the Hong Kong Chinese a certain amount of cultural identity as Chinese, few wanted to fall under the rule of China's Communist Party government. Furthermore, Beijing and London as a rule did not interfere in Hong Kong's affairs, leaving these in the capable hands of the colonial government in Hong Kong. Although the colonial government formally reported to the British Parliament, in practice it was left to handle its own affairs. In 1958, London gave it even greater power by ceding financial authority in Hong Kong to its colonial government. On the other hand, the colonial government did not in turn cede any significant political power to its colonial subjects.[7]

As the years went by, the Hong Kong and foreign business communities grew increasingly concerned about the expiration of the British lease on the New Territories in 1997. The problem was that all land in the New Territories was *leased* to businesses or individuals, not sold outright. But since the New Territories were themselves originally leased from the Chinese for only 99 years, the British colonial government could not grant any land lease that expired after the lease on the New Territories expired. Thus, all land leases—regardless of which year they were granted—would expire 3 days in advance of the expiration of the main lease on the New Territories on July 1, 1997. As 1997 grew steadily closer, then, the British colonial government had to grant shorter and shorter leases. Investors found buying leases increasingly unattractive. By 1980, the British colonial government felt compelled to do something to calm investors.[8]

For this reason, it was the British, not the Chinese, who took the initiative to press for an agreement on the future status of the colony and the rights of its people. Everyone recognized the inability of Hong Kong Island and Kowloon to survive on their own, because of their dependence upon the leased New Territories for food as well as because of the integrated nature of the economies of the colonial and leased parts of Hong Kong. Everyone (everyone, that is, except for British prime minister Margaret Thatcher) also knew that Hong Kong was militarily indefensible by the British and that the Chinese were unlikely to permit the continuation of British administrative rule over Hong Kong after it was returned to Chinese sovereignty.[9] Thus, a series of formal Sino–British negotiations over the future of Hong Kong began in 1983. By 1984, the two sides had reached an agreement to restore all three parts of Hong Kong to China on July 1, 1997.

The Negotiations over the Status of Hong Kong

Negotiations between the People's Republic of China and Great Britain over the future status of Hong Kong got off to a rocky start in 1982. Prime Minister Thatcher set a contentious tone for the talks when she claimed after meeting with Chinese leaders in Beijing that the three nineteenth-century treaties that gave Great Britain control of Hong Kong were valid according to international law, and that China, like other nations, had an obligation to honor its treaty commitments. Thatcher's remarks infuriated China's leaders, who viewed the treaties as the result of imperialist aggression, which has no legitimacy in the contemporary world.

Both sides realized that Chinese sovereignty over Hong Kong would be reestablished in 1997 when the New Territories lease expired, but they disagreed profoundly on what such sovereignty would mean in practice. The British claimed that they had a "moral commitment" to the people of Hong Kong to maintain the stability and prosperity of the colony. Both the British and the Hong Kong population hoped that Chinese sovereignty over Hong Kong might be more symbolic than substantive and that some arrangement could be worked out that would allow for continuing British participation in the administration of the area. The Chinese vehemently rejected what they termed "alien rule in Chinese territory" after 1997.

In the end, the Chinese insisted on sovereignty and ignored the possibly greater economic value of a Hong Kong *not* under its administrative power.[10] Great Britain agreed to end its administration of Hong Kong in 1997, while China agreed to work out a detailed and binding arrangement for how Hong Kong would be governed under Chinese sovereignty. The people of Hong Kong did not formally participate in the negotiations over the colony's fate. Both the British and the Chinese consulted various interested parties in the colony about their views on 1997 and beyond, but they simply ignored many of those viewpoints. China was particularly adamant that the people of Hong Kong were Chinese and that the government in Beijing represented *all Chinese* in talks with the British.

In September 1984, Great Britain and the People's Republic of China initialed the Joint Declaration on the Question of Hong Kong. It stated that, as of July 1, 1997, Hong Kong would become a "Special Administrative Region" (SAR) of the People's Republic of China. The Sino–British Joint Liaison Group was created to oversee the transition to Chinese rule. If they were expected to continue after 1997, any changes in Hong Kong's laws made during the transition period had to receive final approval from the Joint Liaison Group. If there were disagreement within the Liaison Group between the British and Chinese, they had to talk until they reached agreement. This procedure gave China veto power over any proposed changes in Hong Kong's governance and laws proposed before 1997.[11] Once London's newly appointed governor, Christopher Patten, arrived in 1992 and attempted to change some of the laws that would govern Hong Kong after 1997, China had reason to use that veto power.

The Basic Law

The Basic Law is the crucial document that translates the *spirit* of the Sino–British Joint Declaration into a legal code. Often referred to as a "mini-constitution" for Hong Kong after it became an SAR on July 1, 1997, the Basic Law essentially defines where Hong Kong's autonomy ends and Beijing's governance over Hong Kong begins. The British had no role in formulating the Basic Law, as the Chinese considered it an internal, sovereign matter. In 1985, China established a Basic Law Drafting Committee under the direction of the National People's Congress (NPC). The Committee had 59 members—36 from the mainland, 23 from Hong Kong. Of the latter, almost all were "prominent figures belonging to high and high-middle strata," with Hong Kong's economic elites at its core. In addition, China established a Consultative Committee in Hong Kong of 180 members. Its purpose was to function as a nonofficial representative organ of the people of Hong Kong from all walks of life, an organ that would channel their viewpoints to the Basic Law Drafting Committee. By so including Hong Kong's elite and a Hong Kong–wide civic representative organ in consultations about the Basic Law, China hoped to provide political legitimacy to the Basic Law.[12] Once the Basic Law was approved in April 1990 by China's NPC, the final draft was promulgated.

The Basic Law gives the Hong Kong SAR a high degree of autonomy after 1997, except in matters of foreign policy and

The refugees who came to Hong Kong and settled in squatter communities such as the one shown above voluntarily subjected themselves to foreign (British) rule. Government-built housing has largely replaced areas such as the one pictured above.

defense, which are under the direct control of Beijing. The SAR government is made up of local inhabitants and a chief executive "elected by a broadly representative Election Committee in accordance with [the Basic] Law and appointed by the Central People's Government" (that is, the Standing Committee of the National People's Congress).[13] The chief executive was given the right to appoint key officials of the SAR (although they also must be approved by Beijing). Provisions were made to allow some British and other foreign nationals to serve in the administration of the SAR, if the Hong Kong government so desired. An elected Legislature was made responsible for formulating the laws of the SAR.[14] The maintenance of law and order remained the responsibility of the local authorities, but China took over from the British the right to station military forces in Hong Kong. The local judicial and legal system were to remain basically unchanged, but China's NPC reserved the right to approve of all new laws written between 1990 and 1997.[15]

Thus, the Joint Declaration and Basic Law bring Hong Kong under China's rule, with the National People's Congress in Beijing accorded the right of the final interpretation of the meaning of the Basic Law in case of dispute; but the Basic Law allows the Hong Kong SAR considerable inde-

pendence over its finances, budgeting, and revenue until 2047. China is thus committed to preserving Hong Kong's "capitalist system and lifestyle" for 50 years. In other words, China promised not to impose the Communist political, legal, social, or economic system on Hong Kong. It also agreed to allow Hong Kong to remain a free port, with its own internationally convertible currency, over which China will not exercise authority. The Basic Law states that all Hong Kong residents shall have freedom of speech, press, publication, association, assembly, procession, and demonstration, as well as the right to form and join trade unions and to strike. Freedom of religion, marriage, choice of occupation, and the right to social welfare are also protected by law.[16]

Beijing still allows the free flow of capital into and out of Hong Kong, and it continues to allow Hong Kong to enter into economic and cultural agreements with other nations and to participate in relevant international organizations as a separate member. Thus, Hong Kong was not held back from membership in the World Trade Organization (WTO) by China's inability to meet WTO membership qualifications. Similarly, Hong Kong is a separate member of the World Bank, the Asian Development Bank, and the Asian-Pacific Economic Conference (APEC). Hong Kong is also allowed to continue issuing its own travel documents to Hong Kong's residents and to visitors.

When China promulgated the Basic Law in 1990, Hong Kong residents took to the streets in protest by the thousands, burning their copies of the Basic Law. Some of Hong Kong's people saw the British as having repeatedly capitulated to China's opposition to plans for political reform in Hong Kong before 1997 and as having traded off Hong Kong's interests in favor of their own interests in further trade and investment in China. Hong Kong's business community, however, supported the Basic Law, believing that it supported the continuation of a healthy political and economic environment for doing business; and many Hong Kong residents believe it is Hong Kong's commercial value, not the Basic Law, that will protect it from a heavy-handed approach by the Chinese government.

The Basic Law is critical to understanding China's anger in 1992 when Governor Patten proceeded to push for democratic reforms in Hong Kong without Beijing's agreement—particularly since Patten's predecessor, Governor David Wilson, always did consult Beijing and never pushed too hard. After numerous threats to tear up the Basic Law, Beijing simply stated in 1994 that, after the handover of Hong Kong to Chinese sovereignty in 1997, it would nullify any last-minute efforts by the exiting colonial power to promote a political liberalization that went beyond the provisions in the Basic Law. And that is precisely what China did on July 1, 1997. As will be noted below, the changes that Patten advocated were largely last-ditch efforts to confer on Hong Kong's subjects democratic rights that they had never had in more than 150 years of British colonial rule. These rights related largely to how the Legislature was elected, the expansion of the electorate, and the elimination of such British colonial regulations as one requiring those who wanted to demonstrate publicly to first take out a police permit.

The Chinese people were visibly euphoric about the return of Hong Kong "to the embrace of the Motherland." The large clock in Beijing's Tiananmen Square counted the years, months, days, hours, and even minutes until the return of Hong Kong, helping to focus the Chinese people on the topic. Education in the schools, special exhibits, the movie *The Opium War* (produced by China), and even T shirts displaying pride in the return of Hong Kong to China's control reinforced a sense that a historical injustice was at last being corrected. On July 1, 1997, celebrations were held all over China, and the pleasure was genuinely and deeply felt by the Chinese people.

THE SOCIETY AND ITS PEOPLE

Immigrant Population

In 1842, Hong Kong had a mere 6,000 inhabitants. Today, it has about 6.5 million people. What makes this population distinctive is its predominantly immigrant composition. Waves of immigrants have flooded Hong Kong ever since

(United Nations photo/A. Jongen)

Chinese cultural values are still very strong in modern-day Hong Kong. Here, women in traditional Chinese dress take a work break.

1842. Barely half of Hong Kong's modern-day population were actually born in Hong Kong. This has been a critical factor in the political development of this colony; for instead of a foreign government imposing its rule on submissive natives, the situation has been just the reverse. Chinese people have voluntarily emigrated to Hong Kong, even risking their lives to do so, to subject themselves to alien British colonial rule.

In recent history, the largest influxes of immigrants came as a result of the 1945–1949 Civil War in China, when 750,000 fled to Hong Kong; as a result of the "three bad years" (1959–1962) following the economic disaster of China's Great Leap Forward policy; and from 1966 to 1976, when more than 500,000 Chinese fled to escape the societal turmoil generated by the Great Proletarian Cultural Revolution. After the Vietnam War ended in 1975, Hong Kong also received thousands of refugees from Vietnam as that country undertook a policy of expelling many of its ethnic Chinese citizens. Many Chinese from Vietnam risked their lives on small boats at sea to attain refugee status in Hong Kong.

Although China's improving economic and political conditions since the early 1980s greatly stemmed the flow of immigrants from the mainland, the absorption of refugees into Hong Kong's economy and society remained one of the colony's biggest problems. Injection of another distinct refugee group (the Chinese from Vietnam) generated tension and conflict among the Hong Kong population.

Because of a severe housing shortage and strains on the provision of social services, the British colonial government

The refugees who have flocked to Hong Kong during the last few years have often ended up living in squatter settlements and on boats such as these in Aberdeen Harbor.

first announced that it would confine all new refugees in camps and prohibit them from outside employment. It then adopted a policy of sending back almost all refugees who were caught before they reached Hong Kong Island and were unable to prove they had relatives in Hong Kong to care for them. Finally, the British reached an agreement with Vietnam's government to repatriate some of those Chinese immigrants from Vietnam who were believed to be economic rather than political refugees. The first few attempts at this reportedly "voluntary" repatriation raised such an international furor that the British were unable to systematize this policy. By the mid-1990s, however, better economic and political conditions in Vietnam made it easier for the British colonial government to once again repatriate Vietnamese refugees.[17] Before the July 1, 1997, handover, moreover, Beijing insisted that the British clear the camps of all but a few refugees. It was not a problem that China wanted to deal with.

Language and Education

Ninety-eight percent of Hong Kong's people are Chinese, with the bulk of the other 2 percent being European and Vietnamese. Although a profusion of Chinese dialects are spoken, the two official languages, English and the Cantonese dialect of Chinese, still dominate. Since the Chinese written language is in ideographs and the same ideographs are usually used regardless of a dialect's pronunciation of those ideographs, all literate Hong Kong Chinese are able to read Chinese newspapers. Even before the handover, however, students, workers, and officials, especially civil servants, were intensively studying spoken Mandarin, the official language of China.

Since the handover in 1997, a source of bubbling discontent has been the decision of the Special Administrative Region's Executive Council to require all children to be taught in Chinese. The government's rationale was that the students would learn more if they were taught in their own language. This decision caused an enormous furor. Many Hong Kong Chinese, especially from the middle classes, felt that if Hong Kong were going to remain a major international financial and trading center, its citizens must speak English. Many suspected that the real reason for insisting on Chinese was to respond to Beijing's wishes to bind the Hong Kong people to a deeper Chinese identity. In response to strong public pressures, the Hong Kong government finally relented and allowed 100 schools to continue to use English for instruction.

Chinese cultural values of diligence, willingness to sacrifice for the future, commitment to family, and respect for education have contributed to the success of Hong Kong's inhabitants. (The colonial government provided 9 years of compulsory and free education for children through age 15, helping to reinforce these cultural values). Hong Kong's people continue to view education as the key to material success. But their children are educated in schools modeled on a now "out-of-date British grammar school, complete with uniforms, lists of rules, and a packed academic timetable.[18] Since access to higher levels of education is strictly limited, students work hard to be admitted to one of the best upper-middle schools and then to one of the even fewer places available in Hong Kong's universities. An alternative chosen by many of Hong Kong's brightest students is to go abroad for college education. Universities in the West have benefited from the presence of these highly motivated and achievement-oriented students in their classrooms. They have been important in linking Hong Kong to the West.

Living Conditions and the Economy

Hong Kong has a large and growing middle class. By 1995, in fact, Hong Kong's per capita income had surpassed that of its colonial ruler, Great Britain, and there was virtually no unemployment.[19] Nevertheless, Hong Kong's people suffer from extremes of wealth and poverty. The contrast in housing that dots the landscape of the colony dramatically illustrates this great disparity. The rich live in luxurious, air-conditioned apartments and houses on some of the world's most expensive real estate. They are taken care of by cooks, maids, gardeners, and chauffeurs. They enjoy a social life that mixes such Chinese pleasures as mahjong, banqueting, and participation in traditional Chinese and religious rituals and festivals with British practices of cricket, horseracing, rugby, social clubs, and athletic clubs for swimming and croquet[20] (practices that have faded greatly with the exit of the British). There is a heavier concentration of Mercedes, Jaguars, Rolls Royces, and other luxury cars—not to mention cellular phones, car faxes, and fine French brandy—in Hong Kong than anywhere else on Earth.[21] Hong Kong businessmen spend lavishly on mistresses, travel, and entertainment. The wealthiest have at least one bodyguard for each member of their families. Conspicuous consumption and the vulgar display of wealth are an engrained part of the society. Some Hong Kong business tycoons, who have seemingly run out of other ways to spend their money, ask for restaurants to decorate their food with gold leaf. Others spend several hundred thousand U.S. dollars just to buy a lucky number for their car license plate. One successful Hong Kong businessman, confident of the future success of his investments in China, built a lavish mansion in Beijing that features 1,000 brass dragons on the ceilings, decorated with three pounds of gold leaf (at more than $400 per gram).[22]

In stark contrast, the vast majority of Hong Kong's people live in shantytowns and crowded high-rise apartment buildings, with several families sometimes occupying one apartment of a few small rooms and having inadequate sanitation facilities. Since the mid-1950s, the government has built extensive low-rent public housing, which accommodates about half of the population.[23] These government-subsidized housing projects easily become run down and are often plagued by crime. But without them, a not-insignificant percentage of the new immigrant population would continue to live in squalor in squatter villages with no running water, sanitation, or electricity.

In 1998, Hong Kong's chief executive, Tung Chee-hwa, made a commitment to more government-funded housing and social-welfare programs. Furthermore, with an educational system that guarantees 9 years of public education for all children, the children of immigrants receive one of the most important tools for success. Combined with Hong Kong's rapid post–World War II economic growth, such programs have improved the lives of almost all Hong Kong residents and allowed remarkable economic and social mobility. A poor, unskilled peasant who fled across China's border to Hong Kong to an urban life of grinding poverty—but opportunity—could usually be rewarded before he died by a government-subsidized apartment and grandchildren who graduated from high school and moved on to white-collar jobs.

Today, in an effort to protect the Hong Kong SAR from being flooded by mainland Chinese who hope to take advantage of this wealthy metropolis, or just want to look around and shop in Hong Kong,[24] China still maintains strict border controls. The fact that China's economy has grown at a fairly rapid rate for the last 20 years, especially in the area surrounding Hong Kong, has, however, considerably diminished the poverty that leads individuals to try illegally emigrating to Hong Kong.

A large part of the allure of Hong Kong has, then, been its combination of a dynamic economy with enlightened social-welfare policies. The latter were possible not just because of the British colonial government's commitment to them but also because the flourishing Hong Kong economy provided the resources for them. Hong Kong had a larger percentage of the gross domestic product (GDP) available for social welfare than most governments, for two reasons. First, it had a low defense budget to support its approximately 12,000 British troops (including some of the famous Gurkha Rifles) stationed in the colony for external defense (only 0.4 percent of the GDP, or 4.2 percent of the total budget available). Second, the government was able to take in substantial revenues (18.3 percent of GDP) through the sale of land leases.[25] Now, of course, China is in charge of Hong Kong's defense; but because land leases came to an end in 1997 with the return of the leased territories of Hong Kong to China, they are no longer a source of government revenue.

In terms of generating revenue or determining how revenue is spent, Beijing is on record as being in favor of maintaining the status quo. Thus, Hong Kong continues to have "no income tax, no sales taxes, no capital gains tax, no taxes on

In spite of its reversion back to China, Hong Kong still maintains a building boom while maintaining its position as a major player in the world's marketplace.

dividends, a profit tax of 16.5 percent for corporations and a flat 15 percent salary tax starting at thresholds that leave tens of thousands of workers unscathed."[26] The real question is whether Beijing, now that it reviews the preparation of Hong Kong's budget, will continue to endorse as high an allocation of funds per capita to support state welfare in Hong Kong as the colonial government did. Beijing may choose either to scale down the budgetary allocation of funds to Hong Kong's welfare sector or to let the Hong Kong Special Administrative Region continue to have the same budgetary resources in the 50 years of the "one country, two systems" plan. Beijing's greatest concern before the handover in 1997 was that the colonial administration dramatically increased welfare spending costs—65 percent in a mere 5 years.[27] From Beijing's perspective, the British appeared determined to pump all Hong Kong's assets into its people and economy, leaving little for Beijing to use elsewhere in China and setting a pattern that Hong Kong could use to justify continuing expenditures in the next 50 years of protected autonomy.

The Asian financial and economic crisis, however, brought about a severe downturn in the Hong Kong economy. The population pressured the SAR government to step in and do more to ease the pain. Beijing—which has been trying to diminish the role of government in providing welfare to the Chinese people and replace government intervention with market regulation of the economy—had probably never imagined that the capitalist paradise of Hong Kong would move in the opposite direction and seek more government intervention. Certainly Chief Executive Tung Chee-hwa believed that Hong Kong should continue with its free-market policies. The Hong Kong people, however, demanded that the SAR government intervene and take a more activist role in providing greater social welfare and regulating the economy. Thus, Chief Executive Tung announced in 1998 that the government would commit even more to social welfare (especially housing) than it had under British rule. The government also intervened in the financial markets. First, it purchased large amounts of Hong Kong dollars to foil attempts by speculators to make a profit from selling Hong Kong dollars and forcing the currency to lose its peg to the U.S. dollar. Second, it intervened in the Hong Kong stock market, using up some 25 to 30 percent of its remaining foreign-currency reserves to purchase large numbers of shares in Hong Kong companies in a risky effort to prevent a further slide of the stock market. As it turns out, this was not a case of throwing good money after bad; government investments in the stock market had already doubled in value by the end of 1998.[28] This further helped the overall outlook in Hong Kong and aided in the recovery of the economy.

Before the 1997 return of Hong Kong to China's sovereign control, many analysts were predicting that Beijing would undercut Hong Kong's prosperity through various political decisions limiting political freedom, tampering with the legal system, and imposing economic regulations that would endanger growth. So far, however, Beijing appears to have left Hong Kong in the hands of Chief Executive Tung. And, rather than it being Beijing acting in a high-handed manner that imperils Hong Kong's economic prosperity, it is the Asian's financial crisis that has endangered its prosperity.

The financial crisis, totally unanticipated at the time of the handover on July 1, 1997, began to emerge just a month later. It has wreaked havoc on Hong Kong's economy and challenged its financial and economic system. Beijing, instead of interfering with the decisions made by Hong Kong to address the crisis, has taken a hands-off approach. In addition, it offered to support the Hong Kong dollar against currency speculators, if necessary, by using China's own substantial foreign-currency reserves of $150 billion. Furthermore, China did not take the easy route of devaluing the Chinese yuan, which would have sent Asian markets, and Hong Kong's in particular, into a further downward spiral. Indeed, China said that it would not devalue the yuan before the year 2000.

Hong Kong's real-estate and stock markets have recovered a significant amount of the value they lost in the financial and economic crisis in 1997 and 1998; but the crisis and the possibility of a long-term economic recession continue to haunt Hong Kong. For the time being, Hong Kong's greatest protection against substantial turmoil and a prolonged recession is the stability and growth of China. (Although China's own growth had slowed down by 1999 to less than the 8 percent Beijing had hoped for, it has thus far been able to shield itself from Asia's broad recession.)

In truth, however, Hong Kong's and Beijing's best efforts probably will not be adequate to address Hong Kong's recession if Japan, whose economy is larger than all the other Asian economies combined, does not reform its own financial system and pull itself out of its own recession through new policies. Indeed, the major reason why so many of Hong Kong's hotels and restaurants are operating at 50 percent normal capacity, and so many of its retail shops are now bankrupt or on the verge thereof, is because the Japanese are staying at home.

Hong Kong as a World Trade and Financial Center

From the beginning, the British designated Hong Kong as a free port. This has meant that Hong Kong has never applied tariffs or other major trade restrictions on imports. Such appealing trade conditions, combined with Hong Kong's free-market economy, deepwater harbor, and location at the hub of all commercial activities in Asia, have made it an attractive place for doing business. Indeed, from the 1840s until the crippling Japanese occupation during World War II, Hong Kong served as a major center of China's trade with both Asia and the Western world.

The outbreak of the Korean War in 1950 and the subsequent United Nations embargo on exports of strategic goods to China, as well as a U.S.–led general embargo on the import of Chinese goods, forced Hong Kong to re-orient its economy. To combat its diminished role as the "middleman" in trade with the mainland of China, Hong Kong turned to manufacturing. At first, it manufactured mainly textiles. Later, it diversified into other areas of light consumer goods and developed into a financial and tourist center.

Today, Hong Kong continues to serve as a major trade and financial center, with thousands of companies (especially Taiwanese ones) still located in Hong Kong for the purpose of doing business with China. Rather than just being a middleman in trade with China, however, Hong Kong has actually shifted its own manufacturing base into China. Back in 1980, when almost half of Hong Kong's workforce labored in factories and small workshops, Hong Kong was on the verge of pricing itself out of world markets because of its increasingly well-paid labor and high-priced real estate. Just then, China, with its large and cheap labor supply, cheap land, and abundant resources, initiated major internal economic reforms that opened up the country for foreign investment. As a result, Hong Kong transferred its manufacturing base to China, largely to the contiguous province of Guangdong. Today, more than 75 percent of the Hong Kong workforce are in the service sector, with only 13 percent remaining in manufacturing, while some 5 million Chinese laborers work in Hong Kong factories on the mainland.[29]

Hong Kong's investment accounts for some two thirds of China's total foreign investment, and a full 80 percent of Guangdong Province's total. Hong Kong owns 18,000 factories in Guangdong and contracts out processing work to another 20,000 companies.[30] More than one third of China's total trade is through Hong Kong. Whether Hong Kong's transfer of its manufacturing and processing base to China's provinces contributed to its current problems or saved it from greater difficulties during the Asian financial and economic crisis is a matter of debate.[31]

Hong Kong's many assets, including its hardworking, dynamic people, have made it into the world's largest container port; third-largest center for foreign exchange trade; seventh-largest stock market; and until recently, its largest banking and financial center (with 79 of the world's 100 largest banks in Hong Kong). Hong Kong has also been a major processing and re-exporting center, making it the world's tenth-largest trading economy.[32] Considering its tiny size and population, these are extraordinary achievements.

This type of an economy has its own vulnerabilities to international political and economic currents, such as trade restrictions and international monetary fluctuations. In the early 1980s, long before the current crisis in Asia, Hong Kong's economy suffered considerably from the protectionist measures taken by its major trading partners, including the United States. Similarly, the Americans' repeatedly threat-

(Photo courtesy of Bruce Argetsinger)

Even under China's control, the strong work ethics of Hong Kong's small entrepreneurs continue.

point in history, it is Singapore, not Shanghai, that presents the greatest challenge to Hong Kong's position as a financial center. The other two "little dragons" of East Asia, Taiwan and South Korea, have also challenged Hong Kong's growth. In the case of South Korea, once China established full diplomatic relations with its government in 1992, it was allowed to deal directly with China, thereby bypassing Hong Kong as an entrepôt for trade and business with China.

The Special Economic Zones (SEZs)

As part of its economic reform program and "open door" policy beginning in 1979, China created "special economic zones" (SEZs) in areas bordering or close to Hong Kong in order to attract foreign investment. SEZs, until recent years under far more liberal regulations than the rest of China, have blossomed in the last 2 decades. Various parts of China's government have themselves invested heavily in the SEZs, in hopes of making a profit. Even China's military has developed an industrial area catering to foreign investors and joint ventures in one of China's SEZs, Shenzhen, as part of its effort to compensate for insufficient funding for the military. It calls its policy "one army, two systems,"—that is, an army involved with both military and economic development.[34] Brushing aside its earlier concern for a puritanical society, China's military is as likely to invest in nightclubs, Western-style hotels, brothels, and health spas as it is in the manufacturing sector. Although in 1998 China's leader Jiang Zemin ordered the military to rid itself of its economic enterprises, whether it does so remains to be seen.

The bulk of foreign investment in the SEZs and in the rest of China actually comes, however, from Hong Kong Chinese, either with their own money or acting as middlemen for investors from Taiwan, South Korea, the United States, and others. Two thirds of direct foreign investment in China, in fact, comes *through* Hong Kong. In turn, China is the single largest investor in Hong Kong. Thus, this integrated area—encompassing Hong Kong, the SEZs, and Guangdong Province—has the potential to become a powerful new regional economy on a par with other newly industrialized countries (NICs). Indeed, even before China took over Hong Kong in 1997, Guangdong had become an integral part of Hong Kong's empire.

Sensitivity of the Economy to External Political Events

Hong Kong's economic strength rests on the population's confidence in Hong Kong's future, which has fluctuated wildly over the years. Concern over Great Britain's unwillingness to negotiate more democratic rights for Hong Kong before 1997 periodically threatened Hong Kong's economic stability, diminished confidence, and generated an outward flow of professionals from Hong Kong. So did China's economic retrenchment policies and partial closing of the "open door" to international trade and investment. Emigration from Hong Kong (at the rate of about 60,000 per year between

ened withdrawal of "most-favored-nation" (MFN) status[33] for China after Beijing's crackdown on dissidents in Tiananmen Square in 1989 brought as much panic to Hong Kong as it did to China; for as the largest single investor in China's export sector, and because most Hong Kong manufacturing is now done in China, Hong Kong would be badly hurt by the elimination of MFN treatment for China. The favorable resolution of these negotiations by the U.S. Congress each spring since 1989 brings a collective sigh of relief from Hong Kong. Even former Hong Kong governor Christopher Patten, for all his animosity toward Beijing, did not want China punished with economic weapons for its human-rights violations.

Some analysts suggest that Shanghai may soon prove a serious threat to Hong Kong's economic growth and position as a financial and trade center. There is no reason, however, why there would not be room for another major financial and trade center in Asia or that Shanghai's growth would necessarily come at Hong Kong's expense. In any event, at this

1990 and 1997) largely came from among its better-educated, wealthier class.[35] This drain of both talent and money out of the colony was as serious a concern for China as it was for Hong Kong. Once emigrants gain a second passport (a guarantee of residency abroad in case conditions warrant flight), however, they often return to Hong Kong, where there is still money to be made and opportunities available for those in the professions (architects, engineers, dentists, doctors, businesspeople, and so on). In any event, this outflow of talent was largely counterbalanced by an inflow of immigrants as well as by the education of new professionals in Hong Kong's excellent schools.[36] Beijing's verbal intimidation of Hong Kong dissidents who criticized China in the period following the Tiananmen crackdown in 1989, and again when Governor Patten began whipping up Hong Kong fervor for greater democratic reforms from 1992 to 1997, also aroused anxiety in the colony. Earlier, the people of Hong Kong had been afraid that Great Britain would trade the colony's democratic future for good relations with China. Patten's efforts to inject Hong Kong with a heavy dose of democratization before 1997, on the other hand, led to concern that China might restrict its political freedom after 1997. A significant portion of Hong Kong public opinion turned against Patten out of such concerns. Many in Hong Kong (especially the businesspeople who had invested heavily in both Hong Kong and China) wondered whether more democracy was worth the risks.[37]

Since the handover in 1997, Beijing has been extremely cautious. Most observers would agree that Beijing has been a model of decorum and restraint since Hong Kong was returned to its sovereignty. Nevertheless, remaining uncertainty about how China's sovereignty over Hong Kong may affect its economy—and uncertainty as to how China might respond to serious political opposition—has made it more difficult to attract the capital investment necessary for continued strong growth. As a result, Hong Kong's entrepreneurs are among the strongest supporters of China's (and Tung Chee-hwa's) "law and order" approach to governing Hong Kong.

Most businesses are in Hong Kong to stay, including foreign corporations already located there. Indeed, because they are already well positioned in Hong Kong, these foreign corporations will not have to go through the unpredictable, lengthy, and expensive bureaucratic hassle of trying to break into the China market.

Societal Problems

Hong Kong does suffer from significant problems, including serious environmental pollution, which has been ignored in the pursuit of profits. An appallingly high crime rate plagues Hong Kong, with both violent and white-collar crime on the rise. For more than a decade, ordinary criminality has been steadily augmented by crime under the control of competing Chinese criminal societies, called *triads*. Opium, largely controlled by the triads, continues to be used widely by the Chinese. As a commentator once put it:

Opium trails still lead to Hong Kong . . . and all our narcotic squads and all the Queen's men only serve to make the drug more costly and the profits more worthwhile. It comes in aeroplanes and fishing junks, in hollow pipes and bamboo poles and false decks and refrigerators and pickle jars and tooth paste tubes, in shoes and ships and sealing wax. And even cabbages.[38]

Today, Hong Kong is still one of the largest entrepôts for drugs, in no small part because social and economic liberalization on the mainland has permitted human mobility, encouraged some of those with entrepreneurial talent to engage in drug smuggling, and diminished the ability of China's police to control the drug trade. The result is that the number of drug addicts in China is skyrocketing.

Although the Hong Kong and Chinese mainland drug squads cooperate, this association is complicated by Hong Kong's legal system, which still differs from the legal system of the rest of China. The critical difference in criminal law is that Hong Kong does not have capital punishment. And China, committed to not changing Hong Kong's legal system (where Hong Kong's Basic Law takes over), has not pressured Hong Kong to change its law on capital punishment. Thus, a crime such as dealing in drugs, punishable by execution in the rest of China, will result at most in a lifetime sentence in Hong Kong.

Before the handover, when Hong Kong investigators asked the Chinese to turn over drug dealers to the Hong Kong authorities, the Chinese expended significant resources to find the criminals and then turned them over. But when asked to do the same, the Hong Kong drug authorities went so far as to arrest the suspects, but they refused to turn them over to China's public-security office because of the fairly strong chance that a person convicted on charges of selling drugs in China would be executed. (The problems emanating from cross-border crime are discussed further under the topic of "The Judiciary, Law, and Order.")

Hong Kong's organized crime has long been powerful in the areas of real estate; extortion from massage parlors, bars, restaurants, and clubs; illegal gambling; smuggling; the sale of handguns; prostitution; and drugs. And, as is common in other Asian countries (such as Japan), gangs are often hired by corporations to deal with debtors and others causing them difficulties. Triad influence has also expanded into kidnapping for ransom and has taken on some unexpected roles. As an example, when Governor Patten upset Beijing by his proposals for further democratization of Hong Kong before 1997, the Chinese Communist regime (by way of its estimated 60,000 supporters working in Hong Kong) allegedly recruited triad members to begin harassing those within the Hong Kong government who were supporting Patten's proposals. (And when Patten's dog disappeared one day in 1992 during the crisis stage of Sino–British relations, one rumor had it that the Chinese Communists had kidnapped the dog and were going to ransom it in exchange for halting political reform in Hong Kong; the other rumor was that Patten's pet had been flown into China to be served up for breakfast to Deng Xiaoping. Of course, neither rumor was true.)

POLITICS AND POLITICAL STRUCTURE

Hong Kong's colonial government was well institutionalized. The British monarch, acting on the advice of the prime minister, would appoint a governor, who presided over the Hong Kong government's colonial administration. Colonial rule in Hong Kong may be characterized as benevolent, consultative, and paternalistic, but it was nonetheless still colonial. Although local people were heavily involved in running the colony and the colonial government interfered very little in the business activities and daily lives of Hong Kong Chinese, the British still controlled the major levers of power and filled the top ranks in the government.

Hong Kong's remarkable political stability until the handover in 1997 was, then, hardly due to any efforts by the British to transplant a form of Western-style democracy to Hong Kong. Instead, the colonial Hong Kong government sought feedback from the Hong Kong people through the hundreds of consultative committees that it created within the Hong Kong civil service. Similarly, although the British ultimately controlled both the Legislative Council (LegCo) and Executive Council (ExCo), these governmental bodies allowed Hong Kong's socioeconomic elites to participate in the administration of the colony. Some 300 additional advisory groups as well as numerous partly elected bodies—such as the Urban Council (for Hong Kong Island and Kowloon), the Rural Committees (for the New Territories), and district boards—also had considerable autonomy in managing their own affairs. This institutionalized consultation among Chinese administrators and the colonial government resulted in the colony being governed by an elite informed by and sensitive to the needs of the Hong Kong people. As was common to British colonial administration elsewhere, the lower levels of government were filled with the local people. There was, therefore, little need for political dissent to be expressed outside the government.[39]

The relatively high approval rating of British colonial rule helps explain why only a small portion of the mere 6 percent of the people who were registered voters actually voted. With the government assuring both political stability and strong economic growth, the people of Hong Kong spent most of their time and energy on economic pursuits, not politics. In any event, given the limited scope of democracy in Hong Kong, local people had little incentive to become politically involved. And as the 1997 handover came nearer, Hong Kong residents grew increasingly concerned that there were few competent and trustworthy leaders among the Hong Kong Chinese to take over.[40] They also worried that a government controlled by leaders and bureaucrats who held foreign passports or rights of residence abroad would not be committed to their welfare. Although Beijing ultimately withdrew its demand before the handover that all governmental civil servants swear an oath of allegiance to the government of China and turn in their British passports, many did so anyway (including the new chief executive, Tung Chee-hwa).

Hong Kong's colonial government remained stable, then, because it was perceived to be trustworthy, competent, consultative, and capable of addressing the needs of Hong Kong's people. A solid majority of Hong Kong's citizens believed that a strong political authority was indispensable to prosperity and stability; and that the formation of multiple political parties could disrupt that strong authority. Thus, what is seen in the West as a critical aspect of democracy was viewed by the people in Hong Kong as suspect: "Political parties conjure up pictures of conflict, sectional interests, political repression and corrupt government."[41]

Nevertheless, by the late 1980s, many Hong Kong Chinese began to demand that democratic political reforms be institutionalized before the Chinese Communists took over in 1997. The ability of the departing colonial government to deal with these increased pressures to democratize Hong Kong was, however, seriously constricted by the 1982 Joint Declaration and the Basic Law of 1990, which required Beijing's approval before the British could make any changes in the laws and policies governing Hong Kong.

Such was the state of affairs when London appointed Christopher Patten as the last governor general of Hong Kong. Perhaps because of Hong Kong's anger at Great Britain's betrayal, and wanting to erase the stain from Britain's record, Patten decided to ignore the agreements between Great Britain and China concerning Hong Kong's governance after 1997 and to make a last-ditch effort to democratize Hong Kong.

What was "handed over" on July 1, 1997, was sovereign control of Hong Kong by China. Hong Kong became a "special administrative region" of China, with Beijing guaranteeing autonomy for 50 years in the political, legal, economic, and social realms. But Hong Kong would be governed by its new "constitution," the Basic Law written by China's leaders. This document provided for certain changes to be made after the handover. Notably, Article 23 required the Hong Kong Legislative Council to outlaw sedition and other dangerous activities. As of 1999, however, Tung Chee-hwa had done nothing about submitting such a change in the law to the Legislature, and Beijing had not pushed it.[42] Neither the chief executive nor Beijing wanted to risk the public furor that would inevitably accompany any effort to outlaw sedition—which the Hong Kong people would interpret as an effort to outlaw free speech.

Executive and Legislative Branches

At the institutional level, there has been no real change in the government since the 1997 handover—except, of course, that Hong Kong's chief executive now reports to Beijing, not London. Hong Kong's colonial government was structured on a separation of powers among the executive, legislative,

(United Nations, 74037)

The Hong Kong government has constructed new apartment complexes in an effort to address the severe overcrowding in tenements and squatter communities.

and judicial branches of government. This served as a check on the arbitrary use of power by any single individual or institution of the government. The separation of powers in Hong Kong's government, however, never did exist within the framework of a representative democracy.

The structure of Hong Kong's post–1997 government is outlined in great detail in the Basic Law. The governmental structure is similar in many respects to what it was under colonial rule; but China has made changes in it to bring it into greater correspondence with its own structure of government, even if in some cases this is merely a matter of changing names.

The Executive Council is now run by Hong Kong's chief executive, Tung Chee-hwa. Fortunately, continuity was maintained when most of the cabinet heads under British colonial rule (22 of the 25) agreed to serve under Tung. Sole decision-making authority remains vested in the chief executive, although ultimately Beijing must approve of any of the executive branch's policies. So far, Beijing has chosen not to exercise this approval in a way that hampers the chief executive's policy-making authority.

On July 1, 1997, China repealed Governor Patten's expansion of the franchise for the 1995 elections, which had lowered the voting age to 18 and extended the vote to all of Hong Kong's adult population (adding 2.5 million people to the voting rolls, resulting in an electorate of 3.7 million people) in time for the 1995 legislative elections. As the Joint Declaration required that even a small increase in democracy in the Hong Kong colony had to be agreed to by China, Beijing was within its rights when it repealed the changes and replaced the Legislature that had been elected under those rules. China's Preparatory Committee selected a 400-member Provisional Legislature to replace it on July 1, 1997.

What were Beijing's concerns when it canceled the results of the 1995 elections? China's leaders viewed the colonial government's last-ditch efforts to develop a representative government in Hong Kong as part of a conspiracy to use democracy to undercut China's rule in Hong Kong after 1997. They argued—and no doubt believed—that the last-minute political reforms could jeopardize Hong Kong's prosperity and stability by permitting special interests and political protest to flourish; and that Hong Kong's social problems—narcotics, violence, gangs, prostitution, an underground economy—required that Hong Kong be controlled, not given democracy. China therefore adopted a very status quo approach to Hong Kong. After all, Hong Kong's political system under British colonial control was imposed from the outside, a system that kept Hong Kong stable and prosperous. Beijing merely wanted to replace a colonial ruler with a Chinese Communist Party ruler.[43]

Of course, Beijing did not want to face a situation in which one part of the population—those living in Hong Kong—enjoyed many more rights than the rest of China's population. Such a situation could easily lead to pressure on Beijing to extend those rights to all Chinese. If Beijing is going to give greater political rights to its people, it would rather do it on its own timetable and throughout the country.

In the 1995 elections, Hong Kong's Democratic Party, whose political platform called for major changes to the Basic Law to give Hong Kong people more democratic rights, won two thirds of the vote. When Beijing canceled the results of that election, many commentators thought that the writing was on the wall. But as promised, Beijing rescheduled the elections for May 1998, and when those elections led to the reelection of the same number of Democratic Party members as before, Beijing made no effort to remove them from the Legislature.[44] With only 20 of the 60 seats, however, the Democratic Party still does not control the Legislative Council (LegCo).

Thus, the Democratic Party is impotent to change government policy, leaving it in the position of a critic and complainer. In the context of the types of problems that the government has faced since July 1, 1997, its demands for greater democracy have not seemed to be a relevant response in the view of the public. These problems include the "bird flu," which destroyed nearly the entire stock of chickens in Hong Kong and threatened public health; a disastrous opening of the new airport, which suffered from such disarray that cargo had to be processed for months in the old airport; a 50 percent drop in the stock market; a 40 percent drop in real-estate values; increased unemployment; bankruptcies of retail stores; and a dramatic decline in tourism. These were not the sorts of problems for which the Democratic Party's call for changes in the Basic Law were relevant. Instead, 78 percent of the public wanted government intervention in order to address these problems.[45]

As for Hong Kong's chief executive, his near-universal popularity at the time of the handover on July 1, 1997, was seriously eroded by these above-mentioned problems. Tung Chee-hwa was blamed not only for the government's incompetence but also for his reluctance to intervene in order to relieve the people's suffering that resulted from the Asian economic crisis. The fact that he appeared in front of LegCo only twice in the first 16 months after the handover, and that he refused to consult with LegCo representatives in private, caused significant conflict and anger. Although it is the executive branch's role to deal with the financial crisis in Hong Kong, the Legislature still believes they should be consulted.[46] Tung has recovered some of his former popularity with the public as his more interventionist policies have improved economic conditions. Because the source of Hong Kong's problems has not been Beijing's control but, rather, the incompetence of the government, the Asian economic

crisis, and festering problems of social welfare and crime, the critical question for Tung is no longer how autonomous he is from Beijing's control. Instead, it is whether he can maintain his legitimacy through his tenure as chief executive.

The Judiciary, Law, and Order

Under colonial rule, Hong Kong's judiciary was independent, and it should remain so under "one country, two systems." Judges are appointed until they are no longer able to function for mental or physical reasons. English common law, partly adapted to accommodate Chinese custom, has been at the heart of the legal system. Much of the confidence of the international and local communities in Hong Kong as a good place to live and do business has been based on the reputation of its independent judiciary for integrity and competence, the stability of its legal and constitutional system, and its adherence to the rule of law.

China has promised to continue to allow Hong Kong's legal system to rely on such legal concepts as *habeas corpus,* legal precedent, and the tradition of common law, which do not exist in China. Beijing has said that it will not subject Hong Kong's legal system to the Politburo's guidelines for the rest of China. But on political matters such as legislation, human rights, civil liberties, and freedom of the press, there remains considerable concern that the Basic Law offers inadequate protection. For example, the Basic Law provides for the Standing Committee of the National People's Congress (NPC) in Beijing, not the Hong Kong SAR courts, to interpret the Basic Law and to determine whether future laws passed by the Hong Kong SAR Legislature conflict with the Basic Law. Nor are the Hong Kong courts allowed to question whether China's political and administrative decisions are compatible with Hong Kong's Basic Law.

Furthermore, although Beijing had promised Hong Kong that the chief executive would be accountable to the Legislature, the Basic Law gives the Chief Executive (to be appointed by China's NPC until at least the year 2012), the power to dissolve the Hong Kong legislature and to veto bills. Of even greater concern, Beijing has yet to state the relationship of Hong Kong's Basic Law to China's own Constitution; and, now that it has returned to China's sovereignty, whether Hong Kong will be required to recognize the leading role and authority of the Chinese Communist Party, as called for in China's Constitution. A major test of which side would prevail in a conflict between those of China and Hong Kong's Basic Law was decided, by Hong Kong's Supreme Court, in favor of the Basic Law in 1999. In this case, the Court upheld the right of *all* children of citizens of Hong Kong, regardless of whether they were born in the P.R.C. or in Hong Kong, to emigrate to Hong Kong. Beijing disagrees, as it wants to retain the right to decide if its citizens can cross the border into Hong Kong. How this case is resolved will be critical to Hong Kong's perception of whether Beijing is truly not interfering in Hong Kong's affairs. The fundamental incompatibility between the British tradition (in which the state's actions must not be in conflict with the laws) on the one hand, and China's practice of using law as a tool of the state, as well as its conferring and withdrawing rights at will on the other hand, is at the heart of the concern about future Chinese rule over Hong Kong.[47]

The first case to be tried by the Hong Kong courts after July 1, 1997, was that of an American "streaker" who ran nude in crowded downtown Hong Kong and was easily apprehended. In this rather amusing case, he was fined and released. More recently, however, serious questions have arisen about the handling of cross-border crime. As noted above, the source of the problem is that Hong Kong does not have capital punishment, but China does. In the past, when Hong Kong has arrested a P.R.C. citizen wanted for a criminal activity punishable by execution in China, it has refused to turn the person over to China's judicial authorities.

So it is not surprising that in 1998, the Chinese took custody of the case in which they arrested a major Hong Kong criminal who tried to seek refuge from Hong Kong authorities across the border. The gangster, known as "Big Spender," was alleged to have committed a number of crimes, including armed robbery, smuggling, and the kidnapping of two Hong Kong business tycoons. China maintains that some of the crimes were actually committed in China and that the victims of the crimes reported them to China's public-security bureau, not to the Hong Kong authorities. Hong Kong does not believe that Big Spender, a Hong Kong citizen, can be tried for *any* crimes he committed in Hong Kong because of the "one country, two systems" structure.

Many of those concerned about China's conduct demanded that the Hong Kong government ask for Big Spender's return to Hong Kong's jurisdiction, but the Hong Kong government refused to do so. No doubt countervailing pressures on the government, by both his victims and others victimized by triad criminality, to allow Big Spender to be tried under China's more severe Criminal Law caused the Hong Kong government to hesitate. After a brief trial in China, Big Spender was found guilty and summarily executed in December 1998. Another case, in which a Chinese citizen allegedly murdered five people in Hong Kong and was then arrested after he crossed the border back into China, raised no questions of jurisdiction. The problem, in short, is that Hong Kong and Beijing need to come together on the difficult problem of cross-border crime when two different criminal codes may have to be used to deal with a crime.[48] The more porous borders between Hong Kong and the rest of China, the greater mobility of the Chinese people, and the open market economy have seemed like an open invitation to Hong Kong's triads not only to expand their crime rings within China but also to take refuge there.

Finally, as for "law and order," Hong Kong continues to have its own public-security forces; and the British colonial military force of about 12,000 has been replaced by a smaller Chinese People's Liberation Army (PLA) force of about 9,000. The military installations used by the British forces have been turned over to the PLA. In efforts to reassure the Hong Kong populace that the military was there largely to protect the border from smuggling and illegal entry as well as for general purposes of national security, soldiers are mostly stationed across the Hong Kong border in Shenzhen (one of China's special economic zones), but some will also be stationed in the heavily populated part of the colony to serve as a deterrent to social unrest and mass demonstrations against the Chinese government. No doubt the extraordinarily high costs of keeping soldiers in metropolitan Hong Kong were also a factor in the PLA decision to move its troops to the outskirts.

Apart from diminishing the interactions between the PLA soldiers and the Hong Kong people, China has done much to ensure that the troops do not become a source of tension. Quite the contrary; China wants them to aid in developing a positive view of Chinese sovereignty over Hong Kong. As part of their "charm offensive," the soldiers must be tall (at least 5 feet, 10 inches); have "regular features" (translation, be attractive); be well read (with all officers having college training and all ordinary soldiers having a high school education); know the Basic Law; and speak both the local dialect of Cantonese and simple English.[49] In short, the PLA, which has no such requirements for its regular soldiers and officers, has trained an elite corps of soldiers for Hong Kong. No doubt the hope is that a well-educated military will be less likely to provoke problems with Hong Kong residents. In fact, PLA troops are even permitted to date and marry local Hong Kong women!

Press, Civil Rights, and Religious Freedom
China's forceful crackdown on protesters in Beijing's Tiananmen Square on June 4, 1989, and subsequent repression traumatized the Hong Kong population. China warned the Hong Kong authorities that foreign agents might use such organizations as the Hong Kong Alliance in Support of the Patriotic Democratic Movement in China (a coalition of some 200 groups) to advance their intelligence activities on the mainland,[50] and even accused that group of "playing a subversive role by supporting the pro-democracy movement."[51]

Such statements aroused fears that the Beijing regime would use force in Hong Kong after 1997 against politically motivated demonstrations. Beijing has, in fact, used subtle (and not-so-subtle) intimidation to discourage Hong Kong from supporting prodemocracy activities, suggesting that such acts would be "treasonous." In spite of the fact that China had announced before the handover that it would not permit mass rallies or demonstrations against the central government of China after the handover, however, Beijing has done nothing at all to stop the rallies and protests that have occurred on an almost daily basis since then. One freedom that British subjects in Hong Kong cherish is freedom of the press, including television. Hong Kong has had a dynamic press, one that represents all sides of the political spectrum. Indeed, under British rule, it was free to the point of tolerating the Chinese

Communists having their own pro-Communist, pro-Beijing newspaper, as well as a news bureau (the New China News Agency), in Hong Kong, which until the handover, also functioned as China's unofficial foreign office in Hong Kong.

While concerns still remain that China may one day crack down on Hong Kong's press, the possibilities of this happening have been diminished by two factors. First, press freedom in China has made significant progress in the last 20 years; and second, members of the Hong Kong press are masters at knowing where to draw the line in terms of offending Beijing. This is nothing new for Hong Kong's press (or for China's press), and even under the British, self-censorship was necessary. It is not yet clear how Beijing will respond to a Hong Kong press that openly challenges the Chinese Communist Party's right to rule; but in China itself, political analyses no longer merely reflect the Communist Party's line. And beyond politics, just about any type of journalistic article is now tolerated.

In Hong Kong, the press is full of criticism of Tung Chee-hwa and the Hong Kong government, but it exercises more restraint in criticizing China's government. Some analysts have remarked, however, that since the handover, Beijing has given the Hong Kong press very little reason to criticise it, at least in respect to its policies toward Hong Kong.[52] In short, it does not seem likely that China will roll back press freedom in Hong Kong in any significant way. Nor is it likely that information coming into Hong Kong will be cut off, for to do so would jeopardize continuation of the very economic success for Hong Kong that China wants to ensure. A more likely scenario is that Hong Kong will become a center for disseminating information to the rest of China.

As for religious freedom, Beijing has guaranteed that a religious practice will be permitted as long as it does not contravene the Basic Law. Given the fact that China's tolerance of religious freedom within the mainland has expanded dramatically since it began liberalizing reforms in 1979, this does not seem to be a likely area of tension for the post–1997 Hong Kong Special Administrative Region.

In short, Hong Kong still looks much as it did before its return to China's sovereign control. And although some analysts believe that power is imperceptibly being transferred to Beijing, Deng Xiaoping's promise that "'dancing and horse-racing' would continue unabated" has been kept. "U.S. aircraft carriers still drop anchor and disgorge their crews into the Wanchai district's red-light bars. Anti-China demonstrators continue their almost weekly parades through the Central district. . . . Meanwhile, the People's Liberation Army has made a virtue of being invisible."[53] At least on the surface, there is a "business as usual" look about Hong Kong. It may well be that Hong Kong will become the "Manhattan" of China, and not just another Chinese city.

THE FUTURE

Of course, no one can predict Hong Kong's future with certainty. China's leaders have stated that for 50 years after 1997, the relationship between China and the Hong Kong SAR will be "one country, two systems." By this they mean that Hong Kong may maintain its current social, political, economic, and legal system alongside China's system. Yet China is changing so quickly—indeed, it is daily becoming more like Hong Kong in its commercial and economic features as it phases out its state-run economy in favor of a market economy—that the imposition of a socialist economy on Hong Kong is unthinkable.

In spite of the Asian economic crisis, China's extraordinary economic boom in southern China has made the Hong Kong population optimistic about the future. They see a new "dragon" emerging, one that combines Hong Kong's technology and skills with China's labor and resources. For many, the major fear is not political repression and centralized controls imposed on Hong Kong's economy but, rather, that China's bureaucracy and corruption may simply smother the economic vitality of Hong Kong.

Even in the political realm, China is changing so profoundly that the two systems, which seemed so far apart just 20 years ago, are now much closer. China has itself been undertaking significant political liberalization, especially in respect to increasing electoral rights at the local level, permitting freedom in individual lifestyles, and according greater freedom to the mass media. And because of the rapid growth of private property and business interests, China is undergoing major social changes, including the growth of numerous interest groups.

Nevertheless, the legal safeguards of civil rights in Hong Kong are unmatched thus far on the mainland. The Chinese Communist Party has denounced calls for more democracy in Hong Kong, especially multiparty democracy, as "bourgeois liberalization" and reaffirmed its unchallengeable authority. It has repeatedly stated hostility to Western notions of democracy and insisted that any political reforms in Hong Kong must be in line with China's own vision of political reform.

Because China has an important stake in having a successful takeover of Hong Kong, one that does not disrupt the economic sphere, it is concerned that Hong Kong's residents and the international business community believe in its future prosperity. China's rulers know that policies and events that were threatening to that confidence in the future in the 1980s led to the loss of many of its most talented people, technological know-how, and investment. They do not want to risk losing even more. China also wants to maintain Hong Kong as a major free port and the regional center of trade, financing, shipping, and information—although it is also doing everything possible to turn Shanghai into another major center that competes with Hong Kong.

Finally, regardless of official denials by the government in Taiwan, Beijing's successful management of "one country, two systems" in Hong Kong will profoundly affect how Taiwan feels about its own peaceful integration with the mainland. As Beijing wants to regain control of Taiwan by peaceful means, it is critical that it handle Hong Kong well.

NOTES

1. R. G. Tiedemann, "Chasing the Dragon," *China Now,* No. 132 (February 1990), p. 21.

2. Jan S. Prybyla, "The Hong Kong Agreement and Its Impact on the World Economy," in Jurgen Domes and Yu-ming Shaw, eds. *Hong Kong: A Chinese and International Concern* (Boulder: Westview Special Studies on East Asia, 1988), p. 177.

3. Tiedemann, p. 22.

4. Robin McClaren, former British ambassador to China, seminar at Cambridge University, Centre for International Relations (February 28, 1996).

5. Ambrose Y. C. King, "The Hong Kong Talks and Hong Kong Politics," in Domes and Shaw, p. 49.

6. Hungdah Chiu, Y. C. Jao, and Yual-li Wu, *The Future of Hong Kong: Toward 1997 and Beyond* (New York: Quorum Books, 1987), pp. 5–6.

7. Siu-kai Lau, "Hong Kong's 'Ungovernability' in the Twilight of Colonial Rule," in Lin Zhiling and Thomas W. Robinson, *The Chinese and Their Future: Beijing, Taipei, and Hong Kong* (Washington, D.C.: The American Enterprise Institute Press, 1994), pp. 288–290.

8. McLaren.

9. McLaren noted that it was not easy to convince Prime Minister Margaret Thatcher in her "post-Falklands mood" (referring to Great Britain's successful defense of the Falkland Islands, 9,000 miles away, from being returned to Argentinian rule), that Hong Kong could not stay under British administrative rule even after 1997.

10. T. L. Tsim, "Introduction," in T. L. Tsim and Bernard H. K. Luk, *The Other Hong Kong Report* (Hong Kong: The Chinese University Press, 1989), p. xxv.

11. Norman J. Miners, "Constitution and Administration," in Tsim and Luk, p. 2.

12. King, pp. 54–55.

13. Annex I, Nos. 1 and 4 of *The Basic Law of the Hong Kong Special Administrative Region of the People's Republic of China* (hereafter cited as *The Basic Law*). Printed in *Beijing Review*, Vol. 33, No. 18 (April 30–May 6, 1990), supplement. This document was adopted by the 7th National People's Congress on April 4, 1990.

14. For specifics, see Annex II of *The Basic Law.*

15. Article 14, *The Basic Law.*

16. Articles 27, 32, 33, and 36 of *The Basic Law.*

17. When riots again flared in Hong Kong's refugee camps for Vietnamese, Beijing expressed annoyance at the British for not just sending them back to Vietnam and emptying the camps—at least by July 1, 1997.

18. Charmian Suttill, "Chinese Culture in Hong Kong," *China Now,* No. 132 (February 1990), p. 14.

19. In 1995, Hong Kong's per capita GDP was US$23,500. Wang Gungwu and Wong Siu-lun, eds., *Hong Kong in the Asian-Pacific Region: Rising to the New Challenge* (Hong Kong: University of Hong Kong, 1997), p. 2.

20. Tsim, in Tsim and Luk, p. xx.

21. Wang and Wong, p. 3.

22. Keith B. Richburg, "Uptight Hong Kong Countdown," *The Washington Post* (July 2, 1996), pp. A1, A12.

23. Tsim, in Tsim and Luk, p. xx.

24. Chinese cities on the mainland are overrun by transients. On a daily basis, Shanghai alone has well over 1 million visitors, largely a transient population of country people. Hong Kong does not feel that it can handle such an increase in its transient population.

25. Tsim, in Tsim and Luk, p. xxi.

26. Ironically, calls to change the taxation system in Hong Kong have come not from Beijing but from Singapore, Hong Kong's major competitor for the position of financial capital of Asia. Kevin Murphy, "Hong Kong: Taxing Question," *The International Herald Tribune* (March 6, 1996).

27. Keith B. Richburg, "Chinese Muscle-Flexing Puts Hong Kong under Pessimistic Pall," *The Washington Post* (December 26, 1996), p. A31.

28. Richard Baum, "Politics in Post-Colonial Hong Kong," seminar, Harvard University (December 11, 1998).

29. "Is Hong Kong Ripe for a Bit of Central Planning?" *The Economist* (April 12, 1997).

30. Wang and Wong, p. 4.

31. "Is Hong Kong Ripe for a Bit of Central Planning?" *The Economist* (April 12, 1997).

32. Wang and Wong, pp. 2–4.

33. A country with MFN status will not have to face higher tariffs on the exports of its goods to another country than will the most-favored-nation in terms of low tariffs.

34. Tammy Tam, "Shenzhen Industrial Estate Developed to Boost Military Funds," *The Hong-Kong Standard* (September 5, 1989), p. 1.

35. London's refusal to allow Hong Kong citizens to emigrate to the United Kingdom contributed to a sense of panic among the middle and upper classes in Hong Kong, those most worried about their economic and political future under Communist rule. Other countries were, however, more than willing to accept these well-educated, wealthy immigrants who came ready to make large deposits in their new host countries' banks.

36. Yun-wing Sung, "The Hong Kong Economy—To the 1997 Barrier and Beyond," in Lin and Robinson, pp. 316–319.

37. "Sheriff Patten Comes to Town," *The Economist* (November 14, 1992), p. 35.

38. John Gordon Davies, "Introduction," *Hong Kong through the Looking Glass* (Hong Kong: Kelly & Walsh, 1969).

39. King, in Domes and Shaw, pp. 45–46.

40. Prybyla, in Domes and Shaw, pp. 196–197; and Lau, in Zhiling and Robinson, p. 302.

41. Prybyla, in Domes and Shaw, p. 205.

42. Baum.

43. King, in Domes and Shaw, pp. 51, 56, 57.

44. In the 1998 elections, 20 members of LegCo were for the first time elected directly, and of these, 13 seats went to the Democratic Party. Of the remaining 40 seats, which were indirectly elected, seven went to the Democratic Party.

45. Baum.

46. "Silent Treatment: Hong Kong's Chief and Its Legislature Aren't Talking," *Far Eastern Economic Review* (September 17, 1998), p. 50.

47. James L. Tyson, "Promises, Promises . . . ," *The Christian Science Monitor* (April 20, 1989), p. 2.

48. According to Article 7 of China's Criminal Code, China has the right to prosecute a Chinese national who commits a crime *anywhere* in the world, providing the crime was either planned in, or had consequences in, China. "Another Place, Another Crime: Mainland Trial of Alleged Gangster Puts 'One Country, Two Systems' to Test," *Far Eastern Economic Review* (November 5, 1998), pp. 26–27.

49. Kevin Murphy, "Troops for Hong Kong: China Puts Best Face on It," *The International Herald Tribune* (January 30, 1996), p. 4.

50. Miu-wah Ma, "China Warns against Political Ties Abroad," *The Hong Kong Standard* (September 1, 1989), p. 4.

51. Viola Lee, "China 'Trying to Discourage HK People,' " *South China Morning Post* (August 21, 1989). The article, which originally appeared in an *RMRB* article in July, was elaborated upon in the August edition of *Outlook Weekly,* a mouthpiece of the CCP.

52. Baum.

53. "Hong Kong: Now the Hard Part," *Far Eastern Economic Review* (June 11, 1998), p. 13.

Annotated Table of Contents for Articles

People's Republic of China Articles

Topic Guide to Articles

TOPIC AREA	TREATED IN	TOPIC AREA	TREATED IN
Agriculture	13. Breaking the Wall: China and the Three Gorges Dam	Economy	2. China and the World 3. Agent of Change 7. China Moves to Untie the Knots between Military and Industries 9. Which Way for the Chinese Economy? 10. China's Economy: Red Alert 13. Breaking the Wall: China and the Three Gorges Dam 24. Taiwan Survey
Communication	20. Riding the Internet Wave: One Man's Tech Firm Connects China with the Rest of the World		
Communist Party	3. Agent of Change 4. Excising the Cancer 6. Village Elections: Democracy from the Bottom Up? 7. China Moves to Untie the Knots between Military and Industries	Environment	1. China 12. Environmental Taxes: China's Bold Initiative 13. Breaking the Wall: China and the Three Gorges Dam
Corruption	4. Excising the Cancer	Foreign Investment	1. China 3. Agent of Change 13. Breaking the Wall: China and the Three Gorges Dam 24. Taiwan Survey
Cultural Development	6. Village Elections: Democracy from the Bottom Up? 15. Voice of the People		
Cultural Roots	14. Demographic Clouds on China's Horizon 17. What Would Confucius Say Now? 18. Real China: A Firsthand Perspective on Human Rights in Today's China 21. Buddhas of Cloud Hill 22. Script Reform in China 23. Red Envelopes: It's the Thought That Counts	Foreign Relations	1. China 2. China and the World 8. "Chinese Threat" Is Overblown 10. China's Economy: Red Alert 13. Breaking the Wall: China and the Three Gorges Dam 17. What Would Confucius Say Now? 26. Now the Hard Part
Current Leaders	2. China and the World 3. Agent of Change 5. It Looks Like Spring Again in China	Foreign Trade	1. China 2. China and the World 9. Which Way for the Chinese Economy? 11. China's Booming Economy: Do the Risks Outweigh the Opportunities? 24. Taiwan Survey
Diplomacy	25. Breaking the Ice		
Economic Development	1. China 2. China and the World 5. It Looks Like Spring Again in China 9. Which Way for the Chinese Economy? 10. China's Economy: Red Alert 11. China's Booming Economy: Do the Risks Outweigh the Opportunities? 17. What Would Confucius Say Now? 28. How Hong Kong May Vitalize China	Health and Welfare	12. Environmental Taxes: China's Bold Initiative 14. Demographic Clouds on China's Horizon 15. Voice of the People 18. Real China: A Firsthand Perspective on Human Rights in Today's China 19. Holding Up Half the Sky: Women in China
Economic Investment	1. China 2. China and the World 13. Breaking the Wall: China and the Three Gorges Dam	History	1. China 21. Buddhas of Cloud Hill
		Hong Kong's Reversion	1. China 26. Now the Hard Part 27. We Should Not Forget Hong Kong 28. How Hong Kong May Vitalize China

TOPIC AREA	TREATED IN	TOPIC AREA	TREATED IN
Human Rights	6. Village Elections: Democracy from the Bottom Up? 14. Demographic Clouds on China's Horizon 15. Voice of the People 16. New Day in China? 18. Real China: A Firsthand Perspective on Human Rights in Today's China 19. Holding Up Half the Sky: Women in China	**Private Enterprise**	7. China Moves to Untie the Knots between Military and Industries 11. China's Booming Economy: Do the Risks Outweigh the Opportunities? 20. Riding the Internet Wave: One Man's Tech Firm Connects China with the Rest of the World
Industrial Development	8. "Chinese Threat" Is Overblown 9. Which Way for the Chinese Economy? 10. China's Economy: Red Alert 11. China's Booming Economy: Do the Risks Outweigh the Opportunities?	**Regional Cooperation**	24. Taiwan Survey 25. Breaking the Ice 26. Now the Hard Part 27. We Should Not Forget Hong Kong
Military	7. China Moves to Untie the Knots between Military and Industries 8. "Chinese Threat" Is Overblown	**Religion**	23. Red Envelopes: It's the Thought That Counts
		Rural Life	16. New Day in China?
National Reunification	1. China 2. China and the World 8. "Chinese Threat" Is Overblown	**Social Reform**	5. It Looks Like Spring Again in China 14. Demographic Clouds on China's Horizon 15. Voice of the People 18. Real China: A Firsthand Perspective on Human Rights in Today's China 19. Holding Up Half the Sky: Women in China
Nationalism	24. Taiwan Survey		
Natural Resources	12. Environmental Taxes: China's Bold Initiative 13. Breaking the Wall: China and the Three Gorges Dam	**Social Unrest**	6. Village Elections: Democracy from the Bottom Up? 15. Voice of the People
Peasants	14. Demographic Clouds on China's Horizon	**Taiwan Independence**	24. Taiwan Survey
Philosophy	17. What Would Confucius Say Now?	**Territorial Problems**	25. Breaking the Ice 26. Now the Hard Part
Political Reform	4. Excising the Cancer 5. It Looks Like Spring Again in China 6. Village Elections: Democracy from the Bottom Up? 16. New Day in China?	**Trade**	1. China 8. "Chinese Threat" Is Overblown 9. Which Way for the Chinese Economy?
Politics	1. China 2. China and the World 3. Agent of Change 4. Excising the Cancer 5. It Looks Like Spring Again in China 10. China's Economy: Red Alert 11. China's Booming Economy: Do the Risks Outweigh the Opportunities? 16. New Day in China?	**Women**	19. Holding Up Half the Sky: Women in China
		Writing System	22. Script Reform in China

Articles from the World Press

Article 1   *Foreign Policy*, Spring 1998

Think Again

CHINA

China is a giant screen upon which outsiders project their hopes and fears. Expectations of economic gain coexist with worries about financial crisis; shrill alarms about Chinese power with dire forecasts of collapse; visions of democratic change with caricatures of current reality. It is time to step back and look at where China is today, where it might be going, and what consequences that direction will hold for the rest of the world.

by David M. Lampton

China Is a Rogue State with Hegemonic Ambitions

Not true. Strident voices in the West assert that the People's Republic of China (PRC) sees little to be gained from being a good international citizen. This view has three defects: 1) The record of the last two decades does not support it; 2) it is not in Beijing's interest to be perceived and treated as a rogue state; and 3) if other nations begin to regard it in that light, they will help bring about the very Chinese behavior they seek to avert.

Consider China's actions as a permanent member of the UN Security Council. Surely, "the next 'rogue' superpower"—to quote one recent characterization of China in the U.S. press—would not have hesitated to throw its weight around over the years. Yet, since 1972, while China has abstained on some Security Council resolutions, it has cast only two vetoes in open session. Although deeply apprehensive of resolutions condoning sanctions or interventions, the PRC has not sought to stop UN missions in the former Yugoslavia, Haiti, Somalia, or Iraq during the Gulf War and thereafter. As Foreign Minister Qian Qichen said in late 1997 about Beijing's position on sanctions against Iraq: "Despite the fact that we have not supported these [UN] resolutions, they must be respected."

This generally constructive stance extends to the growing number of international organizations that China has joined since former leader Deng Xiaoping's opening to the outside world almost two decades ago. In 1977, China belonged to 21 international governmental organizations and 71 international nongovernmental organizations. By 1994, the respective numbers were 50 and 955. In institutions such as the Asian Development Bank, the International Monetary Fund (IMF), and the World Bank, China has been a model citizen. Beijing has

DAVID M. LAMPTON is George and Sadie Hyman professor of Chinese studies at the Paul H. Nitze School of Advanced International Studies.

also acted responsibly in Asia's recent economic crisis, contributing U.S.$1 billion to the IMF stabilization package for Thailand, clearly conveying its intention to defend the Hong Kong dollar, and (so far) resisting the temptation to devalue its own currency.

Closer to home, the record is mixed. But Beijing's missile exercises in the Taiwan Strait in 1995–96 and its occupation of several reefs in the Spratly Islands must be set next to its concerted and successful efforts during the last decade to improve relations with every country in the neighborhood. In Cambodia, China played an essential role in the settlement leading to UN-sponsored elections. Looking north and west, the PRC has resolved disputes with Kazakstan, Kyrgyzstan, Russia, and Tadjikistan through negotiated agreement. To the south, Beijing has improved relations with Hanoi and New Delhi and joined the Association of South East Asian Nations' regional forum on security.

Beijing's adherence to various international institutions, treaties, and regimes has been best where it has been engaged in writing the rules it is asked to observe and where the international community has made available tangible resources to assist implementation. Indeed, for all the controversy surrounding China's behavior in the field of nonproliferation, it has generally complied with the international nonproliferation regimes to which it has been a full party, including the Treaty on the Non-Proliferation of Nuclear Weapons, the Comprehensive Test Ban Treaty, and the Chemical Weapons Convention. China's relations with Pakistan and Iran have been worrisome. Nonetheless, Beijing addressed these issues during President Jiang Zemin's October 1997 state visit to the United States and reassured the Clinton administration in writing about China's future nuclear cooperation with Iran.

Beijing's compliance has been less praiseworthy in areas where it has not been a member of the rule-writing club, where compliance would conflict with its perceived strategic interests, or where it lacks the necessary resources and enforcement mechanisms. In the case of some missile-related and nuclear technology transfers to Pakistan—long a Chinese strategic ally—Beijing has sought to use its compliance with agreements, or lack thereof, as leverage to obtain stricter adherence in Washington to the Joint Communique on Weapons Sales to Taiwan of 1982. Then again, the transfer of ring magnets to Pakistan probably owes less to government directives than to Beijing's inability to exercise effective supervision and control over industries and companies—a problem that bedevils the United States, Great Britain, and other countries with a strong stake in nonproliferation.

China Is Undertaking a Huge Military Buildup

Wrong. There is little uncertainty about China's modest military capabilities, much speculation about what those capabilities may be 20 years hence, and considerable debate about current and future Chinese intentions.

China's defense budget presents a daunting challenge for analysts, not least because much military spending occurs outside the regular defense budget. Those who wish to point to a Chinese threat often use figures from China's defense budget that show a dramatic rise in official spending from 1988 to 1996. However, a 1997 RAND study of China's official defense budget, which adjusts these figures for inflation, suggests that the increase in official defense spending is much less significant.

The Institute for International Strategic Studies and the Stockholm International Peace Research Institute assert that total spending by the People's Liberation Army (PLA) is four to five times the amount officially reported (which Chinese military officers hotly dispute). If true, this would put actual 1996 PLA spending at U.S.$35.5 to 44.4 billion. The Heritage Foundation puts the upper range estimate at U.S.$40 billion. Japan, in 1996, with the American nuclear umbrella and the U.S.-Japan Security Treaty, spent about U.S.$45 billion. China has a long coastline, land borders with 14 states, many of which have presented, and might again present, security problems, and no protective alliance; the PLA also has domestic control responsibilities (as we saw tragically in 1989). And not only do many of China's neighbors have more modern weapons, but as a report recently issued by the Pacific Council on International Policy and RAND noted, "China's military expenditures as a percentage of total defense expenditures by all Asian countries have been decreasing steadily since the mid-1970s."

What about China's development and purchase of advanced technologies? A 1996 report by the U.S. Department of Defense covering 17 families of technologies with military applications shows that, with a few important exceptions (nuclear and chemical technologies among them), China lagged well behind first- and second-tier countries such as France, Israel, Japan, Russia, the United Kingdom, and the United States.

True, current estimates of Chinese purchases of advanced technology from Russia during 1990–96 ranged from U.S.$1 to 2 billion annually. By way of comparison, however, the U.S. military spent U.S.$11.99 billion with one American prime defense contractor, Lockheed Martin, in FY 1996 alone.

While it would be foolish to dismiss China's increasing ability to project force beyond its borders and to affect U.S. and other interests, it would be even more foolish to allow exaggerated perceptions of Chinese strength to shape U.S. policy—a development that would stoke nationalist resentment in Beijing and likely fuel support for the very buildup that some U.S. commentators regularly decry.

A Peaceful Resolution of Taiwan's Status Is Only a Matter of Time

Maybe not. The conventional wisdom is that the Taiwan Strait missile crisis from mid-1995 to March 1996 had a sobering effect on Beijing, Taipei, and Washington. In Beijing, there had been those who thought that Washington lacked the will to uphold its commitment to a "peaceful resolution" of the Taiwan issue and to stability in East Asia. The March 1996 dispatch of two aircraft carrier groups was a credible assertion of American interest. In Taipei, President Lee Teng-hui and others seemed to have concluded that Beijing could not, or would not, do much about Taiwan's search for a more dignified international role. Beijing's missiles and the resultant dislocations of markets and capital flight were an abrupt comeuppance. And after the PRC missile exercises (particularly those in the spring of 1996), many in the U.S. Congress professed a new appreciation for Beijing's sensitivity to the Taiwan issue. In short, there is now a happy assumption that everyone has become more cautious. One can hope so, but there are other forces at work.

First, something fundamental drives Taipei's search for a greater role in the international community—a changing sense of identity among its population. In recent years, there has been a progressive decline in the percentage of people on Taiwan who consider themselves "Chinese" and a corresponding rise in the percentage identifying themselves as "Taiwanese." Taiwan's ever more competitive political system has given voice to this new, distinct identity. In the Taiwan presidential election of the year 2000, a president may well be elected from the Democratic Progressive Party (DPP), which historically has stood for the island's independence.

Beijing has said it will employ force to prevent independence or outside intervention. How Beijing would actually react to the DPP's assumption of power, how the DPP would lead Taiwan, and how the Taiwanese will respond in an indefinite future are all imponderables. And yet, the answers to these questions will influence whether peace and stability can be maintained in the Taiwan Strait in the years ahead.

There is another part to the equation: How long will Beijing remain "patient?" As Beijing's attention shifts from the return of Hong Kong and Macao (in 1999), it will focus increasingly on "reunification with Taiwan." Not only do PRC leaders worry about trends on Taiwan, they believe that, were the island to achieve de jure independence, their own right to role would be forfeited. Moreover, they fear that areas from Mongolia to Xinjiang to Tibet would use Taiwan's moves to justify their own efforts to break away. Beijing sees everything at stake in the Taiwan issue and is unsure that time works in its favor, despite the ties that about U.S.$35 billion in investment by Taiwan on the mainland create.

In short, continued stability depends on restraint by Beijing, Taipei, and Washington, none of which has an unblemished record of self-control.

China Will Be the Next Asian Economic Domino to Fall

Not necessarily. The financial crash in Northeast and Southeast Asia since mid-1997 is already taking a toll on the PRC. China now faces the prospects of declining regional demand for its exports and stiffening competition from regional economies in other export markets. Its still robust 1997 GDP growth of 8.8 percent was below earlier government forecasts, there are signs that growth will slow further (perhaps to 6 percent), and some Chinese and foreign analysts believe that the PRC may devalue its currency to maintain its export competitiveness. Beijing asserts that it will vigorously resist such a move. Yet, if unemployment rises, growth slows, and domestic exporters apply political pressure, policy could change. Declining asset values in East and Southeast Asia will probably also reduce capital flow to China from the region.

Many of the considerations that have undermined confidence in other Asian financial systems apply to China: a lack of transparency; financial cronyism; banks with huge portfolios of nonperforming loans; poor regulatory systems; property bubbles; heavy borrowing abroad; and new, volatile equity markets.

And yet, China's economy has important differences that may provide a breathing spell. In a forthcoming book, economist Nicholas Lardy lays them out clearly: 1) China's currency is not freely convertible, thereby reducing speculative pressures; 2) Beijing reports hard currency reserves of about U.S.$140 billion, not including the separate resources of Hong

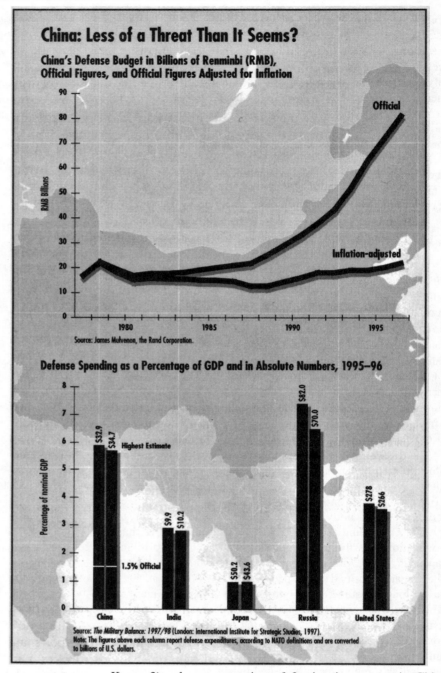

China: Less of a Threat Than It Seems?

China's Defense Budget in Billions of Renminbi (RMB), Official Figures, and Official Figures Adjusted for Inflation

Official

Inflation-adjusted

Source: James Mulvenon, the Rand Corporation.

Defense Spending as a Percentage of GDP and in Absolute Numbers, 1995–96

China $32.9 / $34.7 — Highest Estimate; 1.5% Official
India $9.9 / $10.2
Japan $50.2 / $43.6
Russia $82.0 / $70.0
United States $278 / $266

Source: *The Military Balance: 1997/98* (London: International Institute for Strategic Studies, 1997).
Note: The figures above each column report defense expenditures, according to NATO definitions and are converted to billions of U.S. dollars.

Kong; 3) a large proportion of foreign investment in China has come in the form of direct investment in factories and other assets, not hot money put into more volatile stock markets; 4) although Chinese entities have large foreign debts, most are long-term, unlike elsewhere in Asia; and 5) although foreign direct investment has been important for growth over the last 15 years, the high domestic savings rate has been the principal fuel—growth can continue if savings can be more productively utilized.

The key to avoiding a meltdown will be whether Beijing moves to accelerate reform of the banking and state enterprise sectors—an apparent commitment of the current leadership.

But deciding and doing are two different things: Will Beijing recapitalize its banks and operate them on sound financial principles? Simply training the personnel to accomplish this is a gargantuan task. And will China tackle the problem of state enterprises (at least 40 percent of which lose money), whose bad debts to the banks are a principal cause of the financial system's current woes? The restructuring of state enterprises and the bankruptcy of many others could put millions more workers onto the streets, just as growth slows. Can China meet these challenges and avoid serious political dislocation? Nobody can be sure.

China's Large, Fast-Growing Exports Come Principally at the Expense of Jobs in the West

Wrong. Chinese exports to the United States and Europe have grown rapidly and often dominate in labor-intensive sectors such as toys, footwear, apparel, and textiles. But PRC exports in these areas generally surged after domestic jobs in these industries had already migrated to Indonesia, South Korea, and Taiwan, and elsewhere in East Asia and Latin America. In garment manufacturing, for example, World Bank data suggests that, especially for the European Union, employment had already fallen sharply before Chinese exports achieved even the relatively low penetration rate of 2 percent. And economist Marcus Noland calculated that from 1988 to 1994, almost 90 percent of the increase in the Chinese share of U.S. consumption had merely displaced imports from other countries. The real fear of Chinese export competition ought to be found in low-cost producing economies, not Main Street, U.S.A. or Europe.

China Has Been a Bust for U.S. Firms

Not really. According to U.S. Commerce Department figures for 1990–96, China was the fastest-growing major U.S. export market. During that period, American exports grew at a compound rate of more than 19 percent, if one includes U.S. exports initially exported to Hong Kong but then reexported to China. The PRC is now America's ninth largest export market. By way of comparison, U.S. exports to Japan grew at 6 percent, and those to Brazil by 15 percent, annually. American-invested joint ventures and wholly owned U.S. subsidiaries in China also increasingly sell goods there; although some of the profit is repatriated to the United States, much is reinvested in China, where it can generate future returns.

However, it is also true that the United States has a mounting trade deficit with China—U.S. government estimates peg it at about U.S.$50 billion for 1997—a figure that many economists believe overstates the problem. The reality of these rising exports to China and the simultaneously mounting trade deficit suggest that Washington—quite appropriately—is proceeding to secure more market access.

Those who assert that the Chinese market has been a bust have a deeper, more erroneous point. Their implicit assumption is that the United States and other industrialized economies do not have a lot riding on economic relations with China. Wrong. Everyone has a great deal at stake in whether or not China can sustain (and how it sustains) growth as other economies deflate.

China Is the World's Biggest Intellectual Thief

Wrong, for now. Stealing copyrighted music, software, and movies—the "piracy" of intellectual property rights (IPR)—is a serious and legitimate concern. One 1996 study estimated that "of the 523 million new business software applications used globally during 1996, 225 million units—nearly one in every two—were pirated." China does its share of wrongdoing in this regard. But the sorry fact is that developed nations and Americans themselves inflict the biggest dollar losses on U.S. industry, though the highest piracy rates (the percentage of protected items in use that have been illegally appropriated) are to be found in low-income economies with weak to nonexistent legal structures.

Looking at dollar losses through software piracy in 1996 (and the industry's methodology is subject to criticism for inflating losses), Eastern Europe, Japan, Western Europe, and the United States itself all inflicted greater losses on U.S. industry than China (with 22 percent of the world's population). However, if one looks at the "piracy rate" in 1996, China was surpassed only by Vietnam and Indonesia. Russia and the rest of the Commonwealth of Independent States were close behind.

In short, owners of intellectual property confront a global circumstance in which losses to developed countries (with high rates of personal computer ownership) exceed losses to poorer countries (with fewer PCs, weaker legal and regulatory structures, and more extensive official corruption).

The music recording industry faces similar problems. The Recording Industry Association of America reported in 1996 that lost revenue through CD piracy in Japan came to U.S.$500 million annually—"more than the U.S.$300 million the American record industry says it is losing annually from the far more well-known piracy in China."

China is trying to build an IPR enforcement regime. In addition to constructing a (yet imperfect) framework of domestic law in the late 1980s and 1990s, Beijing signed two agreements with Washington (in 1992 and 1995) and from May 1996 to March 1997 closed 37 factories illegally copying CDs—58 CD and CD-ROM production lines by January 1998. As China develops its own innovators and artists with commercially salable products, demands for stricter IPR protection will grow.

China Is a Totalitarian State

Simplistic. To reject this characterization is not to assert that the PRC is a democracy—it is not. But words should have meaning. Totalitarian refers to a state that has the intention and capability to control nearly all aspects of human behavior, thought, and communication. Totalitarian described the ambitions and, to a considerable extent, the system during much of Mao Zedong's reign, when a trip to Albania was considered broadening and children were expected to inform on parents.

Ironically, many of China's domestic problems and irresponsible behavior abroad—from piracy to proliferation—stem from a lack of central control. Most significantly, between 30 and 200 million people slosh around China in search of temporary employment, encamping in and around cities and creating a potentially volatile pool of poor and discontented citizens.

In fact, for all its imperfections and injustices, China today is freer than it has been at any time in the last five decades. About 40,000 Chinese students are now enrolled in tertiary U.S. educational institutions; during the Soviet Union's entire 70-year history, it never sent that many students to the United States. In 1965, there were 12 television and 93 radio stations in China; today, PLA receiving dishes are sold illegally to citizens who pull in satellite TV. The Internet is growing by leaps and bounds. Newspapers and magazines have become not just more numerous but far more diverse and autonomous. In 1978, the state controlled more than 90 percent of GNP; in 1996, that number was about 45 percent and falling. The state now employs only 18 percent of the work force, compared with more than 90 percent in 1978 (including peasants in communes at that time). In September 1997, at the Fifteenth Party Congress, the concept of "public" ownership was morphed from Marx's concept into "public" in the sense of "initial public offering" of stock. While under Mao the concept of the individual suing the state for damages was inconceivable, it now happens increasingly often.

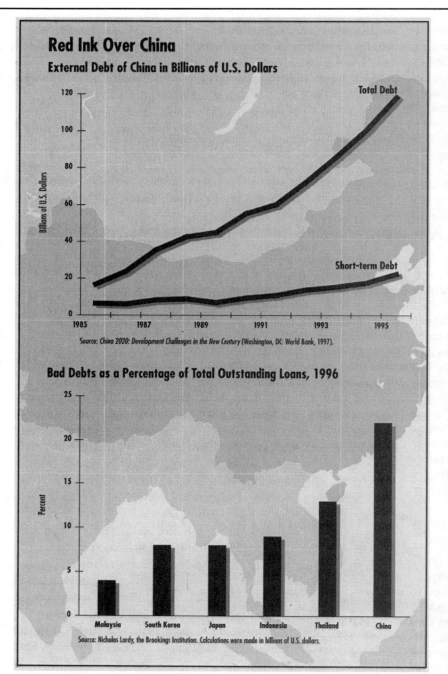

Red Ink Over China

External Debt of China in Billions of U.S. Dollars

Source: *China 2020: Development Challenges in the New Century* (Washington, DC: World Bank, 1997).

Bad Debts as a Percentage of Total Outstanding Loans, 1996

Source: Nicholas Lardy, the Brookings Institution. Calculations were made in billions of U.S. dollars.

China Is Wrecking Hong Kong

No. The broadcast networks that spent large sums covering the July 1, 1997, handover to the PRC left disappointed, not at the absence of disaster but at the absence of a "story." The days since then have been notable for both what Beijing has and has not done.

Beijing has not militarized the city, as some feared. There are fewer army troops there under Chinese rule than there were generally in Hong Kong under British governors—reinforce-

ments are, of course, only a few miles away in China proper. Beijing has not stopped political demonstrations, which have continued on an almost daily basis since the night of June 30–July 1, 1997, when Martin Lee, the leader of democratic forces in Hong Kong, spoke to a crowd from the balcony of the Legislative Council. Although it is hard to measure press self-censorship—and there is some, as evidenced by the reluctance of Hong Kong Chinese to show three controversial movies dealing with sensitive subjects—Hong Kong still has one of the most freewheeling journalism communities in Asia. In terms of governance, it appears that the new chief executive, C.H. Tung, has great latitude in leading Hong Kong.

China through Rogue-Tinted Glasses

Excerpts from House Democratic Leader Richard A. Gephardt's address to the Detroit Economic Club on May 27, 1997:
"The United States has no business playing 'business as usual' with a Chinese tyranny that persecutes Christian and Muslim leaders and leaders from many other faiths, precludes tens of millions from practicing their religion, sells the most lethal weapons to the most dangerous of nations, profits off slave labor, and engages in the utter evil of forced abortion.... Today's China is not content to keep its reign of terror inside its own borders. It blows its storm of calamity into the world's other outlaw nations....

"The totalitarians who rule China—and we should not be afraid to call them that, as Ronald Reagan was not afraid to speak of the Evil Empire—openly express their contempt for the ideals of freedom.... A government that can arbitrarily violate the liberty of its people cannot be trusted to abide by the rules of contract or the rights of companies....

"And what have we gained by trafficking with a tyranny that debases the dignity of one-fifth of the human race? What is gained by a policy that sees all the evils and looks the other way? What is gained by constructive engagement with slave labor? Our trade policy with China has failed. It has failed not only on moral grounds but economically as well. There is nothing 'free' about our trade with China—in fact, it comes to us at great cost and little benefit.... They send more than a third of their exports to our shores while less than 2 percent of our products go there....

"China has said to many of our companies that if they want to sell there, they must produce there. Then they have ordained that in order to build factories there we must transfer our technological know-how to them. Business is being blackmailed into giving China the means and the trade secrets that will make them an economic powerhouse. And in return they will continue to pirate our music, software, and videos...."

U.S. naval ships have been permitted to continue to make port calls—as of January 1998, 34 naval vessels, including two aircraft carrier battle groups and two nuclear submarines. When equity and property markets throughout the region, including Hong Kong, precipitously declined in the latter half of 1997 and early 1998, Beijing let markets work (even though many PRC interests lost heavily). Chinese leaders also quietly let it be known that China's large hard-currency reserves could be brought to the defense of the Hong Kong—U.S. dollar peg.

Less reassuring has been Beijing's determination, expressed well before the takeover, to reverse British governor Christopher Patten's October 1992 speedup in the agreed-upon process of broadening the popular franchise. Instead, immediately after the handover, a provisional legislative council was installed to sit during the interim period before new elections. The elections that Tung has announced for May 1998 will be widely criticized for narrowing functional constituencies and employing proportional representation in ways that can be expected to weaken the power of Martin Lee's Democratic Party.

On balance, however, Beijing has played a responsible role. This pattern of PRC behavior probably will persist, depending on the fate of China's own reforms, regional economic stability, and whether Hong Kong's own people stay out of the business of promoting political change in the PRC.

China Is an Effective, Major Player in the Washington Lobbying Game

Wrong. No misconception is further from reality. Until May 1995, when Lee Teng-hui was given a visa to visit Cornell University as a result of congressional pressure (by a House vote of 396-0), Beijing paid little heed to Capitol Hill. PRC leaders rested secure in the mistaken belief that when U.S. presidents wish to prevail over Congress, they do.

This inattention to Congress is reflected in a number of ways. Beijing has one law firm under retention in Washington—Taipei is reported to have 14. The PRC has (off and on) one public relations firm in the United States—Taipei has many. Even if one adds to the PRC's legal lobbying expenditures the alleged U.S.$100,000 in illegal campaign contributions that the FBI says may have occurred (although the Thompson committee failed to demonstrate this), China does not rank even among the top 10 nations (or territories) in terms of lobbying efforts. Even Haiti (no. 7) and Angola (no. 9) outspend Beijing!

The PRC recently augmented efforts to bring members of the U.S. Congress to China. Beijing knows that there has been high congressional turnover since 1992, that most members have not traveled much, and that seeing China's dynamism leaves few views unchanged. But the PRC efforts lag well behind Taipei's. In 1996, members of Congress took 58 all-expense paid trips to China—still a distant second to the 139 trips they took to Taiwan. When the numbers for 1997 are in, Beijing probably will be seen to have narrowed the gap considerably.

China Is an Environmental Accident Waiting to Happen

Wrong; it is happening. Many concerns with respect to China are exaggerated, but this one is underestimated by most outsiders. The human and economic costs of air and water pollution in China are staggering. China's urban residents breathe air that significantly exceeds the World Health Organization's minimal air quality standards.

The long-term health effects (such as mental retardation attributable to excessive lead concentrations in the blood of children) are becoming all too apparent. The death rate from chronic obstructive pulmonary disease is five times that of the United States. The World Bank says that simply reducing outdoor pollution levels to the Chinese government's standard would save 178,000 lives annually. Beyond the direct monetary expenses (such as additional hospital admissions), there are other costs: lost work time due to sickness; decaying infrastructure from acid rain; lost crops and farmland; and forfeited tourist revenues. The World Bank concluded that "total air and water pollution costs are conservatively estimated at U.S.$54 billion a year, or roughly 8 percent of GDP." China's GDP growth rate has averaged about 10.2 percent over the last 11 years, suggesting a startling conclusion: More than three-quarters of China's real GDP growth has been offset by the above costs since 1985.

Those figures do not account for the costs inflicted by PRC pollution on countries near and far, effects stemming from acid rain, carbon dioxide emissions, and ozone depletion. China's rapidly growing greenhouse emissions, and the burden Beijing should assume to reduce them, were among the principal conflicts at the Kyoto Conference on global warming. And as Charles Johnson of the East-West Center recently observed, "If China follows the pattern of wealth first, cleanup later like its neighbors Japan, South Korea, and Taiwan, even its most affluent coastal provinces probably will not start seriously tackling air pollution for 10 or 20 more years."

WANT TO KNOW MORE?

Rapid changes within China and in its global interconnections are the focus of much new research. One of the most compre-

hensive of such pieces is *China 2020: Development Challenges in the New Century* (Washington, DC: World Bank, 1997), an overview volume that summarizes key findings from six companion volumes. For those interested in governance in China, see Kenneth Lieberthal's *Governing China* (New York, NY: W.W. Norton & Company, 1995). For the best available account of China's foreign policy in the era of reform, see Andrew Nathan & Robert Ross, *The Great Wall and the Empty Fortress* (New York, NY: W.W. Norton & Company, 1997). For a wide-ranging overview of the issues shaping Sino-American relations in the Clinton era, see *Living With China,* edited by Ezra Vogel (New York, NY: W.W. Norton & Company, 1997). To learn more about China's military expenditures and the business enterprises of the PLA, consult James Mulvenon's *Chinese Military Commerce and U.S. National Security* (Santa Monica, CA: RAND Corporation, June 1997). And for a comprehensive, readable overview of China's changing role in the world economy, see Nicholas Lardy's *China in the World Economy* (Washington, DC: Institute for International Economics, 1994).

Finally, for links to relevant Web sites, as well as a comprehensive index of related articles, access **www.foreignpolicy.com.**

Article 2

The World & I, October 1998

China and the World

The global community is seeking to encourage China the aspiring global citizen while avoiding appeasement of China the dictator.

GREG MAY

According to the Beijing leadership, the world has nothing to fear from China's rise. "China," said President Jiang Zemin last year at the Communist Party Congress, "will never seek hegemony. . . . The Chinese people, for a long time subjected to aggression, oppression, and humiliation by foreign powers, will never inflict these sufferings upon others."

The world, however, is not yet convinced. While China believes it is regaining its rightful position as a great nation after a century of "humiliation,"

skeptics see worrisome signs that China, despite its pious denials, aims to dominate Asia. The reality is probably somewhere in between.

The emergence of the People's Republic of China as a major world power has occurred with remarkable speed. In 1978, the year the late paramount leader Deng Xiaoping initiated economic reforms, China was a very weak country, a land of steam locomotives that did a minuscule $19 billion in trade with the outside world. In 1998, China expects to do $345 billion in trade and is on

course to overtake the United States as the world's largest economy in as few as 20 years, according to the *Economist*.

Impressive ascension

As impressive as China's ascension has been, its power must be kept in perspective. While much attention has been paid to China's high economic growth rate, less obvious to outsiders is its hemorrhaging banking system, grossly inefficient state-owned enterprises, and still very low per-capita income. Militarily, despite the recent purchase of some advanced systems, the People's Liberation Army still lacks significant power-projection capabilities.

Meanwhile, the Communist Party has lost much of its ideological legitimacy and the government is dealing with unprecedented problems of labor unrest, mass internal migration, and sporadically violent separatist movements, especially among China's Muslim minority.

China, then, is neither a monolithic threat nor a completely benign power. At times China acts as a responsible global citizen. Although the PRC often takes an aloof posture in the United Nations, it has used its Security Council veto only once since 1981. China maintains an excellent record of on-time repayment of its World Bank loans and has given $4 billion to the IMF to help its neighbors overcome the Asian financial crisis.

China is a member of most arms-control regimes and recently ratified the Chemical Weapons Convention and has signed the Comprehensive Test Ban Treaty. More concretely, China has helped U.S. efforts to maintain stability on the Korean peninsula by participating in the four-party talks with the United States, North Korea, and South Korea.

However, at other times, China seems to confirm the world's worst suspicions about its intentions. While China may be good about signing weapons control agreements, China has provided nuclear and missile technology to countries like Iran and Pakistan. While China acts as a force for stability in Korea, it has done the opposite in the South China Sea, where it has seized disputed islands claimed by Vietnam and the Philippines.

In July 1995 and again in March 1996, China disrupted international shipping and air routes when it test-fired missiles into waters just off Taiwan—a bit of saber rattling meant to warn the island against pursuing independence from China.

Strategic and moral dilemmas

The debate over how to deal with China is much more complex than simply isolation versus engagement. Rather, the global community is trying to find ways to encourage and reward "China the aspiring global citizen" while avoiding any appeasement of "China the brutal dictatorship." This is a problem that in-

Problems in a Worker's Paradise

China's remarkably high economic growth rate is always emphasized.

Less publicized is its hemorrhaging banking system and inefficient state-owned enterprises.

Meanwhile, the Communist Party has lost much of its ideological legitimacy and the government is dealing with unprecedented problems of labor unrest, mass internal migration, and sporadically violent separatist movements, especially among the Muslim minority.

evitably leads to tough strategic and moral dilemmas.

In the international community at large, the issue of whether or not to trade with China is probably the least controversial. Only in the United States are broad sanctions, like the revocation of China's most-favored-nation (MFN) trade status, seriously debated. (MFN was officially changed to *normal trade relations* or NTR as part of the IRS reform package President Clinton signed in late July. The change was put in as a rider. So NTR is now the official term.) The world depends heavily on China as a source of cheap consumer goods (two-thirds of the shoes and over one-half of the toys sold in the United States are made in China) and markets (the PRC is the largest forecasted market outside the United States for Boeing jets and Motorola cell phone equipment.)

But China's economic goals go beyond cornering the stuffed-toy market. One of China's primary motives in participating in the global economy is to gain access to, and the means to pay for, better technology. While China is willing to increase its global integration in some areas of its economy, it also wants to build industrial self-sufficiency in others. For example, Beijing maintains tariffs of 80 to 100 percent on imported cars but offers incentives to foreign companies to produce autos inside China.

China's application to the World Trade Organization (WTO) provides an opportunity to get China to commit to a clear schedule for opening markets and aban-

doning import-substitution policies. The need to get China into the WTO quickly (its application, first made to the General Agreement on Tariffs and Trade, has been under review now for twelve years) must be balanced by the need for China to enter under fair standards that will require sufficient market access.

The United States could offer China permanent NTR as a carrot to encourage swift entry into the WTO. Should China continue to demand overly generous terms, the United States and Europe may need to reconsider their pledge not to let Taiwan into the WTO first, something the PRC vehemently opposes since it considers Taiwan part of its territory.

Regardless of the criteria and timing, China's entry into the WTO will likely expand its access to technologies with dual civilian and military use. Controlling China's access to all dual-use items is simply not possible. For instance, a Global Positioning System receiver, a device with clear military as well as civilian applications, can be purchased anywhere in the world for as little as a few hundred dollars.

Military diversions

Export controls can focus only on the most advanced technologies, the kind that China has a record of diverting to its military. In 1995, advanced machine tools sold to China by McDonnell Douglas were illegally transferred to a factory that makes fighter planes and cruise missiles.

Similarly, in 1997, United States investigators discovered that a Sun Microsystems supercomputer, originally sold to a Hong Kong company, had been installed in a Chinese military facility. Congress and the Justice Department are now investigating Loral Space and Communications Corp. and Hughes Electronics Corp., two U.S. satellite firms, to find out if they illegally supplied missile technology to China.

For the United States, a first step to strengthen control of technology transfers would be to reverse the post-Cold War trend of giving the Commerce Department more and more power over high-technology exports. Many members of Congress have recommended that primary licensing authority for satellites, supercomputers, and encryption technology be returned to the State Department and other agencies with a mandate to protect national security, not boost exports.

Technology transfer is just one of many security issues the United States and its allies must grapple with as China's power expands. During the final decades of the Cold War, Washington wanted China's cooperation to contain the Soviet Union. As part of this policy, the United States built listening posts in China to monitor Soviet missile tests and helped China modernize its F–8 fighter plane.

With the Cold War fading into history, a revival of U.S. military assistance to China seems neither likely nor desirable. But recently, the Clinton administration has emphasized the need to build a "constructive strategic partnership" with China to help maintain regional security, stop weapons proliferation, and fight international crime.

Such cooperation is beneficial in areas where the United States and China have converging interests. China, for example, is growing more dependent on Middle East oil and, like the United States, wants to maintain stability in the Persian Gulf. Stressing such mutual security interests has helped convince China to moderate, though not completely halt, its sales of missiles and nuclear technology to Iran and Pakistan.

Potential conflicts

While there is room for cooperation, potential conflicts between China and the United States, in addition to other uncertainties such as North Korea, mean that a strategic partnership should not come at the expense of America's strategic alliances. The future of the U.S. military in northeast Asia (approximately 45,000 troops in Japan and 36,000 in South Korea) is thus a key question facing Washington, Tokyo, and Seoul.

Beijing opposes American troop deployments in Asia, fearing they are ultimately aimed at China. From the American perspective, the military alliances are needed to maintain a balance of power, prevent an arms race, and discourage China from resolving its lingering territorial disputes, especially its claim on Taiwan, by force. Thus, the major powers of the world, including the United States, all see benefits in fostering both trade and security cooperation with China.

But the harsh reality is that pursuing economic and strategic relations makes it very difficult to take a hard line on human rights. When China was necessary to contain Soviet power, the choice between strategic interests and human rights was quite easy. When President Nixon met Mao Zedong in 1972, he shook hands with a leader who was responsible for the deaths of millions. But doing so was in the compelling interests of both U.S. national security and world peace.

While China's human rights record has improved immeasurably since Mao's time, the world should not avert its eyes from China's present-day abuses. Tibet, for instance, has become a cause célèbre in the West, and Hollywood has portrayed China's harsh treatment of Tibetans in recent movies like *Kundun* and *Seven Years in Tibet*. China's desire to exert control over Tibetan Buddhism led to the bizarre spectacle of the supposedly atheist Chinese Communist Party overseeing the 1995 search for the reincarnation of the Panchen Lama, Tibet's second-highest religious figure.

Trouble with Tibet

Practically every country, including the United States, takes the official position that Tibet is a part of China. Tibet's exiled spiritual leader, the Dalai Lama, does not advocate a separate Tibetan state but rather wants China to give Tibet full autonomy in its internal affairs.

World efforts to improve the situation in Tibet should emphasize the need for dialogue between China and the Dalai Lama rather than calling for Tibetan independence, which prompts even tighter repression by China. Multilateral criticism of China's treatment of Tibet, its religious persecution, its coercive family-planning practices (including allegations of forced abortion), and its jailing of political dissidents is the most effective means to encourage China to improve its human rights record.

Chinese officials now largely shrug off complaints from the United States, but they remain very sensitive to world opinion. This is why China has fought so hard in the UN Human Rights Commission to prevent passage, or even debate, of resolutions critical of its practices.

China's recent release of political dissidents Wei Jingsheng and Wang Dan led the United States to abandon attempts to criticize China at the 1998 meeting of the Human Rights Commissions. Almost a decade after the Tiananmen Square massacre, the world is moving from a policy of stigmatizing China to one of encouraging it to live up to its obligations under the Universal Declaration of Human Rights and the International Covenant on Civil and Political Rights, which China says it will sign.

Drawing China into the world community

Should China backslide on human rights, the world should not hesitate to revive efforts to condemn China in the United Nations, and, in extreme cases, to seek multilateral sanctions.

While each nation has its own unique policy regarding China, a general consensus has developed that China, despite its often cruel authoritarianism, must be drawn into the world community. But, in its desire to hasten China's integration, the world should not give rewards that have not been earned.

Some foreign policy experts have advocated giving China membership in the G–7 group of industrialized nations. But premature membership of China in this body will undermine the notion that great-nation status comes from a combination of economic might and democracy. (A convincing argument can be made that Russia also has no business in the G–7.)

Accommodating China as an emerging power means establishing an unspoken agreement that acceptance of China as a great nation will only come if China strengthens its compliance with international agreements (including those on human rights), reduces its protectionist trade barriers, and halts military intimidation of Taiwan and other neighbors.

The task for the world is to show that greater cooperation and participation in the existing international system will help China obtain the status and respect it desires, while reckless attacks on the interest of other powers will do the opposite. For now, China appears to be getting this message, slowly but steadily.

Greg May is a Chinese studies associate at the Nixon Center, a Washington-based, nonpartisan public policy institute.

Article 3   *Far Eastern Economic Review, July 23, 1998*

CHINA

Agent of Change

Initially dismissed as a transitional figure, Jiang Zemin is now presiding over what may prove to be the most profound changes in China since Deng Xiaoping opened up the economy two decades ago

Susan V. Lawrence in Beijing

On a rainy Saturday in the Chinese capital, the Tree Song Bookstore near Peking University is packed. Customers are leafing through books on subjects that just a year ago were considered taboo. *Farewell to Utopia* documents the failure of socialism worldwide, while in *Ideas and Problems of China,* political scientists Liu Junning argues that "without rights and freedoms for citizens and without limited government, the market economy can only be pie in the sky."

Those books and many like them in the Tree Song Bookstore are testimony to a profound change in the political atmosphere in Beijing over the last nine months. The change has taken place since Chinese leader Jiang Zemin consolidated his power at a party congress and began to put his stamp on China post-Deng Xiaoping. Apparently looking for any help he can get to steer China through the dangerous next stage of economic reform, and to safeguard the gains made in the past 20 years, Jiang has sanctioned an unprecedented public debate about what in which China must change.

Jiang is "looking to see where consensus coalesces," says a seasoned Western observer. Already, the debate has helped create a consensus about the need for rule of law and limits on government power if the market economy is to succeed. Through his advisers, Jiang is hinting at going further, ordering up research projects on how other political systems work.

That's not all. Jiang has made tough decisions about China's economic-reform agenda, giving the go-ahead for a long-postponed overhaul of state enterprises and the financial system. He has shored up China's rocky relationship with the United States. He is promoting transparency and exposing judicial abuses, and he is backing the notion of local accountability through village elections.

Nine years ago, when Jiang first came to Beijing as general secretary of the Chinese Community Party, outside observers did not expect him to last more than a year or two. He was a hastily recruited fill-in for the previous party boss, who was purged in 1989 for siding with the demonstrators in Tiananmen Square. Jiang held office at the whim of his famously mercurial mentor, Deng Xiaoping, who had cashiered two previous choices of successor. And, in meetings with foreign dignitaries and the media, Jiang showed little sign of the steely determination or political skills needed to win the power struggle expected over Deng's death.

Deng held on for nearly eight years after 1989—and Jiang held on, too. But he operated in Deng's shadow, even when the patriarch grew too ill to weigh in on policy. Then, in February last year, Deng finally died, and Jiang began ruling on his own terms. His performance since has proven him to be the canny political operator that his longevity at Deng's side suggested he had to be. Many analysts see in Jiang's recent moves first, an agenda for change, and second, a willingness to break the rules by which China is governed in order to achieve it. He has not yet created a legacy that would put him on a par with Deng, but it now seems at least possible that he might.

Jiang's first priority after Deng's death was strengthening his position in the party leadership. Hong Kong's successful return to Chinese rule a year ago helped. Skilful politicking in the run-up to last September's 15th party congress helped more. At the congress, Jiang dispatched one rival, former National People's Congress Chairman Qiao Shi, and got another, former Premier Li Peng, moved out of involvement in the core portfolios of the economy and foreign affairs and into Qiao's old job. Jiang then embarked on what the Chinese media presented as a hugely successful visit to the U.S., full of photo opportunities portraying him as a statesman who had earned the world's respect.

President Bill Clinton's June 25–July 3 return visit to China strengthened Jiang's position further. Local media made much of the fact that Clinton spent a full eight days in China, and that he brought "half the White House" with him. It was testament, the media said, to American recognition of China's importance, and, by extension, Jiang's.

Jiang is using his newly consolidated power to push forward an agenda set by economic imperatives. At the top of that agenda is the attempt to turn debt-ridden, state-owned dinosaurs into independent, market-driven enterprises. Reforming state-owned industry has long been considered China's most crucial task in its quest to modernize its economy. Leaders had been unwilling to take on the task partly for ideological reasons—public ownership is a cornerstone of socialism—and partly because they knew it would involve massive lay-offs.

But Jiang and his new partner at the top, Premier Zhu Rongji, decided to bite the bullet. Jiang is credited with making the decision at the September party congress to move ahead with state-enterprise reform. Former Shanghai party chief Wu Bangguo has been put in day-to-day charge of the effort.

Such reform requires an overhaul of China's financial system in which banks bail out state firms on orders from the party. Now the market, free from political pressure, must start allocating capital. Another vice-premier, Wen Jiabao, has been named to head a new Central Work Commission on Finance.

Both state-sector and financial reform require changes in the size and function of the party and government bureaucracy. If the economy is run on market principles, it does not need bureaucrats to micro-manage it. Premier Zhu, with Jiang's approval, announced in March a restructuring of government at all levels. By the end of three years, some 4 million officials are slated to lose their jobs in the central government alone.

> 'The leadership now sees the serious consequences of maintaining the old political system while doing economic liberalization'
>
> —A Beijing intellectual

Eventually, Chinese analysts say, Jiang and Zhu would have come around to the idea that for China's economy to function efficiently and rationally, changes are required in noneconomic fields, too—from law to politics. But the Asian financial crisis has lent an urgency to that logic; it points up the perils of economic development without parallel political and legal reform. And it has led Jiang to start flirting with ideas which, if followed through—that's a big if—could change China as profoundly as did Deng's economic changes in the 1980s.

"The disturbances in Indonesia have had a big impact on the leadership," says a former academic who convenes a biweekly discussion group on political change and regularly swaps ideas with policymakers. "The leadership now sees the serious consequences of maintaining the old political system while doing economic liberalization."

He says Chinese leaders saw in Indonesia President Suharto's relatives and cronies using their connections to amass assets, then blocking policies that threatened their interests, but that were needed to make the Indonesian economy healthier. What has particularly shocked the Chinese leadership, he says, is how the crisis has wiped out the fruits of 35 years of Indonesian economic development.

It is far from clear that Jiang Zemin wants to bring fundamental political reform to China. In recent months, however, he has shown at least an interest in alternative models of governance. His point man on such matters is Wang Huning, a professor of politics at Shanghai's Fudan University whom Jiang has recruited to be deputy director of the Policy Research Office under the party secretariat. That office now acts largely as Jiang's private think-tank.

Researchers at the mammoth national think-tank, the Chinese Academy of Social Sciences, confirm that Bai Gang, deputy director of the academy's Institute of Politics, has been assigned to prepare a report on presidential systems around the world. They say that it is widely understood within the academy that the assignment came from Wang Huning.

An academy researcher familiar with the study emphasizes that, so far, it represents just an "exploratory, theoretical forward position" aimed "at the long term." He underlines that "it is not on the agenda of the party or the government."

News of the presidential-systems study is nonetheless being avidly shared among the intelligentsia. Part of the reason for the excitement is that the topic plays into the debate in China about the relationships between party and state. The party and the state operate parallel hierarchies from the highest level of power (the Central Committee and the State Council) to the lowest (the party branch and the village committee). Theoretically, the party sets macropolicy and makes personnel decisions, and the state implements policy. In practice, the party implements policy, too. With their functions overlapping, the two hierarchies have had a history of friction.

As China's leaders have strengthened their support for rule of law—needed to safeguard economic reform—legal issues in the party vs. state debate have taken on a new prominence. It bothers many legalists that Jiang attends international forums in his capacity as state president when, according to Chinese law, the presidency is a ceremonial post with no real powers. By rights, they say, Premier Zhu should represent the state.

Jiang's positions of power are as general secretary of the Communist Party and chairman of the Central Military Commission.

Jiang could create a position of power for himself on the state side—say, an executive presidency on the American or French model. That, Chinese analysts say, could open the way for the party to step back from day-to-day governing. It could confine itself to setting direction for the country and nominating candidates for top posts. The change could stop there. Or, eager liberals say, it could continue. A presidential system would need a legislature with real powers and an independent judiciary. Much later, it might even lead to the sanctioning of opposition parties.

Jiang has given no indication that this is his game plan. Moreover, while establishing a powerful state presidency would require amending the constitution, constitutional scholars say they have heard of no one receiving orders to study such a change. But then, the Western observer notes, "the fact that Jiang Zemin has not made speeches about political change doesn't say anything one way or the other about his views. In that position, you can't and don't want to commit yourself." Jiang, he says, "has people continually testing the waters."

Chinese Academy of Social Sciences researchers say Jiang has also commissioned a study of how different democracies around the world work, and the lessons of their experiences. No one knows what Jiang wants to do with that study, either.

Some analysts see evidence of Jiang's interest in political change in his sanctioning of the public debate about ways forward for China. The debate has produced an intellectual ferment: Liberals, Marxists and nationalists, usually outside the party and government, are now vying in the pages of books, journals and select newspapers to put forward their varying visions of China's future.

He Qinglian's *The Pitfalls of China's Modernization* is one of the hottest new contributions to the debate. It's part of a high-profile series of books edited by an informal adviser to Jiang, Chinese Academy of Social Sciences Vice-President Liu Ji. In her book, He argues that much of the wealth amassed in China since 1992 went to those who exploited official connections and special privileges to gain access to cut-price assets like real estate and stocks. Only with improved moral education and a legal system which guarantees equal access to economic opportunities can China soothe public resentment, she argues.

Staying enigmatic, Jiang has not commented on the public debate, nor allowed those under him to do so. "If you are an official in the government or the party now, you have to be neutral," explains a researcher at the academy. "You are just supposed to support Jiang Zemin and Zhu Rongji. You are not supposed to support the radical Left or the radical Right." The implicit understanding Jiang and Zhu have with those jousting in public, the researcher says, is: "We will say nothing. You can talk. You can debate. You can go

to court. Maybe we'll adopt some of your ideas. We won't interfere."

That makes the debate markedly different from those of a decade ago. In the 1980s, policy discussions took place inside the party, in think-tanks linked to top party officials who used ideas as weapons in internal struggles.

No one is expecting Jiang to put political change firmly on his agenda before the year 2000, at the earliest. The rationale for the current debate—whether it's better protection of individual rights, limits on official power, or the exploration of different models of governance—is that new political solutions are needed to safeguard economic development.

For Jiang, simply steering China through intensifying economic and social dislocation will be a tall enough order. State-enterprise reform could throw as many as 40 million out of work, and Asia's financial crisis is slowing China's growth, hampering efforts to get them re-employed. The potential for unrest is real, and growing.

Jiang is trying to stave off strife by allowing more open debate. If he is the undogmatic reformer liberals hope he is, he may also be looking to the debate to produce a consensus for the political and legal reforms that economic stability demands.

Mao Zedong, says an academic, united China. Deng Xiaoping took China from a period of struggle to one of reform. Jiang, he says, "would just like to have the whole situation stable and growing smoothly." Even if that were all there is to Jiang's legacy, he might yet be ranked in history with China's political titans.

Article 4

Far Eastern Economic Review, August 20, 1998

CHINA

Excising the Cancer

China's Communist Party knows that festering corruption within might kill it. But the patient can't treat itself, especially as the disease has infected crucial organs of the party, including the police and judiciary. Only outside specialists can prescribe the right medicine—but will party leaders allow them to break its monopoly on power?

Susan V. Lawrence in Beijing

It was a scene that China's Communist Party dreads. On August 10, hundreds of angry citizens, many of them laid-off workers, demonstrated outside the red-walled compound in central Beijing where party leaders live and work. The protesters were investors in Xinguoda Futures, a firm affiliated to the People's Armed Police that had allegedly defrauded them of their savings. They had started by demanding their money back outside the firm's offices, but their wrath quickly turned against the party, taking the protest to the leadership compound—a reflex that shows how, to most Chinese, corruption begins and ends with their rulers.

The perception stems from the party's control over all the structures of society—an unbridled power that enables party and government officials to amass fortunes and "become like mafia bosses," says populist writer Liang Xiaosheng in his recent book, *An Analysis of Classes in Chinese Society.* "People fear now for the future, for in China only the Communist Party can check this evolution into a criminalized society," he writes.

And corruption is perceived to be getting worse. The cancer riddles the Communist Party, but—since the patient can't operate on itself—it can only be cured if the party submits itself to surgery by outsiders.

The party knows that corruption could kill it. Party chief Jiang Zemin has for the past year repeatedly called the fight against corruption "a matter of life and death for the party and the state." But if the party has diagnosed its disease as terminal, the old medicine—occasional campaigns, exhortatory slogans, highly publicized executions—isn't working. China's citizens grow ever more sceptical as they suffer rising unemployment and slowing economic growth.

In the search for a way to stem official corruption, a consensus appears to be emerging among China's planners and thinkers, some of them influential party advisers. They see a daring cure: fundamental political reform. Such reform would make the party accountable to outside institutions and groups, and limit the power of party officials.

The question is whether Jiang is willing, or able, to push through such far-reaching reforms that would bring corruption under control. And even if he does, will he move fast enough, or go far enough, to satisfy public expectations? He also has to consider the potentially fatal side-effects: If he does open up the political system, he might win the party a new lease on life. But the political system could then be infected with a different disease—ever more assertive questioning of the party's leading role.

Although the political-reform approach to combating corruption is being broached as never before, there remains opposition to it within the highest party echelons. According to a Chinese academic familiar with the debate, officials in the party's top corruption-fighting body, the Central Discipline Inspection Commission, cling to "traditional thinking"—code for resistance to political reform. Traditional thinking on countering corruption, however, doesn't seem to be getting them anywhere. "This is an urgent issue for them, but they can't find the effective means to deal with it," says the academic.

The commission is soliciting the opinions of two lay people on anti-corruption strategies: Liang, the populist author, and He Qianglian, a Shenzhen academic. Liang's views appeal to anti-market-reform Marxist as he argues that economic reform has made corrupt petty officials wealthy, while ordinary people have benefited the least. He's writings call for getting the party apparatchiks out of the economy, and for more "morality and political responsibility" among officials.

The commission isn't the only official body studying new ways to counter corruption. One centre of feverish theorizing on these matters is the strangely titled Communist Party Central Committee Translation Bureau. Originally an office for translating foreign ideological tracts, the bureau is now also a Central Committee think-tank. One of its researchers, political scientist He Zengke, is a leading thinker on corruption and an advocate of political reform to control it.

What allows the cancer to grow, He argues, is the absence of nonparty mechanisms to check the power of party officials. The Communist Party's approach to fighting corruption has always been to police itself. China has no political opposition or independent anti-corruption agencies. The news media are controlled by the party and civil society is weak. National and local people's congresses, the country's largely toothless legislatures, are meant to "supervise" central and local governments, He notes, but "they can't remove government leaders who abuse their power, without the consent of party leaders." Self-policing, says He, turns on a tenuous premise: "The success of anti-corruption efforts mainly depends on the political will and determination of top leaders," who must themselves be incorruptible.

'If we really want to fight corruption, we must make the transition to democracy'

—He Zengke, a researcher with the

Communist Party Central

Committee think-tank

His prescription for a cure is simple: "If we really want to fight corruption, we must make the transition to democracy." By that, he means competitive elections at all levels of the party and government. Currently, such elections take place only in villages. He thinks it's time for elections to move up to the townships.

He also believes China should open up its policymaking process. In Western countries, he notes, interest groups try to influence decision-making. In China, policy is made in secret, so interest groups exert their influence at the "output" end of the process, trying to affect implementation—often by bribing officials. "We should switch from influencing

implementation to influencing policy-making," He says.

These ideas may be too radical for some at the top levels of the party, but He is no voice in the wilderness. Respected sociologist Deng Weizhi and one of China's most famous economists, Wu Jinglian, both link corruption to political reform in a book, *Governing China: Facing an Era of New Systematic Choices,* released on August 3. "The roots of corruption," Deng says, "lie in the monopoly of power." In the same volume, however, Wang Huning, a political adviser to Jiang Zemin, warns that the political-reformist impulse should be directed towards "upholding and perfecting the party's leadership."

Even as the debate rages, the party is moving forward tentatively to put modest limits on official power, notably in the economy. The reform of China's vast network of state-owned enterprises—most of which will be sold, merged, turned into joint stock-holding companies, or liquidated—will cede to the market decisions now made by party officials. Jiang has also ordered the People's Liberation Army and the criminal-justice system to cease their business activities.

Moreover, the leadership has told party members that they should be bound by the law, and submit to the "supervision" of the media. Such exhortations are less noble than they sound: Both the media and the criminal-justice system remain under the party's grip. The media receive instructions from party propaganda bureaus. The police and the courts take their orders from the party's political-legal committees (*see chart*).

Nonetheless, Chinese, accustomed to reading political tea leaves, see a shift in the leadership's thinking on the party's relationship with the law. They point to Jiang's substitution of one ideogram for another in his report to the party's 15th congress last September: Instead of "rule *by* law," Jiang said "rule *of* law"—meaning that the law should no longer be used to guarantee the party's supremacy; instead, the party should acknowledge the supremacy of the law.

This is easier said than done. The party remains firmly in control of the legal system and law-enforcement agencies. Local party bosses, who appoint lo-

cal police and approve their budgets, often meddle in police work and influence investigations. Murray Scot Tanner, an expert on China's criminal-justice system, points to national plans to professionalize the police force as a possible solution. Under the scheme, local police are to focus on crime prevention and community relations, while criminal cases will be handled by a nationwide network of professional investigators, trained in forensic science. But, says Tanner, a visiting professor at Beijing's Politics and Law University, "it's going slowly. It costs money and it's happening at a time of budget and staff cuts."

The effects of the media's "supervision" of officialdom have been more immediately visible. Today, Chinese newspapers and television are full of detailed reports of official corruption. "Ten years ago, there was no reporting that exposed official wrongdoing," says Xiao Xiaolin, the host of *Law and Society,* a popular Chinese Central Television show watched by 100 million people. She says that many officials are now disciplined after CCTV exposes them.

Xiao adds that she encounters "less and less" editorial interference from above. Like many journalists and scholars, she wants the party to pass a press law that would give legal backing to the media's supervisory role.

In addition to the law and the media, a third weapon against corruption could be competition for official posts. Last year, Xiao took her camera crew into a government office in Hunan province to film more than a dozen candidates debating each other for a bureau chief's job. Applicants for the job, which had been publicly advertised, were assessed both by party officials and outside experts. Such transparency is a departure from the secrecy that previously attended party and government appointments.

Party officials normally appoint bureaucrats of every stripe, opening the way to cronyism, nepotism and the outright sale of official posts. China's liveliest newspaper, Southern Weekend, which is owned by the Guangdong provincial party committee, on July 31 reported the case of a county grain-administration party boss in Anhui province who sold posts. The lucrative position of a grain station chief could be bought for 30,000 renminbi ($3,620)—lucrative be-

Crooked Cops

On a highway in Anhui province last year, police pulled over an out-of-town truck loaded with cigarettes and demanded the driver's documents. The paperwork was in order, according to a report in the *Legal Daily,* but the police impounded the truck anyway. Only after the vehicle's owner presented the police with a 10,000-renminbi ($830) "donation," five bottles of expensive *maotai* liquor and five cartons of cigarettes were the truck and its contents released.

Of all the official corruption in China, the kind that probably stirs the greatest public anger is corruption by the police, often in cahoots with the judiciary. The collusion between them is pervasive because of the way the Chinese Communist Party runs the criminal-justice system.

All over China, policemen, prosecutors and judges sit together on local party bodies known as political-legal committees. If any of them is accused, they can close ranks to prevent the case getting to court. Even when local party bosses decide on punishment of party figures, they, not the courts, usually administer it, enabling the party to protect its own. In the case of the cigarette truck, for example, the local party chief and the county police chief were merely reprimanded. Often, corrupt police and judicial officials go unpunished.

The abuses are so widespread that public respect for law-enforcement agencies is at a dangerous low—a fact recognized by the party leadership. At a national conference of police chiefs in Beijing on July 18, Luo Gan, the party's top point man on legal issues, told his audience they had in their ranks serious problems "especially in having laws, but not implementing them; in implementing laws, but not strictly; in breaking the law in the process of implementing it; in taking bribes to pervert justice; in extorting confessions by torture; and in bullying and oppressing the public."

Since March, the party has stepped up efforts to address the problems. The state-controlled media have been given the go-ahead to expose police and judicial abuses, and do so with relish. Newspapers carry corruption stories daily and television reporters accost red-faced officials on popular news shows.

Ordinary people are being encouraged to turn in crooked cops, prosecutors and judges. Xiao Xiaolin, the host of a popular television programme on legal issues, says she receives 80 letters a day from viewers, the great proportion of them urging her to expose corrupt law-enforcement officials.

In hopes of increasing professionalism among police, judges and prosecutors, the party is producing new training manuals for them that spell out what counts as a confession extracted under torture or an illegal detention. The manuals are required reading for police and court officials nationwide.

Beijing is also encouraging citizens to make more use of the 1989 administrative litigation law, which allows individuals to sue government bodies, including police. A recent case in Hunan province, however, shows the law's limitations.

According to the *Farmer's Daily,* Hunan party authorities received a tip-off that women in the town of Zhongfang were travelling to Guangdong province, seducing businessmen there and then stealing their money. Party bosses told Zhongfang police to crack down on the problem. In late 1996 and early 1997, the police targeted 52 women—their only evidence being that the women had visited Guangdong. In a typical case, police came to Zhong Yuhua's home late at night, ransacked it, held her husband at gunpoint, and took her in for questioning. She insisted that she had been to Guangdong to visit her sister. Only after her husband delivered 2,000 renminbi to the police did they free Zhong the next evening.

Twenty-four of the women sued the police and won. Their money was returned. But the compensation they were awarded was a paltry 15 renminbi for each day spent in illegal detention, and 180 renminbi in court fees. The report mentioned no sanctions against the policemen involved.

Susan V. Lawrence

---

cause a crooked incumbent could line his pockets by buying grain at less than the state-mandated price, resell it at the full price and skim off the difference.

In the past year, party leaders have thrown their full support behind village elections, which raises the hope that at least some local officials will be electorally accountable. Even former Premier Li Peng, a conservative who is now head of China's parliament, the National People's Congress, gave his nod to the experiment when he observed village elections in Jilin province last month. Li also commended transparency as the key to keeping local leaders accountable between elections. He urged them to open the village finances to public scrutiny.

That principle should apply at all levels of government, says Fan Gang, who heads the National Economic Research Institute, a think-tank linked to the State Council's Economic System Reform Office. "We economists say that the first democracy should be public-finance issues in 10 test sites around the country. Fan says local governments should be given the authority to raise local taxes. Currently, local governments can only supplement their budgets through easily abused fines and ad hoc fees.

The party leadership appears ready to allow a modicum of transparency even at the highest levels. At the invitation of Luo Gan, China's top legal official, CCTV crews are filming selected internal sessions of the standing committee of the National People's Congress as it debates new laws. TV host Xiao quotes Luo as saying he wants to "bring the public into the law-making process." That footage will be edited for broadcast. But Xiao says CCTV may broadcast some of the sessions "live," starting this autumn.

Progressive as these moves may be, the party's efforts to fight corruption are met with cynicism by most Chinese. Witness the public reaction to the recent sentencing of former Beijing party boss Chen Xitong to 16 years in prison: People were generally scornful of Chen's long-awaited punishment, which was supposed to demonstrate the party's commitment to excising corruption from even its highest ranks.

Why the disdain? While Chen was still in office, the party blocked the media from reporting his excesses. After he fell, the party assigned itself the task of investigating his crimes. Only after three years did the party hand Chen over to the prosecutor's office, in February this year. Then, despite calls from law scholars for an open trial, the proceedings were held in secret, and lasted just one day.

Many Chinese concluded that had Chen not fallen foul of his longtime political rival Jiang, he might never have been brought down. Corrupt party officials might well figure not that they should fear the law, but that they should nurture their relations with top party leaders—and that could be an invitation to more corruption.

Although the debate on corruption runs far ahead of policy, party leaders nonetheless show signs of recognizing that the cure will only come with risky reform of China's political structures. Certainly Jiang Zemin appreciates the importance of being seen to fight corruption: The 1989 Tiananmen protests, which cost his predecessor his job, were as much about corruption as about democracy.

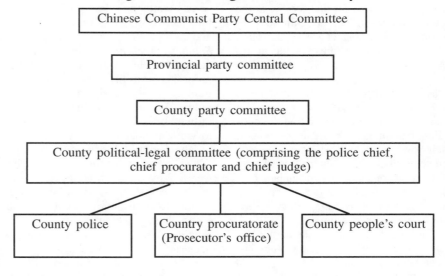

PYRAMID OF CORRUPTION?

Abuse of power pervades the entire body politic of china, starting with the ruling Communist Party

- Chinese Communist Party Central Committee
- Provincial party committee
- County party committee
- County political-legal committee (comprising the police chief, chief procurator and chief judge)
- County police
- Country procuratorate (Prosecutor's office)
- County people's court

CHINA

Rough Justice

The law is no longer an ass, but many judges still are

By Frank Ching in Hong Kong

Corruption doesn't come much more spectacular than a case in Woyang county, Anhui province, that the *Legal Daily* reported last December. The newspaper, published by the Ministry of Justice, related the case of a group of judges who decided to help a businessman friend of one of their number.

The businessman was having a dispute with Duan Shiying, general manager of a trading company in Jilin province. The judges manufactured a case against Duan, fabricated a set of files and had him arrested. After six months they ordered his release—but only after his family and business associates had coughed up 240,000 renminbi ($29,000). The judges split

200,000 renminbi among themselves; the rest went to the businessman.

The judges, all Communist Party members, were later reprimanded, demoted or subjected to public criticism. But only one of them received punishment in court—a one-year suspended sentence.

That's just one example from numerous reports of corrupt judges that have appeared in the Chinese press, portraying a judiciary that often perverts rather than enforces the law. China is building a legal system to support its evolving market economy, with several hundred new laws passed in recent years. But unless reform of the law is accompanied by reform of the judiciary, the rule of law is just as likely to become misrule.

The government has made attempts at judicial reform. The 1995 Judges Law aims to raise the quality of judges by requiring that law graduates have at least two years of work experience before becoming judges. But it also provided a loophole by stating that those without the proper academic qualifications may become judges after undergoing a process of undefined "appraisal."

The new president of the Supreme People's Court, Xiao Yang, has called for further reforms and for the media to supervise the judiciary. He has proposed a hotline and letter box for people to make complaints against judges.

Despite this, evidence still abounds that China's leaders don't fully comprehend the importance of putting the rule of law in the hands of those qualified in law. In March, for instance, the government appointed Han Zhubin head of the Supreme People's Procuratorate, or prosecutor's office. In that job, he is the country's top prosecutor, akin to U.S. Attorney-General Janet Reno. But Han, a former minister of railways, has no judicial experience at all.

The corruption and incompetence of China's judiciary stem from (among other problems) the poor training of judges, their meagre wages, their low status and government interference in their decisions. But underlying all these is something more fundamental: the Chinese attitude that judges should be political instruments rather than skilled and impartial professionals.

The attitude is rooted in the party's history and ideology. When the Communist Party came to power in 1949, it declared that "law is a tool for the oppression of one class by another." The party dismissed qualified judges and lawyers, whose professional training was deemed irrelevant. They were replaced by untrained cadres chosen on the basis of ideological purity and "good" class background.

Many, perhaps most, of the 170,000 judges in China today have little education in the law. Those who have sit on the top benches: The 100 or so judges who preside over the highest court in the land, the Supreme People's Court, all have at least a bachelor's degree in law. Many have master's degrees, too, says Wang Yanbin, a judge in the top court.

In the lower courts, however, a degree of any sort is a rarity. In fact, demobilized military men make up a high percentage of judges at the county level, where the majority of cases are heard. It's hard to say what proportion of China's judges are retired soldiers: The issue is controversial and few dare raise it in public.

He Weifang, a law professor at Peking University, was one of the courageous few. In a January 2 article in *Southern Weekend,* a Guangzhou-based newspaper, He asked whether it was appropriate for military men with no legal training to be assigned to work as judges. Would anyone, he asked, assign military men with no medical training to work as doctors?

The People's Liberation Army published a rejoinder in *China Defence News.* Why can't retired army men join the law courts, it asked, pointing to the military's contributions to the country. Under heavy pressure from the PLA, *Southern Weekend* published an apology, declaring that "the People's Liberation Army [including demobilized soldiers at every historical juncture] has made major contributions at each stage of socialist construction."

Clearly, the PLA considers sterling socialist credentials sufficient qualification for the administration of justice. Indeed, some judges themselves appear not to understand concepts basic to being one. A *China Youth Daily* report in February provides an example of a judge—a president of a court in Shandong province—who seems to have been unaware of the limits of jurisdiction. Informed that he had no authority over an enterprise in another province, he declared that his power extended "to the heavens above and the earth below and the air in between."

And power, of course, corrupts, especially when it is combined with poor pay. A vice-president of the Supreme People's Court is paid a little over 1,000 renminbi a month; a lower-court judge earns 300–400 renminbi monthly. Called on to adjudicate cases involving millions of renminbi, judges are exposed to many opportunities for corruption.

Some try to make opportunities for themselves. In cases involving business disputes, a court receives a percentage of the amount in dispute. So to drum up business, judges make "house calls" on enterprises to inquire about economic disputes. When they learn of one, they suggest legal action, offering their services and often implying a favourable court ruling. To maximize the court's income, a judge may even ask a potential plaintiff to exaggerate the amount in dispute.

Another widely reported problem is what the Chinese call "local protectionism." Since judges are paid by the local government, their rulings often favour their paymaster. And woe to the judge who forgets this. "If a judge rules against the local government," says a Beijing law professor who asked to remain anonymous, "the next day he will get a call from the municipal authorities saying one of the court buildings was constructed without the approval of the bureau of construction and will have to be torn down. There are many such cases."

The concept of judicial checks and balances also seems alien to the Chinese judiciary. Just as Chinese officials are loath to make decisions without consulting their bosses, so, too, judges regularly ask their superiors for "guidance." The result, says He of Peking University, is "to make the appeal process meaningless, since the higher court is unlikely to overturn the original verdict, which it participated in making."

Article 5   *The Washington Post National Weekly Edition,* April 27, 1998

It Looks Like Spring Again in China

There's a hint of greater openness and political reform in the air

By Steven Mufson

Washington Post Foreign Service

BEIJING

The intellectual seeds of liberal political reform are sprouting here, making this the most open spring since the massive pro-democracy demonstrations in Tiananmen Square were crushed nine years ago.

Influential intellectuals here in the capital are talking about promoting individual rights, expanding low-level direct elections, shrinking government and scaling back the ubiquitous role of the Communist Party.

A professor from the elite Communist Party school has blasted the "climate of fear" that he says impedes free speech. A leading business newspaper has hailed a "third liberation of thinking" and devoted two pages to excerpts from "Crossed Swords," a book that harshly attacks orthodox Marxist "leftists."

"Recently, the general environment has relaxed," says Mao Yushi, whose recent essay, "Liberalism, Equal Status and Human Rights," has put him in demand on China's long-dormant college lecture circuit. On a Saturday night in March, 150 students at the Chinese Geological University here crowded into a lecture hall to hear the 69-year-old economist praise Western liberalism, denounce the late Communist chairman Mao Zedong and call for human rights.

Beijing's spring appears to reflect a growing awareness within the party's senior ranks that it must move forward on political reform as Chinese society changes and the economy grows more complex and sophisticated. The party can no longer dictate every aspect of the economy or people's lives, nor easily represent the diverging interests of state workers, entrepreneurs, and city residents.

What started early this year as a debate among a few influential academics has moved this month into the state-run mass media, from Shenyang in the northeast to Shenzhen in the south.

> The opening is limited, and for the time being, true free speech and democracy remain distant. Open debate is a relative concept.

"Only in a democratic environment can people dare to voice new opinions and can their intelligence, wisdom and ability be fully brought into play," central party school professor Shen Baoxiang was quoted as saying by the China Economic Times this month. "If we don't encourage people to think freely and voice new opinions, our society will actually be utterly stagnant, though it may seem tranquil."

Many liberals wield economic arguments, noting that economic progress cannot rely on a handful of officials and experts. China's 1.2 billion people "are not only a 'labor force,' they are also the world's largest thought warehouse and brain. We can thus use the magic weapon of freedom of thought to achieve success," Hu Weixi wrote in a March issue of a magazine called Fangfa ("Way").

The opening is limited, and for the time being, true free speech and democracy remain distant. Open debate is a relative concept. For example, Li Bifeng from Sichuan, jailed for five years after the 1989 demonstrations, was arrested again this month for publicizing incidents of labor unrest. Police also seized written materials from Xu Wenli, briefly detaining the veteran dissident who has called on China's legislature to allow independent trade unions and challenged the government to live up to the United Nations human rights covenant it agreed to sign.

Nonetheless, many intellectuals here say this is the most fertile time in a decade for debate about China's political future.

Mao, the economist with the same name as the Chinese Revolution leader, traces the relaxation to January, when Reform Magazine's 10th anniversary issue featured a hard-hitting article titled "[We Should] Also Champion Political Reform," by Li Shenzhi, 76, a prominent reformer and the retired vice president of the Chinese Academy of Social Sciences.

The "implementation of political reform will determine the ultimate success or failure of economic reform," Li wrote. Rejecting the government line that feeding people is the top human rights priority, Li said China must adopt universal human rights.

In February, Mao, who in 1993 retired from the academy and established an independent economic think tank called

Unirule, organized a forum to discuss a new Chinese translation of "The Constitution of Liberty," a long-banned book by one of socialism's harshest critics—the late Austrian Nobel laureate Friedrich Hayek, a philosopher and economist. In the 1960 work Hayek argued, "A society that does not recognize that each individual has values of his own which he is entitled to follow can have no respect for the dignity of the individual and cannot really know freedom."

About 50 Chinese academics and government policymakers showed up to talk about the book's relevance to China. "Hayek refuted the idea that the ideal system could be artificially designed," Mao says. "He said it comes out of gradual evolution."

In contrast to Communist China's emphasis on class, commune and work units, Mao stresses respect for individual rights, including the right to pursue one's self-interest. "What I'm saying is that in the market economy, the individual has the right to protect the benefits of himself, while at the same time he has to observe others' rights," Mao says. "We need a society of equal status."

That has not always been the case in China, as Mao knows from experience. He was branded a rightist in 1957, his works barred from publication, his salary cut, his job taken away and his rights revoked. It took years to restore his career, and when he was invited to join the Communist Party during the 1980s, he refused.

No longer an outcast, Mao was interviewed recently by Liaoning provincial television on his fast-selling book titled "The Future of Chinese Ethics." In addition to his talk last month at the geology institute, he is slated to appear at Beijing University.

THE MAGAZINE FANGFA PUBLISHED A SPECIAL March issue on political reform, including articles on limited government, property rights, the separation of party and government, and corruption's link to Confucian culture.

"The most pressing issue is the separation of the powers of the government and the party," says Fangfa's assistant editor, Li Ke.

Perhaps for political cover as much as for historical accuracy, editor Li and others in this loosely knit liberal intellectual community argue that their views grow directly from the wishes of China's leadership. Li cites a comment by the late leader Deng Xiaoping, and pulls from a drawer a speech by President Jiang Zemin last September, pointing to a sentence about expanding democracy.

Some people believe Jiang was further encouraged to loosen controls on political debate by his October trip to the United States. In January, Jiang told the Central Discipline Inspection Commission that Asian governments are too "feudal," which some analysts took as another signal of relaxation. In March, newly selected Premier Zhu Rongji held a freewheeling press conference that further emboldened China's liberals.

The recent ferment carries extra meaning because of echoes of the past. In 1988, leading intellectuals debated political reform and held meetings on college campuses. Then, nine years ago last week, the death of Hu Yaobang, the ousted general secretary of the Communist Party and a patron of political reform, sparked weeks of student-led protests in Tiananmen Square that eventually were crushed in the bloody June 4, 1989, army crackdown.

Until this year, Hu has been a taboo subject, and political reform has been a sensitive one. Zhao Ziyang, the reformist Communist Party chief ousted in May 1989 on the eve of the military crackdown, remains under loose house arrest in Beijing.

In 1989, as now, a visit by a foreign leader was seen as a restraint on repressive action by the Chinese government. In May 1989, Soviet leader Mikhail Gorbachev visited Beijing. In June, President Clinton will travel to China, and many analysts predict that China's leaders will refrain from harsh repression before then.

Last week, dissident Wang Dan, a leader of the 1989 demonstrations, landed in Detroit after his release from a Chinese jail. Wang, 29, was freed on "medical parole" and flew into exile as part of a reported deal between Beijing and Washington to smooth the way for the June summit. After receiving a clean bill of health from doctors and being fitted for contact lenses, he said he wants to return to China as soon as possible.

By releasing Wang well in advance of Clinton's visit, China analysts says, Beijing can score political points with Washington and still avoid the appearance of yielding to international pressure. While making a gesture to the United States, China also rids itself of an internationally prominent political prisoner and one of the country's most persuasive and persistent advocates of greater freedom and democracy.

PARTICIPANTS IN THIS YEAR'S DEBATES SAY IT isn't a rerun of 1989. "What happened at the end of the 1980s—the 'political disturbance,' to use the prevailing political lingo—has made people cooler and more reasonable," says Fangfa editor Li, who is a party member.

Another intellectual says, "You can speak about liberalism, but you can't say 'Down with the Chinese Communist Party.' " Change, he says, would come from within the party.

"Both the government and the people learned lessons from that event," says Mao of Unirule. "The government knows that kind of suppression carries a very high cost, especially in terms of the international response, and at the same time the people know that in case of emergency, the government may open fire. So both sides are very cautious."

Article 6   *Current History,* September 1998

> "In the end, the fate of China's experiment in grassroots democracy may hinge on whether Beijing will commit itself to extending the process upward. The risks to the regime in moving forward will be tremendous. But after promoting grassroots democracy for a decade and allowing democratic elections to take root in the countryside, the risks of retreat might be just as high."

Village Elections: Democracy from the Bottom Up?

TYRENE WHITE

During President Bill Clinton's state visit to China in late June, his itinerary included a trip to a village outside Beijing whose leaders were elected by popular vote. For both the Chinese and the Americans planning the president's trip, the village stop was potentially very useful. China could use the visit to highlight its progress in promoting and implementing grassroots democracy, and to suggest the possibility of an expanded agenda of political reform. President Jiang Zemin could also use this public event to silence domestic critics of the grassroots initiative and possibly build momentum for further reforms.

The United States could use the village tour in precisely the same fashion. By exposing a skeptical American audience to signs of incipient liberalization and democratization in rural China, President Clinton might be able to increase domestic support for his trip and deflect his many critics. The village tour could be used to reiterate what has become one of the central themes of Clinton's foreign policy: the importance of freedom and democracy to economic vitality and political stability in the twenty-first century.

As it turned out, the village visit was completely overshadowed by live coverage of a joint presidential news conference and Clinton's question-and-answer session with Chinese students at Beijing University. Yet its inclusion on the itinerary was the logical culmination of a decade-long process that has transformed an obscure rural political reform into a widely touted democratization project with international and foreign

Tyrene White *is an associate professor of political science at Swarthmore College. She has written extensively on China's one-child policy and rural reforms and is coeditor, along with Chris Gilmartin, Gail Hershatter, and Lisa Rofel, of* Engendering China: Women, Culture, and the State (*Cambridge: Harvard University Press, 1994*).

policy implications. How and why did this transformation come about? And how do grassroots elections work in the context of continuing Chinese Communist Party rule? Whose interests do they serve?

MANAGING DISSENT

In the mid-1980s, when China's economic reforms began to take off, the country's rural institutions were breaking down. The reforms had begun to undermine the state's monopoly of economic and political power, and many local cadres saw more profit in working their own fields or starting sideline businesses than in carrying out difficult jobs such as collecting taxes and enforcing birth control. Peasants grew bolder in their resistance to authority, especially as price inflation, tax increases, and corruption began to erode the economic gains of the early 1980s and incomes began to stagnate or fall. Meanwhile, local governments sometimes ran out of money to buy peasants' grain and dared to hand out IOUs instead. Predictably, relations between peasants and cadres, and between cadres at higher and lower levels, grew tense, and skittish party leaders in Beijing began to worry about the prospect of rural unrest.

It was in this context that the foundation for village-level elections was established. In 1986 and 1987, heated debate took place on a draft law on grassroots organization called the Organic Law of Villagers' Committees. Adopted on a trial basis by the National People's Congress (NPC) in June 1988, the law attempted to address the problems of village-level organization and township-village relations by establishing a system of village autonomy (*cunmin zizhi*) and self-management.

The bill was designed to clarify the legal status of the village, which is not a formal level of government (the township, a level above the village, is the lowest official level of government), and to limit the rapacious tendencies of township and county governments to extract as much as possible from villagers to fund local development projects, pad budgets, and boost salaries. By declaring villages to be autonomous and self-managing, supporters of the bill hoped to establish a sound basis for village organization, and to temper the power of township officials by setting clear limits to their authority and defining village obligations explicitly.

If villages were to have any chance of achieving meaningful self-rule, however, they needed leaders who were empowered to defend village interests while still carrying out those unpopular and thankless tasks—collecting taxes, enforcing birth control—that villagers resisted but the state required. This legitimacy could come only through some form of popular representation or election. To that end, the trial law called for the creation of:

- villagers' councils (comprised of all adults or a representative from each household),
- villagers' representative assemblies (comprised of delegates nominated and elected by the villagers), and
- villagers' committees (comprised typically of about five elected village leaders).

Despite intense opposition from conservative county and township cadres—who feared the new law would erode their power over village leaders—the bill took effect in 1988, only to be derailed by the 1989 democracy protests and crackdown. In the repressive climate that followed, conservatives tried to repeal the law, only to find that they were blocked by Peng Zhen, a conservative party elder who had been instrumental in navigating the law through the NPC. Peng was convinced that village autonomy would stabilize the countryside and thereby strengthen, rather than weaken, party rule. In late 1990, a party central directive endorsed the trial law, and in 1991 it began to be enacted in a variety of locations across the country.

The law's implementation over the intervening years has led to the establishment and election of village assemblies, the public posting of village finances, and the drafting of village compacts that cover rules and regulations on all aspects of village life and state policy. What has earned the law so much attention at home and abroad, however, is the practice of direct elections of village officials every three years. While the shadow of Tiananmen still hung over China in the early 1990s, few in or out of the country took much notice of the rural reform, assuming that the countryside was a conservative backwater that served as a brake on democracy, or that any elections under Communist Party rule had to be a sham.

SPREADING THE WORD

The office in the Ministry of Civil Affairs (MCA) charged with the implementation of the village autonomy law, the Department of Basic-Level Government, worked steadily and methodically to establish model sites for villagers' autonomy in every province in the country, cultivating close ties with local authorities who were receptive to the program and attempting to win over those who were not. By 1992, contact with the Ford Foundation's Beijing office had translated into an initial cooperative agreement that allowed the MCA to bring foreign advisers and scholars to China, and to send members of the office staff to the United States for brief investigatory visits. That same year, the National Committee on U.S.-China Relations hosted an MCA delegation and introduced the visitors to the operations of local government in the United States. From this beginning the MCA office began to draw increasing media attention at home and abroad, as reporters started to investigate village self-government on their own, or with the assistance and cooperation of the MCA.

Throughout the early and mid-1990s, as international contacts, scholarly interest, and media attention escalated, the process of village elections became institutionalized in many areas. Although foreign observers, especially in the United States, were skeptical about how democratic the elections were, reporting on the topic began to shift as the shadow of 1989 receded and as more information about the electoral process became available. Chinese officials provided access to a wide variety of village election sites, including some that were exemplars of fair and competitive elections and others where elections had clearly been orchestrated by local party leaders. This gave outside observers the opportunity to gain a balanced view of the reform and draw their own conclusions. By the mid-1990s, officials who had confined themselves to the language of "villagers' autonomy" after the Tiananmen crackdown began to speak more openly about "grassroots democracy," and foreign observers, while remaining circumspect and cautious in their appraisals, began to acknowledge that village elections showed real democratic potential, even if that potential was rarely fully realized.

> The grassroots democratization project is a rare piece of terrain on which Chinese interests and American values seem to converge.

As Sino-American relations plunged to their nadir in the wake of the Taiwan Strait crisis of 1996, and as conservatives in Washington and Beijing pressed to gain the upper hand in domestic policy debates, those on each side seeking to avoid a breach in the relationship began to marshall evidence to support a policy of constructive engagement. By 1996 and 1997 that evidence included documentation of progress in implementing rural elections in Chinese villages, documentation that was leading even skeptical observers to appreciate the Chinese effort, however imperfect and limited it remained.

It was by this path that village self-government made its way into the seemingly distant world of foreign policy and Sino-American relations. In a landscape littered with conflicts over trade, human rights, and security issues, the grassroots democratization project is a rare piece of terrain on which Chinese interests and American values seem to converge.

HOW TO THINK ABOUT VILLAGE ELECTIONS

Village elections may aid Sino-American diplomacy, but are they useful and meaningful to Chinese villagers? Answering that question requires critical examination of some of the claims made about village elections.

Village elections are conducted democratically.
Although the Chinese press consistently makes this claim, it is true only by the narrowest definition of democracy. If by democratic one means that China's villagers get the chance to cast a ballot, then the elections are indeed democratic. If, however, one means that the candidates for village leadership have been democratically selected in a transparent process that meets with villagers' approval, and that elections to each post are competitive, or at least potentially competitive, then many—perhaps most—village elections do not yet qualify as democratic.

There is no question that hundreds of millions of rural residents now have the opportunity to vote for their village leadership team, a group that usually consists of a village chairman plus several deputies.[1] But specific election methods vary a great deal from place to place. All regions are supposed to conduct their elections according to the Organic Law of Villagers' Committees, but this still leaves ample room for provinces, municipalities, counties, and even townships to draft laws, regulations, or guidelines that specify local election procedures. In many regions local people's congresses have drafted laws or regulations, while local branch offices of the MCA have their own set of administrative regulations. This process may eventually lead to a set of harmonized procedures in individual provinces (units equivalent in population to large European nations), but for now there continues to be substantial variety in how the elections are conducted.

The one feature most areas have in common is that the number of people on the ballot exceeds the number to be elected by at least one, thus creating a small element of competition. Villagers are asked to vote for a slate of leaders (for example, choosing five out of six or seven candidates), and

may also be asked to indicate which individual on the slate they prefer as village chairman. A step beyond this is direct competition between two or more candidates for the post of village chairman, with the rest of the leadership team selected from a group of nominees that exceeds the total number to be elected by one or two. This type of competitive election first appeared in northeast China during the initial round of elections a decade ago, and was picked up quickly by other regions, such as Fujian and Hebei provinces, which have been leaders in implementing competitive elections.

Just as important as a competitive ballot is the issue of how nominees are selected. The Organic Law allows for several methods of nomination, including indirect nomination by a villagers' representative assembly, or direct nomination by any group of 10 villagers. Because such public forms of nomination can intimidate villagers or be manipulated by local party officials, some areas have recently moved to a new method of nomination called *haixuan* (literally, election by sea), in which all villagers are allowed to write the names of candidates they would support on a secret primary ballot. Then a process of public winnowing occurs until the two or three most popular candidates have been selected for the final ballot.

No matter what method of selection is used, the test is whether villagers are satisfied with the candidates who emerge, and with the process that produced them. Some provinces and regions score better on this test than others, and there can be wide variation even within the same county on how the nomination process is conducted. Interference by party and government officials at the township and county levels, or unlawful manipulation of elections by corrupt village election commissions, has led some villagers to lodge formal complaints demanding the voiding of election results. If the complaints are a sign of continuing attempts to rig elections, they are also a sign of the growing sense of empowerment some villagers feel in the face of such abuses.

Village elections are designed to prop up a repressive regime.
It is true that the Chinese Communist Party turned to village elections in the hope that they would ease tensions and create the stability that would assure unchallenged party rule. But village elections cannot be labeled a sham merely because they serve the party; they are a sham only if they do not serve the interests of villagers by making local leaders more accountable. On this point the early evidence, although partial and incomplete, suggests that many villagers believe the elections give them an increased stake and a voice in village politics. According to MCA data, voter turnout is high, including participation by absentee ballot, and roughly 20 percent of incumbents are defeated in each round of elections.

Still, it is also true that where local party officials are determined to control an election they may succeed in doing so, especially if no one in the village complains or the officials have powerful allies at higher levels. As a general proposition for all of China, however, the statement that village elections

---

[1]*Estimates of the proportion of China's 930,000 villages that has held elections range from a low of one-third to nearly two-thirds. This means that roughly 300 million to 600 million villagers have been exposed to the electoral process.*

are a sham is false. The fallacy here lies in assuming that the Chinese Communist Party is one uniform, monolithic authority, when in fact it is not. If China's economic reform has given us a strange, hybrid economic system, it has also given us a strange, hybrid communist system, one in which local power, prestige, status, and money are no longer monopolized by the Communist Party. If the party were monolithic, the villagers' autonomy law would not remain controversial in some quarters. Inland agricultural regions continue to drag their heels on implementing meaningful, competitive elections, while coastal areas in northeast and southern China work to improve the process by requiring campaign speeches, ensuring full secrecy in the balloting process, eliminating proxy voting, and providing absentee ballots for residents working outside the village.

The assumption that party power is inconsistent with meaningful elections underestimates the importance of local party sanction and support for getting the process right. Where elections have been successfully implemented and where nomination is fair and competition fully integrated, the county-level party secretary is usually a strong supporter of the process, setting the tone for township and village party leaders. So while it is true that party interference can crush all meaning out of the elections and turn the process into a sham in some locations, it is equally true that a supportive party leadership at the county and provincial levels can restrain township and village officials who might otherwise skew the election results their way.

The best indicator of a democratic process is the defeat of candidates who are party members.

This is one of the most common and most misguided assumptions that foreign observers make when evaluating village elections. Certainly it is important to know that non-party candidates can not only run for election, but sometimes win, turning out incumbents who are party members. This provides outside observers with added assurance that the electoral process is reasonably competitive and fair. Viewed from the point of view of China's villagers, however, the defeat of an incumbent who holds party membership may or may not be a good thing for the village, for several reasons.

First, what villagers want is what most people want in a local leader: someone who is honest, competent, capable of improving the local economy, and efficient and thrifty with tax money. They also want someone who will defend their interests in the face of pressures from county and township officials. Depending on local circumstances, local politics, and the merits of the candidates for village chairman, villagers may choose the candidate who is a party member as their best option. They may calculate that party membership will work in the leader's favor, or that his personal or family ties with township and county officials (or, even better, factory managers) will mean more jobs for villagers in township enterprises and greater economic development opportunities. Although party

membership no longer carries the clout it once did, it can sometimes be seen as an asset, not a liability, where village interests are concerned.

Second, while party members voted out of office will learn one kind of democratic lesson, those voted into office may learn another. Assuming there is open and fair competition from nonparty candidates, party members who must stand for election and reelection may begin to experience in a new way the tension between their roles as party members and as representatives of their village interests. As a result, what the party gains in legitimacy from winning elections it may lose in internal discipline as village leaders resist the implementation of orders that cut against the grain of village interests. Conversely, but equally positive from the vantage point of villagers, local party branches filled with members who must stand for reelection may become more responsive to village needs and interests and less arbitrary in their rule.

Finally, in some rural villages, the party, whatever its limitations, may be the only force that can restrain the power of a strong local clan or village faction that has come to dominate village life at the expense of the weak and vulnerable. From abroad, the party is easily perceived as the only political bully on the block. But other bullies have emerged in recent years as the power of local party branches has declined. For example, complaints are already being heard about attempts by clans to dominate local elections by engaging in intimidation and vote buying. In villages where this is the case, a strong and uncorrupted party presence would be a welcome improvement, especially if it could eliminate clan violence and break up criminal gangs. In short, the diversity and complexity of contemporary village life and politics are easily overlooked by those who see the Communist Party as the only threat to China's prospects for liberalization and democratization.

China is another Taiwan in the making, building democracy out of authoritarianism.

It is true that Taiwan's experience of first introducing elections at local levels has been noted and studied by Chinese officials, and that China's decision to begin at the grass roots echoes that experience. Yet the differences between the two are so great, and the trajectory of the People's Republic still so uncertain, that any attempts at comparison are entirely speculative.

One of the most important differences at this stage is the scope for elections in China as opposed to Taiwan. When the ruling Kuomintang (KMT) began to implement local elections in Taiwan in 1950 and 1951, it simultaneously introduced elections at the village, township, city, and district levels for positions on local councils. Like the Communist Party in China today, the KMT did not allow organized political opposition, and there was wide variation in the quality of the election process, with central and local KMT officials resorting to an array of methods to defeat, intimidate, or co-opt nonparty candidates.

The difference is that elections were not confined to the bottom of the political hierarchy, as they are in China today. The result, for China's village leaders, is that they alone have been elected to serve, while the government leaders they must answer to are appointed, and then confirmed by local people's congresses. Meanwhile, county and township officials, who are not subject to electoral politics, and with their careers, incomes, and bonuses in the hands of other unelected authorities, find themselves increasingly at cross-purposes with village cadres who live in intimate contact with their electorate and are subject, to some degree, to public accountability. Their instinct is to resist village elections altogether, or to manipulate the process in their favor to ensure the election of compliant local leaders who will make their lives easier.

NO GOING BACK?

In the run-up to the fifteenth party congress in September 1997, the issue of extending elections to the township level was debated at senior levels and tentatively endorsed by President Jiang Zemin. And on June 10, 1997, shortly before President Clinton's trip, a Communist Party Central Committee circular announced the party's intention to "make active efforts" to extend elections to the township level. The fears and uncertainties raised by this prospect, however, appear to have forestalled the creation of a timetable for implementation.

Yet unless China moves quickly to extend the electoral process upward to the township and county levels, forcing state officials to face the same public scrutiny beginning to fall on village leaders, the contradiction between the two political cultures will grow sharper. In the end, the fate of China's experiment in grassroots democracy may hinge on whether Beijing will commit itself to extending the process upward. The risks to the regime in moving forward will be tremendous. But after promoting grassroots democracy for a decade and allowing democratic elections to take root in the countryside, the risks of retreat might be just as high.

Article 7

The New York Times International, July 28, 1998

China Moves to Untie the Knots Between Military and Industries

By SETH FAISON

BEIJING, July 27—China's broad array of military-run and military-related enterprises are undergoing a deep transformation that is intended to yield a fighting force that is more professional, less distracted by nonmilitary business and, above all, better controlled by generals allied with President Jiang Zemin.

A series of deep-seated reforms, begun early this year but largely shielded from public view, emerged part way last week when President Jiang publicly ordered the armed forces to relinquish all of their multifarious business operations, ostensibly as a way to combat the military's extensive role in smuggling.

Yet that is only one part of a larger shift under way in China's military, Western and Chinese analysts say. Overall, the idea is to sort out the myriad pieces that make up China's jigsaw puzzle of a military-industrial complex into two sides: military consumers of weaponry on one side, and civilian producers on the other.

While many key personnel shifts have already been made, deeper structural changes may take years. So far, Mr. Jiang appears to have the support of the army's top generals, but potential opposition from middle ranks is harder to gauge.

In theory, the reforms will include these steps:

¶ Making the army more professional, by turning its focus back to military preparedness, and away from money-making.

¶ Making military units more accountable, by more clearly defining lines of control.

¶ Reducing the lawlessness, arrogance and hidden caches of money by officers, who have generated resentment among ordinary people.

¶ Forcing the army to rely on its official budget, $11 billion in 1998, and not on side earnings from the companies it has been operating.

¶ Helping Beijing better control the military's most egregious activities. An epidemic of smuggling goods into China has been dominated by the military in recent years. A spate of free-lance arms dealing, like selling missiles to Iran and smuggled AK-47's in California, has badly embarrassed China's diplomatic efforts to improve its image abroad.

¶ Reducing the overall size of the army to 2.5 million soldiers, from the current 3 million.

Right now, various units of the military control roughly 15,000 mostly small and medium-sized businesses, which experts say range from garment factories to transport companies to hotels.

It is unlikely that anyone inside or outside the military has a clear accounting of how much those enterprises earn, not to mention the money made by illegal activities like smuggling. It is equally difficult to ascertain just how much of this money goes to military operations, and how much simply disappears into the pockets of individual officers.

In a sense, Mr. Jiang is trying to redirect traffic at the chaotic intersection of China's military, politics, law enforcement and money-making, as unruly in recent years as the tremendous traffic jams that paralyze Beijing streets each day.

"The mainland's military-business complex at the beginning of the next decade may no longer be as high-profile, well-connected or sprawling as today," Tai Ming Cheung, an expert on China's military who works in Hong Kong for Kroll Associates, wrote recently. "But it is likely to remain powerful and more focused."

Indeed, Mr. Jiang is up against considerable obstacles. Officers in the army wield considerable influence in a system where access is still more important than talent.

Extracting a lucrative business from any owner can be difficult. In China, the highly secretive nature of the military's financial arrangements may make it difficult to discern real lines of ownership and control over businesses, even if they are ostensibly relinquished.

And in cutting off the military's freelance enterprises, Mr. Jiang may place an added burden on the Government. But it is unlikely that the military budget will be increased by more than 10 percent a year.

Moreover, though Mr. Jiang is pushing military reforms with a political campaign that demands compliance, Chinese officers accustomed to a history of such campaigns have a well-honed sense of how to adjust to the political line of the day, without actually doing much.

Today, apparently as part of the campaign, the authorities released a report, titled "China's National Defense," that for the first time made public the basic operations of the army. Although it contains no significant new information, the report is a symbolic opening for an organization long shrouded in secrecy and is intended in part to ease the concerns of China's neighbors about a military threat.

Mr. Jiang derives his ultimate authority in China as chairman of the Communist Party's Central Military Commission, where he succeeded Deng Xiaoping. Many of the changes under way in the military are a late stage of Mr. Jiang's efforts to gradually replace Deng military allies with his own.

One milestone fell in September, when Gen. Liu Huaqing retired from the Communist Party's ruling Politburo and from the Central Military Commission. General Liu was believed to have overseen many of the military's business operations, and his departure opened the way for significant change.

In March this year, as many of Beijing's central ministries were reorganized, the Chinese authorities made a brief announcement that an organization called the Commission of Science, Technology and Industry for National Defense was being reinvented to gain civilian control over most military-related industries.

The next month, the authorities announced the forming of a new wing of the army called the General Armaments Department, intended to oversee needs for new weapons.

They were small clues to important changes. China's military-industrial complex is so enormous that it is sometimes hard to see where it begins and ends. Yet the thrust of the changes was to divide the military industry into two clear sides, with the army deciding what it needs, and civilians running production.

"It's a push to separate the military buyers from the sellers," said a Western expert in China's military who is based in Hong Kong. "The domestic military manufacturers are extremely poor at delivering product on time. The idea is to make them more efficient."

Realigning the core businesses among China's 15,000 companies owned or controlled by the military will also inevitably lead to deep change involving some of the most lucrative and powerful positions in the country.

Mr. Jiang has said repeatedly that he wants to wean the military from its secondary income from the companies, and to make it rely solely on money from the Government.

Mr. Cheung, the Kroll expert, estimates that more than 95 percent of all Chinese military enterprises are small or medium-sized companies. It may not be difficult to sell or transfer most of these companies into civilian hands.

A more crucial question is what happens to the 500 to 1,000 large enterprises that generate about three-quarters of the untold billions of dollars earned by military-owned or controlled businesses, many of which are being consolidated into conglomerates.

The largest among them, like China Poly Group, Xinxing Group and Carrie Enterprises, are already international corporations with offices around the world, including in the United States. Military leaders will probably be more reluctant to let go of these jewels unless they are given a fair price.

Jonathan D. Pollack, an expert on China's military at the Rand Corporation, said official news accounts of Mr. Jiang's announcement last week were riddled with ambiguities about the scope of the order to separate military from business operations.

"This warrants some skepticism on the parameters of what Jiang is undertaking," Mr. Pollack said, "though I think even a few actions here to curtail some of the friskier business units would resonate with a cynical public."

One of the key factors in the transformation of the military and military-related industries is the reorganization of the Commission for Science, Technology and Industry for National Defense.

REORGANIZATION

China's Military-Industrial Complex to Be Split

President Jiang Zemin announced last week that the country's military would get out of private business. The details of the new structure are just beginning to emerge. Its primary branches are listed here.

Buyers

CENTRAL MILITARY COMMISSION

Military Armaments Department	Military General Staff Department	Military General Political Department	Military Logistics Department
Equipment purchases; research and development.	Existing military technology, equipment and personnel.	Publications.	Food, clothing, construction materials, fuels, vehicles.

Sellers

STATE COUNCIL

Commission of Science, Technology and Industry for National Defense

China National Nuclear Corporation	Aviation Industries Corporation of China	China Aerospace Corporation	China State Shipbuilding Corporation	China North Industries Group
Nuclear technology.	Aircraft builders.	Space program.		Builders of vehicles artillery, weapons ordnance.

Source: U.S. Department of Defense

The New York Times

In the 1980's, with Deng at the helm of China's military, the commission was run like a personal fief of the family of Marshal Nie Rongzhen, a veteran of the Long March, the defining experience for elder leaders of the Communist Party.

Only in 1994, as Mr. Jiang began trying to oppose the widespread nepotism in the military industry, was Marshall Nie's daughter, Nie Li, forced to retire from the board of the commission. Yet her husband, Gen. Ding Henggao, remained in charge of the commission until December 1996.

General Ding was best known outside China for championing the development of long-range ballistic missiles and the Long March series of satellite launching systems. He was replaced by another military leader, Lieut. Gen. Cao Gangchuan, a deputy chief of staff in Beijing.

Yet this year, as the commission was reformed, a civilian was placed in charge: Liu Jibin, a former Deputy Minister of Finance with experience in aeronautics.

In the past, the commission technically answered both to the State Council, China's Cabinet, and to the Communist Party's Central Military Commission, probably the single most powerful organization in China's vast political apparatus. The military commission often overruled or meddled with decisions by the State Council, causing innumerable delays.

Under the new reforms, the Commission for Science, Technology and Industry for National Defense is expected to exercise direct control over key groups in a civilian-run military industry. That includes China Aerospace Corporation, Aviation Industries Corporation, China North Industries Corporation, China National Nuclear Corporation and China State Shipbuilding Corporation.

Article 8   *The American Enterprise,* July/August 1998

The "Chinese Threat" Is Overblown

By Daniel Burstein and Arne de Keijzer

IN THE LAST HALF-CENTURY, America has had to deal with competitors who were either strong economically (like Japan) or strong militarily (like the Soviet Union). As the first new superpower of the twenty-first century, China will wield *both* types of power. Its economy is every bit as effervescent as Japan's or Germany's in their miracle years, on its way to becoming much larger. And its economic might will be matched by plenty of political clout—especially in Asia but also globally—and military muscle (China is in the nuclear club and has the world's largest standing army).

Watching China's rise in the 1990s, some observers have ominously concluded that China is an aggressive power whose drive for dominance could trigger the next world war. But the new China is fundamentally different from earlier global powers: It is powerfully inward-looking. Its main rival, the United States, is also a very different kind of superpower from any that has come before: It is not trying to gain an empire, it is reasonably good at sharing power, and genuinely believes in a self-determining world.

The United States is unique in another way. It may be the first modern great power to enter a downward spiral, then beat the disease of decline. For all these reasons, America and China may be able to enjoy a common future built on free exchange, zestful growth, and mutual prosperity.

China could one day become a Soviet-style geopolitical threat, but we think it unlikely. Fortunately, Americans will have many years to see (and prepare themselves) if this occurs. Meanwhile, as columnist Robert Samuelson has observed, "Treating China as an implacable adversary could become self-fulfilling."

No doubt China will be a nationalistic superpower that looks after its own interests first. Its legitimate pursuit of those interests will pose numerous complex challenges for the United States and others. China will become neither fully democratic nor fully capitalistic at any time in the foreseeable future. Its economic, political, and military relations will be driven by a political economy, a history, and a culture sometimes at odds with our own. This will inevitably lead to differences and clashes. But these need not turn into overall antagonism. China will be a challenge, but it needn't become a threat.

We believe China is mainly concerned with developing its economy, not expanding its empire. This inward focus results from deep forces in its Confucian heritage. Inside Asia, China will exert its clout—subtly most of the time, overtly when it deems that necessary. Still, China is likely to become a responsible power, not a rogue state. If the United States embraces rather than isolates China, extensive benefits can flow to the American people, including the benefit of minimizing long-term conflict.

In short, we differ from the hawks who paint China primarily as a threat to the U.S. Let's look now at their arguments, and explain where we differ.

"CHINA IS A MILITARY THREAT TO THE U.S."

Today's hawks warn that China is engaged in a massive arms build-up. It is said China is "bound" to become America's military adversary. Some imagine a hot war between the U.S. and China, arising over Taiwan.

True, China's annual military expenditures have been increasing, with the 1997 budget 13 percent higher than the '96 budget, which was about 11 percent higher than the year before. Various experts estimate the Chinese are spending somewhere between \$24 and \$87 billion a year on their military (depending on the complicated ways this can be calculated). But if we use one of the more plausible figures of \$36 billion, that means China spends less on its military than does Japan—constitutionally a pacifist state, forbidden to maintain offensive armed forces. And China's defense budget comes to about one seventh of ours.

Some of China's recent military spending represents catch-up after years of budget slashing by Deng Xiaoping while he was trying to free up every available resource for investment in the civilian economy. All through the 1980s, China's military budget was nose-diving as a percentage of GDP—from a onetime high of 16 percent to more like 5 percent today. Over the last 15 years, the Chinese army has declined from 4 million troops to 2.9 million. And at the Fifteenth Party Congress last September, President Jiang vowed to cut an additional 500,000. While military spending has been rising throughout Asia, China's expenditures have actually declined precipitously from 54 percent of the Asian total in 1980 to 34 percent in 1994.

Military experts agree China remains extremely backward in military armaments. When China in 1996 conducted missile "tests" into the Taiwan Strait in a transparent effort to intimidate Taipei, the gravest danger was the munitions' obsolescence. Robert Ross notes: "the missiles were so primitive that they could have veered off course and hit Taiwan." China's most advanced domestically produced fighter, the F8-11, is the equivalent of a late-1960s U.S. warplane, Ross adds, and even this primitive plane has yet to enter fully into production. The SU-27 aircraft China has bartered from Russia are less advanced than what the U.S. sells to Taiwan, and far less advanced than what Japan co-produces with the United States for its defense. Two Kilo-class submarines China purchased from Russia in 1995 were laid up in the harbor two years later with serious problems stemming from poor maintenance.

At the moment, China's naval prowess is dwarfed by Japan's. Beijing clearly desires a more serious blue-water navy, but with nearly 40 percent of its GDP now connected to world trade, that isn't so unreasonable. Some believe China is moving to develop an aircraft carrier, but developing and outfitting even a single 1970s-vintage aircraft carrier is a decade-long undertaking. Developing a carrier *group* is a 20- to 25-year project; so the U.S. has the luxury of a decade or two to observe China's progress before determining whether to treat it as an adversary.

China's occasional uses of force, such as its live-artillery tests near Taiwan and its seizures of disputed islands, obviously discomfit its neighbors. But those of us far away should remember that *every* case of Chinese projection of military power has involved disputed territory, border areas, and what China perceives to be its strategic interests of security and territorial integrity. We may disagree with Beijing's interpretations and criticize the use of force, but it is important to recognize that every such action has been narrowly directed.

The hawks are probably right that at least some strategic thinkers in China aspire, over the long term, to edge the U.S. military out of Asia. The hawks are also right that American armed forces ought to stay in Asia as a critical constraint on China's most dangerous tendencies. But many observers believe mainstream Chinese doctrine still favors a U.S. military presence in Asia, as a check on Japan's remilitarization and other trends Beijing finds dangerous.

The United States should maintain its military prowess and continue developing advanced weapons systems. The many possible dangers in today's world, including the small risk that China will turn into a rogue nation, should keep Washington on this course, but we needn't pretend China is a current threat to our formidable military.

China's increased arms spending bears watching, but we are confident predicting that even from 2010–2025, there will be no comparison between China's military capability and America's.

The world has probably never been so thoroughly dominated militarily by a single nation as it is today by America. China's increased arms spending bears watching, but we are confident predicting that even from 2010–2025, there will be no comparison between China's military capability and America's.

China is a nuclear power, and her warheads are the only ones pointed at the United States. But nuclear forces are not a major area of Beijing's arms build-up. Very few experts believe that China will soon present an aggressive threat in this area that could not be adequately checked by American defensive technology.

"But," argue some hawks, "it is only a matter of decades before China becomes the other military superpower on earth; so it's best to prepare now." To this, Owen Harries, editor of *The National Interest,* retorts that "a matter of decades is a long time in politics. By the time those decades have passed, the United States itself will have made further vast technological advances." The world will be a different place, and we will have a much clearer idea of China's intentions. If China emerges as the threat hawks fear, there will be plenty of time to prepare.

"CHINA IS AN EXPANSIONIST POWER"

Even if China doesn't directly threaten America now, Beijing is an adventurist power eager to dominate Asia, some argue.

If the United States doesn't "contain" China, they warn, China will eventually dominate Asia and endanger American interests.

If the hawks mean China will become the heart and soul of Asia, with many neighboring countries bending to its wishes because of its economic power (as countries all over the globe now bend to American influence), then they had better get used to it, because that is where the world is headed over the next 25–50 years. If the hawks mean China should be discouraged from flexing its muscles as it has recently in the Taiwan Strait and South China Sea, they have a point. But there is little evidence China is bent on making Asian conquests as the former Soviet Union routinely aspired to do.

China's provocations against Taiwan, and her military occupation of Tibet are anything but new. The determination to reincorporate Taiwan is almost 50 years old; the takeover of Tibet took place 40 years ago. China's claim to sovereignty over these areas and its assertion that these are internal and not international matters are persuasive to many.

China's claims of sovereignty over the Paracel and Spratly Islands, asserted against counterclaims by Vietnam, the Philippines, Malaysia, and others, have produced minor military spats over 25 years. These efforts—most recently, the Chinese erection of a reconnaissance station on the aptly named Mischief Reef in the Spratlys—have deeply disturbed the members of the Association of Southeast Asian Nations, who wonder whether China will be a cooperative, benign neighbor or a regional bully.

Legal claims to the islands involve a welter of confusing and ambiguous historical facts, agreements, and surveys. China essentially claims all of both the Spratlys and the Paracels. It has, however, been willing to participate in discussions with its Southeast Asian neighbors. In March 1997, when Vietnam protested the erection of a Chinese oil rig in disputed waters, negotiations ensued. When the Philippine government protested China's activities on another small disputed island in May of that year, China pulled down the hut that had caused the controversy. And the hawks never mention that Taiwan generally concurs with Chinese claims to these islands. Indeed, Taipei agrees in principle with Beijing on most Chinese territorial issues.

There are important long-term issues of possible offshore oil and control of sea lanes. But much of the argument over these particular islands is more symbolic than strategically consequential, part of the give-and-take of negotiating a new order in Southeast Asia—and all claimants understand that. Contrary to alarmist suggestions, the fall of an obscure atoll in the Spratlys is hardly the moral equivalent of Hitler's annexation of the Sudetenland, nor is Beijing a dangerously maniacal regime eager to lash out in all directions. It is a deliberative and conservative power—at least most of the time.

CHINA BEHAVES AGGRESSIVELY TOWARD TAIWAN

Yes, it does. During Taiwan's 1995–96 presidential campaign China was crudely threatening and bellicose toward Taiwan. But stunning and disquieting as those actions were, they were much less consequential than other recent developments in the cross-strait relationship. One hears far more talk in Washington about protecting Taiwan from an aggressive China than one hears in Taiwan, where China is more often viewed as a business opportunity than a threat. Over $20 billion of Taiwanese money flowed into China between 1990–96, and more than 20 percent of Taiwan's vast exports now go to China. Some 40 percent of all companies listed on Taiwan's stock market have mainland operations. Not only are China and Taiwan major trading partners, but Taiwan is sending the mainland a significant flow of technology and managerial know-how.

Much of the Taiwanese shoe industry has moved its operations to China (just as this industry once migrated from America to Taiwan). In Dongguan City, a boom town in China's Guangdong province, an incredible 1,350 companies belong to the local Taiwanese Association. With the complete acquiescence of local Chinese authorities, Taiwanese managers in Dongguan City organize thousands of workers—most of them young peasant women from the Chinese countryside—who make many of the Reeboks, Nikes, and other running shoes sold in America. With on-the-ground cooperation working well, no wonder the Chinese took no punitive economic action against Taiwanese businesses even at the height of the 1995–96 political wrangling.

Taiwanese companies are helping China up the high-tech ladder in everything from cellular phone software to biotechnology. Taiwan's largest company, Formosa Plastics, has put a $3.2 billion power plant in China's Fujian province. Taiwan-based China Chemical & Pharmaceutical Company is building a $50 million biotech facility on the mainland.

A generation of peaceful initiatives has changed the China-Taiwan relationship from one of mutual isolation and artillery shelling to one of dialogue, trade, and tourist exchanges. If anything like today's developing cross-strait relationship existed among former enemies in the Middle East, the foreign policy wisemen would hail it as a triumph for peace. But in China, the same experts can only see conflict.

We do not dismiss the possibility of another Taiwan crisis breaking out—if, for example, Taiwan declared independence and China responded militarily. The intensity of Beijing's belief that reunification with Taiwan is its right, duty, and destiny is undeniable. But a balanced look at all the facts suggests the big story is the way normality and peace are breaking out in China-Taiwan relations, despite some extremely troubling moments.

"CHINA IS A ROGUE NATION THAT REFUSES TO PLAY BY INTERNATIONAL RULES"

Many people have been horrified by elements of Chinese behavior in recent years: selling nuclear weapons-related equipment to Pakistan; helping Iran develop a nuclear reactor; selling chemical warfare components to Iran; smuggling AK-47s into the United States for sale to California street gangs; and committing an assortment of economic sins ranging from running up a giant trade surplus with the U.S. to operating state-owned factories whose main business is pirating American intellectual property.

These behaviors fall far outside the bounds of international acceptability, and must be condemned and punished. Trade sanctions against the Chinese entities selling chemical warfare materials to the Iranians are thoroughly appropriate, for example. But amid the din of criticism some perspective has been lost. China is a country that has gone from near-total diplomatic isolation 25 years ago to being an active and responsible member of the United Nations. In Security Council votes, China has used its veto power extremely rarely. In fact, it has sided with the United States more often than not and has politely abstained rather than use its veto when it did not wish to endorse U.N. peacekeeping missions it judged too interventionist.

China is now a member of numerous other international organizations, ranging from the International Monetary Fund, the World Bank, and the Bank for International Settlements to APEC (the Asian Pacific Economic Cooperation forum) and other regional bodies. These affiliations are weaving the nation into a network of international rules, most of which it follows. Beijing has also become a signatory to numerous global environmental agreements, and even to nine international human rights agreements, although its compliance with these has been very mixed.

China is, unfortunately, a major arms merchant. Some of its weapons are highly competitive in global markets, and its foreign-policy objectives can be bolstered through arms sales. Overall, of course, China is a small arms trafficker compared to the United States; its sales total about 10 percent of American arms exports. China's sales are also considerably less than those of countries like France and Israel. China has sold arms to countries with which the U.S. would prefer it not do business. But every country involved in the arms trade, including the United States, ends up selling to rogue regimes. The story of how the United States built up Saddam Hussein's arsenal in Iraq is well known.

China watchers Andrew Nathan and Robert Ross argue that China's arms sales have recently been relatively clean. They note that "China was negotiating to sell M-9 missiles to Syria, but canceled the agreement in 1992 after lengthy negotiations with the United States. . . . Following the U.S. decision to sell F-16s to Taiwan, Beijing undertook to help Iran develop a nuclear reactor. In response to complaints from the United States . . . China announced in 1995 it would suspend the agreement." More recently, U.S. officials seem to have convinced Beijing to rein in sales of cruise missiles to Iran.

According to Nathan and Ross, the glaring exception to China's willingness to play ball with the United States on arms sales and nuclear issues is Pakistan, where the Chinese have abetted Islamabad's drive to develop nuclear technology. Pakistan, of course, is one of the most important countries in the world to Beijing, which sees it as a strategic counterweight to India, a link to the Islamic crescent in the Middle East, and a bulwark against Russian influence in western Asia. Beijing has

WHY OUR HARDLINERS ARE WRONG

BY ROBERT ROSS

China lacks the ability to conduct sustained military operations more than 100 miles from the Chinese shoreline. China is a formidable land power, but in maritime Southeast Asia, where U.S. interests are most at stake, China is militarily inferior even to such countries as Singapore and Malaysia.

China may succeed in modernizing its military. But it may fail, too—economic and technological modernization is a precarious enterprise. As an export processing zone for the advanced industrial countries, China has succeeded in raising living standards and its GDP, but this is a far cry from developing the economic and technological capabilities to field a twenty-first-century military force.

U.S. military supremacy is so overwhelming that Washington has the luxury of being able to observe Chinese technology development and weapons production before adopting countervailing policies. . . . Washington has global superiority in every phase of warfare, and while China is trying to catch up, the United States is not standing still. . . . U.S. technology and weapons modernization are advancing so rapidly that, in all probability, with each passing day and despite its strenuous efforts, China's technological and military capabilities are losing ground rather than catching up with those of the United States.

Politically, too, the American alliance system in Asia is superior to anything the Chinese can hope to have. Logistically, the U.S. alliance with Japan and its access to basing facilities throughout the region give the United States an enormous advantage. Diplomatically, China is increasingly viewed in the region as a problem to be managed, while the United States is seen as a relatively disinterested powerbroker whose aims are compatible with regional peace and prosperity for all. . . . With such logistical and diplomatic superiority to bring to bear, current U.S. defense spending and weapons acquisitions are already more than sufficient to hedge against China's potential development of advanced military capabilities.

—*Excerpted from the fall 1997 issue of* The National Interest.

had friendly relations with Pakistan longer than it has with the United States or any other country. Whatever aid China supplies to Pakistan is part of a long-term foreign policy, not opportunistic adventurism.

The FBI is still investigating the AK-47 case, but we doubt Beijing has any official plan to profit from American gang wars or to destabilize the United States politically by running guns to gangs. Rather, this looks like other cases in which China's central controls have broken down: units that were formerly part of state enterprises are now trying to fend—and profit—for themselves, with varying degrees of intelligence.

It's not shocking that competing power centers will sometimes abuse their nascent freedoms in the new Chinese economy. Americans should seek the punishment of Chinese individuals or companies that violate U.S. law. But that is very different from imposing economic sanctions on all of China.

On the trade front, there are many reasonable complaints about China's practices—though fewer than there were about Japan a decade ago. China's market for trade, and especially for investment, is far more open than the Japanese market was then. Unlike Japan in the past, which sought to have a positive trade balance with all its partners, China runs a trade deficit with some major trading partners (such as Japan), and only a small surplus with Europe.

China has gone from almost no participation in the world trading system to $300 billion in annual trade, a stunning 50–60 percent of the country's GDP, which is far higher than either the American or Japanese percentage. All this has happened in just 20 years. Foreign investors have been able to invest in companies, buy assets, and even arrange leveraged buy-outs and other Western financial practices that to this day are virtually impossible in Japan.

The debate over China's entry into the World Trade Organization is an extremely important one. China wants to retain the special conditions and exemptions of a developing country; the United States wants it to be treated like any other developed country. What is interesting is that China is arguing its case, and not seeking to join the WTO under false pretenses or trying to assert its right to special exemptions after the fact. It is taking a principled position on its membership from the point of view of its own interests.

American and Chinese interests do diverge on some key points. When tensions arise, China will generally assert its own interests. This does not make it a rogue state, but an independent great power on the road to becoming a superpower. It would be naive to expect such a superpower to simply follow all the rules already written by preceding great powers. China will want to be an insider to the process of global rule making. And American interests will be best served by making it possible for China to become that insider, rather than allowing it to follow some of its more extreme impulses.

"CHINA IS A DICTATORSHIP AND THE WORLD'S LEADING HUMAN RIGHTS VIOLATOR"

China has in the recent past shown a willingness to let might make right. But the picture has grown brighter as China has become the subject of diplomatic criticism from Americans and others. The Chinese people are now more relaxed about individual expression than they have been in their entire history. Information sources have burgeoned, with a recent count of over 10,000 publications now in circulation, compared to the sparse handful of officially approved magazines and newspapers 20 years ago. About 90 percent of the new publications are neither launched nor controlled by the Communist party.

Academic freedom has also expanded enormously. China's think tanks now publish respectably independent studies and papers. Books that are out of favor with the government are published anyway and even become best-sellers. Protest lyrics are heard in Chinese rock songs. Party leaders are unceremoniously dumped in free village-level elections. For the most part, people in China can live comparatively freely, so long as they do not openly challenge the central premises and personalities of Communist rule. That is, of course, a huge speed bump in the middle of this march of progress. It leaves China far, far short of genuine democracy and freedom.

There are several thousand political prisoners held by the Chinese government. Thousands more are under house arrest or are closely watched. Many more have abandoned their dissent because the climate is too repressive. Thousands have gone into exile.

But even if one added up all those who face one form of repression or another, the number of people persecuted for their political beliefs today is the lowest it has been since the 1950s. No one who visited China in the late '60s or early '70s can go back today without noticing the enormous human diversity that was previously repressed. This has happened largely because of the breakup of the "snitch dynasty" (as the Canadian journalist Jan Wong so aptly labeled it) and the old *danwei* (work unit) system. Until recent years, the Communist party controlled the country down to street level, creating "neighborhood party committees" to keep track of everything from individuals' loyalty to the party to their cooperation with family-planning policies. Workers were overseen by the party committee of their factory or work unit as well, which controlled their work and residency permits and compiled dossiers that would have made the East German secret police blush. The loosening of the iron grip of these institutions has brought immeasurable relief to hundreds of millions. Yet it is a story we hear little about.

There are religious believers who are persecuted in China today, and genuine freedom of religion is far from a reality. But there are more people practicing Christianity, Buddhism, and folk religions at present than at any time since the 1950s. Christianity officially has 10 million adherents; researchers in Hong Kong and the United States claim the number to be between 12 and 65 million—and perhaps even as high as 100 million.

China scholar Merle Goldman observes "a qualitative difference between the human rights abuses" of the Mao Zedong era and the current era. Whereas Mao attacked whole classes of people, such as Western-oriented intellectuals in the Cultural Revolution and 30 million peasants during the Great Leap Forward, today's repression of dissidents "is directed against specific individuals, not against their families, friends, and the class to which they belong." Goldman notes that Mao's prisoners were often tortured and died in captivity, whereas today's dissidents usually reappear in public after some jail time. The most famous of those dissidents, Wei Jingsheng—who coined the notion of democracy as China's badly needed "fifth modernization"—was released to U.S. resettlement in 1997 after nearly 16 years in jail.

Owen Harries draws another distinction between China's present oppressors and their precursors:

> There will be some terrible occasions when the violations of human rights will be so horrendous that the absolutist moral approach becomes—or should become—compelling. Such was the case with the murderous regimes of Hitler and Stalin. . . . China today does not constitute such. . . . The best estimate of the number of political prisoners in China currently is 3,000. In a population of 1.3 billion, this amounts to 0.00023 percent, which is hardly the equivalent of the Gulag or Nazi concentration camps. Ironically, back in the early 1970s, when most Americans, liberals and realists alike, were enthusiastically applauding the U.S. opening to China, the Maoist regime *was* in the same league as the Hitlerite and Stalinist regimes.

While the human rights situation in China is not good today by American standards, it is not unlike that of Indonesia, India, or Saudi Arabia. Yet the United States is able to have normal relationships with these countries that are not overwhelmed by human rights concerns.

There is a deeper question here. Is attainment of Western-style democracy and respect for human rights an appropriate expectation for China? Neither China's leaders nor the vast majority of its people have so far set political democracy as a goal. They are clearly focused on achieving a higher standard of living, and mostly succeeding. Even within China's intelligentsia there are few democrats. Most Chinese are consumed with the national project of modernization and economic development, and see campaigns for political rights as a diversion, even criticizing them as impractical. A public opinion poll conducted on the eve of China's takeover of Hong Kong asked whether the takeover was desirable. While only 4 percent of Americans thought so, fully 62 percent of Hong Kong Chinese thought it was.

Stanford professor Henry Rowen argues that those who really believe in bringing democracy to China should hasten it with favorable U.S. trade policies—because social development and middle-class incomes will create the appetite for democracy in China. We agree.

MOST RISING POWERS IN MODERN HISTORY have been keen to extend their global reach. But China has little interest in global issues that don't have a specific bottom line for Chinese interests. Almost all of China's efforts to throw its weight around come when vital Chinese interests are perceived to be at stake close to home, such as in Taiwan or Tibet. "We are too busy with our own internal challenges to threaten other countries economically or militarily," says Zhang Haoruo, head of the powerful State Commission on Economic Restructuring. He adds, "I wish I could say our current agenda will take us only a few years to solve. But realistically, China will be occupied with its internal domestic reforms for half a century."

The huge and knotty problems China faces domestically will constrain her for decades. Bringing the vast peasantry out of its backwardness, modernizing the national infrastructure,

moving the coastal prosperity inland—these are China's main goals at century's end. And that more than anything else makes it unlikely China will threaten anyone else.

Daniel Burstein and Arne de Keijzer are co-authors of the new Simon & Schuster book Big Dragon, *from which this is adapted.*

Article 9

The World & I, October 1998

Which Way for the Chinese Economy?

In the next decade, the Chinese economy is less likely to maintain high two-digit growth, even assuming a stable political situation.

RENHONG WU

China's economy achieved a remarkable two-digit growth (10 percent annually) from 1981 until 1997. But in the first half of 1998, economic growth slowed down and exports drastically dropped. Can China's boom continue in the next decade? And what is the trend of its currency?

In 1998, China's economy is facing great challenges. It is likely that economic readjustment will take two or three years unless the government pushes the GDP growth up to the targeted level of 8 percent.

These challenges are due to not only the external shocks from the Asian monetary crisis but also internal problems. The major challenges are: excessive capacity in industry, increasing unemployment, and lower export growth.

Recent developments

In the first half of 1998, China's GDP growth was 7 percent, 1.8 percentage points lower than the average growth

rate of 1997. The other major macroeconomic indicators are as follows:

Industry grew at 7.9 percent, 3.2 points lower than in 1997. Industry is the leading indicator of China's economic growth, because it is the largest sector in the economy (49 percent of GDP).

Fixed investment increased 13 percent (in real terms), 4.7 percentage points higher than in 1997. Higher investment growth has been pushed by increases in government spending for infrastructure since the second quarter.

Consumer sales increased by 6.8 percent (in real terms), 3.4 percentage points lower than in 1997.

Consumer price index was -0.3 percent, indicating deflation.

Unemployment increased to approximately 8 percent (about 16 million) in cities in the first quarter of 1998, which included about 5.7 million registered unemployed and 10 million laid-off workers. The increase in unemployment was brought about by further reforms of the state-owned enterprises and lower growth of GDP.

Signs of Growth . . . and Slowdown

Positive factors that support China's continued economic growth include: high savings and investment rates, abundant low-cost labor, large domestic markets, and substantial foreign direct investment.

Challenges to economic growth include: excess capacity in the industrial sector, a decrease in exports, inefficient state-owned enterprises, and poor performance in the financial sector.

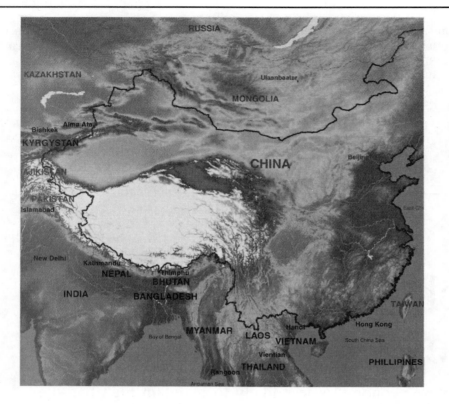

Exports grew by only 7.6 percent, 13 percentage points lower than in 1997. Imports grew 2.2 percent. The trade balance reached a $22.6 billion surplus. The significant drop in exports was mainly attributed to the recessions in China's major trade partners (Japan, Korea, and other Asian countries). Also, the intensified competition from the devaluations of other Asian currencies affected China's export growth.

The Chinese currency (Renminbi/ yuan) remained stable. The exchange rate was 8.2798 Renminbi against one U.S. dollar in June, practically unchanged from January. The foreign reserves reached $140.5 billion in the end of June, slightly higher than that in the end of 1997 ($139.9 billion). This increase was attributed to the continued trade surplus and foreign capital inflow. Direct foreign investment in China reached $20.45 billion, a 1.3 percent drop compared with the same period last year.

The lower economic growth was mainly due to a drop in industrial growth, lower export growth, and decreasing consumer sales. The slowdown of industrial growth can be attributed to excess capacity. The utilization of production capacity in many industries was less than 50 percent in 1995.

Now the situation is worse. The overcapacity is not just a business cycle phenomenon. It has appeared since the end of the 1980s and was intensified by the overinvestments in 1992–94. The adjustment of the excess capacity is slow and will take several years, due to the nature of state-owned enterprises and underdeveloped labor and capital markets.

Lower consumer sales were mainly caused by negative expectations. The large number of layoffs not only directly affected the purchasing power of those involved but also greatly impacted general expectations of future job security and income, which has been reinforced by government announcements of the reform of state-owned enterprises and a 50 percent reduction of the government workforce.

It is expected that 1998 economic growth will be 7 percent. The government may further increase investment to push economic growth, but this will come at a cost of future inflation and a larger budget deficit or government debt.

Future economic growth: challenges and possibilities

During the next decade, the Chinese economy is unlikely to maintain two-digit growth; the expected growth rate will be about 6 to 7 percent, assuming that the political situation remains stable. During this period, some positive factors that supported the high growth of the past 17 years will remain.

But a growth rate as high as two digits will be unlikely because the contributions of some factors will decline: for example, the exceptionally large inflow of foreign capital, the boom of rural industry (township enterprises), and the initial effects of some reforms. More importantly, there will be new and greater challenges for economic growth.

The positive factors that will continue to support China's relatively high economic growth are as follows:

High savings and investment rates. A high savings rate will remain in China because of its culture and tradition; because people expect the cost of education, housing, and medical care to rise in the future; and because of increasing job insecurity as reforms continue. It is expected that China will continue to maintain a rate of over 30 percent gross national savings and a similarly high investment rate in 1999–2010.

Abundant and low-cost labor, as well as the improvement of human capital. Well-educated and trained professionals and workers have been available in China since the mid-1990s.

The dynamic of the private sector. Private enterprises, foreign-funded companies, and stock companies will continue to play an important role in the economy.

Large domestic markets. The huge population and its increasing income offer potentially enormous consumer markets, with consequent advantages in terms of economies of scale and scope.

The inflow of foreign direct investment (FDI). FDI will continue to flow into China, though the absolute amount may decline. This is because China is a potentially large market and China's economic fundamentals, except for the banking sector, have been fairly stable.

The still low-level per-capita stock. This means that China has a potential to achieve relatively high economic growth. The effect of diminishing returns will not be significant until 2010. China's per-capita GDP is low (about $800 in 1997 by current exchange rate), making China far behind the matured economies of Japan

China

Official Name: People's Republic of China.

Capital: Beijing.

Geography: Area: 3,696,100 square miles.

Climate/Topography: Two-thirds of the nation is mountainous or desert; only one-tenth is cultivated. Rolling topography rises to high elevations in the northwest and southwest.

People: Population: 1,221,591,788. Ethnic groups: Han Chinese, 92 percent; Tibetan, Mongol, Korean, Manchu, others, 8 percent. Principal language: Mandarin (official).

Religion: Officially atheism; Confucianism, Buddhism, Taoism, some Islam, Christianity.

Education: Literacy, 82 percent.

Economy: Industries: iron and steel, textiles and apparel, machine building, armaments. Chief crops: grains, rice, cotton, potatoes, tea. Minerals: tungsten, coal, oil, mercury, iron, lead. Per-capita GDP: $2,900.

Government: Communist Party-led state.

and the newly industrialized Asian countries.

Nonetheless, new and greater challenges to economic growth appear on the horizon: There is excess capacity in the industrial sector. Adjustments will take many years. This new problem will hamper economic growth because China has no well-developed mechanisms of liquidation, takeover, and bankruptcy, and its capital and labor markets as well as its social security systems are underdeveloped. Thus, the mobility of capital stocks and labor is very low.

China may find it difficult to maintain a high export growth rate. For this to happen, China needs to upgrade its products and improve its technology. The future market growth for low-end and cheaper textile goods and electronics is limited.

The state-owned enterprises (SOE) are still generally inefficient, and reforming them will take a long time. Quick, radical reform is unlikely because of the risk of social instability resulting from higher unemployment. SOE reform will proceed at a rate mainly dependent on reforms in related areas—social security, labor markets, capital markets, housing, government-business separation, and the legal system.

Economic growth may be slowed by poor performance in the financial sector.

The banking sector is poorly managed and not well regulated. For example, more than 22 percent of loans held by state commercial banks are considered bad. The young stock markets are in the same situation. Thus, financial instability is highly likely.

Unemployment has increased since the mid-1990s. As SOE reforms continue, unemployment will further increase.

> State-owned enterprises (SOE) are still generally inefficient, and reforming them will take a long time.

China is an overpopulated country with 1.2 billion people. About 10 million new laborers join the job markets annually because China's population increases by about 13 million each year. As the state enterprise reform continues, a majority of the current 22 million re-

dundant workers will actually become unemployed. There are 130 million surplus laborers in the countryside.

Income distribution is increasingly unequal. Since the mid-1980s, the gap between the rich and poor has been widening. This inequality, coexisting with the increasing unemployment and government corruption is a potential source of political instability.

For example, there is a big gap in income between the coastal and hinterland regions. In 1996, the average annual wage for a worker in Guangzhou city was 11,801 yuan ($1,420), as opposed to 5,339 yuan ($642) in Guiyang (the capital of Guizhou province). In rural areas, the annual per-capita income was 3,183 yuan ($383) in Guangdong province, while only 1,276 yuan ($154) in Guizhou province.

The trend of Chinese currency

In 1997, several Asian countries experienced dramatic devaluations and fluctuations of their currencies, but the Chinese currency seemed unaffected by the financial disturbances elsewhere in Asia. In 1998, with the drastic decrease in export growth and the fluctuations of the Japanese yen, the Renminbi/yuan seems to be under growing pressure of devaluation. Will the currency be devalued? To analyze this, one should examine both long- and short-term trends of the real exchange rate.

The economist Sebastian Edwards has developed the theory of equilibrium real exchange rate to assess the determinants of real exchange rate in the long run. His theory holds that in the short run, real exchange rate is affected by both monetary variables and fundamentals, but in the long run, it is mainly determined by fundamentals such as the terms of trade, capital inflow, productivity, and government expenditures.

Using this theory, it can be concluded that the trend of China's currency in the long run will likely continue to appreciate, assuming China will maintain a modest economic growth, continued capital inflow, and a favorable trade balance.

In the short run, however, it is likely that a devaluation of the Chinese currency will happen if foreign capital inflow declines dramatically, export growth continues to decrease, economic growth significantly slows down, or there is excessive money supply and the economy suffers heavily from external shocks, such as further significant devaluation of the Japanese yen.

But a devaluation will not help China's export growth or economic growth. This is because the drop in export growth in the first half of 1998 was mainly due to the recessions in two major trade partners (Japan and Korea), not to the devaluations in other Asian countries. The slowdown of the economy has been mainly caused by the decrease in domestic consumption and the excessive capacity in industry.

It should be pointed out that a devaluation is not always beneficial for an economy, especially for the current situation in China. A devaluation may ignite instability in its weak financial sector, especially on the stock markets; it would cause instability in the Hong Kong dollar; it may lead to a new round of inflation because a devaluation causes an increase in import prices; it would increase the trade frictions with the United States; and it may lead to a new round of devaluations and instability in Asian economies. These results would have negative effects on China's economy.

Conclusion

China's economic growth is slowing down. This trend may continue over the next two or three years. The slowdown is mainly due to internal problems. Industrial growth has been hampered by overcapacity, which has dampened investor expectation.

Also, increasing unemployment caused by state-owned enterprise reforms, as well as the negative expectation of future job security, has resulted in a significant decrease in consumer sales. Although not a major factor, lower export growth caused by the Asian financial crisis has also contributed to the economic slowdown.

China's economy needs a period of two or three years to readjust its industry and to reform the weak banking sector. If China makes progress in these efforts, the economy is likely to reach a modest growth rate (about 7 percent) in the next decade.

Renhong Wu is a resident scholar in Asian studies at the Center for Strategic and International Studies in Washington, D.C.

Article 10

The Economist, October 24, 1998

CHINA'S ECONOMY

Red alert

BEIJING

China may be about to catch the Japanese disease. The consequences would be bad not only for China but for all of Asia; and also explosive politically

THE battered leather sofa in the library of Hong Kong's China Club, its horsehair stuffing spewing out, was once Winston Churchill's. Its value at auction was raised by the amorous liaisons he is said to have conducted on it. Perhaps he also found time to lie back and think of China. Many books in the library's magnificent collection, bearing titles such as "Crisis in China", "China in Transition" and "China's Challenge", are the sofa's contemporaries. Those by modern scholars fall back on similar titles. For, as usual, there is plenty to worry about in the Middle Kingdom.

The concern now is that China's economy is entering a dangerous period of sluggish growth. Behind the smog of official statistics the economy may well be growing at only 3–4% a year. For this vast, chaotic land such a slowdown amounts, in effect, to a recession. That threatens China's ability to be able to generate enough new jobs to reduce the growing army of unemployed laid off by the rusting state sector, or to employ the millions of young people who enter the workforce every year.

This has the potential to make China a far more worrying place. Add to the picture a combination of an insolvent banking system, mounting domestic deflation and a sharp divide between the

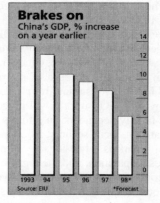

Brakes on
China's GDP, % increase on a year earlier

1993 94 95 96 97 98*
Source: EIU   *Forecast

relatively wealthy parts of the country and the poor regions, and China's stability could be threatened. This year, most regional leaders have been praising China for holding the line in a region devastated by financial turmoil. Such praise is not always blinkered. An unstable China would be among the neighbours' worst fears, not least because it threatens their own ability to recover.

It is remarkable how, in a general sense, China is grappling today with many of the same problems it faced a century ago. Since 1949 the Communists have imposed internal order, at least in comparison with anything that came before them. A powerful brand of nationalism is now backed by a strong national defence. But the biggest difference has been the staggering economic change of the past 20 years which has delivered perhaps the greatest reduction in poverty the world has ever seen.

Yet it took a long time for China to wake. Angus Maddison, an economic historian, estimates in a new paper* that between 1820 and 1952, when world economic output rose eightfold, China's product per head actually shrank. Its share of world GDP fell from one-third to one-twentieth. China's income per head fell from the world average to a quarter of it. This historic perspective is important; it is the humiliation of the past that even today drives China's quest for rapid growth.

Since Deng Xiaoping set China on the path of liberalisation in 1978, its GDP has grown, on average, by 9% a year (see chart on next page). Income per head has grown by 6% a year, faster in that period than any other Asian country except South Korea. China's GDP per head has risen from a quarter to half the world average. And its share of world GDP has doubled, to 10%. China, by some measures that use purchasing-power parity, is now the world's second-biggest economy after the United States.

*"Chinese Economic Performance in the Long Run", by Angus Maddison, OECD, 1998.

What matters, however, is how long this advance can continue. Mr Maddison estimates that even if China's GDP growth slowed to 5.5% a year—realistic goal given higher rates of growth in Japan, Taiwan and South Korea at comparable stages of their development—China would match America's level of GDP by 2015. Its economy would then account for 17% of the world total, while income per head would match the

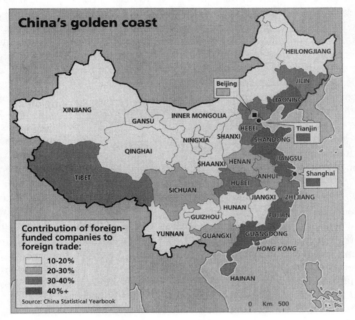

China's golden coast

HEILONGJIANG

Beijing

JILIN

XINJIANG

LIAONING

GANSU

INNER MONGOLIA

Tianjin

NINGXIA

SHANXI

HEBEI

SHANDONG

QINGHAI

SHAANXI

HENAN

JIANGSU

ANHUI

Shanghai

TIBET

HUBEI

SICHUAN

JIANGXI

ZHEJIANG

HUNAN

GUIZHOU

FUJIAN

YUNNAN

GUANGXI

GUANGDONG

HONG KONG

HAINAN

Contribution of foreign-funded companies to foreign trade:

- 10-20%
- 20-30%
- 30-40%
- 40%+

Source: China Statistical Yearbook

0   Km 500

world average. Since a China more integrated into the world economy would presumably be a country more at ease with itself and with its neighbours, the prospect of such an outcome should be welcomed.

Behind the figures

Yet the immediate challenges to this are daunting. For a start, although the government denies it, China appears to be on the brink of a prolonged slump. Growth has already fallen from an annual peak of 13.4% in 1992–94 to an annualised rate of 7.2% for the year so far, making a nonsense of the government's often repeated claims that it will reach the 8% growth target for 1998 that Zhu Rongji, the prime minister, famously "guaranteed" in March.

The difference might appear to be hair-splitting of highly imprecise figures. But

to create those vital new jobs, China needs robust economic growth. A rough rule of thumb is that every percentage-point fall in GDP means 5m more unemployed. As it is, around 70m, almost the population of Germany, are less than gainfully employed on farms or, increasingly, in cities. Hu Angang, a Beijing economist, predicts 18m fully unemployed urban Chinese next year. It is this rising unemployment which helps explain the scramble by President Jiang Zemin and his cohorts since early this summer to find growth, if necessary at the expense of longer-term structural reform.

It is impossible to know exactly how bleak things are. China's growth figures have always been overstated by one or two percentage points, at least. Now there is growing confirmation that China's GDP statistics have become almost meaningless. Although the government reports healthy growth this year in industrial output, electricity output (usually a good proxy for production) has barely risen. Meanwhile, it is hard to square claims of growth in consumer spending of 6.3% in the first nine months of the year with price deflation of around 3%, or with flat or even falling freight volumes. Suspiciously, reports that state-sector profits have fallen by 82% in the first quarter of this year were revised sharply upwards on October 16th, with little explanation.

Last year, when Chinese domestic demand was showing signs of slowing, a 20% spurt in exports helped take up the slack. This year export growth, which looked strong at first, has slowed to less than 4% for the year so far, buckling in the face of collapsed demand from the Asian region. Many exporters have switched to selling their goods at home. That, coupled with a fresh wave of imported goods from the region, many of them smuggled in, has put pressure on manufacturers for the domestic market, most of them state-owned. China's industry is probably working at about half its full capacity. But still factories are churning out goods. Unsold inventories have been growing at double-digit rates. The *China Analyst,* a Montreal-based publication, reckons that, if growth provided by the contribution from inventory accumulation is set aside, China's underlying GDP growth could fall to an annualised 2% in the final quarter of this year.

Though China is at a very different stage of development, its current predicament brings to mind Japan's experience in the 1990s. As in Japan, company profits have collapsed because of over-investment. Both countries have banking systems that are riddled with bad debts. China's banks are burdened with dud loans both to state enterprises and to property speculation made during the boom years of the early 1990s. Having had their fingers burnt twice over, they are in no hurry to lend again. And recent stipulations that threaten to penalise Chinese banks that make ill-judged loans provide a further disincentive to lend to anything but state-sanctioned entities.

As with Japan, China's leaders recognised the deflationary threat too late. They have failed to cut interest rates fast enough (real rates are about 10%) to boost domestic demand, perhaps because they fear that domestic savers will panic and seek hard-currency havens, despite an officially closed capital account. Instead, the government is relying upon additional infrastructure spending, equivalent to a combined 3.5% of GDP for this year and next, to pull the economy up. Yet there is little to suggest that a centrally mandated infrastructure splurge in China will provide much more than a short-term benefit. It will lean against the wind, but that wind, pushing back domestic demand, is a strong one.

Plenty of mainland and foreign economists are cheerier than this; they have an enduring faith in the government's ability to keep the economy growing. But China's structural problems may now be too deep-seated for the government to be able to deliver. Worried about the consequences of unemployment, or about the rising social costs (pensions, schooling, health care) that state companies used to bear, people are becoming afraid to spend—just as they have in Japan.

Several years of Japan-like slow growth, not to mention recession, would be disastrous for the welfare of ordinary Chinese. It would put China's long-term growth assumptions in serious doubt. It would threaten the legitimacy of a leadership whose claim to power is its ability to deliver growth. And it could precipitate a banking crisis that would make Japan's look like a picnic.

Among the most daunting problems is China's sharp west–east divide. This also has echoes from former times, when China was unable to react effectively to the western challenge, backed, as it was, by superior arms. Though many reformers argued for it, China was unable to absorb western, wealth-creating technology and skills. Missionaries aside, the foreigners all lived in extraterritorial "concessions": so-called treaty ports along the east coast.

Across the divide

Rhoads Murphey, a historian, has written that the thriving port city of Tianjin had closer links with the outside world than it had with its own hinterland, and "the foreigners remained outsiders". The biggest reason for this was that China's bureaucratic system held back the emergence of an independent commercial and industrial bourgeoisie. The bureaucracy and the landed gentry of imperial China were not producers of wealth, but consumers of it: they were quintessential rent-seekers.

Today, the eastern cities that Deng Xiaoping threw open to foreign investment are almost exactly those of the treaty ports. Booming foreign investment and the lively international trade that followed have transformed the coastal region, which has become wealthy, outward-looking and cosmopolitan: part of a network of international exchange. Yet the age-old problem remains; the benefits of western investment, technology, management and marketing skills have not spread beyond a coastal zone that threatens to become rigidly divorced from the rest of China (see map on next page).

This coastal region is what many westerners refer to when they talk of the Chinese economy. But it is worth putting China's foreign-investment miracle in context. China's cumulative $270 billion of foreign direct investment has indeed transformed the country's external trade. Foreign investment in 1996 was involved in over 47% of foreign trade, up from just 5.6% a decade earlier. Some 120,000 foreign enterprises or joint ventures employ about 17m people, equivalent to one-tenth of the urban workforce. Yet more than half the multinationals operating in China are not making money, according to A.T. Kearney, a firm of management consultants.

Nevertheless, some observers argue that China's economy has become amongst the world's most open, with exports equal to 18% of GDP. But Mr Maddison argues that the figure, based on current exchange rates, is misleading. On a purchasing-power parity basis, Mr Maddison calculates, China's export ratio is just 4.3% of GDP. This puts into perspective the penetration of foreign investment in China's economy. It also helps explain why genuine private enterprise accounts for no more than 10% of China's national product. Agriculture still represents the biggest part of the economy, and various forms of state-ownership or collectives the remainder.

The impediment to free enterprise, as ever, is a rent-seeking state bureaucracy in much of the rest of the country. Today, it represents the interests of an industrial system of publicly owned enterprises, built by the Communists along Soviet lines. In what Francois Gipouloux, writing in *China Perspectives,* calls the "state planners' special reserve"—the inland provinces of Shaanxi, Guizhou, Yunnan, Qinghai, Ningxia and Xinjiang—the state controls about 60–80% of industrial output. This is a region of satanic pollution, shoddy products, mounting state losses—and little private investment to speak of.

Even if the government in Beijing officially welcomes foreign investment in China's central and western regions—or investment from other parts of China, for that matter—the dead weight of rigid state enterprises stifles the development of the various strands (subcontracting, flexible work practices, competition) that go to make up a modern industrial fabric. In these regions, Mr Gipouloux argues, the debate about development has become nothing less than one of Chinese versus foreign sovereignty. The regions' inhabitants are the losers.

Reading their lips

BEIJING

"STATESMANLIKE" is the term for which editorial-writers reach when describing Chinese leaders' resolve not to devalue their currency, the yuan. China's selflessness, Britain's prime minister, Tony Blair, has said, is something to which tribute should be paid. People fear that if China devalued, Asia would succumb to another round of debilitating devaluations, bringing down even the Hong Kong dollar. In fact, China is following its own self-interest. It knows that to devalue the yuan could do more harm than good.

Certainly, some inside China are lobbying hard for devaluation: China's shipbuilders, for instance, which have been clobbered by the fall in the currencies of South Korea and (until recently) Japan. Moreover, some foreign observers argue that deflationary pressures will make devaluation irresistible, for lower export prices would help combat them. They also point to growing capital flight this year, and a weakening yuan on the black market, as signs that the government's nerve is not expected to hold.

Currency controls, over $140 billion in foreign reserves, and a trade surplus of probably over $50 billion this year: all are reasons for believing that the government will not devalue. Now there is a new reason: concern about China's foreign debt.

This issue has been brought into sharper focus by the recent closure of Guangdong International Trust & Investment Corporation (GITIC), with $2.4 billion in foreign debts. GITIC is one of a network of such groups, mostly owned by provincial governments, that have combined foreign debts of over $10 billion and a history of squandered investments. Now, the central government is set to close more of them. That makes foreign lenders even more nervous; most are stopping new loans altogether. A devaluation would worry them more, because it would undermine the ability of all Chinese entities to pay back debt.

By the official count, neither China nor its lenders should have all that much to worry about. The country's debt ratio—the ratio between external debt and hard-currency income—stands at a comfortable 75% or so, well below the 100% level that starts to ring alarm bells. Moreover, foreign direct investment accounts for four-fifths of all capital inflows to China. The country is not as reliant on short-term borrowing as were its neighbours.

Yet one lesson from the past 15 months is that official debt figures can be gross understatements. The question is how much bigger than the official count are China's reported debts of around $120 billion. Half as much again is a reasonable first guess. Several types of borrowing do not show up in the data. For instance, lending by mainland branches of foreign banks does not, though it amounted to $27 billion in mid-1998.

There are also borrowings by "red chips"—Hong Kong-registered arms of central, provincial or local governments listed on the territory's stockmarket. Strictly, red chips are not mainland firms. But much of what they borrow has been invested in China, so part of their debt ought to count in China's foreign-currency exposure. Also, some foreign direct investment, particularly from Hong Kong, is actually lending in disguise. In several mainland infrastructure projects, the lenders get guaranteed foreign-currency returns: debt by any other name.

China's rising foreign debts clearly worry the authorities. Early this year they tightened rules on the amounts mainland companies can borrow. The State Administration for Foreign Exchange (SAFE) has rattled off a series of measures to plug the holes in China's (officially closed) capital account. One official estimates that a quarter of outflows through the current account is in fact disguised capital flight: dollars earned from false invoicing, illegal foreign-exchange deals and other nefarious activities. With capital flight reckoned to be as big as inward flows of foreign investment ($35 billion–45 billion a year), this official says that plugging just half of the foreign-exchange leaks would be a signal victory.

Further instances of ill-judged lending may well emerge. But a yuan devaluation would greatly aggravate China's foreign-debt problem. It is another reason to think that Communist rhetoric, this time at least, has a ring of sincerity to it.

The sharp dividing-line in China between two incompatible models of development is already a political headache for China's leaders, and is likely to become more of one. They have, in the past year, become more committed to "reforming" the state enterprises, as well as to cleaning up the state banking system that bears the burden of enterprise losses and is, as a consequence, insolvent. Yet the leaders lack the resources to impose their will: the central government's ability to collect taxes, for instance, has shrunk alarmingly. Tax revenues were 30% of GDP in 1989. They are barely 12% today.

Besides, the thrust of reforms is still aimed at improving the socialist "efficiency" of the state system, not at embracing full capitalism. Privatisation of heavy industry, telecoms, energy and the banks is out of the question, even if smaller enterprises are being let go. The legal underpinnings for free enterprise, notably adequate property rights and an impartial judiciary, are still lacking, both in the hinterland and on the coast.

That is not to say that China's enterprises are shunning "reform". Heeding the central government's call for efficiency, workers are being laid off in droves, while many millions more have been sent home with little or no pay. "Reform" has been an opportunity for state managers and their godfathers in local government to swipe incalculable quantities of public property for their own use; what Xiao Geng, of Hong Kong University, calls the "privatisation of profits and socialisation of losses." During two decades of reform, state-enterprise losses have risen 20-fold, to 74 billion yuan ($10 billion) by the government's own, understated reckoning. Surging unemployment, sluggish domestic demand, rising levels of unwanted inventories and an uncertain international economy: the attempted reforms could scarcely be taking place against a harsher backdrop.

The coastal region provides problems of a different kind for a Chinese leadership perennially concerned about national unity and control. The region's pull has attracted the bulk of China's 100m or so migrant workers, roaming the country in search of higher pay. These workers fall increasingly outside the state's supervision. The 3m-odd migrant workers in Shanghai are, for instance, officially nonpersons; nevertheless their daily needs strain the city's resources to breaking-point.

Then there are the provincial political powers themselves to contend with. Recently, the Communist Party secretary of Guangdong was suddenly recalled, under a cloud. Reining in China's most gung-ho province has long been a challenge for Beijing, which is on guard against centrifugal forces in the coastal region. The collapse earlier this month of Guangdong International Trust & Investment Corporation (GITIC) the province's investment arm, highlighted a problem that is as much political as it is financial. Local "warlordism" is a challenge to the central leaders, albeit not on the scale of earlier this century.

Follow the money

The costs of delaying meaningful reform (ie, in most cases, closure) of the state enterprises are being met today in China's banking system. Since 1984, when the government said it would phase out financing enterprises through the central budget, state companies have been borrowing from the banks. By 1988, according to Nicholas Lardy of the Brookings Institution in Washington, DC, state industrial firms' debt-equity ratio had risen to 82%. By 1995, the figure had risen to 570%; it is assuredly higher today, were the figures available.

This means that Chinese companies are more heavily indebted than South Korea's *chaebol* even before taking into account either their overvalued assets and inventories or their unfunded pension liabilities, which the World Bank puts at 50% of GDP. Such high indebtedness makes China's state enterprises acutely vulnerable to an economic slump. But slump or no, China's state enterprises as a group are efficient destroyers of wealth. It would be cheaper to close them all down, and still keep paying the workers.

The condition of the big four state banks mirrors the appalling state of the enterprises, to whom over four-fifths of their lending is directed. The reported profitability of the four banks—which together have 150,000 branches and 1.7m staff—has fallen by five-sixths over the past decade: They have a return on assets of just 0.3% (HSBC's return on assets is 1.6%).

The real picture is undoubtedly much bleaker, for China has a lax system of accounting for bad loans, and unpaid interest on non-performing loans is usually booked as profit. On generally accepted accounting standards, concludes Mr Lardy, at least three of China's four state banks—the Industrial & Commercial Bank of China, the Agricultural Bank of China and the China Construction Bank—are insolvent by a very wide margin indeed. Bad loans, if they were properly accounted for, might be $270 billion–360 billion, equivalent to 30–40% of GDP. One of the gloomiest estimates of Japanese banks' bad loans is 30% of GDP, and Japanese banks are well-capitalised by Chinese standards.

If a meltdown has so far been averted, it is because the stability of China's financial system has been underwritten by a high rate of savings, of almost 40%. Inflows of household savings have ballooned, rising from 18% of all bank deposits in 1980 to around 60% today, and banks are sitting on nearly

$600 billion-odd of household deposits—liabilities for the banking system that are matched by a dud pile of assets. This hugely inefficient intermediation of funds, in effect, represents the massive bilking of urban and (particularly) rural households by the state sector. Presumably, barring serious reform, there will one day have to be a reckoning. Either the government will try to inflate its way out of its obligations, or there will be a run on state banks—or both.

Plenty of mainland and overseas economists are scathing about crisis-mongers who write paragraphs such as those you have just read. How, they ask, can there be a banking crisis if the government stands four-square behind deposits? Besides, has not the banking system survived crises before, notably during the high inflation of the early 1990s? Yet this assessment is blinkered, for a number of reasons. First, a banking crisis, even if today it is a hidden one, already carries great costs for the real economy; by providing capital only for the undeserving, it greatly constrains China's potential for growth and job-creation. Further, it might not take more than a few jolts for China's savers to lose confidence in the banking system; already, there is resentment by depositors told they are unable to withdraw funds at short notice.

No one knows how far China might be from a full-blown domestic banking crisis. But a further slowdown in the country's economic growth will surely bring one closer. The possibility of China devaluing its currency and the level of its foreign debt continue to raise concern, especially as nearly all foreign banks have now stopped lending (see box). This might be just the sort of nudge that can turn nagging doubts about an economy into a crisis. And a crisis big enough to provide the China Club's library with a whole new set of volumes.

Article 11   *USA Today Magazine,* November 1998

USA LOOKS AT THE WORLD

CHINA'S BOOMING ECONOMY:

DO THE RISKS OUTWEIGH THE OPPORTUNITIES?

"Those who take the freedoms of the private enterprise system for granted should not forget that the government still is pulling many of the strings in the Chinese economy."

by Murray Weidenbaum

THIS IS A TIME of fundamental change in the global marketplace. It's like the middle of the 19th century, when European nations dominated the world economy, then the U.S. elbowed its way into the club of industrialized nations.

In the middle of the 20th century, when Western nations dominated the world economy, Japan elbowed its way into the club. In both cases, the world economy continued to grow, if not to accelerate, although the monopoly was broken. In absolute terms each nation experienced growth in its production and exports, although their relative shares of the world market declined.

Today, China stands at the threshold of a similar breakthrough. By some widely used measures, it already is a larger economy than Germany. China, in effect, is in a race with Japan for second place—just behind the U.S. There has been no dramatic equivalent of the Berlin Wall coming down, but, since 1979,

China has been moving toward capitalism and economic expansion—a step at a time and just partially.

Leader Deng Xiaoping was the driving force. He made that decision on practical, rather than philosophical, grounds as the economic superiority of capitalism became obvious. While China had difficulty feeding itself, Taiwan and Hong Kong were booming. Deng substituted economic incentive and technology for Mao Zedong's ideology, unity for class struggle, and experts for "red" loyalists.

It is fascinating to recall that private agriculture—rather than private industry—was the entering wedge. After selling the required amount to the government, a farmer could sell the rest in the market. That is the incentive of capitalism—produce more and earn more—and it worked! To save face, they called it "market socialism." The results were impressive. By 1990, pork consumption doubled; the number of fresh eggs eaten tripled; and luxury fruits and vegetables became commonplace.

The reform of industry followed agriculture, but more slowly. Special Economic Zones were set up to promote exports. Coincidentally, all four were near Hong Kong or Taiwan. Tax breaks and other capitalistic incentives lured foreign business. Deng eliminated the three socialist "irons" that had inhibited economic growth in China: the "iron rice bowl" that

had guaranteed jobs; "iron chains" that had guaranteed management tenure; and the "iron wages" that had guaranteed pay never would be cut.

Most of those foreign businesses were not from the obvious places—Japan, the U.S., or Western Europe. Rather, they were overseas Chinese who were investing in their traditional homeland. The Special Economic Zones were a smashing success. Foreign investment in the zones expanded very rapidly and now accounts for large shares of China's exports. Guangdong Province—adjacent to Hong Kong—became the wealthiest part of China. Guangdong is almost an extension of Hong Kong. Xiamen near Taiwan also has boomed, although not to the same extent as Hong Kong.

Other parts of China seeking to copy the success in the southeast haven't done as well yet. Some of the more urban areas are tied down by socialist approaches to production. The rural areas lack transport and other infrastructure. Nevertheless, substantial amounts of new industry are expanding into the interior, especially along the Yangtze River.

Even before the Hong Kong takeover, Beijing began to hedge its bets. The national government is promoting the economic rebirth of Shanghai, which was China's commercial capital before World War II. Foreign businesses in

Dr. Weidenbaum, Ecology Editor of USA Today, *chairman, Center for the Study of American Business, and Mallinckdrodt Distinguished University Professor, Washington University in St. Louis (Mo.), is co-author of* The Bamboo Network.

Shanghai have more leeway than in Guangdong. They can sell to the local population, while most foreign ventures in China are limited primarily to exporting or providing items not available from domestic producers.

Economic progress in China is uneven. In some areas, Coca-Cola is available—but it is delivered by mule. China has no personal checks and few credit cards, no 800 numbers, and no overnight shipments. Those who have been to a major Chinese city recently will recognize that it is a bicycle society moving up to motor scooters.

To state the obvious, business opportunities in China for Americans are numerous. Nevertheless, cynics abound among Western business executives living in China. They love to quote an imaginary P.T. Wang: "There's a foreigner born every minute." They also will tell you of a T-shirt on sale in Beijing: "If you're too honest, you'll always lose out."

Nevertheless, signs of U.S. companies are frequent: Marlboro Man billboards, KFC restaurants, Motorola cellular phones, Elizabeth Arden cosmetics, and Nike sneakers. McDonald's in Guangdong set a world record—14,000 customers in one day. When the local 7-11 opened, riot police were called in to control crowds.

Guangdong is Procter & Gamble's largest overseas market for shampoo. Coca-Cola dominates the soft drink market with bottlers at 16 locations, and seven more are on the way. Hainan Coconut Juice simply is not a very strong competitor. Other U.S. firms that have invested at least $100,000,000 in China include ARCO, Amoco, United Technologies, Pepsico, Lucent Technologies, General Electric, General Motors, Hewlett-Packard, and IBM.

To be sure, there often is a need to adapt foreign products to China's culture. Hasbro sells its GI Joe doll as an "international hero," having changed the colors to the People's Liberation Army's camouflage green and the Communist Party's red. Maxwell House sells instant coffee—complete with premixed packets of cream and sugar for a market not very familiar with the product.

Those who take the freedoms of the private enterprise economy for granted should not forget that government still is pulling many of the strings in the Chinese economy. Companies that try to compete against domestic firms for the Chinese market may not find the path as easy as those that generate the high-tech products and exports Chinese leaders are so anxious to see expand.

The Chinese are the original Yankee traders. They know the great business potential that will be generated as a country with 1,200,000,000 people industrializes and they are trying their best to take advantage of it. They love foreign investment when it creates new jobs, pays taxes, and generates foreign exchange. Yet, from an American point of view, sometimes those exports compete against the products of the same company's factories located in other countries.

Thus, Motorola is encouraged to sell cellular telephones *and* to produce them in China. McDonnell Douglas and Boeing sell jet airplanes in China, *but* they involve local subcontractors and train local maintenance people. These companies are showing more sophistication than some of the early entrants, such as Schwinn. That U.S. bicycle manufacturer lost its business in China by transferring technology to local manufacturers without adequate protections.

Typically, a U.S. company faces the challenge of developing a presence in the China market in a manner very different from its experience at home or even in Western Europe. In China, there are few 100% American-owned companies. There mostly are joint ventures, often with Chinese middlemen either from the mainland or elsewhere in Southeast Asia.

The Bamboo Network

Guanxi, or personal connections, can help in dealing with the many layers of bureaucracy in China, and the "Bamboo Network" of ethnic Chinese business families in Southeast Asia can be a big help in serving as a transition. Their emphasis on personal relations can clash, however, with the U.S. practice of using lawyers as intermediaries. The head of the Charoen Pokphand Group, the Bangkok-based former joint-venture partner of Wal-Mart in Hong Kong and China, laments that American attorneys can destroy the chemistry needed between partners to make a deal work. One has to wonder whether that is why

that prominent constituent of the Bamboo Network is a *former* joint partner of Wal-Mart—or whether the U.S. firm just did not want to cut too many corners. In any event, Wal-Mart reportedly is off to a good, albeit belated, start in China with both a Supercenter and a Sam's Club in Shenzhen.

Another difficulty that Americans encounter in China and the Orient generally is the Asian model for promoting human rights. In that part of the world, economic freedom comes before political liberty. To put it in perspective, consider an important quote: "I firmly believe that business is the ultimate force for democratic change in China." Who said that? A National Association of Manufacturers official? An export promoter? No, it was Li Lu, an exiled Tiananmen Square student leader who has been studying in the U.S.

Many U.S. firms enter China via joint ventures with a Chinese company that is part of the Bamboo Network. The tales of the work ethic of the overseas Chinese are legendary. The leading Hong Kong billionaire started work at the age of 12 to support his family. The grandfather of a former student of mine generated the original nest egg to finance the family multinational enterprises by ironing shirts in the back room of a Chinese hand laundry. He used his savings to buy a $50,000 rice concession in Hong Kong, which is the basis of the family fortune. Think of hundreds—or thousands—of Horatio Algers repeating these experiences.

A good example is the CP Group of Thailand. It started as a very small seed company in China, then moved to Bangkok. CP now is the biggest agri-business investor in China and perhaps the largest "foreign" investor in China. It was a partner of KFC, 7-11, and Heineken, to get them started in the region.

The Bamboo Network firms are family-oriented. They shy from publicity and take a low profile in the commercial world. They do not produce and distribute consumer products with their own brand names. Instead, they make components, manufacture for others, and/or do sub-assembly work.

These overseas Chinese business firms rely on centralized family control and informal transactions. That minimizes bureaucracy and paperwork. Key information is obtained in conversation and retained in the heads of senior managers. That certainly eliminates the need for a lot of formal reporting. Just compare that with the massive flow of studies, reports, and memos in a typical U.S. corporation.

In the ethnic Chinese firm, transactions often are dealt with by a note jotted in a diary. Money is borrowed from family and friends on trust. Clearly, management styles are far more informal and intuitive than Americans are accustomed to. The Chinese approach to business allows opportunities to be seized as they arise with little need for elaborate consultant reports. Due diligence is not an expensive, legal-oriented process. On the other hand, this management model works better in low-tech than in high-tech businesses, in industrial markets rather than in consumer markets, and in areas with rudimentary legal systems rather than in countries with sophisticated jurisprudence.

The information network of the overseas Chinese business family leaders is unrivaled. They know each other personally, often coming from a common birthplace. They cooperate across borders. For instance, the key ethnic Chinese banking family of Thailand—they control the Bank of Bangkok—provided the initial financing for what presently is the largest Chinese business family in Indonesia. That family, in turn, provided the beginning funding for a major Chinese business family in Malaysia.

The typical Bamboo Network firm operates through an intricate arrangement of enterprises rather than a unitary family company. There is no equivalent of a Ford or Wal-Mart's Walton family focusing on one very large firm. Rather, the typical family groups own percentage interests in a galaxy of medium-size firms. Family members are inserted into key management positions. Cross-holdings are common with other family-controlled firms. This provides both secrecy and diversification in a region where discrimination and threat of expropriation are pervasive. A common saying is, "Keep your bags packed at all times."

A word of warning always is in order. Doing business in China can be very difficult. Don't expect to find a consistent, easily understood, universally enforced judicial system. There are only rudimentary and limited legal protections that foreign ventures can draw on. This can dampen the enthusiasm for making large investments in what is fundamentally a very attractive market. Consider the irony: In the U.S., we are concerned about the *excessive* degree of litigation. Perhaps we should reduce our trade deficit with China by exporting some of our surplus lawyers to them.

Economists are notoriously wet blankets. So, true to form, let me report that business in China is not always profitable. Foreign companies doing business there usually talk about current sales successes and future profit performance. To some extent, that is to be expected with new investments, but perhaps not as universally as seems to be the case in China. Take Volkswagen's joint venture with China's First Auto Works. VW has not reported a profit yet, but sales are high—up six percent in 1996, for instance. That is better than Peugeot's experience—a $100,000,000 loss.

Even fellow ethnic Chinese have difficulty breaking even. Less than 40% of Taiwanese investments in China are profitable. Also, Chinese labor may not always be as productive as expected, although the unit cost is low. They may require more managers than other developing countries. Often, companies doing business in China have to import overseas ethnic Chinese managers.

Even experienced Asian investors can get burned. For example, take the Hong Kongers who opened a restaurant for tourists near Tiananmen Square just a week before the shooting. No amount of due diligence could have prevented that fiasco.

It is helpful to have some historical perspective about China's role in the world. For most of recorded history, it was more developed than the West, more prosperous, more sophisticated, and more civilized. That is why they called themselves the "Middle Kingdom." Only in the past 500 years has the West been ahead. Of course, that's a long time for us, but the Zhou Dynasty in the first millennium BC lasted that long. Naturally, most of us never heard of it.

China is on a road that could restore its earlier greatness. By some economic measures, China is just behind Japan. If current trends continue, it could become number two early in the 21st century, right behind the U.S. in terms of economic output. Some optimists (or, rather, pessimists) think it will be number one later in the 21st century, but here we can take considerable satisfaction with a standard caveat: Trends rarely move in a straight line, especially in China. There is no shortage of serious problems facing the Chinese people and their leadership—energy shortages, environmental degradation, infrastructure inadequacies, and corruption and crime. Then again, there is the famous forecast attributed to Napoleon: "China is a sleeping giant. When it wakes, it will shake the world."

It is vital for Americans to understand events better in that exotic part of the world and not be on the outside trying to look in. China is the prime example of my standard forecast: In change, there is both threat and opportunity. My final point: In *feng shui* (Chinese numerology), eight is a lucky number. Thus, I leave you with my favorite eight letters: Good luck!

Article 12

Environment, September 1998

ENVIRONMENTAL TAXES: CHINA'S BOLD INITIATIVE

by Robert A. Bohm, Chazhong Ge, Milton Russell, Jinnan Wang, and Jintian Yang

China is environmentally stressed. Its air quality is poor to dangerous. Surface and groundwater contamination harms both human health and the sustainability of ecological systems. Wind and water erosion, deforestation, and desertification are serious in many areas. Species are threatened by loss of habitat and other human intrusions.

None of this is surprising because China is both poor and developing rapidly, two conditions that tend to spell environmental trouble.[1] And none of this is news because these conditions have long been known.[2] What is news is the seriousness and creativity with which China has been seeking to prevent further deterioration and to rectify inherited problems.[3] In doing so, it has been a pioneer in the use of nontraditional pollution control measures as well as in adapting traditional ones to the Chinese situation.[4] Judging China's current ecological degradation and health risks against what would have occurred without these efforts and against the performance of other countries in similar circumstances, the country's record is quite credible. But conditions remain grossly unsatisfactory and could get worse unless further action is taken. New and more powerful tools of environmental control are required to meet the goals proclaimed in the 1998 meeting of the National People's Congress; to stop deterioration everywhere before 2015; to show substantial improvement everywhere before 2030; and to meet these goals by 2000 in some regions.[5]

Reform and strengthening of the pollution levy system (PLS), China's emissions tax and pollution control funding system first established in 1979, is one of the paths to achieving these goals.[6] It also presents an example of a process and an approach that may have relevance to other countries facing similar circumstances.[7]

The early adoption of the incentive-based PLS is surprising in the context of the pre-reform, nonmarket Chinese economy, but the need for measures other than command-and-control regulations is not. China adopted the polluter-pays principle early, which in this context means that the production units, not the state, are responsible for controlling emissions. But for this approach to succeed, independent regulatory authority with teeth is needed. In China, however, environmental control authority is highly decentralized. Administration is in the hands of provincial and local officials who are also responsible for goods production—i.e., there is no independent environmental authority.[8] The allocation of responsibilities between government departments and enterprises is often unclear. Furthermore, clear obligations under statutory law and regulations—enforced by an independent judiciary—are only now coming into being. As a result, everything seems to be negotiable. In practice, this means that inspectors and officials have substantial discretion (and often incentives) to overlook violations and that voluntary compliance is unlikely.

PLS fills some of the enforcement gap, however. First, it provides revenues for local Environmental Protection Bureaus (EPBs), which also increases those bureaus' independence. Second, once emissions are estimated, what is required of emitters is unmistakable: The fee is either paid or not. Finally, the bulk of the revenues are recycled back to industry to provide capital for the purchase of pollution control equipment, in effect sequestering funds that otherwise would go to expand production capacity or for other purposes. This recycling has reduced opposition to the tax. PLS thus exists alongside command-and-control regulations, supplementing and reinforcing them (not least by providing local EPBs ample resources for monitoring).

Looking to the future, authorities at the National Environmental Protection Agency (which was renamed the State Environmental Protection Administration after elevation to ministerial status in 1998) concluded that additional pollution control measures were required. They identified reform and strengthening of PLS as a potentially fruitful instrument. After years of effort, that reform is being implemented.

The Path to Reform

The existing PLS was analyzed in 1991 at an international conference on incentive-based regulation organized by some of this article's authors and held in China. At this conference, elements of possible reform (discussed later) were identified.[9] Subsequently, a loan from the World Bank to the National Environmental Protection Agency was negotiated to support intensive study and development of a reform plan. Inclusive from the first, the project was directed by a steering committee chaired by the National Environmental Protection Agency made up of senior officials from China's Ministry of Finance, State Planning Commission, State Economic and Trade Commission, and provincial and local EPBs.

The Chinese Research Academy of Environmental Sciences (CRAES) was selected by competitive bid in 1994 to conduct a study and serve as the staff to the steering committee. Foreign consultants participated in international workshops in China, domestic seminars were held, training programs were conducted

THE ECONOMICS OF EMISSIONS TAXES

The figure presented below shows some of the aspects of emissions taxes that are most important from the standpoint of economic analysis, including the costs and benefits of pollution abatement, the optimal level of emissions, and the tax necessary to achieve that level. To clarify the basic principles involved, only one polluter and one pollutant are considered in this example.

Emissions are measured on the horizontal axis and per unit costs, benefits, and taxes (all in monetary terms) on the vertical axis. The curve labeled MCA represents the *marginal cost of abatement* for a single pollutant.[1] It slopes downward because the cost per unit of emissions reduction is lower the higher the quantity of emissions (or, equivalently, the cost is higher the lower the quantity of emissions). The curve labeled MBA represents the *marginal benefits of abatement*. It slopes upward because the damage from each unit of pollution (and thus the benefits of eliminating it) increases with rising emissions. The area below the MBA curve represents the total value of the damage caused by the pollutant in question, while the area below the MCA curve is the total cost of corrective action.

The optimal level of emissions would be e*, where MCA = MBA. This is the level that minimizes the social cost of pollution (or, put differently, the level that maximizes the net benefits of abatement). If emissions were higher, the benefits of

additional reductions would exceed the costs and it would pay society to undertake those reductions. If emissions were lower, the costs would exceed the benefits and society would gain from tolerating higher emissions. To achieve emissions of e*, society should impose a tax rate equivalent to t*. This would generate revenues equal to t*e*, or the shaded area in the figure.

Although t* would be the optimal tax rate, any rate that exceeded the marginal cost of abatement would lead to emissions reduction. For example, a tax of t′ would result in emissions no greater than e′ because at any higher level of emissions it would be cheaper to engage in abatement measures than it would be to pay the tax.

As noted above, the situation depicted in this figure is for a single pollutant. A system of emissions taxes such as China's PLS would be much more complex, of course. To analyze that situation, one would have to consider how each polluter would choose between adopting abatement measures or paying the tax for each pollutant, recognizing that there could be opportunities to shift from one pollutant to another.

---

1. The principle of marginal analysis, which entails looking at phenomena in terms of incremental changes, is one of the most important insights of economics. See W. Nicholson, *Intermediate Microeconomics* (Fort Worth, Tex.: Dryden Press, 1994), especially page 8.

both in China and abroad, and the experience of other countries was made available through both short-term study tours and longer visits to academic and government institutions. The steering committee was careful to include field-level practitioners in all of these activities to make use of their experience and to build a knowledgeable constituency for the ultimate reforms.

The effort was designed to identify the goals of the reform, to investigate problems and successes with the existing PLS, and to develop the outlines of the proposed reform that could then be tested in practice. More than 100 practitioners and researchers ultimately participated in one or another phase of the project. It was documented in a report (running to 800 pages in English) that was published in October 1997.[10]

In November 1997, the proposal was presented to a special tribunal consisting of senior representatives of all affected government ministries and commissions and the provinces, advised by staff and leading academics. The tribunal approved the proposal and ordered that it be implemented on a pilot basis as soon as practicable. Depending on the results of the trial, the proposal will be revised as necessary and then submitted for formal debate and action by the national government. Then it will be implemented across China.

Objectives of Reform

The advantages of an emissions tax such as that incorporated in PLS are that it provides incentives at all stages of production and consumption to make pollution-reducing decisions. To avoid taxes, individual producers will alter production processes, including maintenance and operation controls, looking at all the opportunities for emissions reductions. (See the box "The Economics of Emissions Taxes" for a formal economic analysis of emissions taxes.)

Under an emissions tax scheme, those producers who are least effective in reducing pollution will suffer a competitive disadvantage and lose sales because of their higher after-tax costs. Consumers, on the other hand, will reduce their consumption of "dirty" products because the relative price of those products will increase. In this way, mar-

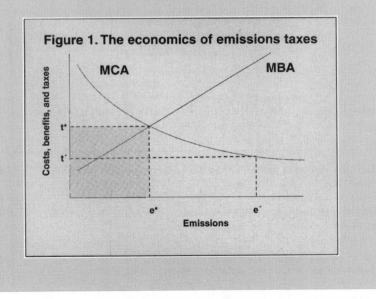

Figure 1. The economics of emissions taxes

ket incentives will both provide information about opportunities for improvement and induce action upon them to a much greater extent than could be mandated by outside authorities.

The in-depth examination of China's existing PLS system found that it was inadequate to meet the country's environmental protection needs. Its rates are too low to provide the needed incentives and adequate revenue, and the tax base is too narrow—it does not cover all pollutants or sources and only covers emissions above the "standard" (as defined by the regulations in place). Furthermore, the rates charged do not discriminate among pollutants sufficiently to reflect the relative harm they impose, nor does the system accommodate the geographic and developmental diversity of China.

To be effective, pollution taxes must be responsive to changes in overall economic conditions and reflect shifting environmental goals. Yet the existing PLS has no mechanism for automatic adjustment. Over time, inflation has eroded both the incentive effects of the tax and the real revenue stream it generates. In addition, the increase in industrial activity and income has both raised the level of total emissions and increased the public's willingness to pay for added environmental quality.

Incomplete capital markets and other institutional factors in China argue for using PLS revenues to support pollution control rather than for general government purposes. The existing PLS recycles funds back to the paying entities to be used for pollution control projects. Although this does channel the funds toward the right goal, it also decreases polluters' incentives to reduce pollution and it does not assure that the funds are used most productively. Furthermore, the system does not provide any funds for projects involving multiple firms or for needs that cross political boundaries, such as water- or airshed improvements. Correcting these problems were the major challenges facing those who designed the reforms that are now being implemented.

Major Provisions of the Reform

The tax base was the first issue to be resolved in reforming PLS. The decision: to adopt a comprehensive system covering all pollutants from all sources. In the old PLS, charges were imposed only on industrial sources and were usually levied only against a single benchmark pollutant per firm—and only on emissions exceeding the relevant standard established under Chinese environmental regulations. The breadth of coverage of the reformed PLS and its major provisions are shown in Table 1.

Determining the tax rates was a major research task involving analysis, judgment, and ultimately attention to political expediency. The goal in this case was to achieve improvement in environmental conditions, and no effort was made to achieve an optimal tax rate in the Pigouvian sense.[11] Indeed, the process is instructive for its pragmatic approach to a difficult and contentious task.

Because the marginal damage from pollution in China is so high, there was little fear of raising rates to the level where total social welfare would be eroded (see the diagram in the box "The Economics of Emissions Taxes"). Below that level, any increase in taxes would certainly lead to reductions in pollution that would (on net) be beneficial. The process thus sought to find an appropriate level within these boundaries. For large industrial dischargers, marginal cost of abatement (MCA) schedules were estimated at the existing levels of pollution by major industries for groups of pollutants with similar control characteristics. This made it possible to estimate the tax levels that would "bite" for major known processes. Based on this analysis and other factors, about a

---

Table 1. Summary of China's proposed pollution levy system

Medium	Pollutants	Tax base	Tax rate
Industrial and urban wastewater	All effluents	Pollution equivalent (PE) quantity	Yuan per PE quantity
Air	All emissions	PE quantity	Yuan per PE quantity
Noise		Decibel level for stationary sources; vehicle type for mobile sources	Flat rate
Solid waste	All industrial and municipal solid waste	Type of waste for industrial and commercial waste; number of households for household waste	Yuan per ton for industrial and commercial waste; per household fee for household waste
Low-level radioactive waste	All low-level radioactive waste	Quantity or level of activity	Flat rate

NOTES: For very small enterprises and some nonpoint sources of pollution, administratively determined fees are imposed in lieu of the tax rates given in this table.

The yuan is China's currency.

A pollution-equivalent (PE) quantity is the quantity of a given pollutant adjusted by its degree of harmfulness. See Table 2 for selected adjustment factors.

SOURCE: Chinese Research Academy of Environmental Sciences, *Study on Design and Implementation of Pollution Levy System in China* (Beijing, 1997).

fourfold increase in the tax rate was determined to be both effective and reasonable for an average suite of pollutants.

Two major concessions to practicality and political expediency were made with respect to entities now covered by PLS. First, the higher rate structure will be phased in over three years. Second, a two-rate system, with a lower rate for emissions below the official standard, will be continued. Both concessions will reduce revenues (the latter permanently), and both will reduce incentives to cut pollution. But they will increase the acceptability of the reforms and by doing so ease implementation. They should also lessen short-term economic disruption and reduce noncompliance and evasion.

Environmental taxes are often criticized for being inflexible and difficult to adjust to changing conditions. Inflation is the culprit most often cited in this regard. Another factor is the growth in number and size of pollution sources and the consequent higher level of emissions. Still another is the increase in the public's willingness to pay for improved environmental quality as incomes rise and environmental sensitivity increases. In a rapidly industrializing and growing economy such as China's, these latter factors are particularly important. The reformed PLS therefore includes annual escalation of the rates (proposed at 9 percent) to deal with these problems. This approach also provides enterprises with information to make investment decisions that will be optimal as time goes by.

The reformed PLS is designed to be a national system, but China's regions vary widely in industrial intensity, income, population density, and their demand for environmental quality. Accordingly, the reformed PLS provides for regional shift factors that incorporate these considerations into rate determination. As a result, the richer, more heavily industrialized regions will pay a higher rate than less developed areas.

Theoretically, optimal tax rates should be keyed to damage avoided, the marginal benefits from abatement (MBA) curve in the diagram in the box "The Economics of Emissions Taxes." There are two difficulties with this direct benefits or "risk tax" approach, however: First, there is little reliable data on the marginal benefits from abatement

for specific pollutants, which in any case would differ at each location and source. Second, finely tuned, multiple rates are administratively impossible.

As indicated in Table 1, the reformed PLS adopts the "pollution equivalent" (PE) concept to provide an administratively feasible benefits basis for the system, an approach that has only been used in isolated instances before.[12] Following this concept, each pollutant is rated according to its harmfulness and assigned a PE index value greater or less than the reference emission, which is assigned the value 1. This factor is then used to adjust the measured quantities of pollutants according to their relative proportions in the overall emissions stream.[13] Because a uniform rate is charged on this constructed tax base, the rate structure itself remains uncomplicated while still accounting for the actual risks of the pollutants in question. Pollution-equivalent index values for several pollutants are shown in Table 2. (In the simpler situations of noise from stationary sources and low-level radioactive waste, it was possible to incorporate risk (damage) information into the tax base more directly, e.g., via decibel and activity levels.)

The reformed PLS simplifies the task of levying and enforcing the tax by ignoring some sources of environmental harm (e.g., carbon dioxide and chlorofluorocarbons (CFCs)). More importantly, it applies a flat rate to sources and pollutants where determining actual emissions is impractical. Per vehicle charges for noise pollution, per capita charges for waste water treatment, and per household charges for garbage are examples.

More daunting, however, is the challenge of expanding PLS to cover not only larger industrial sources but also smaller enterprises and nontraditional emitters, including some non-point sources. While it is essential to bring such sources into the system for political as well as environmental reasons, calculating emissions, monitoring, and enforcement present intractable problems. The pragmatic solution is to use a flat fee only roughly related to emissions. For example, commercial animal husbandry facilities are charged on the number of animals they have, and very small enterprises pay an administra-

tively determined tax until they grow large enough to make taxation on an emissions basis practical.

The obvious questions are how much revenue the reformed PLS will bring in and how that will compare with the environmental damage now being borne by the Chinese economy. Unfortunately, there are no clear answers.

Projecting revenues from the reformed PLS over time is difficult both because data on the tax base are incomplete (and will change) and because the behavioral responses to the incentive to reduce pollution are uncertain. However, a revenue simulation pilot study covering 77 cities and using 1995 data found that receipts would have been about 10 times the amount actually collected by the old system, assuming no changes in behavior due to the tax itself. Using the most likely set of assumptions from the nation as a whole, the reformed PLS would have resulted in revenue of about 0.9 percent of gross domestic product (GDP) in 1995.[14] This falls well short of the estimate of total environmental damage from pollution in 1992, which was about 4.9 percent of national income.[15]

Turning to the revenue use side, funds raised by the tax will continue to support environmental administration at all levels, with about 30 percent (the exact figure is still under negotiation) going for this purpose. With the remaining 70 percent, three funds will be created. The Municipal and County Fund will receive 80 percent, the Provincial Fund 15 percent, and the National Fund 5 percent. These funds are designed to fill the investment gap in pollution control caused by capital shortages and by inadequate general government revenue due to the existing tax structure.

These funds represent a major break with the old PLS. In the old system, money was returned as grants for pollution control projects in the municipality or county where the revenues were raised. While these grants were ostensibly destined for the control of major polluting sources, in practice they were largely returned to the firms paying the taxes as allocations for specific pollution control devices.[16] In contrast, the new funds will be administered as revolving loans with near-market terms. Administrators will be enjoined to make loans on the basis of two criteria: creditwor-

Table 2. Pollution-equivalent adjustment factors

Medium	Pollutant(s)	Adjustment factor
Water pollutants	Chemical oxygen demand[a] for five days	1.00
	Mineral oil	10.00
	Suspended solids	0.25
	Total chromium	25.00
Air pollutants	Sulfur dioxide	1.00
	Dust	0.17
	Carbon monoxide	0.04
	Benzene	13.40
	Methyl benzene	3.70

[a] The quantity of oxygen required to break down chemical pollutants.

SOURCES: Wang Jinnan, Yang Jintian, Cao Dong, and Gao Shuting, "Design for Chinese Pollution Charge Standards," in Chinese Research Academy of Environmental Sciences, *Proceedings of the Seminar on the Reform of Chinese Pollution Levy System* (Beijing, 1997).

thiness and the environmental benefits that are expected to be achieved. Experiences with a pilot fund in Shenyang (Liaoning province) has been good.[17] The three funds will, of course, grow over time as revenues are received and repayments (with interest) occur.

While the Municipal and County Fund will largely be devoted to loans to enterprises and revenue-producing services such as water treatment plants, portions can be used for infrastructure projects for which the polluter-pays principle cannot be applied. More flexibility will be accorded to the Provincial and National Funds because they are designed to support interjurisdictional and multi-regional projects. While loans are appropriate for some such projects (e.g., regional waste disposal facilities), they would not be feasible for others. Such activities were impossible under the old PLS, and indeed, the Chinese governmental structure makes any such projects extremely difficult at present.

Future Implementation

Changes of the magnitude proposed for PLS will be considered carefully, as is appropriate. The initial approval of the proposal is significant because the measure was evaluated by experts and officials from each of the organizations most concerned, as well as by the National People's Congress's Natural Resources and Environment Committee.

Final implementation, however, will require coordination between the departments concerned and approval at the highest levels of the Chinese government. To some extent, it will also require legislative action.

The climate for approval is mixed. In March 1998, the Chinese government was reorganized (which occurs every five years) and new people assumed some leadership positions. A massive restructuring of the economy is under way, which will lead to less government control, more flexibility for industry, and a streamlining of decisionmaking. Unemployment will be a continuing problem because of the rationalization of industry, the reduction in the bureaucracy, and the slower growth rates that are expected overall—and that is assuming that the economic troubles in Asia are contained. The Chinese government's stomach for additional disruptive change in the near future must therefore be questioned. At the same time, however, the visibility of the environmental quality issue continues to rise and PLS reform is seen as a key to taking the next big step in bringing China toward acceptable levels.

As to the reform itself, implementation on a pilot basis (to test the program operationally) began on 1 July 1998 in three large metropolitan areas in different regions of the country—Hangzhou, Zhengshou, and Jilin. For the pilot program, applicable tax rates have been set

at one-half of those proposed for the reformed PLS. The pilot program is set to last one year, and it will be followed by an intense evaluation with subsequent adjustments to the program as needed. Because of the temporary nature of this program, revenues will continue to be handled in the traditional manner. Assuming all goes well, nationwide implementation of the new PLS is scheduled for 2000.

Accomplishments, Lessons, and Challenges

Severe problems require bold actions. The proposed reform is such an action— a bold, comprehensive effort to stop China's environmental deterioration and to place the pollution control enterprise on a sound footing for the future.

While efficiency and effectiveness were guiding principles in the reform's design, the special institutional circumstances of China directed how those principles were actually embodied in the plan. In addition, pragmatic recognition of the prospective barriers to adoption led to many shifts from policy measures that might have seemed preferable theoretically.

One factor in the success of the reform so far is the full participation of field-level personnel, who helped structure a program responsive to the needs of municipalities, provinces, and the taxed entities. Another factor is the inclusion of persons with political experience to temper the enthusiasm of analysts and theoreticians for elegant but perhaps not acceptable solutions. Moreover, participation by key nonenvironmental agencies avoided provisions that otherwise would have been certain to spawn conflict.

Experience with the old PLS will assist in implementing the new program and in gaining acceptance for it. Then too, the revolving pollution control fund in Shenyang should provide substantial lessons in setting up funds that can use the revenues from the new PLS effectively. More will be learned from the trial of the system now under way.

Serious challenges remain, however. As noted above, final approval is yet to come. And even when it does, educating the municipalities and provinces will take time. Informing and gaining at least tacit acceptance by the regulated community will require substantial skill and effort.

Strengthening and expanding the monitoring, inspection, enforcement, and administrative functions and the performance of environmental authorities will also be a monumental task. These challenges, however, should be compared with those of using more intensive command-and-control regulation to achieve the same level of pollution reduction. This comparison may favor the tax approach because of its transparency and reduced opportunities for administrative exceptions. Even so, setting up the three special funds, establishing their operating principles and practices, and recruiting skilled and experienced managers will be difficult.

Research and further analysis are needed in all of these areas. Documentation of China's experience with PLS reform will be especially important because it can assist Chinese authorities and others watching from abroad in making the adjustments that will inevitably be needed.

The Chinese experience offers many lessons for countries seeking to strengthen environmental protection in the most efficient way. In some cases, the PLS program itself may serve as a model. More important, however, is the process through which the program was developed, which stressed learning from the experience of other countries; including field-level people and representatives from all affected government agencies; being pragmatic, i.e., adapting to the political and practical constraints involved and recognizing that the perfect is often the enemy of the good; building on existing institutions and practices to foster acceptance and credibility; doing extensive analysis, including a pilot implementation to assure the program's workability, fine tune the details, and build credibility; and incorporating a schedule for further environmental improvement so that the initial disruption is minimized but long-term goals can be achieved.

The promise of a similar system in countries with poorly developed civil services will be particularly bright if it lessens the differential enforcement of regulations based on special relationships between environmental authorities and firms. Multinational corporations, which have long complained that they are held to higher standards than indigenous firms, will be watching especially closely.

PLS reform in China can be a monumental step forward in the application of economic incentives to the environmental enterprise. It is arguably the largest and most comprehensive test of a new way of achieving environmental quality in recent times.

Around the world, countries are trying to deliver higher levels of environmental quality while under intense pressure to raise the level of goods and services available to their citizens. Policies along the lines of China's PLS reform offer the promise that each goal can be achieved with minimum sacrifice of the other. Environmental authorities and analysts will therefore be watching this process with intense interest as it unfolds.

Robert A. Bohm is professor of economics at the University of Tennessee in Knoxville. Chazhong Ge is an assistant fellow in the Environmental Economics Division at the Environmental Management Institute (EMI) of the Chinese Research Academy of Environmental Sciences in Beijing. Milton Russell is a senior fellow at the Joint Institute for Energy and Environment, a research consortium of the Oak Ridge National Laboratory, the Tennessee Valley Authority, and the University of Tennessee that is based in Knoxville, Tennessee. Jinnan Wang is a professor at EMI and the institute's deputy director. Jintian Yang is an associate professor at EMI and chief of the Environmental Economics Division. The authors may be contacted through Milton Russell at 314 UT Conference Center Building, Knoxville, TN 37996-4138 (telephone: 423-974-4324; e-mail: mrussel4@utk.edu).

Note: So that all authors' names will be consistent, the names of the Chinese authors are given above in Western style, with family names last. In the references below, however, they follow the Chinese custom, with family names first.

Notes

1. China's per capita income in 1997 was about $600 (U.S. dollars) on an exchange rate basis. Even though it was substantially higher on a purchasing power parity basis, China remains in the lower ranks of the world's countries. (In the coastal and developed areas, however, income levels are much higher, approaching those in the newly industrialized countries and not far behind those in Eastern Europe.) As to growth, China's gross domestic product has risen about 10 percent per year in real terms since economic reform began almost 20 years ago. Data on Chinese economic conditions and trends can most easily be accessed from *Economist* Intelligence Unit quarterly country profiles on China. See also S. Shuisheng and Y. Yuqun, "On the Problems of Distribution of Social Income in China," *Chinese Economic Studies* 29, no. 6 (1996): 6.

2. Comprehensive reports on China's environmental conditions are numerous. See, for example, National Environmental Protection Agency, *Report on the State of the Environment* (Beijing, 1997); and National Environmental Protection Agency, *China Environment Yearbook, 1996* (Beijing, 1997). Vaclav Smil and Mao Yushi have coordinated a series of studies that conclude that the economic costs of environmental pollution amounted to 4.9 percent of national income in 1992. See V. Smil and M. Yushi, *The Economic Cost of China's Environmental Degradation* (Cambridge, Mass: American Academy of Arts and Sciences, 1998), 11; and V. Smil, "China Shoulders the Cost of Environmental Change," *Environment,* July/August 1997, 10. For a view of conditions in microcosm, see M. Hertzgaard, "Our Real China Problem," *Atlantic Monthly,* November 1997, 97. Conditions in Beijing have deteriorated to the point where it is now one of the most polluted cities in the world. "Beijing Mops Up after a Mud Bath," Reuters, 16 April 1998.

3. The National Party Congress in September 1997 and the National People's Congress in March 1998 were occasions for Chinese leaders to express determination to rectify environmental problems. See "Chinese Communist Party Opens Its 15th National Congress," *China Daily,* 12 September 1997; and "President Makes Pledge: Habitat Must Be Bettered," *China Daily,* 16 March 1998. In its reorganization after the March National People's Congress, the government elevated the National Environmental Protection Agency to ministry status and broadened its authority.

4. For example, the Chinese have long required environmental impact statements. The "environmental responsibility" system requires city and provincial leaders to make public commitments to specific environmental quality targets (which are negotiated with environmental authorities) for the coming year, with public reports on success or failure. Cities are also publicly ranked against each other annually on an environmental quality index. See, for example, Qu Geping, *Environmental Management in China* (Beijing: United Nations Development Programme and China Environmental Press, 1991); L. Ross, *Environmental Policy in China* (Bloomington, Ind.: Indiana University Press, 1988); State Council, *Environmental Protection in China* (Beijing, 1996); and B. J. Sinjule and L. Ortolano, *Implementing Environmental Policy in China* (Westport, Conn. and London: Praeger, 1995).

5. "Environment Minister Sets Goals," *China Daily,* 2 April 1998; and "President Makes Pledge: Habitat Must Be Bettered," note 3 above.

6. Conceptually, PLS is the equivalent of an emissions tax, and for the convenience of international readers is referred to as such in this article. In China, however, the term *tax* is reserved for revenue sources that feed into general government revenues. The Chinese use the terms levy and fee to refer to earmarked taxes

such as those included in PLS. U.S. practice is similar, with earmarked taxes often being called fees or charges.

7. The efficacy of emissions taxes to control pollution has long been recognized. The theoretical principles were first described by Arthur Pigou and subsequently refined by many others. See A. C. Pigou, *The Economics of Welfare,* 4th ed. (London: Macmillan, 1932); W. J. Baumol and W. E. Oates, *The Theory of Environmental Policy,* 2nd ed. (Cambridge, U.K.: Cambridge University Press, 1988); J. R. Kahn, *The Economic Approach to Environmental and Natural Resources* (Orlando, Fla.: Harcourt Brace and Company, 1998); and Wang Jinnan, *The Theory of Pollution Charges* (Beijing: Sciences Press, 1997). However, such taxes have not been widely employed, mainly for institutional and political reasons. A few European countries, notably Germany, France, and the Netherlands, have adopted emissions of pollutants as the basis for their water management charges, however. See Organisation for Economic Cooperation and Development, *Taxation and the Environment: Complementary Policies* (Paris, 1993); and Organisation for Economic Cooperation and Development, *Environmental Taxes in OECD Countries* (Paris, 1995). And the state of New South Wales in Australia is now implementing a broad-scale system. Simon Smith, manager of regulator innovations, New South Wales Environmental Protection Authority, personal communication with the authors, Beijing, November 1997.

8. K. Lieberthal, "China's Governing System and Its Impact on Environmental Policy," in A. Frank, ed., *China Environment Series* (Washington, D.C.: Woodrow Wilson Center, 1997).

9. National Environmental Protection Agency, *Pollution Charges in China* (Beijing, 1992); and National Environmental Protection Agency, *China Environmental Yearbook, 1992* (Beijing, 1993).

10. Chinese Research Academy of Environmental Sciences, *Study on Design and Implementation of Pollution Levy System in China* (Beijing, 1997). Wang Yangzu and Lu Xinyuan, deputy administrator of the National Environmental Protection Agency and director-general of its Department of Supervision and Management, respectively, directed the project. Yang Jintian and Wang Jinnan of CRAES directed the research and planned and edited the report. The discussion that follows is drawn from the report, from presentations made to the reviewing tribunal and at an international workshop that preceded it, and from personal participation by the authors from the inception of the project. Because the report has had very limited circulation in English, specific references are not given below.

11. A Pigouvian optimum is one in which the total social cost of emissions is minimized.

12. See European Commission, *Tax Provisions with a Potential Impact on Environmental Protection* (Luxembourg, 1996); and Organisation for Economic Cooperation and Development, *Environmental Taxes in OECD Countries,* note 7 above.

13. For example, if actual emissions are 100 tons, of which 60 have a PE of 1.4 and 40 have a PE of 0.8, the tax would be levied on an adjusted base of 116 PE tons $(1.4(60) + 0.8(40))$.

14. Chinese Research Academy of Environmental Sciences, note 10 above; and China Statistics Bureau, *China Statistics Yearbook, 1996* (Beijing, 1996).

15. See Smil and Yushi, note 2 above. Note that GDP and national income are not identical conceptually.

16. State Council, "Tentative Provision for Levy of Fees on Pollution Discharges," in National Environmental Protection Agency, *Pollution Charges in China,* note 9 above.

17. Established in 1988, this fund is managed by the Shenyang Environmental Protection Investment Company. The measures financed by this fund achieved twice as much pollution reduction as traditional grants. See National Environmental Protection Agency, *China Environmental Yearbook, 1992,* note 9 above; and National Environmental Protection Agency, *China Environment Yearbook, 1996,* note 2 above.

Article 13

Harvard International Review, Summer 1998

WORLD IN REVIEW

Breaking the Wall

China and the Three Gorges Dam

November 7, 1997, marked the beginning of the end for a scenic stretch along the Yangtze River in Yichang, China. Groups of giant Caterpillar trucks disposed large boulders into the roaring currents of the world's third longest river. The man-made obstacle sealed off a dike to divert the waterflow, marking an instrumental step toward the completion of China's Three Gorges Dam, slated to be the largest dam in the world.

ALEXANDER KUO

Diverting the river is the first step in preparing the area for the construction of numerous hydropower plants and intricate locks. As President Jiang Zemin and Premier Li Peng looked on over a crowd of 5,000 celebrants, the international media compared the undertaking of this feat to the construction of the Great Wall of China and the pyramids of the Pharaohs.

The prodigious dam is to be built near the center of China, where a valley in the Yangtze narrows to form the Xiling, Wu, and Qutang Gorges. The result will be an enormous reservoir within those gorges. Until the year 2006, the focus of construction will be on the flood discharge system and the actual hydroelectric plant. By that year, the first 14 generators will begin the new distribution of electricity. By the year 2009, 12 additional generators will begin operating, as well as two massive locks and ship lifts. Bringing the generators to full capacity will symbolize the project's successful conclusion. The year 2009 will also mark the culmination of an unprecedented human endeavor—the assemblage of a 900 cubic foot dam. But perhaps more importantly, the beauty of the Yangtze River, a treasure trove of Chinese mythology, will also cease to exist. More than a decade prior to the dam's completion, it is already evident that the environmental and social consequences of the construction of the dam outweigh the expected benefits of energy distribution and modernization.

Beyond the Building

The world's largest dam will figuratively and literally swamp existing human structures in all dimensions. The 600 foot tall, 1.2-mile wide structure will tower over the world's third-largest river. The lake created by the dam will extend 650 kilometers upstream, creating an immense reservoir that will submerge approximately 50,000 acres of land, 19 cities, 150 towns, and 4,500 villages. The relocation process for the 1.2 million people who will be forced out of their homes has already begun.

Yet one of the most staggering figures attributed to the dam is its cost. At a minimum, dam supporters expect the entire process to cost at least US$24.5 billion; some have predicted that the cost will exceed US$70 billion. The Chinese government has sought at least US$8 billion from foreign investment to help finance this project. While companies in Europe and Japan have actively signed construction contracts, their US rivals have unwillingly been left out of the frenzy. The French and German governments, unlike the US government, have given their corporations the financial guarantees that the Chinese govern-

ment requires from contractors working on the dam. Due to environmental concerns, however, the United States has withheld Export-Import Bank export credit guarantees for US companies, including Rotec Industries and General Electric. But the Export-Import Bank is not the only institution preventing investment in the dam. After conducting a four-year study through the Canadian International Development Agency that examined the financial risks of the project, the World Bank also refused to aid the project.

In the face of these roadblocks, China has taken additional measures to minimize criticism of the project. The Chinese government has persecuted and imprisoned Chinese scientists for questioning the technological feasibility of the project. Since 1989, the government has also banned public debate on the dam. The comments of Dai Qing, a journalist and one of the most vocal critics of the dam, cost her ten months in prison. The government also banned the

journalist's book of essays. The book, *Yangtze, Yangtze,* crystallized the various problems with the dam. The journalist explicitly cited the dam as a dangerous product of a socialist economic system. Some critics note that the pace of work on the dam recently accelerated to ensure that the construction reached an "irreversible point" before Premier Li Peng's term expired in March 1997. It is likely that the fear of reprisal has prevented many potential high-ranking detractors from publicly criticizing the project.

Expected Returns

Certainly those responsible for squelching criticism of the dam embrace the projected benefits it is expected to bring to the people of the Yangtze River valley. One of the primary advantages of the project is the control of periodic flooding of the river, which has killed tens of thousands of people in the three great floods of this century. Most nota-

China has invested in massive hydroelectric projects in the past, but the costs of the Three Gorges Dam may outweigh the benefits. (File Photo)

bly, in 1931, the Yangtze submerged what is now the industrial center of Wuhan for three months.

Additionally, the dam's supporters expect the 26 giant generators to account for close to a tenth of China's energy output. The hydropower is viewed as a more efficient and cleaner source of energy than the sulfur-laden coal that is currently used in the area. Some engineers estimate that the dam will annually generate an amount of energy equivalent to the burning of forty million tons of coal. Thus, if successful, the dam's energy output will be environmentally advantageous over the current release of destructive sulfur dioxide and carbon dioxide gas emissions. This cleaner supply of energy will be available within a 1,000 kilometer radius of the dam, as far as Shanghai and Guangzhou.

While seasonal flood control of the Yangtze and maintenance of a more efficient energy supply are persuasive arguments for the dam's construction, its economic possibilities are what have piqued corporate interest. A major motivation for many outside corporations to engage in expensive and risky dam construction is the potential of gaining future contracts with China. For example, firms such as Germany's J.M. Voith hope to gain a foothold in China's future hydropower sector because of their involvement in the Three Gorges. Thus, the dam represents a gigantic entry point for many corporations to do business with China; the sheer size of the project represents a possible leap to a market-oriented economy for China. From the nation's perspective, a parallel economic benefit is the drastic reduction in shipping costs after the dam's construction. The increased water level in the reservoir would improve river navigation, allowing for heavier vessels to sail up the Yangtze. Shipping capacity could increase by as much as 400 percent; the change would be magnified because the river is responsible for about 65 percent of the country's riverborne cargo. Despite widespread feasibility concerns, many Chinese leaders remain convinced that the dam is essential for China's transition into an age of modern efficient energy distribution and into a more prosperous economic era.

Concrete Costs

Before one can gauge the dam's success it must first become functional. Unfortunately, the structure's current design has already incurred incalculable human costs. Furthermore, any engineering defects will doom any hopes for energy efficiency or flood control. One potential problem is that the dam will be sprawled out over a seismically active area; the reservoir will lie over an active fault line. The weight of the water could trigger an earthquake, which would devastate the entire structure. Such a calamity would dwarf the 1975 collapse of the 62 iron dams in the Henan province, which killed over 85,000 people. The floods also rendered millions homeless, and triggered famine and disease. If the Three Gorges were to meet a similar fate, the result would be 40 times worse.

Another major problem that will undercut the dam's effectiveness is the high degree of sedimentation in the river. Since the sediment suspended in the water currently flows downstream, critics fear that the dam will cause it to build up around the installations at the end of the reservoir. One result of this buildup is that the particles can clog filtering pipes, causing sewage backups in Chonqing. The sheer amount of gravel and sand suspended in water—approximately 540 million tons—will overwhelm any dredging effort. The sediment buildup could even block the Chonqing harbor, thus flooding the land upstream, which will be compounded by the immense amount of existing sewage. In addition to turning the reservoir into a reserve for gravel and sand, the sewage problems may cause more pollution. Unfortunately, and perhaps too late, these costs will only be realized after the dam's construction is complete.

The process of construction has raised other environmental concerns which cannot be measured in relation to any future output the dam might bring. For example, environmentalists have warned that the river blockage will endanger many species indigenous to that particular ecosystem including the Chinese alligator, the white crane, and the Chinese sturgeon. The creation of the reservoir could likely lead to the extinction of these species. Another unquantifiable cost is the loss of precious

historical artifacts and relics, which enshrine ten centuries of Chinese history. Archeologists are scrambling against time to comb over 250 square miles of the riverbank for ancient tombs and writings before they become permanently submerged.

Tangible human costs of the construction exist as well. One problem is the disregard for the rights of the workers on the dam. Several provinces involved in the project have put political and religious prisoners to work in labor camps. The viability of the government's massive resettlement initiative has also been questioned. Many of those who have been forced to higher ground face harsher economic circumstances, which compounds the difficulties of their abrupt displacement to new areas. Of the 92,000 people resettled so far, a majority have had difficulty in adjusting to the new communities in the already densely populated areas. The forced settlement has sparked serious social unrest and resistance. Outrage at the relocation initiative has led to numerous assaults and lootings, and these uprisings will only worsen once the resettlement engulfs the rest of the 1.4 million people living in the path of the reservoir.

Piecemeal Possibilities

Despite the monetary risks involved in investing in the dam, possible financial benefits for corporations remain tempting; the structure is an economic "showpiece" that invites outsiders to quickly establish vital business networks that will pave the way for future dealings. The Caterpillar Company, for example, went so far as to showcase the Three Gorges on the cover of its annual report, after selling US$15 million of equipment to developers. With European and Asian corporations massively gaining ground in the race to supply the project, the frustration of American firms is understandable. Notably, the engineering firm Rotec Industries has lost business to a Mitsubishi-led group, backed by Japanese export credit guarantees. Rotec, because of the Export-Import Bank's ruling on assistance to the project, does not enjoy the same guarantees as Japanese industries.

Political motives have complemented the economic motives that have gar-

SIZE MATTERS

The construction of the Three Gorges Dam is not the first controversial hydroelectric project. About 40,000 dams with heights of 15 meters or more are currently operating globally. Numerous non-governmental organizations have attempted to delay some of these major projects, including the Sardar-Sarovar Dam in India and the Arun Dam in Nepal. Efforts to halt such massive projects, though, have often failed.

But the Three Gorges Dam will outdo all past hydroelectric projects in every respect. Not only will the projected US$29–75 billion cost be higher than any other, the approximate 1.2 million people that will be resettled represents a figure significantly higher than any other resettlement project.

Approximately 3.6 billion cubic feet of rock and soil will be excavated, 900 million cubic feet of plain and reinforced concrete will be poured, and an enormous 300,000 tons of metal structures will be installed, with each individual turbine weighing roughly 400 tons.

Regarding benefits, the 500 foot deep lake that will be created should allow for 10,000-ton ocean-going cargo ships to navigate as far as 1,500 miles inland to Chongqing. If the dam successfully prevents flooding of the Yangtze, it could potentially prevent thousands of deaths. In 1931 and 1935 flooding killed over 280,000 people. Most recently, in 1954, the death toll from the Yangtze River was 33,000.

nered support for the dam. The colossal project, apart from modernizing China by increasing the nation's access to efficient electricity and by decreasing transport costs, stirs some nationalistic pride. President Jiang Zemin has pronounced that, "blocking the Yangtze is a great moment in the modernization of our country . . . it vividly proves once again that socialism is superior in organizing people to do big jobs." Because the project has called for so many resources and support, and because the implications for its completion have such wide-reaching effects, no one closely involved in the construction would dare to turn back at this point.

This situation is a case where political hubris has trumped practical considerations. For government officials who have espoused the dam since its inception, halting construction would deliver a terrible blow to Chinese modernization and to their own perception of self-importance. Yet, by focusing on the future prospects of a singular monument that will satisfy energy needs and ego in one sprawling project, the advocates of the dam have failed to support alternatives to the current project. Detractors support the building of smaller power plants along the tributaries throughout the river system, including the Jinsha and Wujian Rivers. By constructing medium-sized energy outlets, flood control could still be achieved, but at a much lower cost. Additionally, the risk of a massive flood from a giant reservoir could be averted. Finally, the construction of these smaller dams would also preclude having to relocate massive numbers of people to unfamiliar territories.

Opponents of the megadam generally sympathize with the need to aid the tens of millions who are without efficient electricity. They are not against the ideas of spurring development and modernization in China through improved shipping pathways and cheaper electricity. They are not against stopping the destructive flooding of the Yangtze. But, they also understand that these admirable goals should not be obtained through a risky project that will trigger social unrest, more flooding, and immeasurable human costs. These goals will not be realized through a project that garners its momentum from politicians and investors who seek economic advantage and place their own pride on the line. Unfortunately, those who advocate the more sensible, cost-efficient, albeit incremental steps to these goals are being drowned in a raging effort to suppress opposition and maintain a one-sided debate focused on the dam's merits. The Three Gorges Dam represents a unique cross-section of cultural, environmental, economic, and political interests. Opponents of the project who recognize the implications of the dam's construction beyond the economic and political considerations have been systematically prevented from expressing the necessary criticism.

Comparisons between the Three Gorges Dam and the nation's other great colossal structure, the Great Wall of China, have already been made. Whereas architects of the Great Wall attempted to shun foreigners, the planners of the Three Gorges Dam have invited foreigners to assist in erecting another monument of majestic value. But the Three Gorges Dam has only succeeded in eroding the majestic beauty along the Yangtze. And unlike the Great Wall, which supposedly provided security to the Chinese people, the Three Gorges Dam may well spell ruin for millions of Chinese inhabitants.

Alexander Kuo, World in Review Editor, *Harvard International Review.*

Article 14

The American Enterprise, July/August 1998

DEMOGRAPHIC CLOUDS ON CHINA'S HORIZON

by Nicholas Eberstadt

While there is little about China's position in the year 2025 that we can predict with confidence, one critical aspect of China's future can be described today with some accuracy: her population trends. Most of the Chinese who will be alive in 2025, after all, have already been born.

The most striking demographic condition in China today is the country's sparse birth rate. Though most of the population still subsists at Third World levels of income and education, fertility levels are remarkably low—below the level necessary for long-term population replacement, in fact. This circumstance of course relates to the notorious "One Child" policy of China's Communist government, applied with varying degrees of force for nearly two decades.

> **By laboring so ferociously to avoid "overpopulation," Beijing has ensured that other, even more daunting, problems will emerge in the decades ahead.**

Ironically, by laboring so ferociously to avoid one set of "population problems"—namely, "overpopulation"—Beijing has helped to ensure that another, even more daunting set of problems will emerge in the decades ahead. Those population problems will be, for Beijing and for the world, utterly without precedent. While impossible to predict their impact with precision, they will impede economic growth, exacerbate social tensions, and complicate the Chinese government's quest to enhance its national power and security.

How can we know fairly well what China's demography will look like 25 years from now? Because according to the latest estimates by the U.S. Bureau of the Census, about a billion of the 1.2 billion Chinese living on the mainland today will still be alive in 2025—accounting for about seven out of every ten of the 1.4 billion Chinese then alive.

The main population wildcard in China's future is fertility. The Census Bureau suggests that the nation's total fertility rate (TFR) now averages a bit under 1.8 births per woman per lifetime (significantly below the 2.1 births necessary for long-term population stability). For broad portions of the Chinese populace, fertility appears to be even lower—as depressed as 1.3 lifetime children per woman in some cities. In Beijing and Shanghai, TFRs may actually have fallen under one by 1995!

The Census Bureau assumes Chinese fertility will average about

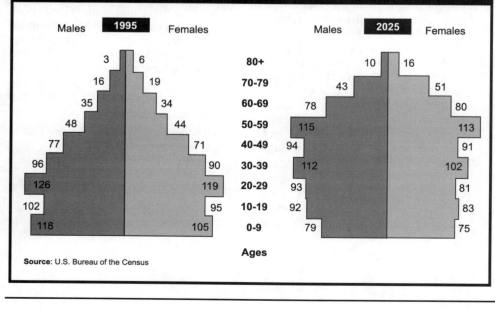

CHINA'S AGE PYRAMID 1995 & 2025

1995 — Males / Females

Males	Ages	Females
3	80+	6
16	70-79	19
35	60-69	34
48	50-59	44
77	40-49	71
96	30-39	90
126	20-29	119
102	10-19	95
118	0-9	105

2025 — Males / Females

Males	Ages	Females
10	80+	16
43	70-79	51
78	60-69	80
115	50-59	113
94	40-49	91
112	30-39	102
93	20-29	81
92	10-19	83
79	0-9	75

Source: U.S. Bureau of the Census

1.8 births per woman through 2025. But today's child-bearing takes place under the shadow of the country's severe—and coercive—anti-child campaign. Might not the birth rate leap up if that program were discarded or reversed? It's impossible to be sure, but bits of evidence suggest that a revolution in attitudes about family size has swept China since Mao's death—and that this would prevent fertility from surging back toward more traditional patterns, even if all governmental controls were relaxed. Consequently, the Bureau projects that China will be reaching zero population 25 years from now.

But China's population will look quite different than it does today, as the nearby chart reveals. China in 2025 will have fewer children: The population under 15 years of age is projected to be almost 25 percent smaller than today. The number of people in their late twenties may drop nearly 30 percent. But persons in their late fifties stand to swell in number by over 150 percent, and there will be more people between the ages of 55 and 59 than in any other five-year age span. Persons 65 years or older are likely to increase at almost 3.5 percent a year between now and 2025, accounting for over three-fifths of the country's population growth.

In short, if Census Bureau projections prove correct, China's age structure is about to shift radically from the "Christmas tree" shape so familiar among contemporary populations to something more like the inverted Christmas trees we see out for collection after the holidays. While in 1997 there were about 80 Chinese age 65 or older for every 100 children under age five, by 2025 China would have more than 250 elderly for every 100 preschoolers.

China's coming demographic transformation will bring three sets of serious social problems: rapid aging, declining manpower, and a protracted bride shortage.

China's "graying" will be as swift as any in history. In 1995, the median age in China was just over 27 years. By 2025 it will be about 40.

Although several European nations are already at China's 2025 median age, they got there much more slowly, and with much more societal wealth available to cushion the effects. A similar "graying" over the last four decades in Japan has emerged as an intense concern of Tokyo policymakers, who wonder how the nation is going to manage its growing burden of pensioners. Like the China of 2025, Japan's median age is currently around 40 years. But Japan is vastly richer today than China could hope to be by 2025. Even if its current brisk pace of economic progress continues, China will still be by far the poorest country ever to cope with the sort of old-age burden it will face.

For despite its recent progress, China remains a land of daunting economic disparities and crushing poverty. World Bank research has indicated that the proportion of Chinese suffering "absolute poverty" (defined by the Bank as living on less than $1 a day) was nearly 30 percent from 1981–95. Though that figure is undoubtedly lower today, under almost any plausible scenario for future income growth, China in 2025 will still have hundreds of millions of people with incomes not much different from today's average ones—but with a dramatically older population.

How will such a nation care for its elderly? Under current arrangements, the only social security system for most of the country's poor is their family. Scarcely any public or private pension funds operate in the remote rural areas where the overwhelming bulk of China's poor reside. In 2025, grandparents will by and large be the parents of the "One Child" era, so they will have few offspring to offer them shelter in old age. A small but significant group will have no surviving children. A fourth or more could have no surviving sons—thus finding themselves, under Chinese culture, in the unenviable position of depending on the largesse of their son-in-law's household, or, worse, competing for family resources against their son-in-law's parents.

Problem two will be declining manpower. Over the past generation, China's brisk economic growth has been partly due to an extraordinary increase in the work force. From 1975 to 1995, China's "working-age population" grew by over 50 percent (or nearly 300 million persons). In a final burst due to population increase, it will grow by over 12 million persons a year at the beginning of the 2000's. Then the growth of potential workers will abruptly brake. By around 2015, China's working-age group will have peaked at just under 1 billion. In 2025, it is projected to be about 10 million persons smaller than a decade earlier. Thereafter, the decline may accelerate, with the workforce shrinking by as many 70 million people over 15 years.

Having fewer workers may complicate China's quest for economic growth. Younger people tend to be better educated than their elders, and as they stream into a work force this increases its average skill. But China's demographic trends will slow down the improvement in education and skill-levels among the working-age population. Today. the rising cohort of 10- to 14-year-olds represents roughly a seventh of the country's working-age population. By 2015 it will be only a twelfth. This presages a sharp slowdown of education-based improvements in labor productivity.

China will not be the first country in the world to wrestle with an aging populace, or a shrinking workforce. But China's third major demographic challenge is unprecedented: a coming imbalance between men and women of marriageable age.

Beginning with the advent of the nation's "One Child" policy, Chinese sex ratios began a steady, and eerie, rise. By 1995, a Chinese sample census counted over 118 boys under the age of five for every 100 little girls. Part of this imbalance is a statistical artifact—the combination of strict government birth quotas and the strong Chinese preference for sons has caused some parents to hide or "undercount" their newborn daughters, so that they might try again for a boy. But the larger portion of the reported imbalance appears to be real—the consequence of sex-selective abortion and, to a lesser extent, female infanticide.

This tragic imbalance between boys and girls will mean a corresponding mismatch of prospective husbands and brides two decades hence. By Chinese tradition, virtually everyone able to marry does. But the arithmetic of these unnatural sex imbalances is unforgiving, implying that approximately one out of every six of the young men in this cohort must find a bride from outside of his age group—or fail to continue his family line.

In China's past, any problem of "excess" males was generally solved by the practice of marrying a younger bride, which worked well when each new generation was larger than the one before. But with today's low fertility, each new generation in China will typically be smaller than the one before. So if young men try to solve their marriage problem by pairing off with a younger woman, they will only intensify the "marriage crisis" facing men a few years their junior. Nor will searching abroad for a Chinese wife be very promising: By 2020,

the surplus of China's twentysomething males will likely exceed the entire female population of Taiwan!

In early modern Europe, bachelorhood was an acceptable social role, and the incidence of never-married men was fairly high. In China, however, there is no such tradition. Unless it's swept by a truly radical change in cultural attitudes toward marriage over the next two decades, China is poised to experience an increasingly intense, perhaps desperate, competition among young men for the nation's limited supply of brides.

A 1997 essay in the journal *Beijing Luntan* predicted direly that "such sexual crimes as forced marriages, girls stolen for wives, bigamy, visiting prostitutes, rape, adultery . . . homosexuality . . . and weird sexual habits appear to be unavoidable." Though that sounds overly dramatic, the coming bride shortage is likely to create extraordinary social strains. A significant fraction of China's young men will have to be re-socialized to accept the idea of never marrying and forming their own family. That happens to be a condition in

which men often exhibit elevated rates of crime and violence.

Many of China's young men may then be struck by a bitter irony: At a time when (in all likelihood) their country's wealth and power is greater than ever before, their own chances of establishing a family and comfortable future will look poor and worsening. Such a paradox could invite widespread disenchantment.

There is little any future Chinese government will be able to do to address this problem. China's involuntary bachelors will simply have to "handle punishment they have received as a result of . . . the mistakes of the previous generation," suggests the *Beijing Luntan*. How they will accept this remains to be seen—and it will bear directly on the character and behavior of the China that awaits us.

Nicholas Eberstadt is a visiting scholar at the American Enterprise Institute and a visiting fellow of the Harvard Center for Population and Development Studies.

Article 15　　　　　　　　　　　　　*Far Eastern Economic Review*, May 7, 1998

Voice of the People

As people band together to try to improve their lives, they're spawning thousands of grassroots organizations. A wary Beijing is tolerating some, but mowing many others down.

By Matt Forney in Beijing

The Divorced Women's Teahouse was a cosy place to drown broken marriages in cups of jasmine tea. Members of the Beijing self-help discussion group ranged from distressed women on the verge of leaving abusive husbands to divorcees looking for help finding dates. In a society notoriously inattentive to the plight of women, "we gave them a place to talk," says founder Shi Jian-

ping. "It had nothing to do with government or policy."

Not according to the government. In late 1996, a year after the divorcee association was formed, officials demanded it register. That was no easy task. First, the group needed a government sponsor. Then it needed $24,000 in capital reserves—an astronomical sum for Shi, who once found it difficult

to scrounge together $20 to treat members at McDonald's. Unable to muster the necessary sponsors or funds, the teahouse closed last year.

Civic organizations like the teahouse are emerging across China—much to the consternation of a government deeply suspicious of any group outside its control. As the Communist Party reluctantly withdraws from people's daily lives, a multitude of new associations are forming to represent the interests of their members. The new groups are helping the poor, providing health tips to homosexuals, protecting the environment, safeguarding the rights of women and migrant workers—emerging wherever they see a need for teamwork.

The government says there are 200,000 registered "mass organizations." There are surely at least that many unregistered groups that are technically illegal, including anything from a sewing circle to a triad society. Jude Howell, a specialist in Chinese civil society at Britain's University of East Anglia, compares the desire to set up new groups to "a boiling pot, and it's difficult for Beijing to keep the lid on."

Indeed, civic organizations like the teahouse are struggling against a government that still wants to stay in charge. That tension is likely to intensify. A fearful Beijing has set up a Byzantine registration system to weed out any organization it deems threatening—and that includes just about every independent civic group.

For a party that once controlled everything from coal production to what peasants ate for dinner, organized groups beyond its control constitute a clear challenge. China's leaders recall with dread how quickly the independent Solidarity labour union undermined Poland's communist government in 1989.

At the same time, Beijing knows that executive fiat won't drive this newly emerging "civil society" out of existence. Bai Enpei, governor of Qinghai province, acknowledged as much to China's legislature in March: "Things the government shouldn't manage, or can't manage, or manages badly, should be given to enterprises, society and relevant institutions to manage themselves."

Beijing, therefore, allows the existence of groups with agendas that dovetail with its own, such as protecting the environment. But it has been remarkably successful in constraining broad-based networks that could one day oppose the government. The government figures that even though it could come into conflict with these groups at least it has identified the people it is conflicting with," says University of East Anglia's Howell. "That's easier for the govern-

ment to deal with than mass outpouring like the Tiananmen demonstrations."

Meaningful nonstate organizations were unheard of from the day Chairman Mao announced a communist victory in 1949 to the dawn of Deng Xiaoping's reform era in 1978. Then the 1989 Tiananmen uprising occurred, and frightened party leaders moved to control grassroots movements from which popular dissent could emerge. State Council Order No. 43 banned any "social organization" that fails to "protect the unity of the state and the solidarity of the nation." More perniciously, it banned "identical or similar social organizations . . . within the same administrative area." That outlawed any group serving a function ostensibly filled by a government-registered organization. There can be, for instance, no labour alliance to compete with Beijing's officially sponsored union.

The order ruined Luo Qichun's chance of forming an association to help protect people's historic homes. Luo, an engineer, boned up on property law in December 1996 after workers pasted a notice on the wall of his family's graceful residence in western Beijing announcing its scheduled destruction less than a month later. Luo refused to budge. His family had fought for its home before. Ultra-radical Red Guards had squatted there during the Cultural Revolution, and Luo's father had regained control only after Mao's death in 1976.

Luo knew the city had to provide market-based compensation. His family had held a deed since 1944, and new laws in 1986 protected homes bought before the revolution. All the city offered, however, was a small apartment miles away and $4,000—a hundredth of the family residence's market value by Luo's estimate. He sued for greater compensation, representing himself, and lost. Police forcibly removed him last year, and his home is now rubble.

But the story didn't end there. His experience prompted Luo to spend his free time offering legal advice to people facing similar evictions. He says more than 100 are suing the city based on his counsel. Luo considered starting a formal organization, but decided against it because "we'd never find approval from the government we're suing."

The city already has an organization to safeguard its older neighbourhoods:

The Beijing Association for Preservation of Cultural Relics is supposed to be independent—even though its members are former officials and its offices are in the city government. By law, its existence means Beijing can't allow Luo's group to serve the same function.

It's not always easy to tell how independent a group is. All legal organizations have official approval, and report to a specific government department (which bears responsibility for the group's "mistakes"). Some use government office space; others receive official stipends. China, therefore, has few truly nongovernmental organizations. On the other hand, mere registration doesn't indicate a puppet, and many organizations set up by the government operate with a measure of autonomy.

Take the Centre for Legal Culture, which was formed in 1995 by a group of Beijing law professors who registered it with the Ministry of Civil Affairs. The centre has no offices and its first round-table discussion had an innocuous theme: "Mores and Law in Traditional Society." Since then, however, the centre has been pushing the limits of what is permissible. A recent discussion was of a new translation of a book by Friedrich Hayek, the late Austrian Nobel laureate who was perhaps the world's most eloquent critic of socialism.

The Centre for Legal Culture has also begun sending members to evening guest lectures at Beijing University, China's top school, to speak to packed auditoriums about how "a strong legal system can protect civil rights," says He Weifang, the centre's co-founder. Most importantly, the Ministry of Civil Affairs "doesn't seem concerned with what we're doing," He says.

Perhaps sensing that the growing number of semi-independent groups erode the party's control over society, Beijing has tried to strengthen its hand. The official Xinhua news agency recently released a circular declaring that any social group with members from the Communist Party must form party committees within the organization. Rigorous enforcement is unlikely, but the circular reflects the party's anxiety about losing control.

Yet grassroots groups continue to grow. In the past few years, migrants from the countryside to the cities have begun to organize. Since many have no residence permits and no legal right to stay in urban areas, the migrants are vulnerable to extortion by police or periodic roundups and forced repatriation to the countryside.

In Beijing, migrants from central Zhejiang province live in a southern district of the capital informally called Zhejiang Village, where most of them run small textile businesses. In 1994, the area's more prominent businessmen formed the Loving Hearts Society to mediate disputes between the community and officials.

It scored some successes. A year after it was formed, a policeman savagely beat a village resident. The society brought medical help and laid plans to bring a lawsuit, but backed down under pressure from managers of the local marketplace, who didn't want trouble. On another occasion, the same managers suddenly evicted village vendors from their stalls to develop a piece of land. The Loving Hearts Society mediated, but by then city officials were involved. The group was simply declared illegal and closed in May 1995.

Yet members of the society still live in the village, and will likely re-emerge. Their presence is simply too necessary. In addition to providing a service, they are needed by the community to create an elite that will fight for the people's rights and interests, says Xiang Biao, a Beijing University expert on migration and himself a transplant from Zhejiang. But he warns that "the government is especially afraid of these groups—just as a manager is afraid of unions."

Social groups enjoy little access to the government. The Women's Telephone Hotline, registered in 1992 to advise women on a host of troubles ranging from abusive husbands to poor sex lives, has been advising China's legislature on a new marriage law. Hotline members have argued for making marital rape, as well as other forms of domestic violence, a crime. The marriage law's drafters have promised to "consider our opinions," says Wang Xingjuan, the hotline's founder. "But it will be up to them how much they use."

The most successful organizations are those promoting causes that fit in neatly with Beijing's own policies—environmental protection, for instance. Beijing finds itself unable to prevent local leaders from chopping down trees, polluting rivers and fouling the air in the name of regional development. Locally, there's not much tree-huggers can do. By forming national networks, however, they are faring better.

Take the coalition that formed around Yunnan province's endangered golden monkey. A county government had sold loggers the right to clear 160 square kilometres of forest—an order that would have led to the destruction of the reclusive primate's migration route to Tibet. The first activist was Xi Zhinong, a nature photographer who had spent several freezing months on the Tibetan plateau taking pictures of the monkeys.

Xi inspired students at the Beijing Forestry College into forming the Green Students' Forum. It, in turn, got in touch with Friends of Nature, Beijing's only registered environmental-protection group, which was formed in 1993. Xi was soon joined by environmental author Tang Xiyang, and together they wrote a letter to China's top environmental official, Song Jian. Last year, Song pressured the province to cancel its logging plans. Just to be sure, the students organized a month-long trip to "investigate."

The green network continues to expand. Until recently, residents of Panjin city on the northeast China coast hadn't realized that their summertime visitors were the highly endangered Saunders' Gulls. Only 3,000 of the birds exist, and not until 1990 did ornithologists discover their salt-marsh roosting site in Panjin. Locals called the gulls "Old Black Heads" for their distinctive plumage, and thought their uses were predicting rain by their evening wails and providing eggs for food.

Liu Detian, a journalist from a local newspaper, thought otherwise. In 1991, he registered the Saunders' Gull Protection Commission, and convinced a vicemayor to chair the group. Despite the high-level names on the board, the reserve hasn't proscribed development—shrimp fisheries and oil rigs dot the area, and more are to come. Last year, Liu contacted Friends of Nature and was given some advice: "more publicity." Liu has since sponsored domestic press tours, and arranged for local schools to teach about the gulls. It's not clear flying yet, but Liu is optimistic. "Before the Beijing connections, I was lonely," he says. "Now I feel support."

Despite the successful outcome of these preservation campaigns, China's social organizations remain tethered. "The government wants us to be part of its system," says a women's-rights activist who requested anonymity. "We can just hope for more influence as the government tries to shed some of its responsibilities." So far, that influence has been slow in coming.

Article 16   *The Washington Post National Weekly Edition,* June 29, 1998

A New Day in China?

Beijing's baby boomer generation builds democracy one village at a time

By Steven Mufson

Washington Post Foreign Service
BEIJING

In July 1989, about a month after Chinese troops killed hundreds of civilians in a crackdown on student-led protests in Tiananmen Square, a little-known official named Wang Zhenyao from China's Ministry of Civil Affairs traveled to a village in the northeastern province of Liaoning to oversee a democratic election.

Wang traveled with one of the vice ministers, who nervously wondered aloud whether it wasn't an inopportune time to be promoting grass-roots democracy. "The word democracy had become unmentionable," Wang recalls.

Not to worry, Wang reassured the vice minister. If the local officials were supportive, there would be no problem, he said. The balloting went off without any serious hitches.

Nearly a decade later, genuine elections have become commonplace in roughly half of China's 928,000 villages, thanks in large part to the self-effacing Wang, who has crisscrossed China's vast countryside training local officials in the most elementary principles of democracy and democratic procedures.

That may seem like an uncommon achievement for a bureaucrat in what is still a Communist state. But Wang is just part of a remarkable new elite in and outside China's government that is beginning to transform the country at the turn of a new century.

They are the most talented portion of the Cultural Revolution generation, a group comparable to the baby boomers of the West that for the most part lost its way amid the political and economic upheaval that racked China from 1966 through 1976. The few who, like Wang, managed to claw their way back into universities and get their careers back on track are self-starters who learned hard lessons about their society and its political system.

NOW, THEY'RE HITTING THE PEAKS of their careers, carrying with them the indelible marks of that earlier time. Though less well-known internationally than the country's senior leaders, these people in their late thirties and forties are reshaping China's one-party politics, its booming businesses and its culture. Many of them believe that in the next century, they are likely to make China a more stable country with greater democracy, a more open and capitalist economy, and far greater personal freedom.

In the case of the village democracy program that Wang has championed, the changes are in some ways subtle so far. The experiment has been confined to communities averaging about 1,000 residents, and political parties other than the Communists are not allowed. In many places vote-buying and ballot-rigging are problems. Still, any resident may be a candidate for the freely elected village council, which has the power to levy taxes and manages local services and schools.

Wang estimates that he has visited about 1,000 villages, from Gansu province, the gateway to China's far west, to Shaoshan in Hunan province, where villagers gave him a small copper statue of

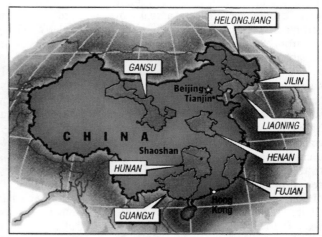

(BY ROBERT DORRELL—THE WASHINGTON POST)

their famous native son, Communist Party Chairman Mao Zedong, who ruled China like a latter-day emperor until his death. The statue stands on his bookshelves at home, near an encyclopedic series on Chinese history and a Chinese translation of the 19th-century classic by Alexis de Tocqueville, "Democracy in America."

In every place he has visited, Wang has approached local officials with a disarming, "aw shucks" air about him, prodding them to adopt more open primaries and procedures to ensure voter privacy. At the same time, he has deftly worked China's bureaucracy, tapped into different personal networks, and at times called on old friends in provincial governments or in the national media to pressure recalcitrant local officials.

Building democracy, Wang says, "is like rolling snowballs. At first you have just a little bit. Then more and more."

In early 1995, the weather in Jilin province was certainly cold enough for snowballs. Wang trekked there to observe elections in Lishu, a county Wang was cultivating as a model of rural democracy. Though it seemed as though the cold would lower voter turnout, Wang had learned that during good weather peasants are too busy in the fields to vote.

IN DONGBAISHAN, POPULATION 1,300, people braved subfreezing temperatures to listen to candidates in a decrepit schoolroom with faded pictures of Albert Einstein, Madame Curie and other scientists staring down from the walls. Smoke seeped from a coal stove and mixed with cigarette smoke billowing from peasants. Soon it was barely possible to see across the crowded room.

The three candidates delivered campaign speeches. One spoke with a folksy, unprepossessing style, and one sounded as though he were giving a Mao-era harangue. All obliquely criticized the financial expertise of the outgoing village party chief, who had frittered away $1,200 on an ill-conceived pig-raising venture. It was a prodigious sum in a poor area where per capital income averages only $120 a year. The incumbent party chief, the local leader for 20 years, dropped out after a disappointing showing in the primary.

"My thinking can't keep up with the current thinking," he said.

"We need to build a democratic culture," said Wang. "Our tradition is that you don't speak out loud, you wait some years, have a revolution and overthrow the government. We're saying that in three years you can throw out the government."

It is one of the ironies of Communist China that a government that proclaimed the wisdom of peasants during the Cultural Revolution, which took refuge among the peasants during the civil war with the Nationalists,

in fact places little faith in peasants and frequently cites the rural dwellers' lack of education as a reason that Western-style democracy can't be introduced here. Chinese leaders fear that open elections would lead to irresponsible populism or, worse yet, chaos.

Wang, however, has never doubted the common sense of people from the countryside. He's one of them. During his life, chaos has come from above. Born in 1954 in a village in Henan province, Wang's first political memory is hunger. Mao's economic program, the Great Leap Forward initiated in 1958, had failed spectacularly. Though Mao wouldn't admit that the economy was collapsing, in villages like the one where Wang grew up it was no secret. Fuel and cooking oil were in short supply. The cooking pots had been melted down to meet Mao's unrealistic steel production targets.

To survive, Wang ate raw tree bark. "We ate it raw, right off the tree," he says. "For my generation, the first deep impression is hunger. We were very, very hungry."

His area barely had time to recover from the Great Leap Forward when the Cultural Revolution began. In November 1966, at age 12, Wang spent two weeks in distant Beijing with his classmates to

catch a glimpse of the revered Mao in Tiananmen Square. When Mao appeared in the square, he was greeted by Wang and half a million other screaming youths waving their little red books of Mao's quotations and chanting "Long live Chairman Mao."

"My generation really believed we were red," Wang recalls. "We believed in Chairman Mao and that we should devote ourselves to Chairman Mao."

Wang went back to his village. Each Sunday he would walk 15 miles to school, stay there for the week and walk back on Saturdays. Soon classes stopped, and the students planted crops instead. He was essentially self-educated, having borrowed the few books permitted at the time, mostly classic Chinese novels or books about Marxism or Maoism.

In 1972, Wang joined the army. He stood guard in four-hour shifts at an airport near Guilin, in Guanxi province. To keep his mind alive, he studied at night and on Sundays, reading the only books available. One was an official diatribe against Confucius. In 1976, he was promoted to platoon leader and sent to work in a factory.

Mao died the same year. Youths like Wang, who worshiped him at the outset

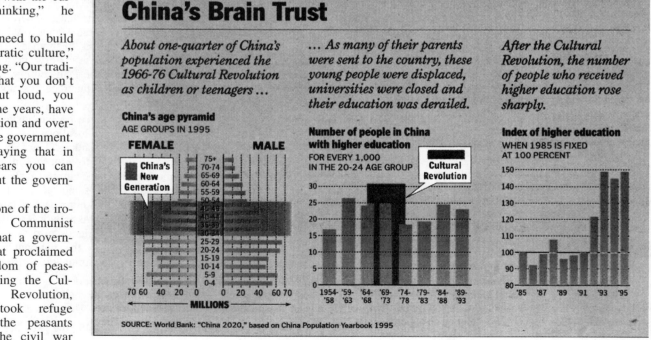

China's Brain Trust

About one-quarter of China's population experienced the 1966-76 Cultural Revolution as children or teenagers ...

... As many of their parents were sent to the country, these young people were displaced, universities were closed and their education was derailed.

After the Cultural Revolution, the number of people who received higher education rose sharply.

China's age pyramid
AGE GROUPS IN 1995

FEMALE   MALE

China's New Generation

75+
70-74
65-69
60-64
55-59
50-54
45-49
40-44
35-39
30-34
25-29
20-19
15-19
10-14
5-9
0-4

70 60   40   20   0   0   20   40   60 70
◄——— MILLIONS ———►

Number of people in China with higher education
FOR EVERY 1,000 IN THE 20-24 AGE GROUP

Cultural Revolution

30
25
20
15
10
5
0

1954- '59- '64- '69- '74- '79- '84- '89-
'58   '63   '68   '73   '78   '83   '88   '93

Index of higher education
WHEN 1985 IS FIXED AT 100 PERCENT

150
140
130
120
110
100
90
80

'85 '87 '89 '91 '93 '95

SOURCE: World Bank: "China 2020," based on China Population Yearbook 1995

(BY DITA SMITH AND ROBERT DORRELL—THE WASHINGTON POST)

of the Cultural Revolution, had started to question Mao's godlike stature as the infighting of the Cultural Revolution dragged on and the proletarian utopia Mao promised failed to materialize.

When senior Chinese leader Deng Xiaoping was rehabilitated the next year, he reintroduced an examination system for university admissions. Wang was one of a half-dozen selected from a group of 100 soldiers. In 1978, he enrolled in the prestigious Nankai University, with its impressive Soviet-built façade, in Tianjin.

"THE OLDER GENERATION REmembers the 1950s when life was going well, and they can compare before and after liberation," Wang says. "But for my generation, it is very, very different. We felt emancipation in 1979," when Deng introduced his economic reform program.

After graduate school, Wang went to work for the rural policy institute of the State Council, China's cabinet, and was put to work doing rural political reform. Economically, Mao's communes were finished by the mid-1980s. Land once managed collectively was contracted to individual households. Communes were renamed townships, and production brigades rechristened villages. But politically, the old, appointed cadre structures were still in place.

The real impetus for village elections wasn't a liberal reformist impulse, but rather the desire among Chinese leaders to regain greater control of the countryside. In the 1980s, discontent was spreading like a prairie fire. Peasants were ignoring family planning guidelines, physically assaulting tax collectors and refusing to hand in to state depots the minimum quantities of grain required under government-set quotas.

"In the rural areas, democracy may have originated in a dispute about taxes," Wang says, not unlike the Boston Tea party.

Wang researched local elections and wrote reports to rally support within the party for change. In the winter before the Tiananmen uprising, Wang studied two unruly villages in Heilongjiang province. In one village, the party appointed a leader to reimpose order. But the peasants continued to boycott tax payments, burned the village cadre's

house and cut down his trees. In the other village, order was restored after a competitive election.

In a report to the party's central committee, Wang concluded that "by introducing competitive elections, we can gain the peasants' support and avoid the danger of loss of control in the countryside." A key party elder, Bo Yibo, endorsed the report.

"This was not going against the Chinese Communist Party line," Wang says. "These were the facts."

Over time, the idea of rural elections attracted an odd alliance. Peng Zhen, a conservative who was then chairman of the National People's Congress, rammed a village election law through the reluctant parliament. Wang says party elders like Peng "believed that the Chinese Communist Party would rule forever, but that they needed democracy to protect themselves." To win over waverers, Peng dubbed the law "experimental." Eleven years later, it still is.

Some election supporters were true democrats who hoped the elections would spread to the more populous townships and cities, and ultimately include national offices like the presidency. Other supporters, like Bo, were party faithful who saw the elections as techniques for ridding the party of corrupt and unpopular officials and spotting new talent. Roughly 40 percent of the candidates elected in village balloting aren't party members, Wang says. But half of those people are successfully recruited by the party within a year. Wang calls the process "mutual and spontaneous."

Despite broad support at the top, many local officials feel threatened by elections or loathe sharing power with the electorate. Wang needed broad support because he couldn't do it alone. His 1995 visit to Lishu county was part of a calculated gamble. Wang wanted to drum up more support by getting publicity from Chinese media about the elections, but Chinese reporters balked for fear of offending Marxist ideologues.

So Wang took along three American reporters whose articles were later reprinted in a Chinese party newspaper, Reference News, devoted to reprinting foreign dispatches. The Foreign Ministry, realizing the elections could be good publicity for China overseas, then wrote a report to the party's central committee.

Chinese journalists soon followed up with articles of their own.

China's Communist Party central committee now seems more committed to the process. On June 11, the front pages of the leading state-run newspapers led with news of a new central committee circular ordering all villages to comply with the election law, and saying that the party would "make active efforts" to introduce elections at the township level, the next highest rung of government.

NO ONE IN CHINA BELIEVES THAT the world's most populous nation is on the verge of democracy as the West knows it. The most prominent democracy dissidents remain in jail, under surveillance or in exile. Asked at his maiden news conference as premier about the possibility of holding elections at higher levels of government, Zhu Rongji said that the government would study and consider it. But he didn't suggest it would happen any time soon.

Wang says that if far-reaching political change ever comes to China, it needs a foundation. "If there is no foundation, there will be no pluralism," he says.

The experience of the former Soviet Union, viewed by the Chinese as a combination of political instability and economic collapse, serves as a cautionary tale. "[Former Soviet leader Mikhail] Gorbachev's biggest problem was at the grass roots. He didn't build any political culture for pluralism at the grass roots. He tried to impose it from above," Wang says.

"This [holding elections] worth doing whether it results in a more democratic [Communist] party or a democracy with many parties," Wang says philosophically. When, how or if multiparty democracy might come about is out of Wang's hands. "Who can predict?" he says.

China's experiment with village democracy has become a favorite cause among Americans looking for a reason to hope that China is becoming more democratic. For a time, Wang became a common name on American guest lists. On his bookshelf, he has photos of himself meeting Vice President Gore and former national security adviser Brent Scowcroft.

But last year, Wang was suddenly reassigned to a job running disaster relief. Some people who know him say it was a normal job rotation. Others say he fell victim to jealous colleagues at the civil affairs ministry. Now he does everything from coordinating aid to flood areas to building a social safety net for the poor and unemployed in the cities. On the side, he still consults with local election officials and researches local elections.

"Disasters are no problem," he says. "They're not like democracy. They're not as dangerous."

Article 17

The Economist, July 25, 1998

ASIAN VALUES REVISITED

What would Confucius say now?

SINGAPORE

Asian values did not explain the tigers' astonishing economic successes, and they do not explain their astonishing economic failures

MAYBE the cycles of intellectual fashion are speeding up. Just 20 years ago, Chinese communists and many western historians alike blamed the set of moral teachings and social mores known as Confucianism for China's backwardness. Despite its ancient civilisation and technological breakthroughs, it had been humbled in the 19th century by western barbarians, partly, it was argued, because of the Confucians' contempt for trade. Then, in the early 1990s, some Asians argued that those same intellectual and social traditions, now subsumed into a broader concept—Asian values, they were called—helped explain East Asia's remarkable economic success, and prepared the region for global dominance in what was to be the "Pacific century". The aftershocks from the region's economic earthquake of the past year now rumble through this debate. Those Asians—and some westerners—who argued that there was something inherently superior about Asia's social structures have been proven wrong. Indeed, the very values they touted have contributed to the collapse.

Or perhaps not. To believe that Asian values caused either miracle or crash is to accept two dubious premises: that there is a common core of distinctively Asian principles, and that this core has been accurately defined by the most outspoken and articulate Asian participants in this debate, most of them from South-East Asia, notably Malaysia and Singapore.

According to Kishore Mahbubani, a Singaporean diplomat and writer, Asian values include "attachment to the family as an institution, deference to societal interests, thrift, conservatism in social mores, respect for authority". This list is not exhaustive. Indeed, Asians are also said to prize consensus over confrontation, and to emphasise the importance of education. Put together, these values are held to justify regimes which, to the West, look illiberal. Invoking Asian values, authoritarian governments are said only to be providing their people with what they want. While they delivered unprecedented economic success, the claim was taken seriously.

Asians moved off the back foot, and on to the offensive. Westerners, they argued, had confused ideas rooted in their own traditions—about individual freedom and liberal democracy—with universal truths. Asians, however, stick to eternal verities forgotten by western countries in their headlong pursuit of individualism, and their descent into a morass of broken families, drug-taking, promiscuity, mud-slinging and violence. In 1996, after the first Asia-Europe summit, Malaysia's prime minister made the bold assertion "Asian values are universal values. European values are European values."

So it appears both that there is something different about Asian values, and that they, unlike western ones, are somehow "universal". The picture is further muddied by occasional suggestions that these values change with time, but are appropriate for Asia's present stage of economic development, just as "Victorian values" suited 19th-century Britain. But Asians, broadly defined, make up more than 60% of the world's population. Any attempt to distil essential, but non-universal, beliefs across such a huge swathe of humanity is ambitious to say the least. And in practice, the debate has concentrated on East Asia, largely ignoring South Asia, except in negative comparisons sometimes drawn between India's rumbustious democracy and its relatively poor economic performance on the one hand, and the tough but successful systems to the east on the other.

Even in East Asia, talking of a single set of values involves blending many of the world's intellectual traditions—Confucianism, Buddhism and Islam, to

The sage, 2,549 years on

FOR most of the 25 centuries since Confucius was alive, scholars have been debating what he was on about. As with any influential thinker, people tend to pick and choose which elements of his ideas most appeal. In recent years, he has been cited favourably by those on both sides of the debate about Asian values.

The only (nearly) direct source of Confucius's thoughts is "The Analects", a collection of his *obiter dicta* compiled by disciples after his death. It is more of a scrap-book than a thesis. Its classical Chinese is terse and elliptical. Some of it is hard to interpret. Indeed, some passages are understood in diametrically opposed ways by different scholars.

Confucius lived at a time when the old feudal order had disintegrated into warring satrapies. His advice to the rulers he sought to influence reflected a conservative hankering for the old rituals, the old certainties and the old stability. Modern exponents of Asian values like to stress his emphasis on "filial piety", scholarship and meritocracy.

But others point out that "the rectification of names" (a son should behave like a son, a subject like a subject) was a two-way street: fathers and rulers also had obligations. In this sense, argues Simon Leys in a recent book*, "Confucius was certainly not a Confucianist . . . More essential notions were conveniently ignored [by him]—such as the precepts of social justice, political dissent, and the moral duty for intellectuals to criticise the ruler." Confucius believed in a loyal opposition. Asked how to serve a prince, he replied: "Tell him the truth even if it offends him."

Lee Kuan Yew, Singapore's senior minister, is accepted even in China as a great Confucianist: he spoke at a big conference in China in 1994 to celebrate the 2,545th anniversary of the great man's birth. But others use the sage's words to argue a different line from Mr Lee's. Malaysia's Anwar Ibrahim, for example, cites Confucius to denounce the idea that "the state must always precede the individual". Another scholar argues that Mr Lee's policies owe less to Confucianism than to the rival Chinese tradition of "legalism". A Confucian state, he says, would not need to pass a law, as Singapore has done, requiring children to look after elderly parents.

The legalists were famous for laying the intellectual basis for the rule, through strict laws, of China's first emperor, Qinshi Huangdi—he of the terracotta warriors, the Great Wall, the burning of books and the burial alive of Confucianists. Nowadays, legalism, mercifully, takes milder forms.

---

* "The Analects of Confucius, Translation and Notes" by Simon Leys. W.W. Norton, New York, 1997.

---

name but three. However, it was not in doubt that the region had produced many authoritarian regimes and, until last year, some fantastic rates of economic growth. First, Taiwan, South Korea, Hong Kong (all of which industrialised before they democratised) and Singapore; and then China, Indonesia, Malaysia and Vietnam.

But now some of the sins laid at the doors of the region's economic systems look suspiciously like Asian values gone wrong. The attachment to the family becomes nepotism. The importance of personal relationships rather than formal legality becomes cronyism. Consensus becomes wheel-greasing and corrupt politics. Conservatism and respect for authority become rigidity and an inability to innovate. Much-vaunted educational achievements become rote-learning and a refusal to question those in authority.

Goenawan Mohamad, an Indonesian writer, tells a story of his country during President Suharto's last months in office. A young journalist came across some traffic policemen engaged in the odd pursuit of drying out banknotes at the roadside. On inquiry, it emerged the money came from bribes routinely paid by bus and lorry drivers. To shorten procedures, they stuffed the cash in cigarette packs and threw them from their cab windows. The banknotes were wet because first they would spit on them.

It is a tale of petty, futile yet rebellious compliance that could be told of many corrupt and arbitrary regimes in the world. Yet it casts doubt on the proposition that Asians have a greater respect for authority—however exercised—than do westerners, as does other evidence. In the past 12 years, the region has seen a series of mass protests: in the Philippines in 1986, South Korea in 1987, Myanmar in 1988, China in 1989, Taiwan in 1990, Thailand in 1992, Indonesia in 1998. Some of these popular protests were manipulated by factions among the elite, but that was possible only because of the large pool of disaffection to draw on. Their success or failure depended, ultimately, not on the inherent support enjoyed by the government, but on the willingness (as in China), or otherwise (as in the Philippines) of the army to shoot civilians.

Nor is such protest just a phenomenon of a "westernised" middle class. In 1990, even the people of Myanmar, among the world's poorest, voted decisively against the military junta and for the party of the western-educated, "liberal" Aung San Suu Kyi. In 1993, the benighted, long-suffering people of Cambodia also voted against the established powers-that-be and, despite threats of intimidation and threats of violence, may do so again in the general election to be held there on July 26th.

Nor do Asia's intellectuals and politicians come close to unanimity about the notion of Asian values propagated by the concept's leading promoters, Lee Kuan Yew, Singapore's senior minister, and Mahathir Mohamad, the prime minister of Malaysia. Among the many Asians who have argued that "human rights" and "freedom" are universally held aspirations are Miss Suu Kyi, Kim Dae Jung, the veteran campaigner for democracy elected in December as president of South Korea, and Wei Jingsheng, a well-known dissident expelled from China. In apparent defiance of his boss, Malaysia's deputy prime minister, Anwar Ibrahim, claims that "no Asian tradition can be cited to support the proposition that in Asia the individual must melt into a faceless community."

The argument about Asian values is usually presented as an intellectual joust between Asia and the West. But it is probably more important as a political debate going on in Asia itself both among leaders (like Mr Anwar and Dr Mahathir) and between governments and their opponents. It is notable that so much of it is conducted in—or with—Singapore. Singapore is the youngest, richest, smallest (Brunei aside) and most westernised country in South-East Asia. No other is so dependent on international trade and investment from multinational companies, giving it, you might have thought, an incentive to pipe down a bit.

Mr Mahbubani explains Singapore's assertiveness as in part shrugging off a colonial chip—"an effort to define [Asians'] own personal and national identities in a way that enhances their sense of self-esteem where their immediate ancestors had subconsciously accepted that they were lesser beings in a western universe." But that explains only national values, not Asian ones. Tommy Koh, another Singaporean diplomat and Asian-values theorist, says he once asked one of his Japanese colleagues why they were so quiet in this debate. "We're more Asian than you," was the reply. It meant, apparently, that the Japanese were less confrontational. Another interpretation is that they are surer of their identity and place in the world.

A multi-media exhibition currently running in Singapore is part of a recent effort to foster an understanding of the island's history. The visitors sit on a mobile "people carrier" which transports them through a series of tableaux designed as a "journey through time", from the arrival of Britain's Sir Stamford Raffles in 1819 to the glorious, three-dimensional (special glasses are provided) but "challenging" future. There are gory pictures of past communal riots, and an explanation of how vulnerable Singapore felt after its expulsion from federation with Malaysia in 1965. Singapore itself is an accident of history in a dangerous part of the world. Complacent young Singaporeans, the display suggests, could do with some of their elders' edginess, as well as a commitment to a "shared pledge" beginning "Nation before community and society above self".

The internal stresses

In spreading that message across the region, other factors may have come into play, such as the desire to seek a shared

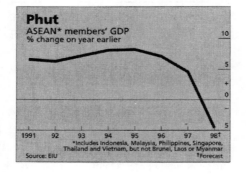

Phut
ASEAN* members' GDP
% change on year earlier

1991 92 93 94 95 96 97 98†
*Includes Indonesia, Malaysia, Philippines, Singapore, Thailand and Vietnam, but not Brunei, Laos or Myanmar
Source: EIU   †Forecast

view of the world with countries which in the past have been hostile. Singapore, a small and mostly Chinese island surrounded by largely Muslim Malaysia and Indonesia, hopes that its neighbours, seeking an alternative to wholesale westernisation, will not veer towards more extreme forms of Islam; Mr Anwar in Malaysia, and B.J. Habibie, Indonesia's new president, evoke some alarm—not so much because both seem to have rather "liberal" views, but because in both their backgrounds is a link with Islamic groups. The recent orchestrated rape and murder of ethnic Chinese in Indonesia's riots is a grim enough reminder of the lingering dangers of ethnic and religious antipathies as economic hardships worsen.

Asia has rarely been without intraregional tension, and much less in any sense united. Indeed Asia itself is a western concept: the Chinese word for it, *Yazhou,* is a coinage translating a foreign notion. Even South-East Asia is a remarkably diverse and potentially fractious region. The assertion of Asian values partly represents a desire to increase regional cohesion, both to ease tensions between the countries of the region, and to put on weight internationally. Whereas, say, the European Union is a collection of largely Christian, democratic countries, the regional club, the Association of South-East Asian Nations, includes communist states (Vietnam and Laos), a military dictatorship (Myanmar), an "Islamic monarchy" (Brunei) and parliamentary democracies of varying sorts. ASEAN has countries with Buddhist, Muslim and Christian majorities. Hinduism from India and Confucianism from China have left deep imprints. So have periods of Dutch, British, Spanish, French, German, Portuguese, American and Japanese rule.

There is nothing wrong in seeking some common ground in such diverse terrain, especially given the instability

and mutual hostility that until recently marked intraregional relations. But, to quote Mr Anwar again, "It is altogether shameful, if ingenious, to cite Asian values as an excuse for autocratic practices and denial of basic rights and liberties." That, nevertheless, is what many Asians believe has happened.

Don't interfere

The debate may seem to be over. It is not. Both Mr Mahbubani and Mr Koh have this year produced books* collecting their essays. But the discussion is now taking rather different forms. One will be felt at the meetings that begin this week in Manila, among ASEAN's foreign ministers and later with their foreign partners in the security talking-shop, the ASEAN Regional Forum. Since its foundation in 1967, ASEAN's most fundamental policy has been "non-interference" in its neighbours' affairs. This, "the ASEAN way", applied Asian values—even before the term was coined—of consensus and non-confrontation to diplomacy. But in the past two years it has been under threat.

The admission of Myanmar to ASEAN a year ago has created trouble in the group's relations with Europe and America. Without an effective mechanism for telling Myanmar its behaviour is unacceptable, ASEAN is powerless to resolve the dispute. Similarly, the contagious effect of the region's financial turmoil has shown how vulnerable members are to their neighbours' policy mistakes. But, without "interfering", it is hard to exert influence. Thailand and the Philippines have argued for a new policy of "flexible engagement" among members. This is unlikely to overcome the objections of Indonesia and Malaysia, let alone ASEAN's newer recruits, like Vietnam and Myanmar, which would resent any attempt by such a convivial club wanting to change its rules so soon after they have joined.

Nor has economic collapse led to a sudden rush to embrace liberal democracy, although it has entrenched democratic change in some countries. Only in South Korea, with the once-imprisoned Mr Kim now president, is a former inmate running the asylum. Thailand has

---

* "Can Asians Think?" by Kishore Mahbubani. Times Books International, Singapore.
"The Quest for World Order" by Tommy Koh. Federal Publications, Singapore.

adopted a constitution that should lead to a more representative, less corrupt, form of democracy, and the economic mess encouraged Fidel Ramos in the Philippines not to try to amend the constitution last year and run for a second term as president. Mr Habibie is introducing liberal reforms in Indonesia. Some of the intellectuals advising him have long taken issue with what they call "the Singapore school" of Asian values, as have some of those close to Mr Anwar. But the country's political future remains beholden to the army.

And in Singapore and Malaysia, the proponents of Asian values are unrepentant. Dr Mahathir continues to rail against decadent western liberals. This week he accused the opposition leader, Lim Kit Siang, of simply mouthing any criticism he found in the foreign press. Two newspaper editors have resigned because, many believe, their loyalty to the prime minister is less than wholehearted. In Singapore, there is not much opposition left. Two leading government

critics, Chee Soon Juan and Tang Liang Hong, who have lost lawsuits brought by the government, are in Australia. A third, J.B. Jeyaretnam, recently saw the court of appeal increase fivefold the damages awarded to the prime minister by a lower court in another defamation suit. If the judgment is enforced, he will be bankrupted and lose his seat in Parliament.

Elsewhere—especially in the worst afflicted economies, Thailand, and Indonesia—there remains a big risk of an anti-western backlash, as people lose their jobs, see foreigners buy up local companies, and generally force tough policies on weakened national governments. The next time the Asian-values debate flares up, it may be in a new guise, concentrating not so much on individual freedom and human rights, and whether or not they are universal, but on the global financial system and its dominance by the West. Now is not the time for westerners to crow about their superior ways. Such triumphalism has,

in fact, been rather muted. Yet noting how some western commentators have reacted to the disaster, Mr Mahbubani's book argues that "the desire to bury Asian values revealed the real pain" inflicted during the debate.

Yet that pain was felt not just by smug westerners whose ingrained sense of superiority was challenged. It was shared by Asians who believed their values were being misrepresented, and their traditions selectively culled to justify policies. In Asia, as everywhere, there is disagreement about which traditions are worth preserving and nurturing. South-East Asia, for example, with its history of maritime trade, has in some ways an admirable record of tolerance and openness to foreign influence. The urge to avoid wholesale westernisation is understandable. But it need not mimic former colonial prejudices about the ineffable otherness of the East. Dr Mahathir was right: Asian values are universal values. But he should have added, vice versa.

Article 18

Harvard International Review, Summer 1998

HUMAN RIGHTS

The Real China

A Firsthand Perspective on Human Rights in Today's China

BY GEORGE KOO

In the autumn of 1993, the chief executive and the executive vice president of sales and marketing of a small Tennessee firm visited Shanghai with me to explore a business relationship with a local company. Early during our stay, I took them for a walk on the

famous Shanghai Bund by the banks of the Huangpu River. The walkway along the river was full of local Chinese enjoying the warm, sunny Sunday afternoon. Young couples wandered aimlessly or simply stood shoulder to shoulder to gaze across the river without

really seeing the busy river traffic below. Children out with their parents ran around shouting, chasing after balls, or simply letting out their exuberance and delight. Senior folks sat in twos and threes watching the lively scene and sipping tea or eating a frozen dessert pur-

(Photo courtesy of George Koo)

The Western media often fails to recognize the relative freedom of daily life in China.

chased from the many vendors stationed nearby.

While these US executives, visiting China for the first time, were soaking in the good cheer, I asked them if the scene before them exhibited any signs of the police state that had been depicted by the American media at home. They had to admit that what they saw bore no resemblance to their preconceived notions of China.

In October 1996, another Chinese-American and I were invited to Xian, the ancient capital of China, to lecture. Over a casual lunch hosted by local government officials with an official from Beijing in attendance, the conversation was informal and lighthearted. One of the senior dignitaries reminisced about how he was successful in persuading some of the student leaders to tone down their protests during the "June 4 movement"-the Chinese euphemism for the Tiananmen protest of 1989. Thus their political activism did not lead to arrests even though they were blacklisted from pursuing careers in government. Instead, the students directed their energy elsewhere and became highly successful entrepreneurs, as the official noted with a touch of paternal pride.

While we were sightseeing in the countryside, a funeral dirge wafted from the public announcement system of a

nearby village. One of the accompanying young officials in our group said, "This is the funeral music played whenever somebody important dies. Maybe it is for Lao Deng"—a familiar but hardly respectful reference to Deng Xiaoping, the former Chinese leader. Another member of the group replied, "Probably not. Nowadays anybody can use that music, including anyone in the village." Sure enough, at the conclusion of the solemn piece, the "village disc jockey" said that he simply played it for enjoyment. The official who took the music to heart became the butt of some good-natured ribbing from his colleagues.

These are casual conversations of the sort that could not have taken place a few years earlier. Conversely, such conversations are no longer noteworthy today because they have become commonplace—indicating how relaxed China has become. Americans with the opportunity to visit China invariably return home saying they saw the vitality of a purposeful people but did not see or feel the presence of an authoritarian state. Sadly, not enough Americans can go and see for themselves and must depend instead on the words of pundits and politicians, many of whom have been harshly critical of China ever since the Tiananmen protest in 1989.

20 Years of Change

My first trip to China was a personal visit with family members in 1974 when China still was tightly controlled by the infamous Gang of Four. China then was drab—nearly everyone wore the same blue or white shirt. While the people were friendly, they were guarded in what they said. Friends did not socialize except on rare occasions, such as welcoming a returning classmate from abroad.

When I started to advise US companies on doing business in China in 1978, China was just beginning to emerge from the uniform drabness I had previously observed. There were no high-speed expressways, only a few locally-made "Shanghai" sedans; there were no traffic jams, no fancy Hong Kong-style restaurants, no five-star hotels, no high-class department stores brimming with shelves of imported luxury goods, no McDonald's stands, and nobody wearing anything that could be described as colorful, much less fashionable. Thanks to China's nearly double-digit economic growth since it instituted reform in 1979, all of those things have become commonplace. Twenty years ago, foreign visitors shopped in government designated "friendship stores" that were off-limits to local people. Today those same friendship stores are fighting to survive against the proliferation of fancy department stores that are joint ventures with outside partners. Local citizens are no longer barred from friendship stores but prefer to frequent the high fashion stores operated by owners from Hong Kong or Japan.

The one constant about China over the last 20 years has been change. Economic reform has been the driving force. While the economic change is easiest to spot, the change has been accompanied by widespread social and political changes. While the Chinabashers in the West dwell on and are fixated by the images from Tiananmen on June 4,1989, China has moved on.

At the national level, the National People's Congress (NPC), formerly a rubber stamp for the Chinese Communist Party, has been taking more independent action and getting away with it. In April 1995, for the first time, an unprecedented one-third of the delegates rejected Jiang Chunyun for Vice Premier, notwithstanding the fact that he was Chairman Jiang Zemin's choice. In the latest *pro forma* election of Li Peng, the sole candidate for president of the Congress, over 300 delegates—about 11 percent of the NPC—showed their disapproval by abstaining or voting against him. The willing disclosure of this embarrassing deviation from lockstep unanimity for the second most powerful position in China's hierarchy is in itself a noteworthy step toward increasing transparency. In early 1997, the NPC drafted and passed amendments to the criminal procedure code greatly liberalizing the provisions handling criminals. These procedures were passed despite opposition and displeasure from the Ministry of Public Security.

On the local level, China has shown further liberalizing tendencies. Elections have been held in the countryside in recent years; the most recent ones have been observed by representatives of the Carter Center, sent from the United States. The essential point of these elections is not whether they meet Western standards—probably most do not—but that they are taking place. Eventually elections will be held at the township and county level and perhaps will continue even higher. The countryside still accounts for 75 percent of China's population. Taking the rural population through the

democratic process is an important step toward true political reform. Rural populations in developing countries are not usually well educated. When a country with a predominantly rural population adopts elections in haste without proper preparation, the country is practicing merely sham democracy, a sham because a largely uneducated and ignorant population is easily manipulated by a crafty and corrupt few.

American Impatience

The recent progress in China has been scarcely noted in the Western media and overshadowed by the focus on the human rights abuses as perceived by the West. For example, most of the US public do not know that China's former Minister of Justice, Xiao Yang, has publicly stated that China needs to govern all its affairs by the rule of law. He also admitted that China has not achieved this goal yet. In the June 18, 1996, issue of *China Daily,* the quasi-official English daily of the Beijing government, Xiao indicated that "the aim [of the Chinese government] is to ensure [that] over 80 percent of the villages, 80 percent of state-owned enterprises, and 70 percent of other institutions conscientiously administer affairs by law by the year 2000."

The typical US reaction would be: if China recognizes the need for rule of law, why not one hundred percent now? Such an expectation typifies the lack of understanding of the complexities of today's China. Accompanying the economic reform has been a steady loosening of control by the central government. No longer can Beijing rule by edict and expect instant or total compliance. On the other hand, the rise of regional control is uneven, as is local commitment to the rule of law. Some local courts are fair and professional while others are still not trained in the subtleties of the rule of law and may be partial to local parties regardless of the merits of the dispute.

The United States' impatience with China's pace of reform overlooks its own history. The United States has been a free republic since 1776, but it was not until 1865 that slavery was abolished, not until 1920 that women were granted the right to vote, and not until the 1960s that civil-rights legislation began to address racial discrimination in a

serious way. Compared to the US experience, China's progress over the past 20 years has been lightning-quick.

Chinese Values of Human Rights

Impatience aside, China's priority on human rights also differs from that of the West. While the United States considers the rights of the individual sacred, China, along with many other Asian nations, prizes the stability of the entire society over the welfare of the individual. For example, recently in the city of Zhengzhou, a former head of public security, equivalent to a police chief in the United States, was executed for killing a 15-year-old boy while driving under the influence of alcohol, and leaving the scene without rendering assistance. No doubt this is considered a harsh sentence from the US perspective. Even worse, at China's current imperfect state of applying the law, a similar incident in another locale would not always result in the same sentence. On the other hand, most visitors to China would agree that the roads congested with many inexperienced and reckless drivers could stand a strong dose of law and order. If the execution has the desired sobering effect on the drivers of Zhengzhou, why not let the traffic fatalities prevented outweigh the hapless life of one drunk?

China also looks at human rights at a more fundamental level, which includes such provisions as the right to life, freedom from starvation, the right to shelter and clothing, the right to an education, and the right to employment and a means of self-support. When individuals are deprived of these basic rights, they do not necessarily care about voting and having the freedom to express their opinions. With economic growth, the general population begins to enjoy a higher standard of living. Only after they have their basic human rights satisfied, then and only then do they start to look for more and demand more. They expect more alternatives and choices in lifestyle, if not for themselves, then for their children. The progressive liberalization that follows may not be part of the plans of the political leaders, but it is inevitable.

US critics, however, insist on dwelling on the treatment of a handful of prominent dissidents, to the exclusion of an objective evaluation of the total picture in China. A particularly extreme demonizer of China has been the so-called human rights activist Harry Wu, who has long been making outlandish comments and outrageous statements about China, none of which stand up to even perfunctory scrutiny. For example, Wu claimed to have videotaped the removal of kidneys from prisoners in China's prison before these prisoners were led away to be executed. He never explained, however, how he was invited to take such pictures. Wu devoted a great deal of space in his article in the Winter 1997/98 issue of the *Harvard International Review* to Hitler and Nazism for no obvious purpose except as a feeble attempt to associate today's China with a target that the US public hates.

Wu has been making a big deal about China's *laogai,* a Chinese abbreviation for their prison system based on the idea of "reform through labor." He has been campaigning tirelessly in the West to depict China's prison system as hell on earth. Yet the United States has 565 prisoners per 100,000, ranking highest in the world, more than five times the reported incarceration rate in China. The failure of the US prison system is well known—recidivism remains over 40 percent. The only response from US government officials has been to enact laws which attempt to reduce recidivism by imprisoning criminals longer, and thus ensuring the construction of jails as a new growth industry. China claims to have one of the lowest recidivism rates in the world, between six and eight percent. Someone more objective than Wu is needed to make a determination on whether the United States has something to learn from China's approach to reforming convicts.

Finally this year, the Clinton administration has decided to forego the futile annual attempt to censure China through the UN Human Rights Commission in Geneva. Last year the effort ended in dismal failure when countries such as Australia, Canada, France, Germany, and Japan declined to join the US-backed resolution fronted by Denmark. This year even Denmark has decided to abstain from this foolishness. Congresswoman Nancy Pelosi promptly criticized the Clinton decision as one motivated by money interests at the expense of US values on human rights. The representative from San Francisco could not be more wrong. Western participation in China's economy has done far more for improving China's human rights than all the carping and posturing about human rights abuses.

The Role of the West

Apart from helping to raise the standard of living in China through investment, multinational corporations insist on clear guidelines that would protect their investments. Consequently, Beijing's drive for joint ventures with foreign companies has led to the formation of laws and regulations on foreign-owned ventures. These laws are not perfect, but they do represent a huge step in getting China accustomed to the benefits of the rule of law. Similar economic pressures have also led to the formation of laws protecting intellectual property and subsequently the enforcement of such laws. The drive to put economic laws on the books spilled over to the establishment of a host of new civil and criminal laws in China. In fact, China today has become the only country other than the United States where the courts will hear class action suits.

Joint ventures with Western partners are also important stimuli for change. By having US citizens working in China and training some of the Chinese staff abroad, the Chinese gained an opportunity to witness directly and appreciate the typical US egalitarian attitude, concerns for the environment, views on equal opportunity, sense of fair play, and respect for due process. With daily contact, the joint ventures provide a means to introduce Western values by example, rather than by rhetoric, and to exert a positive influence on the Chinese people.

Of course, I am not suggesting in any way that China is free from human rights problems, but I do believe that China's problems will become increasingly similar to the problems experienced in the United States. Economic boom has led to a widening gap between the haves and the have-nots. Consequently, there are now as many as 100 million migrant workers from the rural areas seeking work in the cities. They frequently sleep in hovels or in the open, as do the homeless in the United States. With the threatened wholesale closing of inefficient state-owned enterprises, prospects loom of a huge unemployed workforce clashing with the migrant workers. Unscrupulous outside investors have already taken advantage of the cheap migrant labor and porous regulations on labor protection to set up sweat shops operating under inhumane and unsafe conditions. With the loosening of government controls, drug addiction is on the rise, a problem thought to have been eradicated when the Communists took over.

> I am not suggesting in any way that China is free from human rights problems, but I do believe that China's problems will become increasingly similar to the problems experienced in the United States.

Will familiarity with China's human rights problem lead to sympathy from the United States instead of castigation? It is useful to bear in mind the observation made by Professor John Bryan Starr, in his recently published book, *Understanding China:* "In looking at conditions in another country, Americans often measure real conditions abroad against an idealized vision of conditions at home, and thus seem blind to violations of human rights in their own society at the same time that they ferret out evidence of violations elsewhere."

Dr. George Koo is former President of the U.S./China Business Association and an international business consultant.

Article 19

Current History, September 1998

> "In analyzing the impact of economic reforms on women's lives in China, the government would evidently prefer to discuss its achievements in promoting gender equality and not the chronic discrimination problems that remain. At the other end of the spectrum, Western feminist discourse on China often presents an alarming portrait, replete with stark statistics on the skewed male-female birth ratio, domestic violence, and increased trafficking in women." Exactly how far have women in China come? And how far will Beijing let them go?

Holding Up Half the Sky: Women in China

SUSAN PERRY

As the members of Gao Yinxian's family prepare to take a family photograph, thousands of years of Chinese culture are evident in the seating arrangements. Gao, whose husband has died, is the family's oldest member; she is seated in the middle. Her eldest son, who positions everyone for the photograph, is seated to her right, and her first grandson is to her left. Gao's daughter-in-law and granddaughters remain standing behind the seated members of the family: they have second-row status. They will not earn the right to be seated until their own sons assume the responsibilities of family leadership.

First in an Occasional Series: Focus on Women

Although Gao's family lives in a remote corner of Hunan province, these gender dynamics are universal in China. Women have been relegated to second-row status throughout the country's history, with their social standing determined by their reproductive role and the clout wielded by their husbands and sons. Yet the last 50 years have seen the role of women in China change more than during the last 5,000 years. These changes result from a variety of factors, the most important

SUSAN PERRY is an assistant professor of international affairs at the American University of Paris. She co-organized a three-day conference on "Women, Culture, and Development Practices" at the French Senate with UNESCO and the OECD in November 1998.

of which have been the modernization of Chinese society and the 1949 Communist revolution. Women have moved out of the home and into agrarian and industrial production—and into the professional spheres traditionally reserved for men. In doing so, they have been both assisted by the government and hampered by recent economic reforms.

While women have benefited from an increasing array of new opportunities, their liberation remains incomplete. Since 1990 there has been a noticeable nationwide slowdown in the move toward gender equality. This stems in large part from the economic reform program that has transformed China from a poor, isolated nation into a burgeoning economic powerhouse. The reforms have widened the gap between the urban and rural populations in terms of access to education, health services, and technology. At the same time, booming private businesses and farming for profit have created a new class of urban and rural elites whose exploitative tendencies recall feudal China. The government now acknowledges that men and women have also been affected differently by the introduction of free market policies.

THE BEGINNING OF CHANGE

Most women rarely ventured beyond their own doorsteps in imperial China, their feet bound and their lives one of domestic drudgery. They had few possibilities of earning an income aside from household handicraft production and, in extreme cases, prostitution. Marriage was designed to control female labor; the young bride was immediately transferred to her husband's family home, where she assumed domestic and reproductive obligations that lasted until old age.

During the late nineteenth century, foreign incursions into China's coastal cities resulted in their partial industrialization and altered traditional marriage patterns. In the Canton delta, foreigners and Chinese alike owned textile factories employing thousands of young women. Their nimble hands and good eyesight were essential attributes for silk reeling, which earned them a cash income. Consequently, many of these workers practiced a form of marriage resistance or delayed marriage; they continued working for three years after their wedding, at which point they would move to their husband's village and begin childbearing.

For Chinese women this is a time of opportunity and exploitation.

The increasing modernization of urban China, symbolized by the 1919 May 4th Movement and its call for China's political, social, and cultural transformation, created new opportunities; schools and universities were founded to train female students as teachers, social workers, nurses, doctors, activists, and politicians. The nascent urban communist movement gained considerable female support because it called for a change in the traditional Confucian gender relations that relegated women to a subservient existence. Beginning in the late 1920s, the Chinese Communist Party promoted liberal marriage laws in its peasant base areas, which generated support for the movement among rural women. With the 1949 Communist revolution, both urban and rural women were expected to participate fully in the socioeconomic transformation of society. Because Marxism emphasized class as the agent for change, however, Chinese women were encouraged to enter the workforce to gain their liberation. They were mobilized to contribute to socialist construction, rather than fight for gender equality.

The upheavals of the Cultural Revolution between 1966 and 1976 made the majority of Chinese women eager to embrace Deng Xiaoping's brand of "market socialism" in 1978. Yet it was during the Cultural Revolution that many women came to the forefront of political decision making. During this period femininity was criticized as a "petty bourgeois characteristic." Female Communist Party members were expected to be mili-

tant and ambitious. Shrill but effective political propaganda emanating from Chairman Mao Zedong's wife, Jiang Qing, helped double the number of women in local, provincial, and national government. Later, many of these women admitted that they had felt compelled to serve the Chinese Communist Party and had entered politics with little enthusiasm.

Today 14 percent of the Communist Party's membership is female, but only 7.5 percent of the Central Committee is made up of women. Female deputies constitute 21 percent of the National People's Congress, but only 9 percent of its powerful Standing Committee. Three female ministers have been appointed to the State Council, the country's main administrative body; they represent 7 percent of all ministers, commensurate with the world average.

The most influential female minister is undoubtedly Wu Yi, who heads China's Ministry of Foreign Trade and Economic Cooperation. She has reached the highest echelon of political power because of her competence and ability to weather political storms. While she might serve as an example to younger women working their way up through middle-level management and government positions in China, overall interest in politics appears to be waning. Many urban professional women appear unwilling to make the necessary sacrifices to climb the political ladder when their time could be better spent making money.

GENDER ECONOMICS

For Chinese women this is a time of opportunity and exploitation; those with a good education or strong motivation are most likely to succeed. Women managers have proved to be extremely effective at running large and small-scale enterprises in the new market economy. A recent study by American and Chinese scholars has shown that they score the same level of managerial motivation as male colleagues in organizational behavior tests, especially on the desire to exercise power and stand out from the group. Opportunities fostered by economic reform and the government's one-child policy, which effectively limits women's child-care responsibilities, have clearly had a positive impact on their managerial motivation. These women form an elite class, set apart from the masses by their university education and professional experience.

At the other extreme are women who work on the assembly line. China's export drive during the 1990s has been dominated by goods traditionally produced by female workers. In southern China women make up the bulk of the labor force in light manufacturing—especially in textiles, which is one of the country's major exports. Many of these workers are young peasants who have fled agrarian underemployment for cash jobs and a bit of excitement in the cities and towns. In the southern city of Shenzhen, for example, women make up one-half the migrant workforce.

Some of these women will return to the countryside with considerable savings. Nearly 50,000 women who have returned to their villages in Guangdong province are now the owners of individual or private businesses. According to one study published in China, "when [women] return to the village, not only has their appearance changed but they have also become stronger in character, are no longer afraid of going out in public, are more poised and independent. They have a relatively stronger sense of business and affairs."

Businesses created by the returning women workers form the backbone of the expanding private sector. Throughout China, women account for approximately one-third of the 14 million self-employed rural individuals engaged in commerce and service trades. In the villages, female employers favor female workers for services and light industrial production because, as one woman factory owner noted, they are "obedient, detail-oriented, and do not get into fights." They are also cheaper, earning less than 77 percent of the pay given to men doing the same work. Like their great-grandmothers in the textile mills at the turn of the century, these young peasant workers are a malleable workforce, with few dependents and a willingness to work long hours for low wages.

The new private sector frequently denies women health benefits and maternity leave. Working conditions are unsafe, since national and provincial safety standards are not enforced. In 1992, for example, dozens of women were killed when a fire broke out in their Guangdong toy factory; windows had been barred and doors locked to prevent them from leaving before their 12- to 15-hour day was over.

Women working in the shrinking state sector still receive health services and three months guaranteed maternity leave. Nonetheless, unequal pay and fewer chances for promotion are also chronic in this sector; women workers are perceived as less reliable than their male colleagues because of their household responsibilities. This perception is misguided, since urban Chinese men are far more likely to share household and child-care tasks with their wives than their American counterparts; according to one official study, men in the city of Shanghai perform up to 80 percent of household and childcare chores.

Unemployment is disproportionately high among women. National surveys indicate that the average laid-off worker in China is female (60 percent), works in an industrial enterprise (60 percent), is between the ages of 35 and 45 (67 percent) and has a junior high school level of education. Moreover, Prime Minister Zhu Rongji has targeted the largest female employer, the state-owned textile sector, for major structural reforms. In the next three years, new jobs must be found for 1.2 million female state textile workers.

The All-China Women's Federation, generally considered a mouthpiece for party policy, has been surprisingly sharp in its criticism of inadequate government programs for the retraining of unemployed women. The "Pioneers Project," run by the federation since 1995, offers professional retraining for nearly half a million women each year; 230,000 were placed in new jobs in 1997. Many of these women move into the service sector, seeking employment in fields as varied as hairdressing and computer programming. Economic security is considered so vital in today's rapidly changing social climate that several female college graduates interviewed for this article claimed that taxi driving and prostitution—the old stand-by in times of extreme duress—were the only jobs that would guarantee them a high cash income and no layoffs.

"FEMINIZED" AGRICULTURE

Nearly 80 percent of China's female population lives in the countryside, where gender equality has been slow to develop. The launching of the household responsibility system in the early 1980s as part of China's reform program has helped maintain rural gender inequality. The system disbanded agrarian collectives and allowed peasant families to grow crops both for themselves and for the state. In many respects, this policy has reinforced the traditional social structure, which also relies on female labor. Women continue the Confucian tradition of "marrying out": moving into their husband's household after marriage, where their status remains that of a secondary family member even after the birth of their first son.

With the integration of women into the agrarian workforce, all but elderly women and very young girls bear the burdens of farm work, child rearing, and domestic chores. Moreover, with the increase in migration to urban areas by men and young women, middle-aged married women have taken over the bulk of farm work in all but the poorest areas, resulting in a "feminization" of agriculture. The Chinese government estimates that women shoulder between 40 and 60 percent of the workload in the fields, while some Chinese scholars believe that women now perform between 70 and 80 percent of all rural work.

The feminization of agriculture may, in the long run, adversely affect traditional patriarchal values. Many women who become the heads of their household when their husbands depart as migrant laborers often retain their position once their husbands return.

WOMEN AND THE STATE

The government's one-child campaign is a long-standing example of effective state intervention in the lives of Chinese women. Introduced on a broad scale in 1980, this nationwide campaign has attempted to reduce China's galloping population growth by restricting couples to only one child. The government's draconian measures appear to have lowered fertility in urban areas. Women who become pregnant a second time must pay a substantial fine; risk losing their employment, housing, or health benefits; and may be required to undergo forced abortion or sterilization. Their husbands may also be penalized at work. These potential sticks, along with the carrots of pay bonuses and promotion eligibility that accrue to one-child families, have altered fertility behavior to the extent that the majority of city couples willingly have only one child.[1]

Although the campaign has altered fertility behavior, it has done little to educate urban women about their sexual identity.

Despite the diversity of new material on sex-related issues and a great deal more discussion on the subject in the 1980s and 1990s, the dominant discourse on female sexuality still promotes women's subordination as a natural condition of their existence. This discourse is reinforced by the policies used in promoting the one-child campaign. Nonetheless, Chinese publishers have recently purchased translation rights to classic self-help books, such as *Our Bodies, Ourselves* (minus the American edition's sections on lesbianism and masturbation) or psychologist Francoise Dolto's texts on the family and child rearing, which indicates that they anticipate the growth of a new market.

Rural areas remain removed from elite urban discourse on female sexuality. The convergence of the household responsibility system, urban male migration, and the one-child campaign has put unprecedented pressures on peasant women. The household responsibility system, designed to encourage peasants to farm for their own profit, places a premium on the number of family members able to farm, while urban male migration and the one-child campaign reduce the number of laborers per household. Peasants obviously oppose both the coercive methods and the logic of the campaign. Couples continue to have more than one child in hopes of producing one or more sons, who are considered essential help with the heavy farm work and in providing a daughter-in-law to take care of parents in their old age. The exception to this trend occurs when peasant women seek employment in rural industries; since hiring priority is given to women with only one child, these positions have become a major family planning incentive.

Overall, peasant couples have proved adept at managing the economic penalties imposed on families with more than one child. Nonetheless, the psychological costs incurred by rural women are inordinately high. The All-China Women's Federation has publicly condemned family violence against women because of the birth of unwanted baby girls, the use of ultrasound to "select" a child's sex, and female infanticide. Peasants have also chosen more benign methods to circumvent the one-child policy, such as not registering the birth of a female. Without a birth certificate, however, the hundreds of thousands of unregistered girls born annually will be unable to receive state health care, enroll in school, or vote as adults.

Despite a renewed drive to limit births in 1992, the Chinese government, because of widespread peasant discontent, has had to officially sanction in rural areas the birth of a second child in cases where the first child was female. The government also tolerates the small-scale, peaceful demonstrations that occur with increasing frequency in front of the gates to the State Family Planning Commission. In private, many educated Chinese women bluntly question how much state coercion is legitimate in trying to arrest population growth, and they criticize the government's heavy-handed methods.

Studies by Chinese scholars show that female education is the single most important predictor of fertility. China claims that 96.2 percent of its 7- to 11-year-old girls are registered

AT THE GRASS ROOTS

THE MOST NOTABLE TREND in gender relations in China today is not the return of patriarchal traditions, but the sustained support women have begun to extend to one another across urban and rural landscapes. The United Nations Conference on Women, held in Beijing in 1995, was a watershed experience for the development of the women's movement in China. The push toward learning from and networking with women's movements worldwide was the single most important legacy of this extraordinary international gathering.

During the preparatory stages to the conference, slogans such as "connect the rails" with the international women's movement appeared. The government, however, attempted to rein in preparations once officials became aware of the possibility of human rights demonstrations at the accompanying International Forum for Non-Governmental Organizations. The forum was moved 30 miles outside Beijing, to Huairou, and the 47 panels to be presented by Chinese women were screened by the government through "rehearsals."

Nonetheless, many Chinese men and women observed for the first time how nongovernmental organizations function and the role these organizations can play in empowering women. More important, these men and women also managed to convince Chinese officials that the women's movement would not form an independent power base in China and hence was not a threat to the government.

Fresh from this experience, women have begun to explore how best to promote gender equality in China. Because the government has been unwilling to sanction the formation of independent women's associations, activists must find an officially approved umbrella group that is already registered, or strike out on their own to form an unofficial association.

Examples of innovative individual initiative abound. A banner embroidered by over a thousand rural women from the Shanxi area and displayed at the Huairou forum has been sold to benefit Shanxi rural development programs for women. A support group for female migrant workers in Beijing helps these women find jobs in understaffed city hospitals. A successful urban lawyer runs a legal consultation service out of her home to assist battered wives and their children. That so many women are willing to devote their time toward building an ad hoc grassroots women's movement indicates that sustainable gender equality will not be imposed from above, but demanded from below. *S. P.*

for school. Yet, although education is theoretically available to all regardless of gender, female literacy rates continue to be lower than the national average. Of the 200 million illiterate Chinese, 70 percent are female. Often a woman burdened by farm chores will keep her daughter at home to assist with the multiple workloads. The children of urban migrants are also less likely to be schooled, since enrollment would call attention to their "illegal" residency.

In rural areas, the government has responded to this problem with the "Spring Bud" program, which is designed to put girls back in school by helping with their school fees, including lunch, textbooks, shoes, and eyeglasses. Many adult women have benefited from literacy programs sponsored by nongovernmental organizations or the All-China Women's Federation. Little has been done to provide public schooling for the unregistered children of urban migrants.

At the other end of the spectrum, Chinese women who study through the master's and doctorate degree levels are outnumbered by their male counterparts—in some cases, by as much as ten to one. Professors complain that female graduate students are informed outright that prospective employers are interested only in hiring male graduates in their field. Still, female students are encouraged to pursue graduate work in the sciences, particularly in medicine. China has a higher number of female graduate degrees in engineering and other sciences than the United States.

A NEW IMAGE EMERGING?

Urban popular culture has focused new attention on women's issues. Once taboo subjects, including marital sex, divorce, and domestic violence, are now thoroughly explored in a growing body of women's radio talk shows and magazines, such as the favorite *Jiating* (Family) magazine. According to an official from the All-China Women's Federation, demand for weekly or monthly publications devoted to women's issues is growing. The federation and its branches currently edit 47 periodicals, up from just a handful during the Maoist years.

Television has also moved to accommodate the expanding female viewer market. The extremely popular show *Dajia tan* (Everybody's Talking) pits husbands and wives against one another in a mock trial setting in which they hurl accusations regarding one another's chauvinism, infidelities, and spending habits. The show's high ratings indicate that the topic offers more than entertainment value: Chinese viewers are exploring the boundaries of the "modern couple." Recently, a media partnership of Chinese businesswomen has proposed a television project titled *Women in the World*, a series of documentaries designed to introduce Chinese women to support systems as varied as model French day-care centers or Emily's List, the election fund for women running for political office in the United States.

MAKING THEIR VOICES HEARD

In analyzing the impact of economic reforms on women's lives in China, the government would evidently prefer to discuss its achievements in promoting gender equality and not the chronic discrimination problems that remain. At the other end of the spectrum, Western feminist discourse on China often presents an alarming portrait, replete with stark statistics on the skewed male-female birth ratio, domestic violence, and increased trafficking in women.

In determining how far China has come in terms of real gender equality, Chinese women themselves are likely to focus their attention on the development of pragmatic strategies for improving women's lives locally. Although outright criticism of central government policy is discouraged, women are making their voices heard by using those avenues for dialogue that the government has made available.

According to the State Council, the most pressing problems concerning Chinese women include their legal status, equal access to employment, involvement in politics, and the right to organize and participate in international women's activities. Officially recognized nongovernmental organizations, along with the growing number of unregistered women's groups, have expanded the limits of debate, bringing in new issues, such as the feminization of poverty and reproductive rights. Their tactics, which encourage respect for national law, enable them to push for enforcement of existing legislation without appearing to threaten political orthodoxy.

Many Chinese activists believe that the seeds for real gender equality were sown at an NGO forum in Huairou during the United Nations 1995 Beijing Women's Conference. Since then a movement that encourages individual initiative has taken shape, with motivated urban and rural women working to assist those who have not benefited from China's economic expansion. Inspired by their own grassroots experience and a growing interaction with women's associations worldwide, these informal women's networks signal the beginning of what may become a modern civil society in China.

---

[1]*The one-child campaign has slowed China's population growth to a gross fertility rate of 2 births per female, while producing a statistical anomaly: China had 118 male births for every 100 female births in 1992. Since most nations produce 105 males for every 100 females born, this warped statistic indicates that 12 percent fewer girls are born in China annually than anywhere else.*

Riding the Internet Wave

One man's tech firm connects China with the rest of the world

By Steven Mufson

Washington Post Foreign Service
BEIJING

America in the imagination of Tian Suning had always been a place of bright lights and big cities. So it was a shock to Tian when he arrived in Lubbock, Tex., in 1987 with $45 in his pocket and a full scholarship to Texas Tech. There were no skyscrapers. No Fifth Avenue. No White House. No night clubs. Instead, he found prairies, churches and ranches.

The tallest building was 10 stories high. When he asked for a beer, he got root beer.

For the next five years, he studied the ecology of the prairie, making mathematical and statistical models of the growth of bromegrass. He counted leafy stems and saw how bromegrass weeds compete in nature with sand drop seeds. He also spent several months studying the environmental impact New York City sewage would have if, as proposed at the time, it were dumped on the Texas grasslands.

For Tian, however, isolation was the mother of invention. To stay connected with the rest of the world, he became proficient with computers, and he caught the wave in the rising American Internet craze.

Today, Tian Suning, a k a Edward S. Tian, PhD, is back in Beijing where, at least when it comes to business, the grass is greener. In a little more than three years, he has become one of China's leading entrepreneurs. His company, AsiaInfo Group, has built much of China's Internet backbone by installing the American-made equipment needed to connect more and

more Chinese Web surfers at higher and higher speeds. And it is now branching out into new areas by providing software solutions to big Chinese enterprises.

Founded by Tian in early 1995 with just four employees, AsiaInfo now has 320 employees, $45 million a year in revenue and an impressive array of backers and projects. He has provided the Internet infrastructure for Sichuan province, which has a population of more than 100 million. He is doubling the speed of the Net in Beijing, in an effort, he says, to prevent the information superhighway from becoming a parking lot. He's helping Chinese banks, which still do much of their business in cash, devise online "e-commerce" systems. He's advising a Shanghai securities firm about online trading. He's putting newspapers in Shanghai and Heilongjiang online. And to help him with future ventures, he recently arranged financial backing from three leading American venture capital firms.

IN JUST 3½ YEARS OF DOING business, Tian has already met the goal shared by most of his generation and followed the advice of the late senior Chinese leader Deng Xiaoping, who said that "to get rich is glorious." But as with many of the most successful members of the Cultural Revolution generation, Tian views his mission as something even bigger.

"I want to bring the best part of America to China: an efficient information infrastructure that will change people's minds and people's ways of doing things," he says. "This is the responsibility of our generation."

Sitting in his modest office in Beijing's computer software district, Haidian, Tian brims with a sense of historic opportunity.

"I'm very confident," says Tian, who is reading Daniel Yergin's "The Prize" and just published a Chinese translation of Ron Chernow's "The House of Morgan." China, he says, "is like America at the turn of the last century. There is the opportunity to build a Standard Oil and giant companies that American founding fathers built, because China is in the midst of an economic revolution and a technological revolution."

The numbers back him up. In China, 11 million new telephone lines are installed every year, equal to starting a new Baby Bell operating company every 12 months. The Internet is booming. Nationwide there are about 1 million accounts. In Guangzhou, 1,000 new users sign up every month. Within five years, the number of users is expected to hit 10 million. Intel estimates that China will overtake Germany this year and become the world's third-largest market for personal computers.

"The Internet is today's equivalent of the steam engine," Tian says. "At the turn of the century, it was the sewing machine instead of information technology. This," he says, meaning China and the information technology revolution, "is like the Industrial Revolution, and that's whey I feel very passionate about it."

PASSION WAS ONCE SOMETHING reserved for devotees of Chinese Communist Party Chairman Mao Zedong. Tian was born three years before the

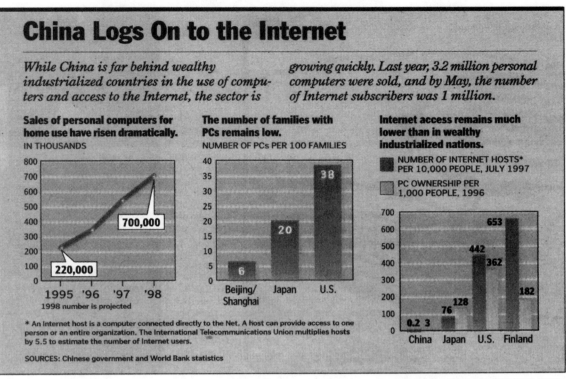

China Logs On to the Internet

While China is far behind wealthy industrialized countries in the use of computers and access to the Internet, the sector is growing quickly. Last year, 3.2 million personal computers were sold, and by May, the number of Internet subscribers was 1 million.

Sales of personal computers for home use have risen dramatically.
IN THOUSANDS

700,000
220,000

1995 '96 '97 '98
1998 number is projected

The number of families with PCs remains low.
NUMBER OF PCs PER 100 FAMILIES

Beijing/Shanghai 6
Japan 20
U.S. 38

Internet access remains much lower than in wealthy industrialized nations.

■ NUMBER OF INTERNET HOSTS* PER 10,000 PEOPLE, JULY 1997
□ PC OWNERSHIP PER 1,000 PEOPLE, 1996

China 0.2 3
Japan 76 128
U.S. 442 362
Finland 653 182

* An Internet host is a computer connected directly to the Net. A host can provide access to one person or an entire organization. The International Telecommunications Union multiplies hosts by 5.5 to estimate the number of Internet users.

SOURCES: Chinese government and World Bank statistics

(BY DITA SMITH—THE WASHINGTON POST)

Cultural Revolution began and millions of young Chinese descended on Beijing's Tiananmen Square waving their little red books of Mao's quotations.

Tian's parents were two of China's leading ecologists. Educated in forestry, they were sent to study in the Soviet Union, which was then China's main ally. But in 1961, relations with the Soviet Union soured, and his parents reluctantly returned to China. Two years later, when their son was born, they named him Suning, which means, roughly, "thinking of Leningrad," the city they associated with their romantic young adulthood.

Back in China, they were sent to a desert research institute in Lanzhou, capital of Gansu, a backward province at the edge of China's far west. At the beginning of the Cultural Revolution, Tian, only 3, was sent to live with his grandparents across the country in Shenyang, a northeastern industrial city. Except for short visits, he would be separated from his parents for 11 years.

The situation in Shenyang wasn't much better than in Lanzhou. His mother's family had been wealthy and educated, which made them suspect during the Cultural Revolution's enthusiasm for peasant virtues. Despite the

family's earlier wealth, they lived simply. They didn't dare use money they had stashed away.

THE FAMILY HAD GOOD REASON to be nervous. When Tian was 11, he returned to Shenyang from a stay with his parents in Lanzhou carefully carrying a basket of eggs. A neighbor spied the eggshells in the garbage and interrogated his grandmother about how she could afford such a delicacy.

"This is a very bitter memory for me," he recalls. "The neighbor was so jealous when he saw the eggshells in the garbage and said, 'You must be very rich.'"

But the persecution of his family and the disruption of Chinese schools also gave the young Tian an unusual introduction to learning. By candlelight, his aunt, who had a degree in Chinese literature, would teach him poetry from the Tang and Song dynasties. His grandmother, who once tutored the children of rich families, devoted herself to her grandson's education.

After the Cultural Revolution, life became easier. Tian went back to high school and in 1981 enrolled in Liaoning University to study environmental biology. Environmental biology wasn't the most important thing he learned in

Liaoning, however. English, the language of the Internet, was.

One day in the university library he met a disaffected Englishman who had moved to China during the Cultural Revolution. He turned out to be a good English tutor, introducing Tian to John Lennon records and George Orwell's "1984." "He opened my eyes and opened my mind," Tian says.

While a graduate student in Beijing at the Chinese Academy of Sciences, Tian dabbled in publishing. He published a translation of Lee Iacocca's book "Talking Straight" that was completed in only four days by a team of 12 student translators to beat another Chinese publisher.

One problem: how to translate "pickup truck." Another problem: copyright.

With some money in his pocket, he and a friend took their girlfriends to the Great Wall Sheraton Hotel, the first major Western-style hotel in Beijing, for a drink. But it was 1985, and the hotel was trying to cater to foreign business people. Tian and his friends didn't look the part for the hotel's clientele. In the lobby, they were asked for their passports and turned away.

"I was very humiliated," he recalls. "We were so angry. We had a beer in a small restaurant, and my friend said, 'We have to make money and feel that we are something.'"

Eleven years later, after Tian came back from the United States, his friend called. The friend had made millions of dollars running a trading company that is now listed on a Chinese stock exchange. He said to Tian that they needed to go back to the Great Wall Sheraton.

"I said, 'This is stupid,'" Tian recalls. "He asked me what kind of car I had. I said, 'I drive a VW Jetta.'" The friend scoffed. "I said, 'We spend our money on computers instead of cars,'" Tian recalls. "He said he'd pick me up in his Mercedes 600." By that time, after the boom in the Chinese economy, the hotel was full of Chinese customers. Tian and his friend were seated and treated like the other guests, but that wasn't good enough. "My friend called the manager and made a big fuss," Tian says.

Still, the earlier incident at the Great Wall Sheraton and some other embarrassing meetings with foreign businessmen convinced Tian that he needed to learn more about the West. So he took the standardized English test for foreign students and applied to schools in the United States.

And so, on to Lubbock, where he drove a pickup for four years. In Lubbock, Tian says, the best hour of the day was sitting with a beer and watching "The MacNeil/Lehrer NewsHour" on public television.

But some of that bromegrass got under his skin. He was concerned about the environment and felt that he should follow in his parents' footsteps and make it his career. He felt a responsibility to the people at Texas Tech who had invested time and scholarship money in him. So he went to work for a year for something called the Green China project in Washington, D.C., but it didn't click. He still feels guilty about it.

"There are lots of hopeless battles for people who want to do environmental projects in China," Tian says. "One reason is that China doesn't allow real nongovernment organizations. Another is that industrialization and economic growth are the country's top priorities. But if we continue the current growth pattern there will be no way to avoid environmental disaster."

The solution: What else? The Internet. "The only way is to alter technology and alter the economic growth pattern," he says. "One fundamental problem is that the economy is built on energy, not on information."

In China, however, information has been treated as political propaganda, not as a marketable commodity. So the same equipment that Tian sells to make the Internet work faster is also being used by the government to block access to sensitive Internet sites. Only those who are adroit with computers can still find ways to circumvent the electronic barriers.

Tian compares the Internet to the invention of the printing press. "People were afraid then too that information would not just be for the elite," he says. "People could read Confucius and get the wrong idea."

Tian himself is still full of wonder about the Internet. He had a business meeting in San Jose; he booked a beach house online. He couldn't get home for his daughter's birthday, so he sent her flowers by connecting to *www.flowers.com*. He sent a note: "Your daddy is building the Internet in China, and you got this flower."

LIKE TIAN, ASIAINFO IS A STRANGE hybrid. in the early 1990s, a Chinese American in Dallas offered to give Tian money to start a company on condition that Tian return to China. "I said, that's exactly what I want," Tian recalls. So he started a company in Dallas that was designed to do business in China.

Because AsiaInfo is American, it has broad access to technology. Because Tian is Chinese, it often has an edge on American companies competing for contracts here. AsiaInfo buys equipment from such giants as Cisco Systems Inc. and Sun Microsystems Inc., and it buys from smaller American software companies that are not familiar with the Chinese market. Tian's company also has 170 of its own programmers finding software solutions for Chinese firms.

"If we bid against IBM, what's the difference we offer? We're small, and they're big. We're three years old, and they're 70 years old," Tian says.

But, he adds: "China is our only market. And one thing we represent is a new generation of Chinese companies and a new generation of Chinese entrepreneurs."

Is he Chinese or American? "I really consider myself both. China gave me my birth and early education. America opened my mind and gave me the opportunity to start a company very easily. And it gave me the confidence about what a young man can accomplish."

China's values have changed, he says. "We used to be such an idealistic society. After the Cultural Revolution, however, we believed in nothing. We were like the Beat Generation. I was one of them. Materialism became the natural choice for us."

Tian says most people feel their best days were at college and that he's trying to re-create a campus atmosphere at his company. He pays workers $500 to $1,000 a month, plus that much again in retirement benefits—good wages by Chinese standards.

"We very forcefully want to create a new culture," he says. "In this changing environment and society, you can't rely on anybody. Only on ourselves."

When Tian worries about the future, he's not thinking about unrest, protests or political instability. He's not thinking about Mao, broken eggshells or even bromegrass. Asked about his biggest problem of the future: "Management," he says.

"The market is no problem. The market is tremendous. But can you find enough personnel? How do you manage a high-growth company in China. Can we manage a $200 million or a $1 billion company? How can we transform from entrepreneurs to managers? That worries me."

Article 21

Archaeology, September/October 1996

Buddhas of Cloud Hill

China's earliest cave-temples reflect the imperial ambitions, religious sentiments, and sculptural artistry of a fledgling dynasty.

James O. Caswell

James O. Caswell, a professor in the department of fine arts at the University of British Columbia is author of Written and Unwritten. A New History of the Buddhist Caves at Yungang *(Vancouver: University of British Columbia Press, 1988).*

About A.D. 460 Tanyao, the head of the Buddhist church in the court of the Northern Wei dynasty, petitioned the emperor Wencheng to "open up five caves and carve a Buddha image in each of them, the tallest to be 70 feet high, the next tallest 60 feet high, with superb carvings and decorations, a crowning glory to the world" ("Treatise on Buddhism and Daoism," *History of the Northern Wei*). Skilled artisans flocked to the one-half mile of porous sandstone cliffs at Yungang, or "Cloud Hill," in northern Shanxi Province. There they carved out five caves, each with a central colossal Buddha or Bodhisattva (a savior-like figure), representing the power and authority of the first five Northern Wei emperors. Scholars believe there was a precedent for such an effort in the casting of five bronze Buddha images honoring the emperors at a temple in the nearby capital of Pingcheng. The head of the church at the founding of the dynasty in 386 was reported to have said, "I am not worshiping the emperor, I am only paying respect to the Buddha." The later collaboration between Tanyao and the court indicates a relationship had been established between the power of the Buddha and Northern Wei rulers.

Today these five imperial caves are numbered 16–20. Other caves (5–13) in the central area of the site are of almost equal size and sculptural richness but, though stylistically related to the imperial five, are quite distinct. The 14 caves (there are also minor grottoes and niches) constitute the earliest extant Buddhist site of major significance in China, and are comparable in importance to India's magnificent Buddhist cave shrines at Ajanta (see ARCHAEOLOGY, November/December 1992).

When I first visited Yungang nine years ago, I was intrigued by the carved images of Buddhas and Bodhisattvas as well as other figures and decorative motifs on the cave walls. The calculated austerity and programmatic coherence of the carvings

in the imperial caves contrasted sharply with the florid, even joyful exuberance of those in caves 5 through 13. It was difficult for me to imagine that these images were as close and

(Larry Gartenstein)

Scores of Buddhas, Bodhisattvas (savior-like figures), apsaras (angel-like figures), celestial musicians, and other images adorn the walls and ceilings of cave 12's anteroom.

An Endangered Sanctuary

Over the centuries wind erosion, rock fractures, water seepage, and the depredations of thieves have taken their toll on the Yungang cave-temples. So have coal mines from the nearby city of Datong, source of the soot that covers much of the statuary. In 1988 the Chinese State Bureau of Cultural Relics invited the Getty Conservation Institute to suggest strategies for preserving the sculpture. Most of the carvings exposed to the elements, such as those on pillars outside caves 9 and 10, had been destroyed by weathering, and much of the remaining paint was in danger of flaking. Restorations beginning in the seventh century had mainly addressed cosmetic problems; eroded or flaking surfaces, for example, were plastered over with mud, then decorated with paint and gilding.

The Getty's first task was to assess the extent and impact of weathering caused by pollution, wind, and rain. It determined that the deterioration of paint on carved surfaces had been aggravated by the presence of coal dust. It also found that regular dustings by maintenance workers were inadvertently removing paint. Studies by the Environmental Laboratory of the California Institute of Technology in Pasadena revealed that a great deal of soot had accumulated on the sculpture, in some cases forming a layer several millimeters thick. The lab estimated that reducing the amount of soot in the air could limit dust in the caves by 38 percent. It suggested covering loaded trucks to prevent coal from spilling onto roads, paving streets in the village of Yungang, and paving or spray-washing dirt roads in front of the caves.

The Chinese plan to install shelters in front of some of the cave entrances to reduce the soot problem. Caves 5 and 6 still retain ancient wooden pagoda facades mounted against the cliff to provide the interiors a measure of protection against the elements. The new shelters will be constructed of fabric and mimic the design of the traditional wooden ones. Miguel Angel Corzo, director of the Getty Conservation Institute, says the site is also threatened by

(Courtesy The J. Paul Getty Trust)

Severe weathering has eroded carvings on pillars of cave 10.

sequential in date as other scholars said they were, that they were products of the same religious vision, or that they served the same ends. I felt that the caves must have been built for different reasons, using Buddhist imagery in different ways, perhaps at different times.

There are only scant references to Yungang in the mid-sixth century imperial annals known as *History of the Northern Wei*. Two of Wencheng's successors are said to have visited the site, Xianwen in 467, possibly to dedicate the finished imperial caves, and the boy-emperor Xiaowen, in 480, 482, and 483.

Thereafter the imperial record says nothing about the caves until the early sixth century, when they are cited as a precedent for the Longmen grottoes near the new capital at Luoyang where the court moved in 494. Only two inscriptions survive from before 494, one dated 483 and the other 489. The earlier one reports the donation of a large wall composition by 54 villagers, and the latter indicates the support of a nun for a smaller one. Both may represent gifts from nonimperial Buddhists hoping to gain divine merit. There were clearly two distinct major cave building phases at Yungang: the imperial

(Courtesy The J. Paul Getty Trust)

California Institute of Technology professor Glen Cass takes a reading from a particle analyzer monitoring concentrations of soot in cave 9.

(Courtesy The J. Paul Getty Trust)

Restorers examine the eroded remnants of small niches carved into the wall between caves 19-B, left, and 19.

the remains of a Ming fortress on the plateau above it. "The walled perimeter of the fort acts as a catchment basin," he says. "When it rains the walls create a pond and the water filters down. Salt in the rock is dissolved by water and then crystallizes on the stone surface, promoting the exfoliation of the painted layer of the statues and the exfoliation of the stone itself."

The Getty team studied the site's drainage in an effort to control the spread of damaging salts. In the past 30 years the Chinese have installed surface drainage channels above the grottoes to alleviate the problem, but their effectiveness has not been monitored. In a successful experiment, the Getty buried drainage pipes to collect and channel the run-off. According to Corzo, "Several drains need to be installed to divert water from the fort and away from the caves. Unfortunately the Chinese are having problems obtaining government funds, so installation may be delayed."

Perhaps the Getty's most important service was to co-sponsor a program with the Australian Heritage Commission advising the site's caretakers on the nuts and bolts of site conservation. The team offered a series of on-site lectures "trying to instill a clearer sense of site management at Yungang," says Corzo. "The Chinese have to figure out the best way for tourists to visit the site." Tourism is a growing factor in China's economy, and conservation of the Yungang caves serves not only cultural interests but those of China's pocketbook as well.

Spencer P. M. Harrington is an associate editor of ARCHAEOLOGY.

caves, ca. 460–467, and after a hiatus of some 16 years nonimperial caves, from ca. 483 to no later than 494.

The Northern Wei dynasty was established by the Tuoba Tartars, a people of Turkic stock from central Asia who had invaded China in A.D. 386. Adopting the name Wei from a Chinese dynasty that had ruled over roughly the same territory some 150 years earlier, they took advantage of China's political weakness in the aftermath of the collapse of the Han dynasty (206 B.C.–A.D. 220), establishing an empire that extended across northern China, mostly south of the Great Wall, from Gansu Province in the west to the Yellow Sea in the east. Seeking to legitimate their rule and at the same time maintain their identity, they adopted Buddhism as a state religion. By doing so, they could claim they were culturally distinct from Chinese subjects who practiced ancestor worship, while using the organization of the Buddhist monastery as a model for their administrative bureaucracy.

Buddhism was at first an uncomfortable fit for the Chinese. The Indic languages of its texts were alien, as were many of its ideas; for example, believers were asked to sever their con-

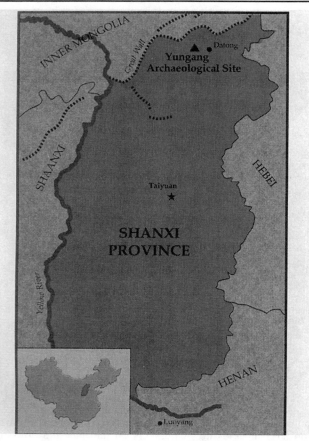

(Lynda D'Amico)

reports that there were 6,478 temples with 77,258 monks and nuns. Another, in 513, lists 13,727 monasteries. By the end of the dynasty there were some 30,000 temples housing roughly two million monks and nuns. The growing number of Buddhists, with their voracious appetite for new temples and the consequent waste of both human and financial resources, was lamented by a court officer in a memorial written toward the end of the dynasty. In spite of regular court edicts prohibiting temple construction, the officer concluded that "the [imperial] restrictions of earlier days were given no heed." The court itself joined in this building frenzy when it moved the capital to Luoyang. According to a nearly contemporary account known as the *Luoyang qielan ji (Record of the Monasteries in Luoyang),* the building program at Luoyang was probably the most profligate waste of resources on the most splendid buildings ever known in the history of Chinese cities. The account listed some 1,367 temples in the city of Luoyang alone.

Caves 5 through 13 are probably evidence of the construction boom that began after the court had abandoned Yungang and lasted until the capital was moved. They were the work of nonimperial patrons who dug cave-temples for religious rather than political reasons. While the art of the imperial caves is solemn, the carvings in the later caves reflect greater thematic and artistic variety. Some of the Buddhas in the later group, particularly in cave 6, are clad in Chinese dress, making them more comprehensible to native Chinese. Visitors to the imperial caves probably kept a deferential distance from the colossi. The later caves were more spacious, afforded more intimate viewing, and paid greater attention to religious themes and iconography. Cave 6 is full of scenes from the life of the Buddha, while carvings in caves 7 and 8 show multiarmed and multiheaded figures derived from Indian images, though direct formal precedents are lacking. Chinese motifs such as dragons and phoenixes also appear in the later caves.

Thus what began at Yungang as political statements exalting imperial authority by equating the emperor with the Buddha became, in the second phase, statements of religious devotion. Concurrent with this transformation was the explosion of Buddhist temple-building throughout the empire. The human and financial investments in Buddhist buildings, the worship commitment required by Buddhist practice, and friction between the court and the landed gentry, who gradually withdrew from official life and refused to pay taxes, contributed to the collapse of the Northern Wei in 535. Almost forgotten after the dynasty's fall, the caves at Yungang remain a silent witness to the exercise of both political authority and uncontrolled religious enthusiasm.

nections with the world and even give up their surnames. In A.D. 446, in an effort to dislodge the religion, two Chinese ministers employed by the Northern Wei court deceived the emperor Taiwu (reigned 423–452) into believing that Buddhists were planning an armed revolt. To counter such sedition, the emperor ordered the killing or defrocking of monks and nuns and the destruction of monasteries and their contents. The persecution lasted until Taiwu's death in 452. "His body had scarcely cooled," as one contemporary historian wrote, before Buddhism was restored. Wencheng's decision to build the five imperial caves at Yungang may have been an act of atonement for the persecutions carried out by his predecessor.

After the last visit of a Northern Wei emperor to the site in 483, the court appears to have lost interest in Yungang, focusing its attention instead on beautifying the capital of Pingcheng with splendid structures. At the same time both lay and clerical Buddhists with no attachment to the court were building their own monuments throughout the countryside. A census of 477

Article 22

The World & I, October 1989

Script Reform in China

Victor H. Mair

Victor H. Mair is professor of Chinese in the Department of Oriental Studies at the University of Pennsylvania. He is a specialist on early vernacular texts and Sino-Indian cultural relations. Among his publications are Tung-huang Popular Narratives (Cambridge, 1983). Painting and Performance: Chinese Picture Recitation and Its Indian Genesis *(Hawaii, 1988), and* T'ang Transformation Texts: A Study of the Buddhist Contribution to the Rise of Vernacular Fiction and Drama in China *(Harvard, 1989).*

| Battle | Solitary | Dragon | Old | Nation | Disaster or Difficulty |

Samples of complicated or full forms of the tetragraphs on the top line, with the simplified modern forms on the bottom line.

Nearly everyone who has seen Chinese characters is deeply impressed by them. Even without being able to read a single graph, one is struck by their longevity, beauty, complexity, and numerousness. Indeed, all these qualities are true of the Chinese writing system and account for the strong feelings it evokes. These emotions are particularly intense for those who consider the script to be one of the primary symbols of Chinese cultural identity. There is a great fear that, without this distinctive set of graphs, Chinese civilization as such would cease to exist.

Yet, during the past century, there have been persistent and equally urgent calls for radical changes in the script—including its abolition—from other segments of society. The traditionalists strive to maintain a proud and unique heritage that goes back over three millennia. The reformers worry that, unless their country modernizes its cumbersome, out-of-date script, everything—including the script itself—will be lost in an unsuccessful race to keep up with the rest of the world. A dispassionate look at the history and nature of writing in China may help to reconcile these two contradictory attitudes.

The Chinese writing system first occurs in virtually full-blown form around 1200 B.C. in the oracle bone inscriptions of the Shang dynasty. Scholars are perplexed by the suddenness with which the script appears; prior to the oracle bone inscriptions, there were only a few isolated and still undecipherable marks on pottery and occasionally on other objects. Hence the origins of the Chinese script remain a mystery. Its basic characteristics, however, do not. From its very inception as a tool for recording facts and ideas, the same fundamental principles have governed both the shape and the function of the individual graphs. In spite of widespread belief to the contrary, there seems never to have been a purely pictographic or ideographic state of full writing in China. The earliest connected texts contain sizable proportions of signs that communicate meaning through sound (the so-called "cyclical stems and branches," the graph for "all" [*xian*], the graph for "come" [*lai*], and so forth).

John DeFrancis and others have convincingly shown that it is actually impossible to record all the nuances of speech without substantial recourse to phonetic indicators. Certainly, for at least the last twenty-five hundred years, by far the largest proportion of Chinese characters was made up of a component that conveys meaning and another component that conveys sound, though neither does so with precision alone. Since these components are gathered together in a consistently quadrilateral configuration, Chinese refer to them as tetragraphs (*fangkuaizi*, literally "square graphs" [a cluster of four successive letters in cryptography]).

REASONS FOR LANGUAGE REFORM

Perhaps the single most outstanding dissimilarity between the Chinese writing system and alphabets is the vast quantity of separate units in the former compared to the strictly limited elements of the latter. In contrast to the 26 letters of the English alphabet, for example, there are over 60,000 discrete tetragraphs in the Chinese script, and new ones are being added continually. Mastery of such an enormous assemblage of individual shapes is beyond the ability of any mortal. For practical purposes, literacy in Chinese requires the passive recognition of approximately 2,000 tetragraphs and the active ability to write about 1,000 of them. Even the most learned persons are rarely able to read more than 5,000 tetragraphs and can reproduce only about half that amount without the aid of a dictionary. The other 50,000-plus tetragraphs consist largely of obscure variants, shapes whose sound or meaning (or both) is not known, and classical terms seldom or never used in modern parlance. Unfortunately, once a tetragraph has entered the lexicon, it becomes embedded there permanently. Typesetters, teachers, and translators must be prepared to cope with all 60,000 of them when the occasion demands.

Such large figures immediately lead to one of the most difficult questions about the tetragraphs: how to order them. It is easy to store and retrieve information in languages using an alphabetical script. The systematic nature of straightforward alphabetical ordering is one of the hallmarks of modern civilization. The case is entirely different with the tetragraphs. There is a large variety of traditional ways for arranging them, and they are very hard to control. The most common method is to break down each of the tetragraphs into a semantic classifier (also popularly called a radical or key) and a number of residual strokes. There are still several problems: The semantic cluster is not always readily identifiable, counting the residual strokes is both time-consuming and fraught with error, and the exact sequence of the semantic classifiers (usually 214) can be memorized only with tremendous effort.

Another complaint of the script reform advocates is the excessive amount of time and energy students have to spend in their early years to acquire minimum reading and writing skills. Several steps have already been taken to alleviate the burden placed upon young schoolchildren during the first few grades of their studies. In Taiwan, the National Phonetic Alphabet is used as an auxiliary to help beginners remember the sounds of the tetragraphs, and in the People's Republic of China, the initial lessons are given in Pinyin (romanized spelling). An increasing number of children's books written entirely in the National Phonetic Alphabet or in Pinyin are made available for students in elementary grades. Wide-scale experimental projects in Pinyin only or Pinyin mixed with tetragraphs for elementary education have been initiated in China. Results thus far show unmistakably that

students learn to read much more quickly through Pinyin than when they are exposed to the tetragraphs alone.

Even more dramatic is the drastic reduction of the strokes in many tetragraphs and the limitations on the total number of tetragraphs officially accepted by the government of the People's Republic. These steps, particularly the former, fall under the rubric of "simplification." By 1964, altogether 2,238 tetragraphs, most of those that are frequently used, had been simplified. Nearly another 900 were scheduled for simplification in 1977, but the scheme was withdrawn when it met with stiff opposition from those who asserted that it would lead to intolerable confusion. Because of the disparity between the original, complicated forms used in Taiwan and the simplified forms employed on the mainland, there now exist, in essence, two sets of tetragraphs. This has caused some obstacles to communication between peoples from the two areas.

Another very important sphere of language reform activity in China centers on efforts to increase familiarity with the national language, Modern Standard Mandarin, and to diminish reliance upon regional languages such as Cantonese, Taiwanese, and Shanghainese. The latter are often referred to erroneously as "dialects," but this is due to misinterpretation of the Chinese term *fangyan* ("topolect" [speech pattern of a place]) as well as to certain nonlinguistic, political constraints. Even within the Han or Sinitic group, there are dozens of mutually unintelligible tongues, most of which have never been written down. This is not to mention the non-Sinitic languages such as Mongolian, Tibetan, Uighur, Zhuang, Yi, and the like, many of which have their own alphabets or syllabaries. The linguistic map of China is thus quite complicated. Statements to the effect that there are a billion speakers of "Chinese" are therefore as misleading as to say that there are a billion speakers of "European" worldwide or a billion speakers of "Indic." Pinyin has played a vital role in attempts to unify the pronunciation, vocabulary, and grammar of the various Han languages, but there is still a tremendous amount of work that needs to be done before someone from Peking will be able to converse with someone from Amoy, Swatow, or Fuchow.

This is the cover of volume eleven of the Mandarin language text used in the six-year elementary school curriculum of the People's Republic of China. Note the use of Pinyin.

The governmental organ charged with overseeing language reform in China is the Script Reform Committee (Wenzi Gaige Weiyuanhui), whose name, significantly, has recently been changed to the State Language Committee (Guojia Yuyan Wenzi Gongzuo Weiyuanhui). The new name may be interpreted as reflecting either decreasing government involvement in script reform or a resolve to broaden the committee's work. Judging from discussions with ranking members, it would seem that the chief aim of the reconstituted body is to transfer reform initiatives to the private sector, leaving the committee to act merely in an oversight capacity.

RESISTANCE TO TAMPERING WITH THE SCRIPT

The government was prompted to downplay its championing of language reform because of the strong opposition to it from certain circles of society. Particularly during the period of liberalization that began after the close of the Cultural Revolution, the hostility toward officially sponsored changes in the script became more vociferous and more determined. It is curious that the most out-

(Van Phillips/Reflexion)

The Vertical message in Canton is an exhortation to the people in Canton to remember those who worked hard and overcame many struggles in the oil fields. For political messages, the Chinese prefer simplified characters, which ably lend themselves to the horizontal widening that has become commonplace for such purposes. The first and fourth characters are the same as in the past; the remaining ones are simplified and originally contained from six to twelve additional character strokes. Although one of the reasons for using these simplified characters was to save ink (and paint) and to ease comprehension, many Chinese actually have greater difficulty in distinguishing the meaning of look-alike character sets or their elements. Note, for example, the similarities between the fourth and fifth character.

spoken adversaries of language reform are to be found among the overseas communities. Living in countries where they are a minority, these émigrés keenly feel the need to assert their cultural identity. The tetragraphic script, as one of the most remarkable attributes of Chinese civilization, makes an excellent vehicle for the expression of nationalistic sentiments. Overseas spokesmen against language reform have contributed sizable sums of money toward the campaign to prevent further erosion of their cherished script. They are regularly given ample opportunity to express their opinions in such prominent newspapers as the *Peoples' Daily* and the *Guangming Daily*. By contrast, proponents of additional modifica-

tions of the script no longer have a nationwide forum in which to air their views. Instead, they work in small semi-official or unofficial groups at the city or, at best, provincial level.

Echoing the overseas opponents to script reform are classicists and other conservative factions within China proper. They decry the publication of ancient texts in simplified characters, pointing out that such practices often lead to ambiguity and distortion. There are, as well, those who propose a return to more ancient styles of writing and the reintroduction of more classical materials in the curriculum. The nearest parallel that can be imagined for the West would be the restitution of Greek and Latin as a requirement for all pupils.

Whether living abroad or within the homeland, critics of language reform declare that further adjustments to the script will only serve to cut young Chinese off from their past even more decisively than they already are. Although all middle and high school students are minimally acquainted with ancient Chinese through exposure to set passages, much as we might learn a few lines of *Beowulf* or Chaucer in the original, only highly trained specialists can read the Confucian *Analects* or a T'ang essay with any degree of facility. The gap between Classical Chinese and Modern Standard Mandarin is at least as great as that between Sanskrit and Hindi or between Latin and Italian. If additional changes are imposed upon the Chinese script, traditionalists argue that it will be impossible for all but paleographers to make any sense whatsoever of the old texts.

The antireformers are also alarmed by the flood of vernacular translations of classical texts issued in Taiwan, China, Hong Kong, and Singapore. This tendency is tantamount to admission that Chinese can no longer read the original texts anyway and only adds fuel to the fires of those who demand a complete revamping of the script. In truth, the trend toward greater use of the written vernacular at the expense of the classical goes back over one thousand years and would appear to be irreversible. With the final collapse of the imperial structure of government in 1911 and the abandonment of the examination system that went hand in hand with it, the demise of Classical Chinese as the officially sanctioned written medium was inevitable. This has naturally had a huge impact on the status of the tetragraphs, which are so perfectly well suited to Classical Chinese but are demonstrably less congenial to the vernaculars.

PROSPECTS FOR THE FUTURE

The principles governing the operation of the Chinese tetragraphs are almost identical to those on which the ancient Sumerian, Egyptian, and Hittite scripts were based. All four writing systems relied heavily on a mixture of phonophoric (i.e., "sound-bearing") components and semantic classifiers to convey meaning.

于貢問曰有一言而終身行之者乎子曰其恕乎
己所不欲勿施於人

Original Classical Chinese text written in the full (i.e., complicated) forms of the tetragraphs.

子贡问，"有可以一辈子奉行的一句话吗？"
孔子说，"就是宽大吧！自己不喜欢的事儿，
也不加在别人的身上．"

Translation of the above into Modern Standard Mandarin and written in simplified tetragraphs.

Zigong wen, "You keyi yi beizi fengxing de yi ju hua ma?" Kongzi shuo, "Jiushi 'kuanda' ba! Ziji bu xihuan de shir, ye bu jiazai bieren shen shang." Romanized Modern Standard Mandarin.

[The disciple] Zigong asked, "Is there a motto which one can follow all one's life?" Confucius said, "How about 'generosity?' Do not do unto others what you yourself do not like." English translation.

It is no wonder that the Chinese people are experiencing hardship in trying to make their archaic writing system compatible with modern information procession technology, which is geared to phonetic scripts. Here lies the real source of the debate over the future of the tetragraphs: Can technology bend to accommodate the tetragraphs, or must the tetragraphs make concessions to technology?

Their affection for the beloved tetragraphs notwithstanding, the Chinese people as a whole have already permitted Pinyin to displace the traditional script in many applications, simply because it is more convenient and efficient. Hotel and hospital registration, Chinese braille and semaphore, book indices, library catalogs, and dozens of other instances could be cited. It is particularly revealing that both the Modern Standard Mandarin translation of the *Encyclopaedia Britannica* and the new *Great Chinese Encyclopedia (Zhongguo Da Baikequanshu)* have selected the Pinyin alphabetic order for their entries. This choice is sure to have a deep influence on the way Chinese view Pinyin vis-à-vis the characters. Above all, it is the

computer that is pushing China further and further down the path to phoneticization. For modern word processing, the most user-friendly inputting methods, such as those devised by Tianma, Great Wall, and Xerox, all use Pinyin entry by word (not by syllable) and automatic conversion to tetragraphs. The danger, of course, is that there is but a short step from Pinyin in and tetragraphs out to Pinyin in and Pinyin out.

It is highly unlikely that China will ever legislate the romanization of its national language in the sweeping manner adopted by the Turks on January 1, 1929. Instead, there will undoubtedly be a gradual spread of Pinyin in those areas where it is warranted for strictly economic reasons. For example, international Chinese telegraphy is largely carried out in Pinyin because it is much cheaper than paying operators to memorize and transmit accurately the arbitrary code consisting of 10,000 numbers that has hitherto been used to send tetragraphic telegrams within China. Alphabetic telegraphy has already begun to make inroads in China proper. Pinyin has also been used for more than twenty years in experimental attempts at machine translation.

At present, there in only one romanized journal, *Xin Tang,* published in China. Yet nearly all Chinese journals give their titles in Pinyin and in tetragraphs. Barring unforeseen political upheavals, it will not be long before other scattered Pinyin magazines spring up in various parts of China. A few mostly independent, locally financed newspapers employing a mixture of Pinyin and tetragraphs have begun to appear in the past few years. Educational authorities in the province of Honan have stressed Pinyin heavily in grade schools, and many parents, along with their children, are learning it enthusiastically.

A momentous step toward romanization was quietly taken in August 1988 when the rules for Pinyin orthography were promulgated without fanfare in *Language Construction,* the official organ of the State Language Commission. With these rules, word boundaries were established, punctuation was regularized, and grammatical usage defined. Pinyin now has the potential to become a fully functioning alphabetical script. Whether it does or not depends on many factors, including the extent to which English is used instead of Pinyin Mandarin in international networks and other instances where an alphabetical script is deemed superior to the tetragraphs. The most likely scenario is a long period, at least fifty to a hundred years, of digraphs in which the tetragraphic script and Pinyin coexist. During this period of digraphs, use of the tetragraphs and Pinyin will probably be restricted to those applications for which they are best suited—Pinyin for science, technology, commerce, and industry; the tetragraphs for calligraphy, classical studies, and literature.

The fate of Chinese characters has yet to be decided. Vietnam and North Korea have outlawed them, South Korea spurns them for most general purposes, and Japan restricts their number severely in favor of its two syllabaries (*katakana, hiragana*) and *romaji* (romanization). Only in the land of their birth, China, do the tetragraphs still hold sway. Even there, however, these extraordinary signs have come under attack. They have been simplified, reduced in number, phonetically annotated, analyzed, decomposed, put in sequence according to hundreds of different finding methods, and otherwise abused by reformers whose sole purpose is to make them more amenable to the needs of modern society. However, the tetragraphs will not fade from the scene without a struggle. Regarded even by illiterates with utmost veneration, their disappearance would constitute a mortal blow against what many hold to be the very soul of Chinese civilization. It is a gross understatement to say that traditional Chinese intellectuals have a large stake in maintaining their tetragraphic writing system intact for as long as possible. On the other hand, China's most celebrated writer of the twentieth century, Lu Hsün, is reported to have declared that "if Chinese characters are not annihilated, China will perish."

Where the tetragraphs are concerned, emotions run high both among those who want to reform them out of existence and among those who wish to preserve them eternally. Both sides are earnestly committed to their cause and honestly believe they have China's best interest at heart. Ultimately though, one side will lose. Regardless of the outcome, China is undergoing a painful process of self-discovery. The tumultuous events that have recently wrecked China are part of a continuous adjustment to modernity. At the vortex of these struggles may be found the Chinese script and all that it represents.

ADDITIONAL READING

John DeFrancis, The Chinese Language: Fact and Fantasy, University of Hawaii Press, Honolulu, 1984.

—, Nationalism and Language Reform in China, Princeton University Press, Princeton, 1950; reprint: Octagon, New York, 1972.

—, Visible Speech: The Diverse Oneness of Writing Systems, University of Hawaii Press, Honolulu, 1989.

I. J. Gelb, A Study of Writing, University of Chicago Press, Chicago, 1963, revised edition.

William Hannas, The Simplification of Chinese Character-Based Writing, University of Pennsylvania Ph.D. dissertation, 1988.

Robert K. Logan, The Alphabet Effect: The Impact of the Phonetic Alphabet on the Development of Western Civilization, William Morrow, New York, 1986.

Tom McArthur, Worlds of Reference: Lexicography, Learning and Language from the Clay Tablet to the Computer, Cambridge University Press, Cambridge, 1986.

Victor H. Mair, "The Need for an Alphabetically Arranged General Usage Dictionary of Mandarin Chinese: A Review Article of Some Recent Dictionaries and Current Lexicographical Projects," Sino-Platonic Papers, 1 (November 1986).

Jerry Norman, Chinese, Cambridge University Press, Cambridge, 1988.

S. Robert Ramsey, The Languages of China, Princeton University Press, Princeton, 1987.

Robert Sanders, "The Four Languages of 'Mandarin,'" Sino-Platonic Papers, 4 (November 1987).

James Unger, The Fifth Generation Fallacy: Why Japan Is Betting Its Future on Artificial Intelligence, Oxford University Press, Oxford, 1987.

Article 23

Sinorama, January 1992

Red Envelopes: It's the Thought that Counts

Melody Hsieh

Past or present, in China or abroad, it is unlikely you could find a gift like the "red envelope," which in Chinese society has the capability of ascending to heaven or plumbing the depths of hell.

To attach a piece of red paper to a sacrificial offering depicts sending a red envelope to the deity, symbolizing a request for expelling evil or granting of good fortune. On Ghost Festival (the fifteenth day of the seventh month on the lunar calendar), you may burn some paper money wrapped in red paper to bribe the "good brothers" (ghosts), in hopes that they will be satiated and do no more mischief.

In the corporeal world, the red envelope is even more versatile: as a congratulatory gift for all manner of auspicious events, as a New Year's gift given by adults to children, as a "small consideration to the doctor before surgery or the birth of a child, as an expression of a boss's appreciation to his employees.... For whatever the giver may desire, the red envelope is just the thing to build up personal sentiment in the receiver.

In fairy tales, the fairy godmother can wave her magic wand and turn stone into gold or a pumpkin into a luxurious carriage. But calling it a magic wand is not so good as seeing it as a wand of hope for all mankind.

The red envelope is like the Chinese wand of hope, and it often carries limitless desires. To give a red envelope at a happy occasion is like embroidering a flower on a quilt; when meeting misfortune, to receive a red envelope is a psychological palliative which just might change your luck.

Whether it be congratulations, encouragement, sympathy, gratitude, compensation ... just give a red envelope, and not only will the sentiment be expressed, substantive help will also have arrived.

The fact that the red envelope opens so many doors and is so versatile today also naturally has practical advantages. For marriages, funerals, birthdays and illness, send a gift. But choosing a gift is an art in itself, and you can wrack your brains and spend a whole day shopping, and you still won't know if the other person will like it or need it. That's not nearly as good as wrapping money in red paper, which on the one hand saves work and on the other is useful, so everybody's happy. Compared with the way Westerners give gifts, giving a red envelope may be lacking in commemorative sentiment, but it's a lot more practical.

Nevertheless, Chinese haven't always been so substantive." In fact, it is only in the last few decades that red envelopes have become so commonly used.

A Brilliant Fire Neutralizing the Year: Kuo Licheng, a specialist in popular culture who is today an advisor to *ECHO* magazine, points out that traditionally Chinese did not present gifts of money. For example, when a child reached one month old, friends and family would send a gold locket; when visiting a sick person, people would bring Chinese medicine; upon meeting for the first time, people would exchange rings or jade from their person as a greeting gift. . . . None of these carry, as the Chinese say, the "unpleasant odor of brass," implying penny-pinching greed.

No one knows when money began to replace these traditional gifts. The only certain continuous tradition of using money to express sentiment—perhaps the origin of the practice of combining usefulness and sentiment, material and spiritual—is the tradition of the "age neutralizing money" (cash given on New Year's day to children), which has been carried down to this day.

"In the past, the New Year's money was simply a piece of red paper attached to a gold yuan, or the use of a red twine to string together cash. When eating New Year's dinner, the money would be pressed beneath the stove, representing 'a brilliant fire, abundant wealth;' only after dinner would it be pulled out and handed out to the small children. The meaning is that, after undergoing a baptism of fire, it was hoped that it could

expel evil and resolve dangers, so that the children could put the past behind them ("neutralize" the past) and grow up strong and healthy," says Juan Changjuei, director of the Anthropology Committee of the Provincial Museum, laughing that in fact "age neutralizing money" should be called "age extension money."

The writer Hsiao Min lived in Peking before 1938. At that time she was just a little sprite of less than ten years old, but because the New Year is quite different today from what it was in the past, she has a very deep impression of the New Year's money.

She recalls that it was not easy to get the "age neutralizing money" in those days. The children had to kneel on the floor and kowtow, and your forehead had to touch the floor, and it would only count if it was hard enough to make a sound. "In the past, floors were made of rough concrete, and we kids often had to kneel until our knees hurt and knock our heads until we were dizzy, before we could get our New Year's money."

It was only with the spread of paper currency that the New Year's money became paper cash wrapped in red envelopes. The reason why the paper is red, or why in early days red thread was used, rather than white, green, or black, is from religious rituals.

Better Red Than Dread: Juan Chang-juei suggests that in primitive times, when man would see a bright red flower in a green field, he would find it quite eye-catching and delightful. so maybe this is why red is an "auspicious" color.

Further, red is the same as the color of blood, and since a sacrifice of blood has a lucky effect, red came to be ordained as having the meaning of avoiding ill-fortune.

"Before the red envelope form appeared, people 'carried red' to represent auspiciousness and evading evil," says Juan. He says that in previous generations people would attach a piece of red paper to a religious offering or to a wedding dress, in both cases having this meaning. It was only after cut-paper techniques had been invented that the red piece of paper was changed to the "double-happiness" character. Before paper was invented, perhaps they used red cloth or painted on some red pigment instead.

Juan Chang-juei reminds us that because red symbolizes the vitality of life, and all mankind in early times had their magic ways to expel evil, it was by no means unique to China, and in the distant past Westerners also considered red to represent auspiciousness.

For example, shortly after Columbus landed in America, he gave the local natives red cloth to wrap around their heads to show celebration. For this reason, in the past red was always the color used to wrap presents in the West, and only later did it evolve that many colors were used.

But Chinese are relatively more concerned about colors, as Confucius has said: "I hate the way purple spoils vermilion," Colors are divided into "appropriate" colors and "deviant" colors. Red in this sense is the orthodox representation for good fortune, which cannot be altered lightly.

A Not Unreasonable Perquisite: As for using red envelopes as a small consideration in order to get the other person to do something on your behalf, very early on there was the "gratuity" for servants.

Kuo Li-cheng indicates that in novels like *The Golden Lotus,* you can often see in old style banquets that when the chef serves the main course the guest of honor must give the cook a "gratuity," using silver wrapped in red paper, to express appreciation to the host.

Or, family or friends might dispatch a servant to deliver a gift to your door. For the person giving the gift, it's only natural that they would send a servant, but for the person receiving the gift, the emissary is performing an unusual service, "so the recipient always had to ask the servant to bring back a letter of thanks, and to give a red envelope, which was called a *li* [strength] or *ching-shih* [respect for the emissary], to express gratitude for his legwork and provide transportation expenses." Kuo Li-cheng adds that the *ching-shih* was usually about 1/20th the value of the original gift, so this kind of red envelope was a reasonable perk as far as the servant was concerned.

"The ching-shih was originally a gift of money replete with sentiment, and it's only because modern people use it erroneously that the significance of the red envelope has become muddled," notes Kuo, who cannot help but lament that today "sending a red envelope" is synonymous with giving a bribe.

Some Chinese have adapted to circumstances, and since a red envelope can bribe a living, breathing human being, the effect should be no less in sucking up to the ghosts of the nether world. Today, in some rural townships in south and central Taiwan, especially at Ghost Festival, people wrap up the spirit money in red paper and burn it as an offering to the "good brothers" (spirits), hoping that after they get a red envelope and become a local god of wealth, they will no longer tamper with the affairs of men.

Juan Chang-juei says that in the past there was by no means the custom of sending red envelopes to ghosts, and this is a product of circumstance invented by Chinese in recent years.

Evangelical Red Envelopes: "The red envelope in and of itself is not to blame, and originally it was just to express a friendly intent, a symbol of sentiment," states Juan. Those who can afford to give red envelopes are always the older generation or the boss or the leader. He raises an example, noting that over the New Year's holiday in 1991, the Provincial Museum sponsored an opera appreciation activity for children. The day work began, the museum curator gave every one of the people who worked on it with him a red envelope, to thank his colleagues for giving up their holiday to work for the museum.

Hsiao Min also believes that there have also been some positive changes in the red envelope as it has evolved.

"In the past, the red envelope was just a simple red packet, without any characters printed on it. Today a lot of organizations, like restaurants or hotels, will imprint relevant auspicious phrases, and will give a set of red stationery to customers as a small gift at New Year's, to add a little more human feeling." For example, the Lai Lai Sheraton prints "May good fortune come, May wealth come, May happiness come" on its red envelopes, a play on the word lai (to come) in its name; steakhouses may print a golden bull, to make a deeper impression on their customers.

It's worth noting that even evangelical organizations cannot underestimate the attraction of a red envelope. Hsiao Min, a Christian, says that every time the passage to a new year approaches, churches will print their own red envelopes, which congregants can use at no charge. Because propitious proverbs from the Bible have been imprinted on the set, they are very popular among the congregants, so that supply can't keep up with demand. Since they integrate traditional customs, they can also help the evangelical church spread and adapt to local conditions.

"However, no matter how much money is in the red packet, how can a few pieces of paper currency take the place of or outweigh the feeling in one's heart?" says Hsiao Min. She concluded, that a small gift given with a big heart, the act of giving and receiving, and mutual affection are the real meanings of giving a red envelope.

Article 24   *The Economist,* November 7, 1998

TAIWAN SURVEY

The survivor's tale

If you want to copy Taiwan's model, remember to add a bit of luck

IF AN economy is doing well, it is tempting to think that it can do no wrong. Tempting, but dangerous. Whereas in the 1980s the world marvelled at Japan's economy, now it pities the nation for keeping its discredited model for so long. Similarly, it may turn out, some time in the future, that Taiwan's economic arrangements are not clearly as prescient and wise as they appear today. With that caveat, however, it is illuminating to consider the factors that have shielded it from the Asian storm.

As this survey has already argued, Taiwan's greatest strengths are a healthy paranoia in combination with the best of Chinese business acumen. These qualities show up in lots of ways, from conservative government policies to prudent corporate financial management. But there are also some more prosaic reasons why it dodged the bullet this time, including good old-fashioned luck.

For one, Taiwan is fortunate in that it trades mostly with America and China rather than the rest of Asia. Between them, those two countries account for more than half of Taiwan's exports, and neither has so far been pulled into recession by the crisis. Where Taiwan is exposed to South-East Asia, it is largely as an investor, not as an exporter counting on the local markets. Taiwanese companies have set up factories in Malaysia, Thailand, Vietnam and even Indonesia to take advantage of cheaper labour there. When those countries' currencies devalued, it made the labour cheaper still. What Taiwan does export to South-East Asia is mostly raw materials and components for those factories, so its regional exports have not fallen as much as those of countries that sell mainly to consumers.

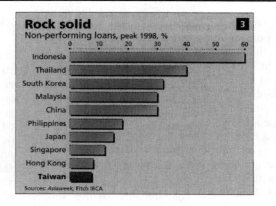

Rock solid `3`
Non-performing loans, peak 1998, %

Sources: Asiaweek; Fitch IBCA

Taiwan is also lucky that its business cycle happened to be out of phase with the rest of the region. It has seen mad property inflation and stockmarket booms, just like Thailand, Hong Kong and the rest, but that was in the late 1980s and early 1990s. In 1989, for instance, Taiwan's stockmarket had the world's second largest turnover, behind New York but ahead of London and Tokyo. An estimated quarter of the adult population (many of them housewives) was playing the market full-time, creating a serious labour shortage, among other problems. In rural areas, stock listings were colour-coded so that illiterate farmers could join in, and an industry emerged to allow the bull-market millionaires to flaunt their wealth.

Since then Taiwan has had several corrective crashes, the most recent one caused by a crisis of confidence when China conducted military exercises and missile tests in the Taiwan straits in 1995 and 1996. So when the regional crisis hit last year, Taiwan's stock and property markets were already more than 30% down from their peaks. There was simply less of a bubble to burst.

Bug-resistant

Luck may explain why Taiwan was not a glaring devaluation target in the early days of the crisis, but sounder reasons help account for its resilience to the contagion that later struck the rest of the region. Taiwan's macroeconomics are fairly reassuring. Its foreign-exchange reserves stand at $84 billion, exceeded only by China and Japan. Its foreign debts are a trifling $250m or so, including old Agency for International Development

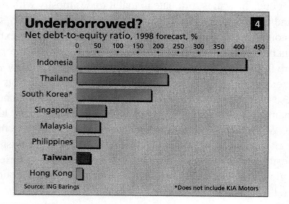

Underborrowed? `4`
Net debt-to-equity ratio, 1998 forecast, %

Source: ING Barings   *Does not include KIA Motors

loans. GDP growth this year is likely to be around 4–5% (just a percentage point or two lower than in recent years), which considering the grim environment is remarkable. As always, it has a large trade surplus. Indeed, the only significant black marks are its chronic budget deficits and its relatively high national debt (about 20% of GDP), explained mostly by the vast sums it spends on F16s and other arms to keep China at bay.

Likewise, the corruption, nepotism, egomaniacal infrastructure building and overcapacity that (eventually) offended the international bankers in countries such as Indonesia and Thailand were simply not such big issues in Taiwan. Because of its rapid transition to democracy and the emergence of a strong opposition, the KMT is far less corrupt than it was just a decade ago. Transparency International, a consultancy that publishes an annual corruption survey, now gives Taiwan a ranking of 5.3 (out of ten for squeaky clean), closer to the United States (7.5) than Indonesia (2.0). That may be a bit generous—according to one estimate, 30% of all government infrastructure spending is still lost in kickbacks—but it is generally agreed that things used to be worse. Although the KMT, as a party rather than as the government, still owns a good chuck of corporate Taiwan, it has gradually been divesting in response to public outrage over conflicts of interest.

But some of the other factors that have protected Taiwan are less commendable. In particular, it has been slow to open its financial markets, which meant that even if currency and stockmarket speculators were unimpressed by its economy, there was not much they could do about it. Although Taiwan's currency is convertible, its central bank imposes so many restrictions on commercial currency trading that, in effect, it sets the exchange rate. It has allowed the NT$ to devalue by about 20% to help Taiwan's competitiveness, but draws the line there.

Again partly because of restrictions on foreign banks, international investors make up just 3% of Taiwan's stockmarket holdings, so cannot influence the index much. Besides, they are a pretty docile bunch: mostly pension funds, which tend to take a long-term view and stick with their holdings. Hedge funds and most of the other overt speculators are banned.

Regulators are now congratulating themselves for dragging their feet on the financial liberalisation that America and other western nations have been urging for years. There are even signs of reverting to tighter regulation. Aside from the damage this may do to Taiwan's hopes to join the World Trade Organisation, it does not bode well for its somewhat dreamy ambitions to crank up its service sector by encouraging companies to pick Taiwan for their regional operations centres.

The same conservative tendencies have also spared Taiwan the sort of banking meltdown that most other Asian countries are now suffering. A high level of bad debt is a regional affliction that can turn a few bank failures into a chain reaction. But at the start of the Asian crisis, Taiwan's non-performing loans accounted for just 1.5% of total assets, compared with Thailand's 30%. Even in the darkest days of this year, peak levels reached only 7.5% in Taiwan, half the official figures in Japan and less than anywhere else in Asia, according to Fitch IBCA, a credit-rating agency (see chart 3).

The reason is not far to seek: paranoia again. As recently as the mid-1990s, most of Taiwan's banks were state-owned and lent mostly to other state-owned enterprises, which by definition are unlikely to go under. The security-obsessed KMT valued stability above all. It still has painful memories of the waning days on the mainland, when its attempts to print money to finance the war against the communists triggered hyperinflation that hastened its retreat. It has usually kept a miserly hand on the money supply since then.

To prevent leakage of precious hard currency, the government early on introduced strict capital controls to prevent Taiwanese companies from taking on cheap foreign-currency loans for speculative projects. "Capital is like blood. If you use too much of it, it will cost you your life," says Chiang Pin-kung, head of the government's Council for Economic Planning and Development.

Starvation diet

For anything but the biggest companies, this meant that bank loans were simply unavailable. Instead, smaller firms turned to friends and family, and to the so-called "kerb market", meaning anything from loan sharks to community lending associations that auctioned off loans to the highest bidder. In either case, the price was steep (often three times the official interest rate, which was itself higher than the regional average), so companies borrowed as little as they could and paid it back quickly.

The legacy of this credit shortage is that Taiwan's firms have one of the lowest debt-to-equity ratios in Asia: about 30% for listed Taiwan as a whole, compared with more than 400% for Indonesia (see chart 4). Without easy access to cheap capital, they have never been able to chase market share with massive investments, like the expansion-mad Korean conglomerates, or *chaebol*. Instead, they have had to finance growth from cash flow, which made them concentrate on profits. The average Taiwanese electronics company, for instance, showed a return on equity of 23% last year. In South Korea and Japan the average return was in single digits.

In the region's boom times, this financial conservatism limited Taiwan's growth and drew criticism. "In the high-economic-growth days, people said we were very inefficient from a financial standpoint, since we were so underleveraged," says C. Y. Wang, chairman of China Steel, which has usually kept its debt-to-equity ratio below 50%. By comparison, POSCO, South Korea's own national steel maker, typically had debt ratios five times that. Although the two firms started at the same time, POSCO has grown to twice China Steel's size; but it is lumbered with expensive capacity it cannot use, whereas China Steel's capacity utilisation is still near 100%.

"We always felt that the Japanese and Korean models were too dangerous," frets Chien-Jen Chen, head of the govern-

ment's information office. The largest Korean company is 16 times as big as the largest Taiwanese firm, he notes, and for Japan, the figure is 80 times. Such giants "have a collusive relationship with the banks that gives them the confidence to expand abroad quickly," Mr Chen says. "This is fine when the wind is in your favour, but that is not always the case."

With hindsight, all this caution looks inspired. But the KMT's motives were not always economically pure. One of the reasons for limiting the private companies' credit was its fear that a strong merchant class could arise that might challenge the KMT's hold on power. And it distrusts the Korean *chaebol* model in part because it worries that such big companies can become a force unto themselves. Indeed, Taiwan's government is now doing battle with Formosa Plastics, the island's largest industrial conglomerate, over the firm's plans to build a power plant on the mainland, which the government fears could help China's military capabilities.

When government officials are asked what country in the world is most like Taiwan, they usually single out Israel. It, too, is small and under constant threat from its neighbours, and has a paranoid government that places national security above all else. Like Taiwan, Israel was created under a political cloud which still looms, and has survived for the past five decades in large part because of assistance from America, its most important economic partner. And perhaps for some of the same reasons, both have emerged with an entrepreneurial business culture and an industry that is increasingly high-tech. Like Israel, Taiwan sees this as the model for its future, and for good reason: it has been fabulously successful. If there are lessons other nations should draw from Taiwan these days, they lie more in the character of its high-tech industry than in the fortuitously successful policies of its often illiberal government.

Silicon Valley (East)

Making computers for other people may not be glamorous, but it has shown Taiwan its future

IN HIS temporary office in a building still covered with bamboo scaffolding, Wen-Hsiung Huang is having another tough day. The workmen have found ancient bodies while digging, and the archaeologists will have to come in to inspect them; in the meantime the trenches have filled with rainwater. Moreover, the local farmers want compensation for the electromagnetic damage their crops may suffer from the high-voltage power lines that have been strung above them. Building a replica Silicon Valley from scratch in a sugar cane plantation in Taiwan's rural south is not easy.

Mr Huang is serious. He aims to recreate the suburban Northern California essence of Palo Alto, complete with townhouses and American-style schools, alongside all the semicon-

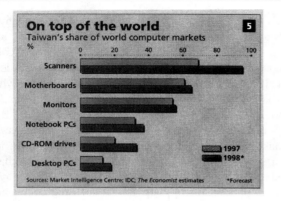

On top of the world 5
Taiwan's share of world computer markets
%

| | 0 | 20 | 40 | 60 | 80 | 100 |

- Scanners
- Motherboards
- Monitors
- Notebook PCs
- CD-ROM drives
- Desktop PCs

1997
1998*

Sources: Market Intelligence Centre; IDC; *The Economist* estimates   *Forecast

ductor factories, software start-ups, venture capitalists and cappuccino counters that make the real Silicon Valley hum. It might seem a silly idea if Taiwan had not done it once already. The Hsinchu Science Park near Taipei in the north is the core of the world's third-largest high-tech industry, accounting for a third of Taiwan's manufacturing exports and a huge share of the world's computer production (see chart 5). Now Hsinchu has run out of space, a victim of its own success, and Taiwan's government technocrats, led by Mr Huang, are building a second science park near the southern city of Tainan.

Never thought of Taiwan as a technology superpower? Start reading the labels in the back of your PC. From the circuit boards, CD-ROM drive and monitor to the mouse, keyboard and case, the odds are that most came from Taiwan or the Chinese factories of Taiwanese firms. If your computer is a laptop, it was probably entirely made in Taiwan; the "Dell" or "Compaq" labels were stuck on by employees of little-known companies such as Asustek, Mitac, FIC and Compal. This year Taiwan became the world's leading producer of notebook computers, ahead of both America and Japan. "Silicon Island" may be a marketing slogan, but it is not far from the truth.

Most countries would kill for such a big share of one of the world's strongest and fastest-growing industries; indeed, there is hardly a developing country in the region that has not tried to emulate high-tech Taiwan. But it is a hard model for governments to copy, mostly because it owes little to ambitious five-year plans and brilliant technocrats. Compared with the hugely expensive government-led high-tech efforts of Japan and South Korea, Taiwan's bottom-up success has surprised even its government planners.

Taiwan owes most of its success to two factors. The first is its close links with America, particularly through the thousands of young people that go each year to study at American universities and end up working in Silicon Valley. The second is the commoditisation of the PC in the early 1980s, which divided the industry into big brand-name companies that concentrated mostly on marketing and sales, and a horde of no-name component suppliers who could supply generic parts, even completely assembled machines, at low prices. It was the Taiwanese already in Silicon Valley who spotted this commoditisation trend first, and recognised that their home country was

a good place to set up all those no-names. Their efforts set off an explosion of entrepreneurial activity that has made this island across the Pacific into Silicon Valley's hinterland, an essential extension of America's high-tech industry.

In fairness to Mr Huang and his colleagues, Taiwan's government has played a role, too, although it deserves more praise for recognising its limitations. Kwoh-Ting Li, a former minister now considered the father of Taiwan's high-tech industry, travelled regularly to America in the 1970s and early 1980s, seeking the advice of Taiwanese-Americans in industry and academia and luring back some of the best to practise what they preached. Taiwan had already gone through the usual development phases of making things locally to save hard currency, attracting export-oriented foreign firms and developing its own export industries. But its labour was no longer cheap compared with its neighbours', and it needed to move up the technology ladder to industries that rewarded brains more than brawn.

Mr Li did four things which Taiwan's thousands of electronics companies now thank him for. He started a national laboratory, called the Industrial Technology Research Institute, from which many of Taiwan's most successful high-tech firms have been spun off. Around the lab he secured scarce land and built on it the beginning of Hsinchu, helping companies settle it by offering tax incentives and shared factory space. He beefed up the engineering side of Taiwan's already numerous universities. (Today Taiwan churns out nearly 50,000 new engineers a year, more than a quarter of all graduates.) And he encouraged the creation of a venture-capital industry, convincing a Taiwanese executive from Hambrecht & Quist, one of Silicon Valley's top investment banks, to set up a venture fund in Taiwan which spurred a host of imitators.

Fortunately, Mr Li stopped there. Now 89, he says he saw his role as accommodating the natural growth of the industry by providing the infrastructure it needed, rather than steering it: "We knew we were not smart enough to do more than that." The result is that, unlike Japan and South Korea, where the government encouraged concentration on a few technologies chosen by the rocket scientists in the economic ministries, Taiwanese firms have largely made their own way, helped by a large pool of talent, fairly easy access to capital, and a critical mass of like-minded companies around them.

A giant sucking sound

Today, Taiwan's high-tech industry is a model for the country's economic future, and a management guru's dream. By instinct more than by reading the *Harvard Business Review,* the average Taiwanese electronics company has managed to embody practically every globalisation trend going, from horizontal integration to virtual organisations.

Much of this comes from making virtues of Taiwan's main liabilities: a small domestic market, expensive labour, little available land and few natural resources. These limitations told Taiwanese entrepreneurs that they should dispense with any ambition to become the next Sony or IBM. Instead, they would have to make a living in the shadow of foreign giants—as the pilot fish, not the shark. This proved liberating. Once a company gets over corporate vanity, it can get on with the real business.

For Taiwanese high-tech firms, that turned out to be the so-called Original Equipment Manufacturer (OEM) market. This is the well-guarded secret of all sorts of industries, from bicycles to consumer electronics: the company whose name is on the box may have never touched the product inside. OEM manufacturers make goods to other firms' specifications, sometimes even helping to design the product. They labour in obscurity while their customers get all the credit and most of the profit. Unfair? Maybe. But Taiwanese firms were not too proud to grab a good business opportunity. Three-quarters of Taiwan's electronic production today is eventually sold under someone else's brand name.

For all the hard work and low wages of the OEM business, there are two particularly good things about it. The first is that its practitioners learn a lot from their customers, which helps them come up with their own technology and products. The second is that they can ignore the tricky marketing side of the business, from demand forecasting to advertising and distribution, and just concentrate on making the stuff as efficiently as possible.

It soon became clear that this often meant leaving Taiwan. Wages in mainland China and parts of South-East Asia, such as Vietnam, are one-twentieth of those in Taiwan, and land is affordable and available. So companies moved their older, more labour-intensive factories to somewhere cheaper. Over the past eight years, some 80,000 businesses have moved offshore, about half to China and half to South-East Asia, and today more than half of Taiwan's electronics production is off the island. "We don't compete with neighbouring countries— we use them," says Stan Shih, boss of Acer, Taiwan's biggest PC manufacturer. The result is that Taiwanese firms are insulated from competitive devaluation, having already moved most of their labour-intensive plants to the countries that are now becoming cheaper by the day.

This not only made Taiwanese companies into some of the most cost-efficient in Asia, it also allowed them to grow far larger than they could on the island itself. For example, Taiwan's small pool of labour and limited land can support a shoe industry of only about 10,000 workers. But by moving most of its factories to China, just one company, Paochen, was able to expand to 120,000 workers. It is now the biggest shoe maker in the world, producing millions of Nike, Reebok and other brand-name sport shoes. The same is true for industries from umbrellas to handtools, none of which make sense on Taiwan itself these days.

Taiwan Inc is becoming a virtual company. A small headquarters in Taipei now supports vast manufacturing and distribution facilities around the world. Profits are made abroad and increasingly reinvested abroad as well. Over the past eight years, Taiwanese companies have invested $80 billion outside

of the country, and 300,000 of their best people have followed to manage these investments. Many electronics firms do their research in Silicon Valley, and some are even planning to move their nominal headquarters there so they can hire a presentable western stand-in as chief executive and list on Nasdaq.

No wonder fretful planners worry that Taiwan is "hollowing out". For a government concerned about national security, having to watch a growing proportion of the economy move out of its reach may be a frightening prospect, but the companies themselves see it differently. As the more basic production moves offshore, what stays behind is increasingly sophisticated: the newest products with the highest technology and the most automated production.

Ten years ago, for instance, San Sun Hat & Cap's Taiwan factories were competing with companies in Bangladesh and Sri Lanka for caps that sold for under $6 a dozen. Those other countries are still making caps for that price, but San Sun has moved on. It has shifted the cheap stuff to China, and is now producing caps in Taiwan that sell for $40 a dozen, thanks to automation that makes them good enough for brands such as Nike and Polo.

Outside tiny Hong Kong, no other country in Asia has shown such manufacturing flexibility. Taiwan's domestic industry is being forced to advance faster than any of its neighbours, simply because the weak are so quickly shoved out of the nest. That does not leave an empty nest, but rather a stronger breed of bird. Where will it fly to next?

Little Taiwan

It is getting harder to see where Taiwan's economy ends and China's begins

LUNCHTIME on the day of the mid-autumn festival in Dongguan, an industrial region in China's Pearl River basin, and all should be well. But not for Hayes Lou, who is talking worriedly on his mobile phone. A Taiwanese businessman in Dongguan has been murdered a few days earlier by his girlfriend's brother, cut into pieces, put into bags and tossed on to nearby railway tracks. Now his grief-stricken family are coming over and arrangements must be made to console them. This sad task falls to Mr Lou, deputy secretary of the Taiwan Businessmen Association of Dongguan. Sadder yet, it is not such an unusual occasion.

The association's 24-hour emergency centre, manned by a staff of 12, gets 10,000 calls a year, ranging from car accidents and bar fights to disasters such as today's. In the first seven months of this year, according to Taiwan's Straits Exchange Foundation, eight Taiwanese businessmen were killed in China, another eight disappeared and four were kidnapped. The coastal factory towns of mainland China are Taiwan's Wild West, with the same gold-rush excitement—and corresponding risks.

In places such as Dongguan, it is hard to remember that it is only a decade since Taiwan's government allowed its citizens to do business in China. In this sub-province of 1m permanent inhabitants, 25,000 Taiwanese businessmen run 4,000 factories that together employ 2m mostly migrant workers. In one township there are hundreds of shoe factories, in another similar numbers assembling computers or sewing hats. A web of Taiwanese suppliers and subcontractors have come over with them, replicating (often on a much larger scale) most of industrial Taiwan. Taiwanese investment in China has reached an estimated $38 billion.

It is a hard life for the Taiwanese businessmen (and almost all of them are men). Like their workers, they usually live in their factories. They work almost all the time. It is no place for families, since it is not safe to leave the walled factory compounds after dark. But the rewards are commensurate: high management salaries, booming business and limitless cheap labour. For light relief, there is frontier karaoke nightlife (which accounts for many of those calls to the emergency line: the locals sometimes find the rich Taiwanese a bit loud). "We drink together, sing together and [enjoy the charms of Dongguan's many inexpensive hostesses] together," says Mr Lou. "And the next day, when we need a supplier at short notice, we just call each other up and it is done."

The importance of Dongguan, and other centres of Taiwanese investment in China, can hardly be overestimated. Today China seems to hold the future of Taiwan Inc—an almost limitless hinterland, with some of the lowest wages in the world, and a huge pool of educated technical workers ready for the next step up. And that is just as an export base. China is already a big and growing market too, and nobody knows it better than the Taiwanese. Investment in China has allowed Taiwan to leverage its strengths in a remarkable way, giving it a high standard of living at home while retaining the competitive labour advantages of its poor and underdeveloped past.

Milking the dragon

Multinationals from other countries complain about the conditions in China that keep them from turning a profit, but the Taiwanese just quietly go about their business of making money. If the system works through bribes, they bribe. And, not to put too fine a point on it, they are not unduly burdened by western standards of employee or environmental protection. Ailing Lai, boss of Thunder Tiger, which makes model airplanes in its China factory, scoffs at those who claim the mainland is a tough place to turn a buck. "Opening a factory in China today is easier than opening a factory was in Taiwan 20 years ago. It's got better infrastructure, highways, ports, and the cost of labour is one-twentieth that of Taiwan." No wonder nearly half of all listed Taiwanese firms have manufacturing operations on the mainland, and investment in China rose 22% in the first seven months of the year.

The result of this rush across the straits is that Taiwanese businesses have created a huge parallel economy in China, almost indistinguishable from China's own. By some estimates, up to a third of consumer goods for export marked "Made in China" are actually made by Taiwanese-owned firms. Analysts attribute more than 70% of the growth in America's trade deficit with China to the exports of Taiwanese firms. Yet to outside eyes this parallel economy is almost invisible: ethnic Chinese working with ethnic Chinese, speaking the same language (Mandarin, although Money runs a close second). There are few outward signs of Taiwanese ownership aside from the occasional "KTV" signs that give the game away. Karaoke TV is a Taiwanese passion.

But many in Taiwan worry that the China trade may be the seed of their destruction. The more Taiwan becomes an island of hollowed-out headquarters dependent on factories in China, they fear, the more power the rulers in Beijing will have over it. The Taiwanese government's official policy is to "go slow", and it specifically bans big infrastructure projects such as roads, power plants or anything else that might help the mainland's military machine. Quite apart from general unease about China's intentions, officials say that overdependence on any one country is simply unwise. They also worry that the ability to stay in labour-intensive industries by moving across the straits makes Taiwanese companies lazy about claiming the technology ladder to more automation and innovation.

But the government is also pragmatic, and knows better than to get in the way of Taiwanese business instincts. "For small firms, China is often their only choice," says Kuo Wen-jeng, a research fellow of the Chung-hua Institute of Economic Research. "We need to be realistic: China is a big market and it helps us attract foreign investment. It's natural that the government should be more conservative than industry, but they must make concessions to market forces. Without a China connection, the attractiveness of Taiwan would diminish. Isolating ourselves from China is not an option." Even as politics struggles to keep the countries apart, economics pulls them ever more strongly together. What kind of future does this predict?

Same again, please

For better or worse, Taiwan's future rests with China

FIFTY years ago, who could have foreseen today's Taiwan? Then it was a poor island occupied by the demoralised forces of a corrupt and discredited government. Mao's armies of millions were massed on the coast, ready to administer the *coup de grâce*. And even if the KMT survived that, Taiwan was just a temporary place to regroup before continuing the civil war on the mainland.

Fifty years on, the range of possibilities is mostly happier. A reforming China could one day let Taiwan become the sovereign nation it already is in all but name. Or it could reform so much that Taiwan could stomach being part of it again. Or—no more unlikely than it seemed 50 years ago—the status quo could continue for decades more.

But there is still, always, the possibility of war. China, its officials never fail to point out, does not have infinite patience. The current generation of leaders are probably reconciled to not seeing reunification in their lifetime, but the next may not be so understanding. Should an independence-minded party be elected in Taiwan and actually declare independence, an invasion would not be far off. And China itself, now undergoing reforms that by its standards are benevolent, could go horribly wrong.

For all Taiwan's development and democratisation, it still lives in the lengthening shadow of the mainland. If China also democratises and continues to develop, it will be harder for Taiwan to find fervent anti-communists to count as friends. Conversely, if China turns vicious, Taiwan's dabblings with independence look unsafe. As long as Taiwan remains top of the mainland's wish list, the desires of the 22m people on the island will always be tempered by those of the leadership in Beijing.

Apart from more of the same in one shape or another, these are the three main scenarios:

• China reforms enough for the two to agree to **unify peacefully**. Its good behaviour in Hong Kong, if kept up for five or ten more years, will start to put Taiwan's and the world's mind at rest about the notion of one country, several systems. As yet, it is too soon for that: Taiwan is still too hung up about the fundamental differences between a British colony and a fully fledged democratic state to consider whether, and under what conditions, a "handover" on the Hong Kong model might be appropriate. But there could be a day when the economic ties between China and Taiwan have become so close that agreeing to match them politically at a date, say, 50 years hence seems more palatable to Taiwan's citizens than another five decades of diplomatic purgatory and threats of war.

• China reforms even more, **letting Taiwan go.** By leaving Hong Kong's system alone, China has made itself vulnerable to infection from the free-wheeling territory. Already most of Guangdong, the province just across the border, is almost as exuberantly capitalist as Taiwan, not least because it is full of Taiwanese and Hong Kong firms. This could spread, along with the virus of democracy. If the only thing holding China back from reaping the international rewards of this reform in full is its continuing persecution of Taiwan, perhaps its people will decide one day—hard though it is to imagine today—that this crusade is more trouble than it is worth.

• China's reforms backfire, leading to a rise in militant nationalism and **possible invasion.** Taiwan's President Lee sees in the torn fragments of the former Soviet Union a likely end to communist China, too: he describes the mainland as a "tottering pile of bricks." Throughout China's history, the ends of dynasties have tended to unleash centrifugal forces, leaving breakaway republics; Taiwan would then be just another one.

The difference is that the 12th-century warlords did not have nuclear weapons.

Which of these is the most likely? For the foreseeable future, say the next ten years, the best answer is none of the above. Taiwan will muddle through pretty much as it has for years, and China will not feel brave enough to do much about it. "It's like living together," says one international observer. "You're effectively married. You can deal with the flag later. True, there are really no precedents for this in the world, but Taiwan has broken all the moulds already and it continues to function well."

Last month the chairman of Taiwan's Straits Exchange Foundation met a series of important Chinese officials, including President Jiang Zemin—the highest-level talks for five years. The meetings made headlines, although apart from the fact that the world feels safer when Taiwan and China are talking than when they are not, it is not clear that any progress was made. China offered new semantic variations on its one-country, two-systems theme, promising Taiwan unprecedented levels of autonomy if it joins the fold. And, no surprise, Taiwan rejected the offer. On the important issues, Taiwan and China have nothing to talk about. On both sides of the straits, it is political suicide to deviate from the stand-off script: neither independence nor reunification, in any guise, are on the table, nor will they be for years to come.

For all the talk of independence, what the Taiwanese really want is prosperity and safety. There is no groundswell for change; the vast majority of people are for the status quo. The missile tests reminded the Taiwanese of the risks associated with exercising their new-found democracy too freely. They like the idea of independence, but would rather not die for it.

Since Taiwan really is a democratic society, any change would require a popular perception that there was more to be gained from doing something new than from retaining the status quo. The island's pariah status in world affairs may be irksome for its people, but its practical effect is minimal, especially set against the possibility of war.

To understand Taiwan's future, simply follow the money. It is going to the mainland: economically, "one China" is getting closer by the day. Taiwan's high-tech industry sees its future as the Silicon Valley of China. Much of its manufacturing sector has already crossed the straits. Taiwan and China are already half-wed.

If China continues its reforms, this link offers Taiwan a glorious future: gateway to what will be the biggest economy in the world. But if China stumbles, Taiwan will stumble too. Fear of China made Taiwan tough enough to survive the Asian crisis; now its businesses are becoming bolder and asking the country to do the same. For example, they want the ban on transport links to be relaxed, and Taiwanese banks to be allowed to operate in China. It is a scary thing for Taiwan, dancing with its worst enemy. But even paranoia has its limits.

Article 25 *Far Eastern Economic Review*, October 15, 1998

TAIWAN

Breaking the Ice

After a long silence, Beijing and Taipei have decided to start talking again. They're both under pressure to be more flexible than before, but they remain deeply suspicious of each other.

by *Julian Baum* in Taipei and *Susan V. Lawrence* in Beijing

The last time China's Wang Dao-han met Taiwan's Koo Chen-fu, media excitement ran high but mutual suspicion ran deep. So it was not surprising that those historic talks in Singapore yielded extremely modest pacts, on documenting marriages and paying for registered mail. Five years on, the same two envoys are preparing to meet again—on Chinese soil and without an agenda. This time the stakes are higher since they have agreed that political issues can be raised, and not just civil affairs.

Beijing and Taipei—as well as Washington, the absent third party in the cross-strait dialogue—also better understand the importance of settling their differences peacefully. With economic crisis gripping most of East Asia and requiring regional cooperation, no one wants a return to the military confrontation of 1995–96. Then, Beijing protested against Taiwan's allegedly pro-independence policies with military exercises and missile "tests" in the Taiwan Strait, forcing Washington to respond with the largest mobilization of U.S. naval forces in Asia since the Vietnam war. To avoid more confrontations, U.S. President Bill Clinton has urged both sides to talk "sooner rather than later."

The two envoys will meet in Shanghai in mid-October. Wang, head of China's Association for Relations Across the Taiwan Strait, is a former mayor of Shanghai and a close adviser to President Jiang Zemin. Koo, chairman of Taiwan's Straits Exchange Foundation, is a member of the ruling Kuomintang's inner circle. Significantly, Koo is also scheduled to meet Jiang, Premier Zhu Rongji and other senior leaders in Beijing—the highest-level public contact between the two sides in half a century.

Both sides are playing down the notion that Koo's ice-breaking visit will move the relationship dramatically forward. Given the glacial pace of cross-strait diplomacy, many observers doubt that the meeting will produce much progress. Still, Koo's trip to China marks a firm step away from the tensions of 1995–96 towards a more stable relationship. Optimistic observers hope for even more: the start of a process that could culminate in a face-to-face meeting between President Jiang and Taiwan's President Lee Teng-hui.

Taiwanese officials exude none of that optimism. Premier Vincent Siew told Taiwan's legislature in late September not to have high expectations of the outcome. It's a "first step" for both sides to normalize their exchanges, he stressed. "It's a meeting, not negotiations; it's a visit, not talks." Koo has been authorized only to have "exploratory conversations" with his hosts, an official at Taiwan's National Security Council told the REVIEW.

Similarly, mainland scholar Su Ge, a vice-president of Beijing's Foreign Affairs College, says the limited goal of these talks is to "maintain the status quo, facilitate understanding, and make confidence-building efforts." Adds Su, a specialist on Taiwan: "The point is to stay engaged."

Taipei's caution over engagement springs from Beijing's uncompromising stance, say officials in Taipei. "There's been absolutely no shift in their strategy," asserts Lin Chong-pin, deputy chairman of the cabinet-level Mainland Affairs Council, which coordinates policy towards Beijing. Among other things, Beijing insists on the "one-China principle" as a condition of political talks. Taiwan's leaders accept the term, but not what they perceive as Beijing's definition of "one China" as the People's Republic.

Beijing also refuses to recognize Taiwan's de facto sovereign status and won't renounce the use of force if the island declares independence. Unless Beijing first accepts the principle of political equality, Taiwanese officials say, political talks would not be a dialogue among equals; it would signal the capitulation of the ruling Kuomintang and a retreat for Taiwan's democracy.

Taipei's official position is that China should be unified as a democracy and a free-market economy. Taipei no longer contests Beijing's rule over continental China, and wants Beijing to reciprocate by not contesting Taipei's rule over Taiwan. "We are masters of our own house under conditions of freedom and democracy," says a senior government official. "We are not going to give this up to suit the fancy of people in Beijing."

Beijing's official position is that political dialogue should focus first on "officially terminating hostilities across the strait under the principle of one China." Beijing regards Taiwan as a renegade province which should be peacefully reunited with the mainland under the "one country, two systems" formula—the formula under which Hong Kong returned to mainland rule.

Chinese Foreign Ministry spokesman Tang Guoqiang on September 29 restated Beijing's position that after unification, Taiwan would be allowed to keep its own military and Taiwanese leaders could be appointed to central-government positions. "The degree of autonomy enjoyed in Taiwan will be even greater than that enjoyed in Hong Kong," he pledged.

Beijing's caution stems mainly from its deep suspicion of President Lee. Although Lee has never openly called for Taiwan's independence from China, mainland officials and scholars believe that his actions add up to a bid for independence. While Lee remains in charge, mainland experts do not believe that cross-strait talks can make significant progress.

Despite their mutual distrust, however, both sides have in the past year made concessions to get talks going again. Beijing has bowed to Taipei's demand that it should issue the invitation to resume the dialogue, which it had suspended. Beijing also softened its earlier insistence on having political talks. In Su's words, it agreed to settle for a dialogue that at least "leaves room for political issues."

Taiwan softened its stance, too, saying that it would not exclude the possibility of a political dialogue, but that the two sides needed to work out practical issues first, such as agreements on settling fishing disputes and hijacking cases which were negotiated in the past but never signed.

Analysts on each side cite differing factors that persuaded President Jiang to reach out to Taiwan. What set the stage, Su says, was Jiang's state visit to the U.S. last year. "Stable Sino-American relations provide a healthy and stable framework so that cross-strait relations can proceed," says the mainland scholar. "You cannot proceed when the U.S. and China regard each other as a major menace to national security."

But observers in Taiwan believe that the decisive factor was the rise of the pro-independence Democratic Progressive Party, Taiwan's leading opposition group. In municipal elections last December, the DPP won 12 of the 23 top local-government posts and slashed KMT-held posts from 15 to only eight. The DPP's surprise victory raised the prospect of a DPP-controlled central government sooner than expected.

Presumably adding to Beijing's worries are opinion polls in Taiwan which show a steady rise in support for outright independence. "They see time is running out," says Liang Su-yung, president of the Association of Peaceful Unification, a private group of retired KMT officials. A former speaker of the legislature, Liang was recently received by Jiang in a new bid to cultivate private organizations in Taiwan which are sympathetic to Beijing's policies.

Liang urges political dialogue as a way of preventing Beijing from again resorting to military force if it sees the prospects for unification slipping away. "Two years ago they had no timetable for unification, but now we're not sure," he warns, implying that Beijing's leaders could set a deadline for a political solution which could be followed by more serious military threats than in the past.

Experts in Beijing insist, however, that the mainland is in no rush to settle the Taiwan issue. They say President Jiang signalled as much last year, at the Communist Party's 15th Congress, which he declined to name an army representative to the party's top decision-making body, the politburo standing committee. If serious military threats against Taiwan were being contemplated, they say, Jiang would not have excluded the military from the body.

The mainland's outreach policy was most recently boosted by comments made by President Clinton when he visited China at mid-year. For the first time, an American president stripped away the ambiguity from the U.S. position by saying publicly that Washington did not support Taiwan's independence, "two Chinas," or Taiwan's membership in international organizations requiring state sovereignty. Tang Shubei, vice-chairman of China's Association for Relations Across the Taiwan Strait, said that Clinton's "three no's" statement made it possible for Beijing to "normalize" cross-strait relations. Beijing is looking for a similar statement from Japanese leaders during Jiang's planned visit to Tokyo later this year.

But Taiwan, too, is feeling pressure to revise its policies, especially its 50-year-old ban on direct links with the mainland. Last year Taiwanese business leaders publicly criticized the restrictions. This year even the American Chamber of Commerce, Taiwan's most influential foreign business lobby, urged Taipei to open direct links to serve its goal of making the island a regional operations centre for multinational corporations.

Lee's "go slow, no haste" policy for Taiwanese companies investing on the mainland has also come under fire. Formosa Plastics Chairman Y. C. Wang, who is being told to pull out of a $3 billion power-plant project in Fujian, has said this policy should be scrapped.

China-watchers in Taipei say Beijing set the timing for the resumption of cross-strait meetings with Taiwan's next national election in mind. With less than two months to go before the December poll for an expanded 225-seat legislature, some analysts believe the KMT could lose its majority in parliament. By giving the KMT credit for improving the cross-strait relations, Beijing may hope to enhance the ruling party's support among voters and at least delay the arrival of an opposition-led government.

Taiwanese analysts surmise that Beijing would prefer bargaining with the KMT, which is still officially committed to unification, rather than the pro-independence DPP. They believe Tang implied as much when he told Taiwanese journalists that it was not his government's intention to open talks with the DPP.

However, a senior Chinese analyst counters that China prefers to deal with people who are "straight up." He contends that President Lee pretends not to support independence, while pursuing pro-independence policies. The analyst suggests that China might make more progress negotiating with the DPP, which at least does not make any pretence about its pro-independence policy. He draws a parallel to Beijing's successful cooperation with the virulently anti-communist, yet pragmatic, U.S. President Richard Nixon.

Su also does not rule out the possibility that Beijing might find itself negotiating with the DPP. "If the DPP is going to be elected, we need to keep contact now," he says. It's important that they "understand our positions."

Beijing's deep antipathy toward Lee has in the past five years been the biggest stumbling block in the cross-strait relationship. Chinese propaganda has described Taiwan's first popularly elected president as "the sinner of all millennia" and consigned him to "the dustbin of history." Those who distrust Lee argue that China should wait out the remaining months of his term before reopening talks. Lee has said he will step down when his term expires in 2000. So Su says some people in Beijing are asking "What's the hurry?"

But the improvement in U.S.-China relations offered an opportunity for cross-strait engagement that others did not want to pass up. "At the end of last year, we were not sure how to deal with Lee Teng-hui," Su comments. "However, we just could not let the status quo go into a downward spiral again." Su argues that contact before Lee leaves office is important. "If you don't have any contact, how can you influence Taiwan?" he asks.

Would Lee and Jiang go so far as to exchange visits, as recently mooted in the news media in Taiwan and Hong Kong? In his inaugural speech two years ago, Lee proposed to make a "journey of peace" to the Chinese mainland, although Beijing is adamant that he cannot visit in the capacity of a national leader. A Hong Kong newspaper recently floated the idea that Lee could be welcomed as the "supreme leader" from Taiwan, one of several new proposals coming from unnamed sources.

But Taiwan's China-watchers suspect such proposals are part of Beijing's campaign to convince the world that it is being more conciliatory. At best, they say, the proposals show a divergence of views, such as the "one country, three systems" idea which presumably offers

Taiwan a more distinctive niche in a future unification scheme. (Taiwan has steadfastly rejected the "one country, two systems" formula.)

Taiwan's Lin says such proposals are meaningless unless they come from key decision makers and address the core issues. "We'd prefer something more substantive, such as an offer to end the strangulation of Taiwan's international diplomacy and end the military preparations which threaten us," he says.

Premier Siew told Taiwan's legislature on September 29 that the most "natural" setting for a meeting between Jiang and Lee would be at the summit of leaders of the Asia-Pacific Economic Cooperation forum in Kuala Lumpur in November. (Beijing has blocked Lee's attendance at previous Apec meetings.) But most Taiwanese officials worry that such a grand gesture could put Taiwan on the defensive. Says a presidential staff member: "We are aware of the potential risks. That's why we insist on parity in our relationship."

For Taiwan, the bigger question is whether Beijing is ready to resume talks on civil affairs broken off in 1995. "We're still in the dark about this," says Jean-Pierre Cabestan, director of the French Research Centre on Contemporary China in Hong Kong.

As for political talks, he believes that neither side appears seriously ready to open such a dialogue. "These meetings are just a beginning; it's not even a negotiation about negotiations." Cabestan adds: "It's even possible that after these meetings both sides will feel that they have met their obligations to the U.S. and go back to sleep."

Article 26   *Far Eastern Economic Review*, June 11, 1998

HONG KONG

Now the Hard Part

In its first year as sovereign, China has assumed near-colonial control over Hong Kong. But with economic woes prompting calls for more responsive government, that control may be challenged sooner than expected.

By *Bruce Gilley* and *Joanna Slater* in Hong Kong

The symbols have changed, but the ritual remains the same: On July 1, about 100 Hong Kong people will gather at the former colonial governor's residence to be honoured for their service to Hong Kong and loyalty to the sovereign. As an honour guard stands rigidly by, Hong Kong leader Tung Chee-hwa will decorate each winner. One of the few differences from colonial days: Instead of the British crown, the medals will depict bushy sheaves of wheat and square-jawed socialist faces looking skyward.

For China, the symbolism is perfect. In the year since it regained sovereignty amid promises of "Hong Kong people ruling Hong Kong," it has allowed individual and economic freedoms to flourish as before. But quietly, the city's Beijing-backed authorities have orchestrated legal and institutional changes that essentially give China the same kind of control over Hong Kong that Britain enjoyed as a colonial power.

China, however, may find itself challenged to use that control sooner than it may have calculated. Any illusion that Hong Kong people were going blithely along with the game plan was swept away in May, when a record 1.5 million people, or 53% of registered voters, cast ballots in legislative elections—sweeping a raft of pro-democracy politicians into office. Less than a week later, the Hong Kong government announced that GDP shrank by 2% in the first quarter. The downturn is almost certain to stoke popular discontent with the government, whose legitimacy is based largely on its ability to deliver the economic goods. If

the financial crisis feeds demands for political change, Hong Kong could be steering into a stormy sea.

Martin Lee, the Democratic Party chairman, warned of as much after his party captured nearly half of popularly elected seats to the legislature. "The Hong Kong people have spoken with one voice to say that we want to choose our own leaders through democratic elections," said Lee, whose party will push for a fully elected legislature by 2000 and an elected chief executive by 2002. "If the chief executive goes against the will of the Hong Kong people, he is actually leading Hong Kong forward by taking a very dangerous course."

At street level, such warnings sound extreme. A walk in the sultry tropical air of Hong Kong Island, the British colony's original site, suggests that little has changed in a year. U.S. aircraft carriers still drop anchor and disgorge their crews into the Wanchai district's red-light bars. Anti-China demonstrators continue their almost weekly parades through the Central district.

An annual march to commemorate the Tiananmen Massacre took place on May 31, while a candle-lit vigil that in past years has attracted tens of thousands of people was due to take place on June 4 as usual. Meanwhile, the People's Liberation Army garrison has made a virtue of being invisible.

The business community's biggest concern is a grinding economic recession which blew in from Asia, not privilege and corruption from the mainland. "Beijing has done nothing drastic to

meddle in Hong Kong affairs since the handover," notes local political analyst Andy Ho, managing director of PA Professional Consultants.

Some overt threats to freedom have been scuttled by protests. In March, for example, local patriot Xu Simin demanded during a visit to Beijing that the Hong Kong government broadcaster, RTHK, should tone down its criticism of government policy. After a local outcry, Beijing and then the Hong Kong government told him to be quiet. "If anything, RTHK's freedom is more assured than ever," says a senior reporter at the station.

Beijing, clearly, has kept Deng Xiaoping's promise that "dancing and horseracing" would continue unabated in the New Hong Kong, along with a raft of political freedoms unknown in mainland China. Yet almost imperceptibly, as pundits combed the outspoken *Apple Daily* newspaper to see if it had lost its punch, or watched to see whether Chinese dissidents were evicted from the territory, real political power has been transferred to Beijing. It has happened through a series of legal and systemic changes that are too complicated—or too subtle—for many to even notice.

China's motives are clear: to ensure that Hong Kong continues to be ruled by elites who will keep the territory's economy ticking and its popular—and often anti-China politics—under control. But a simple reassignment of colonial power was not, on the surface, the intent of the agreements that governed the territory's transformation into a Special Administrative Region of China.

"Hong Kong's relationship to China was not supposed to be the same as its relationship with Britain," says Yash Ghai, a law professor at the University of Hong Kong and occasional legal adviser to the government. China promised Hong Kong a "high degree of autonomy" after 1997; Beijing would handle only foreign affairs and defence under the "one country, two systems" formula. "But the SAR government has ignored that fact and taken a very mechanical view that sovereignty has changed but that nothing else has changed," says Ghai.

Indeed, the Chinese state has assumed privileges in Hong Kong previously reserved for the British crown—with significant implications for Hong Kong's constitutional relationship with China.

Under British rule, all British government agencies in Hong Kong were immune from local laws. But after 1997, most observers expected that only China's foreign-affairs office and army garrison would enjoy such immunity. Instead, the Hong Kong government went further, granting the local office of the Xinhua news agency immunity.

The move was significant: Xinhua is widely believed to be the headquarters of the Hong Kong Work Committee of the Chinese Communist Party, whose existence was acknowledged by the party newspaper, the *People's Daily*, only as recently as October. This exemption of the party branch in Hong Kong has been a stark symbol of the seeming return to colonial status, since it suggests Beijing expects to be involved in administering all aspects of Hong Kong.

Other events are equally worrying: In May, two youths were convicted of desecrating two small Chinese and Hong Kong flags under new flag laws. Their action, at a January protest, was judged to be a prelude to "riots." "If the logic of the magistrate were to carry," commented defending lawyer Albert Ho, since re-elected to the legislature for the Democratic Party, "many dissenting voices in Hong Kong . . . should be silenced because it may lead to riots."

The new legislature was elected on May 24 under arrangements that diluted the power won by the popular pro-de-mocracy forces in favour of establishment groups close to China; these pro-Beijing bodies are expected to become pro-government bodies. Under British rule, government officials appointed to the legislature served the same function. The new attitude of the pro-Beijing Federation of Trade Unions, for example, whose political party, the Democratic Alliance for Betterment of Hong Kong, or DAB, won nine seats in the elections, is summed up as "supporting the government on major issues while disagreeing on minor issues," according to the Beijing-run *Wen Wei Po* newspaper. "This is progress in civilization! This is the new SAR culture!" the newspaper declared in early May.

Hong Kong government officials, perhaps unsurprisingly, echo past British governors—save the last one, Chris Patten—when justifying democratization's slow pace. "We may be very advanced in terms of our business and finance, but democracy is still something where we are in a learning process," Secretary for Home Affairs David Lan said after officiating at a pre-election rally. "Perhaps we are not moving as fast as people overseas would like, but it's because we are still at the learning stage."

The government has adopted an executive-led approach. New rules governing the legislature's powers oblige both pro-Beijing and pro-democracy parties to look to the government for policy leadership. Under British colonial rule, any bill involving public spending had to have the governor's consent to be introduced; under Chinese sovereignty, two other subjects have also been placed out of bounds: Bills that concern government structure or government policy will also need the chief executive's written permission before they can be introduced. These conditions effectively strip legislators of the ability to propose bills on any important issues.

Beijing has left nothing to chance: There is also a new way of voting on government-policy amendments. Legco will split into two: the 30 seats from functional, or professional, constituencies on the one hand, and on the other the 30 seats returned by two other voting methods—the direct elections (20 seats) and a small poll conducted by an election committee (10 seats). Passing an amendment will require a majority of both groups, throwing yet another spanner in the pro-democracy camp's works.

The local courts, meanwhile, have provided another crucial key to Beijing's colonial-type controls over Hong Kong. In a series of judgments, the lower courts have ruled that, since the Chinese parliament, the National People's Congress, represents the sovereign power, China, it can overrule the Basic Law, the mini-constitution for Hong Kong that China devised before the handover.

Ghai of the University of Hong Kong hopes the judges might narrow the Chinese parliament's carte blanche by asserting its right to override the Basic Law only in cases of "necessity." "If the earlier decision stands," warns Ghai, "it will represent a very significant weakening of the Basic Law."

What does it mean for the future? With these powers in place, China can do as it likes in Hong Kong—including passing more restrictive laws. Hong Kong's autonomy and freedoms are no longer guaranteed in writing but are now enjoyed only on the sufferance of Beijing. "The promises of autonomy and eventual democracy in Hong Kong will depend on the willingness of authorities in Beijing and Hong Kong to uphold these promises," commented the Washington-based National Democratic Institute in a May report that summarized many of the changes.

The first real blow to freedoms could be struck later this year when the new legislature is expected to pass laws against "subversion" as part of a national security bill. The law is expected to signal a clampdown on some forms of free expression. "This will be a litmus test for whether the government has any respect for freedoms of expression in Hong Kong," says political commentator Andy Ho.

There are indications, however, that Hong Kong people will not simply resign themselves to being treated as colonial subjects. True, satisfaction levels with China's handling of Hong Kong affairs have risen continuously since the handover, reaching 67% by April compared with 45% at the handover, according to the Hong Kong Transition Project, a respected local academic group. But as economic recession takes hold—unemployment is at a 15-year high of 4%—demands for more help for the jobless, among others, is expected to grow.

If Beijing and the Hong Kong government remain aloof from popular demands, anger at the polls may turn into anger on the streets. Just one week after the elections, for example, Democratic Party member Albert Chan led a demonstration of angry property-owners in danger of losing their homes. "We have worked very hard," says C. K. Lee, his voice trembling with emotion as he marches outside the main government building. "We have no confidence at all in the government—they only help the developers, not the citizens."

Tung now finds himself in the unfortunate position of welcoming a feisty new legislature just as he delivers Hong Kong's worst economic news in a decade. These two factors will test his leadership skills and his executive-led style of government, which now must compete with different factions in the legislature for public support for its policies.

It also remains to be seen if and how the government will cooperate with its newly minted opposition, for whom the economic crisis is also a challenge: the pro-democracy camp will have to demonstrate that it can be a credible opposition on all issues, not just those that deal with political reform.

Democrat Martin Lee quotes Tung as saying the downturn "will last at least two years; we'll all tighten our belts together." But, Lee adds, "it's not very convincing, because Hong Kong people say, 'I didn't even put you there.'" The Democrats say they will use their electoral triumph as a licence to hound the government on everything from the economy to the territory's democratic development.

They're not wasting any time: Two days after Tung hinted that Hong Kong's first-quarter growth might be negative for

BACK TO THE FUTURE

A year after the handover, Hong Kong's system of government looks a lot like the one it had at the height of British colonial rule—only more so

Colonialism . . .
- Legal immunity transferred from the British crown to the Chinese state
- System of executive-led government and election system tailored to produce a weak legislature
- Slow pace of democracy

. . . with Chinese characteristics
- Power of legislators to propose bills severely constrained
- New law outlawing 'subversion' to be introduced
- Courts rule that acts of National People's Congress can take precedence over Hong Kong's constitution

(REVIEW GRAPHIC/DICKY TANG)

the first time in years, the Democratic Party announced plans to host a forum for all the political parties to come together to discuss ways to boost the economy. Pro-Beijing and pro-democracy groups alike have agreed in principle to attend. Whether or not the forum succeeds, its connotation is obvious: Democratic legislators intend to shadow the government's every move.

Hong Kong people, it seems, want them to do just that. "The Democrats will watch the Hong Kong government," said 39-year-old marketing manager Chung Fuk Hing on election day. And does the government need to be watched? Chung and his wife Nora nodded vigorously.

The pro-democracy camp will certainly perform that watchdog function assiduously— even though the recent modifications in the legislature may block them from making concrete changes. "We are very much aware that we are in a minority and we will always be outvoted," says Emily Lau, leader of the Frontier. "But we hope the administration will not just brush us aside." Tung has promised to meet all party leaders in July to discuss future policy, but experts are not optimistic about the prospects for cooperation.

"There will be a lot of frustration; there will be no give and take," predicts Joseph Cheng, a professor at the City University of Hong Kong. "If the vocal minority in the legislature manages to show it has the support of the ordinary people, it will be very different. . . . You can't simply ignore the democrats every time."

Even pro-Beijing groups are a force to be reckoned with. Asked how his party would influence policy, Tsang Yok-sing, leader of the pro-labour DAB, replied: "The legislature is not exactly toothless—if the government is always seen to be acting against the wishes of the legislature, then of course they cannot expect the legislators to support them in return."

Tung will have to run a lot faster to stay in front of Legco if he wants to maintain executive-style government. He risks being forced onto the defensive, with a newly active Legco setting the pace. For example, how will Tung deal with a potential alliance of the pro-democracy camp (19 seats) and the DAB (10 seats, after an independent joined their ranks), who share similar views on issues such as the importation of labour and the possibility of increasing social assistance? "I have yet to see the chief executive adopt a proactive strategy," says Lau Siu Kai, a professor of sociology at Chinese University and a member of the Preparatory Committee, a Beijing-appointed body that helped set up the post-handover government. "If he doesn't, he'll be at a disadvantage compared to the legislature." Beijing may have quietly amassed the powers it needs to exert its influence over Hong Kong. But even its anointed leader, Tung, almost certainly failed to recognize the power of the people's will. "The more who come out to vote, the more discontented they are," Martin Lee commented after the surprisingly high turnout for the legislative elections. "These are just the ABCs of politics. How can the chief executive not know that?"

Article 27   *The World Today*, April 1998

WE SHOULD NOT FORGET HONG KONG

John Gittings

Hong Kong is about to have its first political test since sovereignty reverted to China. The May elections raise again the uncomfortable question of democracy, and whether the international community—and Britain in particular—still cares.

THE CYNICAL VIEW of the Hong Kong handover and what would happen afterwards has proved correct. There was no great upheaval; the world media packed its bags and left; and the problems of Hong Kong faded fast from international consciousness, demonstrating the truth of that old saying: Ah, How quickly one forgets!

Will more than passing attention be paid to next month's elections for the Legislative Council (Legco)—the first to take place under the rules which were rejigged to please Beijing? What is certain is that controversial preparations for that election have attracted little comment outside Hong Kong. Nor has much notice been taken of the low-key attitude already adopted by Britain, which undermines its responsibility under the 1984 Joint Declaration to continue to play a special monitoring role.

Yet it would be a great mistake if Britain, or Europe, or the US—or for that matter the Chinese leadership in Beijing—were to remove Hong Kong and its people from the map of important world issues. Even if the question of moral obligation is left on one side, there is more than one scenario which could force Hong Kong back into awkward focus: all the more reason not to lose sight of the territory and its unclear future now.

First, the issue of democracy is not going to go away as easily as apologists for the new arrangements (including senior figures formerly involved on the British side as well as in Beijing) may hope. The elections on May 24 are only the beginning of a process of electoral reform mapped out by the Basic Law over the next ten years—and sketched more vaguely further into the future. The next election will take place in only two years: however tiresome it may be for Beijing and Chief Executive Tung Chee-hwa, the pace and extent of further democratic change will remain naggingly on the agenda.

Second, while it may be a truism that Hong Kong's future depends on the future of the mainland, the implications of this are far from clear. There is a reluctance to ask serious questions about 'what will happen' in China—perhaps for fear of inviting unsettling answers. Yet there is no need to subscribe to any doomsday scenario to conclude that huge social and economic forces are at work in China which must before too long impact upon the political scene. The result of such an impact must also have repercussions on Hong Kong, whether for better or for worse.

Third, Hong Kong—along with mainland China—is already rocked by external events which were not even glimpsed on the horizon when the handover took place last year. So far both have withstood the Asian economic crisis well: can they continue to do so if it intensifies? Even if it does not, what has happened should be a sobering reminder that in the new globalised world one should always expect the unexpected.

SETTING MINDS AT EASE

Finally, it would be very unwise to assume that because the handover went smoothly, and Hong Kong has coped fairly well with the economic crisis, Hong Kong minds will remain—to use Deng Xiaoping's phrase—'at ease.' In the past Hong Kong has more than once surprised those who took its people for granted. The British assumed they could manipulate local opinion after concluding the 1984 Agreement; the Chinese that they could ignore it after the Beijing Massacre in 1989.

Loyalties and expectations, within a community where both have been turned upside down in the last two decades, may be fragile and changeable. The Social Indicators Programme at the Chinese University recently reported a gradual build-up of social discontent since the late 1980s and suggested that this is likely to intensify.

THERE FOR HONG KONG?

In Britain there has been a conspicuous lack of interest in Hong Kong since the tearful departure of Governor Chris Patten. The Labour government has scaled down its own interest without any critical notice being taken. British policy towards Hong Kong has now reverted to the mainstream perspective before the interlude of the Patten governorship (1992–97), namely that Hong Kong is only part—and now an even smaller part—of British policy towards China. The Foreign Office takes the fairly amazing view that the handover and its consequences have been a triumph for British diplomacy.

Britain's obligations as a co-signatory of the Joint Declaration under international law, and the special role—though more limited in time—which it should perform in monitoring developments through the Joint Liaison Group (JLG) until the work of this body comes to an end in the year 2000, are now played down. 'The Special Administrative Region has got off to an extremely good start', the new British JLG head said at the first post-handover meeting in November, 'and the Chinese government is pursuing wise and enlightened policies.'

Britain's new consul-general, Sir Andrew Burns, stresses that he is just an ordinary diplomat, and will watch the May elections 'like other members of the international community.' These are clear signals to Beijing that Britain will not insist on the special responsibility in the Joint Declaration.

Occasionally something more is said: Britain, after all, does have an ethical foreign policy now. After his visit to Beijing in January the Foreign Secretary denied that Britain had softened its stand and said it had 'real concerns' with the electoral arrangements for the May elections. This was after Mr Cook had thanked China for observing the Joint Declaration, and for introducing 'progressive democracy' in Hong Kong.

In a year when the Prime Minister is to visit Beijing, London's voice will not be raised very loud, unless China or the Hong Kong government violates the procedures which they themselves laid down when they discarded those used for the previous elections in 1995.

It will be a serious mistake if Britain abdicates its special role—it has already said that it will not monitor the Legco elections—or muffles criticism of the inequitable features of the current electoral system. Ritualised regret at the reduction in size of the functional constituencies is hardly enough.

There should have been loud concern, for example, when the bizarre arrangements for those constituencies—which allow foreign firms and shell companies to hold a significant number of votes—were revealed, and at the low rate of registration in which one million potential voters have failed to register. The results of this election, and the attention which they attract, will materi-

ally influence the terms of debate for further reform.

It is instructive to recall the pledge by former Prime Minister John Major on his last visit to Hong Kong that the Special Administrative Region 'will never have to walk alone', and the assurance from his foreign secretary Malcolm Rifkind that London would always 'be there for Hong Kong on the issues that matter.' This election does matter: if Britain will not make its interest clear when things are running smoothly with Beijing, what confidence can the people of Hong Kong have that London will be of any help in a crisis?

WATCHING THE BIG ISSUES

It will take a major act of miscalculation or heavy handedness on the part of the Chinese government to refocus world attention on Hong Kong—and we can be sure that this is well appreciated in Beijing. Their behaviour so far has been scrupulously correct on the record: any clumsiness has been on the part of the Hong Kong administration.

There has been no hint of interference over Hong Kong's handling of the financial crisis. The provinces have been told to stay away, and have done so with such discipline that it has become another factor depressing Hong Kong tourism. This does not mean that on the important issues China's wishes are not observed. They are and they will be.

Chief Executive Tung, however inept he may be in his public relations with the Hong Kong people, has not put a foot wrong in his private relations with Beijing. Whether walking deferentially behind President Jiang Zemin on the morning of the handover, or paying complimentary remarks about the Chinese economy when visiting Beijing in December, Mr Tung knows to please. He has only come under serious criticism in Hong Kong over internal issues—the mishandling of the 'chicken crisis' caused by the new flu outbreak, and his ambiguous attitide towards Radio Television Hong Kong.

If political life continues to go smoothly in Beijing, the Chinese government's attitude will continue to be that of *da tong xiao yi:* not fussing about the small issues as long as the big ones

go its way. This was noticeable in the selection of Hong Kong delegates to the National Peoples Congress which met last month: it went without saying that the Democrats could not be admitted, and that the director of the New China News Agency in Hong Kong, Jiang Enzhu, had to come top of the poll—but the rest of the placings were of much less concern to Beijing.

Yet no one should be in any doubt that Beijing regards Hong Kong as subordinate. The two systems may co-exist but they are not on the same level. In this respect Hong Kong is no different from any other Chinese province: the art for Mr Tung is to find ways, as provincial officials elsewhere do, of working his way around the formal hierarchy. He also has to contend with mainland provincial rivals who will use any shortcomings in his administration to press their own claims on Beijing.

CHEERFUL VIEW?

The longer term question is whether China will change—or rather, how it will do so, since change is bound to come in Beijing and what effect this will have on Hong Kong. In theory the Chinese government could become weaker and therefore less able to enforce its will on important issues. But weakness in Beijing, or the apprehension of it, is in practice more likely to increase the demand for Hong Kong to conform.

In a serious political crisis on the mainland, Hong Kong opinion will therefore be torn between rival arguments: whether to keep quiet or to claim greater autonomy. It may also be subjected to rival pressures from competing interests on the mainland, whether national or provincial.

The more cheerful (and still perhaps more likely) scenario is that Chinese political culture will evolve in a more open direction—one hesitates to use the word democratic—becoming more radical and therefore more willing to tolerate a substantial degree of political heterodoxy in Hong Kong.

If either possibility is to be discussed seriously now, it is necessary to do what everyone in Hong Kong hates—making a serious attempt to predict what may happen in mainland politics.

Almost without exception since 1949 China has managed to convey the impression of stability even when on the verge of great instability. And in more recent years many outsiders, particularly those in foreign business and diplomacy, have acquired a vested interest in asserting that the Chinese system is stable and will not change.

It is true that a less isolated, much less revolutionary, China is probably more stable than in the past. Yet by refusing to discuss the possibility of another upheaval, are we really saying that the Chinese Communist Party has found the secret which eluded the Soviet Union and Eastern Europe? And in a world where change of all kinds, political, economic and social, is taking place at ever-increasing speed, how long can Jiang Zemin and his 'third generation' of leaders keep their hand on the brakes?

At the moment China maintains an uneasy balance both in its economic and political spheres. It is a country with a fundamentally strong and productive economy yet this is offset by huge infrastructural deficiencies, widening income disparities, deterioration of the urban fabric, the dilemma of state-owned industries, and—probably the most significant factor in the long run—a rapid worsening of the environment.

Politically, China also displays some strengths. The Communist Party has re-invented itself as the guarantor of entrepreneurial activity, and as the vehicle for personal advancement. It has successfully exploited symbols of cultural and national unity.

Despite growing provincial assertiveness, the Party backed by a strong state and military apparatus still exerts far more control than generally realised. Yet this too is offset by the loss of a unifying ideology, by pervasive corruption, by generational tensions particularly with those who have been educated abroad, and above all by a general sense that it cannot go on like this for ever. It is hard to believe that the Chinese 'system' which forms one part of the 'two systems' with Hong Kong will not be very different from today in ten years time—the question is how different?

THE NEXT DECADE

In Hong Kong this brings us to the critical year of 2007 when, according to the Basic Law, there will be an opportunity to consider how to move towards what is described as the 'ultimate goal' of 'universal suffrage'. Next month's voting, however defective the current franchise, is being held within this time-frame of progressive development through subsequent elections to the point where the ultimate goal may be considered. It is a powerful inducement to the Democratic party and its allies to put up with the system as currently weighted against them, and work for improvement from within.

Chief Executive Tung has carefully refrained so far from making any commitment to press eventually for a wholly elected Legislative Council. The Chief Secretary Anson Chan has spoken more positively—but her relations with Mr Tung may not survive that long. The wording of the Basic Law suggests that

there must be some improvement after 2007, but that it need only be very gradual.

Hong Kong society too will undergo many changes in this period. It would be surprising if these were less than the changes it has undergone in the past decade. The bulk of Hong Kong opinion might be expected to identify increasingly with the mainland as long as there are no great upheavals there: there will certainly be a greater sense of cultural belonging. Yet it will remain important—and for a minority of Hong Kongers essential—to maintain a distinct identity both socially and politically.

Furthermore, if an administration led by Mr Tung or his successor fails to meet expectations, then such failure is likely to be blamed before long on Beijing. Any serious impact upon the Hong Kong economy of the Asian crisis—such as job loss, inflation, and widening income disparities—will also intensify social discontent.

To conclude, the pace of change in Hong Kong will depend crucially on that of China and those concerned with Hong Kong's future should be making every effort to understand where China is likely to be heading. Significant social change in Hong Kong, and perhaps social conflict, is also an important factor to be considered when looking ahead.

However none of these uncertainties should absolve the outside world from taking a lively and explicit interest in how Hong Kong develops. Britain in particular, for reasons of history and conscience, owes it to Hong Kong not to forget.

Article 28

The World & I, February 1998

ANALYSIS

How Hong Kong May Vitalize China

by Paul Murphy

Hong Kong is somewhat like a life preserver for the People's Republic of China—whose economy is in some ways ailing, contrary to popular perception.

From providing a prodigious bailout for restructuring China's bloated state sector to making available a deep pool of talent to sate the mainland's ravenous appetite for infrastructure experts to stemming Beijing's alarming brain drain, the former British colony is proving to be a godsend to China.

Illustrative of the brain drain is Gao Xiangzhu, who, back in 1993, was a laser science lecturer at one of Beijing's main colleges. In common with teachers across China, his salary was tiny.

To supplement his income, he would pedal across the city on his Red Flag bicycle, visiting the homes of foreign expatriates to give tutorials in Mandarin. Every academic in his college was moonlighting. One of his colleagues, a mathematics professor, boosted his bank balance as a street-side pancake vendor.

But Gao was accepted for a postdoctoral course in computing at an Australian university and became part of a brain drain of talent from China over the last two decades. The favored place for further study is the United States, and even the progeny of Beijing's top leaders attend colleges there. A large proportion who leave never come back.

China is a society of paradoxes. On the one hand, as the world's largest developing country, there is still much rural poverty, with peculiar statistics such as tens of millions of Chinese who live in caves. On the other hand, it has a history of technological invention—from the Great Wall to the creation of gunpowder to the damming of the Yangtze, the world's third-largest river, a project that began in October.

The country's president Jiang Zemin, himself an engineer by profession, often talks about his technological vision for China, which is promoting the idea of sending its first astronaut into space early next century. It is forging ahead in many

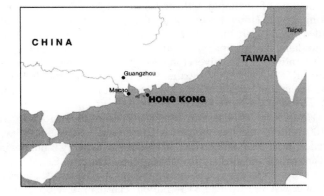

areas, from successful satellite launches to an Asia-Pacific fiber-optic network currently in progress.

But technology is also crucial for another reason. When Gao was preparing to fly to Sydney, Australia, at the end of 1993, the buzzword in Beijing was *xia hai*, or "leap into the sea"—taking the risk of going into business. The removal of the "iron rice bowl" has resulted in millions of Chinese being laid off from unprofitable state-owned firms.

Now the key phrase is *xia gang*, which was originally a military term for going off duty but now refers to being unemployed.

HONG KONG: PILLAR OF FINANCE

Beijing's political leadership believes that technology holds the answer to saving the country's growing army of xia gang. And since Hong Kong's return to Chinese sovereignty on July 1, the former British territory, with its 6.5 million people, has been regarded as an important pillar in building this technological dream.

China aims to restructure 150,000 state-owned enterprises, and financial experts have put the price tag at $389 billion. Hong

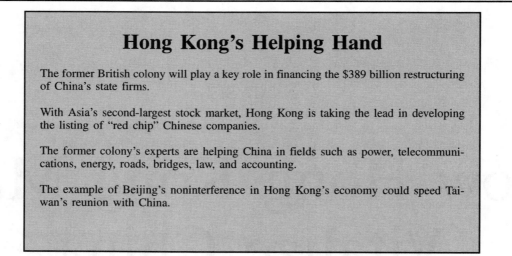

Hong Kong's Helping Hand

The former British colony will play a key role in financing the $389 billion restructuring of China's state firms.

With Asia's second-largest stock market, Hong Kong is taking the lead in developing the listing of "red chip" Chinese companies.

The former colony's experts are helping China in fields such as power, telecommunications, energy, roads, bridges, law, and accounting.

The example of Beijing's noninterference in Hong Kong's economy could speed Taiwan's reunion with China.

Kong, being a world leader in finance and closely bound up with the mainland, is in the best position to help.

Scores of examples illustrate the close mainland–Hong Kong bond. Hong Kong companies, for instance, have provided nearly half the contracts to the fledgling mainland satellite-launch company, China Great Wall Industrial Corporation. So far, five Hong Kong satellites have been put into orbit by the company, the most recent being the Ap Star-2R Telecommunications satellite, successfully placed into orbit by a Long March 3b rocket on October 17.

Hong Kong's total investment in China is well in excess of $100 billion, and this process is fast-growing. The close cooperation was exemplified when many of the territory's billionaire businessmen attended a post-handover conference in Beijing. The main item on the agenda: how Hong Kong, whose gross domestic product last year totaled $154 billion, can help develop China's economy.

While computer factories are rising above China's hand-tilled rice paddies—China has become Asia's largest market for personal computers—the mainland still suffers from a lack of first-rate computer engineers with the experience to place the country in a cutting-edge position to compete with places like Singapore, where electronics accounts for 70 percent of non-oil exports. The exodus of talented figures such as Gao hasn't helped.

Tung Chee-hwa, Hong Kong's chief executive, has pledged to fully develop the territory's own high-technology capabilities. The creation of a science park is one major plan, he said in his maiden speech, delivered 100 days after the British colony of Hong Kong became the first special administrative region (SAR) within China on July 1.

Predicting that the Asian market outside Japan for communications technology and services will grow to $1 trillion by 2010, five times the 1995 level, Tung said information technology is the tool that will shape the twenty-first century. He pledged to make Hong Kong a world leader in the field. Help will come, he said, from Hongkong Telecom, one of the world's most advanced telecommunications companies.

"There's no question that China would like to develop high-tech industries and is interested in technology transfer," said Frank Martin, president of the American Chamber of Commerce in Hong Kong. "The SAR government appears to be heading in the right direction in developing research and R&D capability. And that's going to help put China on the right track."

AREA'S HIGH-POWERED UNIVERSITIES

Hong Kong's seven major universities will also play a central role in promoting the flow of ideas and expertise to China. The mainland's key universities have all forged close cooperative links with them in scientific research.

Prof. Tam Sheung-wai, president of the Open University of Hong Kong, sees his institution as a gateway of ideas to China, noting that it has many students from all over the mainland.

King Cheng, spokesman for the Hong Kong University of Science and Technology, which is also noted for its high proportion of mainland Chinese students, said: "We have identified high inter-areas to initially help develop China. These include construction and structural engineering, electronic packaging and assembly, language and speech technology, structural science and technology, and transportation systems."

In November the university signed an agreement to help develop a "Silicon Valley" in Guangdong, the wealthy south China province adjacent to Hong Kong.

Nothing will be achieved without political stability, but the Hong Kong–China marriage so far looks like a success story. The reason is the pragmatism of the "one country, two systems" philosophy conceived by Deng Xiaoping, China's paramount leader, who died a few months before the handover.

There are, however, still many who are wary of China's takeover of Hong Kong. They point to Beijing's tightening of the screws on political freedoms as foreshadowing a clampdown on business freedoms, as well.

For instance, Hong Kong has set up a Beijing-approved chief executive and provisional legislature. The legislature, in turn, has adopted rules for May's legislative council elections—the first vote under Chinese auspices—that critics say severely curtail democracy.

Pedal power. Bicycles remain a primary mode of transport in China, including the capital of Beijing (above).

Under the rules, only 20 of the 60 seats will be decided by universal suffrage. Thirty of the council members will be elected by industry groups, which are expected to vote pro-China so as not to rock the business boat. Before the handover, these 30 seats were voted for by 2.7 million people. Only about 250,000 will be eligible to vote this time. The final 10 seats will be decided by an 800-member electoral college that is expected to be mostly pro-Beijing.

Martin Lee, leader of Hong Kong's powerful Democratic Party, has charged that the rules are designed to squeeze out his party's influence.

Moreover, Tung has imposed limits on the formation of political parties and their right to protest. He has frozen a gaggle of labor laws, weakening trade unions.

FROM CROWN COLONY TO COMMUNIST DEPENDENCY

Contrary to many media predictions, in the months since the handover, there has been no attempt to pluck the goose that lays the golden egg. Life goes on as it did. Crown mailboxes may have been painted green when before they were red, but coins bearing the head of the British queen still circulate. The main difference is that a British governor has been replaced by Tung, the locally appointed Chinese governor who is a billionaire shipping magnate.

Jiang's pledge, given at the handover ceremony, that Hong Kong's people would enjoy autonomy and no infringement of their economic liberties under the Basic Law that operates until 2047 has been honored so far in the opinion of many.

Hong Kong has always been an important bridge linking China to the outside world. The path ahead, most experts agree, will feature even closer integration between the two economies than already exists.

The mingling process is well advanced, with Hong Kong relying upon the mainland for most of its water and food. Ninety percent of the SAR's manufacturing activities have been relocated to the mainland, where Hong Kong businessmen own 25,000 factories employing four million people.

"Culturally, there's a natural affinity between Hong Kong and China, particularly in southern China," noted Michael Leary, vice president of the Hong Kong division of the New York-based investment banking company Lehman Brothers. "The two have already been developing a close relationship over many years, and future trade growth hangs on that relationship."

As the financial outlook in Southeast Asia turned somber in October, Hong Kong's Hang Seng stock market suffered a temporary setback at a time when the island's property prices were tumbling. But the International Monetary Fund on November 7 released a positive assessment of Hong Kong, stressing that the SAR's economic fundamentals remain strong.

Hong Kong is economically a world away from the crisis-hit Southeast and Northeast Asian states.

Booming: Hong Kong, whose downtown area is shown here, is a world-class metropolis that is also a first-rank financial powerhouse. Moreover, it has a stellar university system.

(PAUL MURPHY)

HONG KONG IN THE DRIVER'S SEAT?

Many in the West had been incredulous over the wedding between Hong Kong—recently crowned by the Heritage Foundation as the world's freest economy—and the world's last major communist nation. But China's leaders met in Beijing in October for the fifteenth National People's Congress, which urged a rapid, radical reversal from old ways to new ones.

Under this new order, Hong Kong in many cases is in the driver's seat. For example, the former colony's new $20 billion airport, due to open in April, will manage air-traffic control for the entire Pearl River delta region of south China, covering five airports.

With Asia's second-largest stock market, Hong Kong is also playing a key role in developing the listing of Chinese state companies. There has been massive interest in Hong Kong in "red chip" shares—locally listed companies backed by mainland Chinese parent firms. Citi Pacific is the most prominent of the "red chips" and China Telecom the newest.

International bankers see this new form of "red capitalism" as providing a big potential market for them, with benefits from exposure to China's fast economic growth.

Hong Kong's most direct input into China will undoubtedly be in the service sector, which now constitutes 83 percent of the SAR's GDP. The sector ranges from banking and accounting to insurance and legal services.

With millions of Chinese losing their jobs, Beijing has signaled that priority should be given to the service sector, especially technology-intensive areas. But it badly needs an input of knowledge skills, and Hong Kong can provide this, said Terence Cuddyre, senior vice president and country manager of the Bank of America in Hong Kong, which has become a growing presence in investment projects in China.

"In service businesses, there are clearly a number of ways Hong Kong will assist in China's development, apart from provision of expertise," said Cuddyre. "Hong Kong plays a critical role in China's insatiable appetite for infrastructure development.

"In fields such as power, telecom, energy, roads, bridges," he continued, "there's a great deal of work to be done, and Hong Kong can provide leadership and growth for all that. Hong Kong can also provide leadership in developing China's legal and accounting systems."

EFFECT ON TAIWAN

Most important, however, China hopes that Hong Kong could smooth the way for the economic and political prize of Taiwan to be reunited with the mainland. Observers say that, if Beijing scrupulously observes the Basic Law and refrains from interfering in Hong Kong's economy, suspicious Taiwan will be mollified.

Beijing has offered Taipei "a high level of autonomy," its own administrative and legislative powers, and an independent judiciary—the same setup established in Hong Kong. But the offer goes further: Taipei would be allowed to run its own military, keeping its current forces.

Beijing has pledged that the People's Liberation Army (PLA) would not be dispatched to Taiwan—in contrast to Hong Kong, where the PLA occupied the former British garrisons after the handover.

City-state Macao, in south China, ruled by Portugal since the sixteenth century, returns to the mainland's fold on December 20, 1999, when it will become the second special administrative region. Deng's concept of "one country, two systems" was not originally developed for Hong Kong or Macao but for Taiwan.

When Taipei rejected the SAR model, Deng proposed it to then British Prime Minister Margaret Thatcher, who lauded the principle as "ingenious" when the Joint Declaration was signed in 1984.

As Leary noted, "If you look at the relationship of China with Taiwan, the biggest issue is not politics but the increasing access to Taiwan of trade through China's ports. The 'one country, two systems' approach in Hong Kong is being watched very closely all over the world, and the experience that Hong Kong has had since July 1 has communicated a positive signal to Taiwan as much as it has to the rest of the world."

The stakes are high, and China has many reasons for ensuring that Hong Kong remains on a pedestal as a model for "one country, two systems."

Paul Murphy, based in Hong Kong, is a writer who has traveled extensively in Asia.

Credits

Page 96 Article 1. Reprinted with permission from *Foreign Policy,* Spring 1998. © 1998 by the Carngie Endowment for International Peace.

Page 102 Article 2. This article appeared in *The World & I,* October 1998. Reprinted with permission from *The World & I,* a publication of The Washington Times Corporation. © 1998.

Page 105 Article 3. Reprinted by permission from *Far Eastern Economic Review,* July 23, 1998. © 1998 by the Review Publishing Company, Ltd.

Page 108 Article 4. Reprinted by permission from *Far Eastern Economic Review,* August 20, 1998. © 1998 by the Review Publishing Company, Ltd.

Page 113 Article 5. © 1998, The Washington Post. Reprinted by permission.

Page 115 Article 6. Reprinted with permission from *Current History* magazine, September 1998. © 1998, Current History, Inc.

Page 119 Article 7. From *The New York Times,* July 28, 1998. © 1998 by The New York Times Company. Reprinted by permission.

Page 121 Article 8. From *The American Enterprise,* July/August 1998. Adapted from *Big Dragon* by Daniel Burstein and Arne de Keijzer. © 1998 by Simon & Schuster, Inc.

Page 127 Article 9. This article appeared in *The World & I,* October 1998. Reprinted with permission from *The World & I,* a publication of The Washington Times Corporation. © 1998.

Page 130 Article 10. © 1998 by The Economist, Ltd. Distributed by The New York Times Special Features.

Page 135 Article 11. © 1998 by the Society for the Advancement of Education. Reprinted by permission.

Page 138 Article 12. From *Environment,* September 1998, pp. 10-13, 33-38. Reprinted with permission of the Helen Dwight Reid Educational Foundation. Published by Heldref Publications, 1319 Eighteenth St., NW, Washington, DC 20036-1802. © 1998.

Page 144 Article 13. Alexander Kuo, "Breaking the Wall," *Harvard International Review,* Summer 1998, Vol. 20 (3), pp. 28@ndash@;31.

Page 148 Article 14. From *The American Enterprise,* July/August 1998, pp. 54@ndash@;56. © 1998 by The American Enterprise.

Page 150 Article 15. Reprinted by permission from *Far Eastern Economic Review,* May 7, 1998. © 1998 by the Review Publishing Company, Ltd.

Page 153 Article 16. © 1998 by The Washington Post. Reprinted by permission.

Page 156 Article 17. © 1998 by The Economist, Ltd. Distributed by The New York Times Special Features.

Page 159 Article 18. George Koo, "The Real China," *Harvard International Review,* Summer 1998, Vol. 20 (3), pp. 68–71.

Page 163 Article 19. Reprinted with permission from *Current History* magazine, September 1998. © 1998, Current History, Inc.

Page 168 Article 20. © 1998 by The Washington Post. Reprinted by permission.

Page 171 Article 21. Reprinted with permission of *Archaeology* magazine, Vol. 29, No. 5, September/October 1996. © 1996 by the Archaeological Institute of America.

Page 175 Article 22. This article appeared in *The World & I,* October 1989. Reprinted with permission from *The World & I,* a publication of The Washington Times Corporation. © 1989.

Page 179 Article 23. Reprinted by permission of *Sinorama Magazine.*

Page 181 Article 24. © 1998 by The Economist, Ltd. Distributed by The New York Times Special Features.

Page 188 Article 25. Reprinted by permission from *Far Eastern Economic Review,* October 15, 1998. © 1998 by the Review Publishing Company, Ltd.

Page 191 Article 26. Reprinted by permission from *Far Eastern Economic Review,* June 11, 1998. © 1998 by the Review Publishing Company, Ltd.

Page 194 Article 27. © 1998 by The Royal Institute of International Affairs. Reprinted by permission.

Page 197 Article 28. This article appeared in *The World & I,* February 1998. Reprinted with permission from *The World & I,* a publication of The Washington Times Corporation. © 1998.

Sources for Statistical Reports

U.S. State Department, *Background Notes* (1998).

C.I.A. *World Factbook* (1997–1998).

World Bank, *World Development Report* (1998).

UN *Population and Vital Statistics Report* (January 1998).

World Statistics in Brief (1998).

The Statesman's Yearbook (1998–1999).

Population Reference Bureau, *World Population Data Sheet* (1998).

World Almanac (1998).

Glossary of Terms and Abbreviations

Ancestor Worship   Ancient religious practices still followed in Taiwan, Hong Kong, and the People's Republic of China. Ancestor worship is based on the belief that the living can communicate with the dead and that the dead spirits to whom sacrifices are ritually made can bring about a better life for the living.

Brain Drain   A migration of professional people (such as scientists, professors, and physicians) from one country to another, usually in search of higher salaries or better living conditions.

Buddhism   A religion of East and Central Asia founded on the teachings of Siddhartha Guatama (the Buddha). Its followers believe that suffering is inherent in life and that one can be liberated from it by mental and moral self-purification.

Capitalist   A person who has capital invested in business, or someone who favors an economic system characterized by private or corporate ownership of capital goods.

Chinese Communist Party (CCP)   Founded in 1921 by a small Marxist study group, its members initially worked with the Kuomintang under Chiang Kai-shek to unify China and, later, to fight off Japanese invaders. Despite Chiang's repeated efforts to destroy the CCP, it eventually ousted the KMT and took control of the Chinese mainland in 1949.

Cold War   A conflict carried on without overt military action and without breaking off diplomatic relations.

Communism   Theoretically, a system in which most goods are collectively owned and are available to all as needed; in reality, a system of government in which a single authoritarian party controls the political, legal, educational, and economic systems, supposedly in order to establish a more egalitarian society.

Confucianism   Often referred to as a religion, actually a system of ethics for governing human relationships and for ruling. It was established during the fifth century B.C. by the Chinese philosopher Confucius.

Contract Responsibility System   A system of rural production in which the land is contracted by the village to individual peasant households. These households are then responsible for managing the production on their contracted land and, after fulfilling their production contracts with the state, are free to use what they produce or to sell it and pocket the proceeds. Such a system has been in place in China since the late 1970s and has replaced the communes established during the Maoist era.

Cultural Revolution   Formally, the Great Proletarian Cultural Revolution. In an attempt to rid China of its repressive bureaucracy and to restore a revolutionary spirit to the Chinese people, Mao Zedong (Tse-tung) called on the youth of China to "challenge authority" and "make revolution" by rooting out the "reactionary" elements in Chinese society. The Cultural Revolution lasted from 1966 until 1976. It seriously undermined the Chinese people's faith in the Chinese Communist Party's ability to rule and led to major setbacks in the economy.

De-Maoification   The rooting-out of the philosophies and programs of Mao Zedong in Chinese society.

Democratic Centralism   The participation of the people in discussions of policy at lower levels. Their ideas are to be passed up to the central leadership; but once the central leadership makes a decision, it is to be implemented by the people.

Exco   The Executive Council of Hong Kong, consisting of top civil servants and civilian appointees chosen to represent the community. Except in times of emergency, the governor must consult with the Exco before initiating any program.

Feudal   In Chinese Communist parlance, a patriarchal bureaucratic system in which bureaucrats administer policy on the basis of personal relationships.

Four Cardinal Principles   The Chinese Communists' term for their commitment to socialism, the leadership of the Chinese Communist Party, the dictatorship of the proletariat, and the ideologies of Karl Marx, Vladimir Lenin, and Mao Zedong.

Four Modernizations   A program of reforms begun in 1978 in China that seeks to modernize agriculture, industry, science and technology, and defense by the year 2000.

Gang of Four   The label applied to the four "radicals" or "leftists" who dominated first the cultural and then the political events during the Cultural Revolution. The four members of the Gang were Jiang Qing, Mao's wife; Zhang Chunqiao, former deputy secretary of the Shanghai municipal committee and head of its propaganda department; Yao Wenyuan, former editor-in-chief of the *Shanghai Liberation Daily*; and Wang Hongwen, a worker in a textile factory in Shanghai.

Great Leap Forward   Mao Zedong's alternative to the Soviet model of development, this was a plan calling for the establishment of communes and for an increase in industrial production in both the cities and the communes. The increased production was to come largely from greater human effort rather than from more investment or improved technology. This policy, begun in 1958, was abandoned by 1959.

Great Proletarian Cultural Revolution   See *Cultural Revolution.*

Gross Domestic Product (GDP)   A measure of the total flow of and services produced by the economy of a country over a certain period of time, normally a year. GDP equals gross national product (GNP) minus the income of the country's residents earned on investments abroad.

Guerrilla   A member of a small force of "irregular" soldiers. Generally, guerrilla forces are used against numerically and technologically superior enemies in jungles or mountainous terrain.

Han   Of "pure" Chinese extraction. Refers to the dominant ethnic group in the P.R.C.

Ideograph   A character of Chinese writing. Originally, each ideograph represented a picture and/or a sound of a word.

Islam   The religious faith founded by Muhammad in the sixth and seventh centuries A.D. Its followers believe that Allah is the sole deity and that Muhammad is his prophet.

Kuomintang (KMT)   The Chinese Nationalist Party, founded by Sun Yat-sen in 1912. Currently the ruling party on Taiwan. See also *Nationalists*.

Legco   Hong Kong's Legislative Council, which reviews policies proposed by the governor and formulates legislation.

Long March   The 1934–1935 retreat of the Chinese Communist Party, in which thousands died while journeying to the plains of Yan'an in northern China in order to escape annihilation by the KMT.

Mainlanders   Those Chinese in Taiwan who immigrated from the Chinese mainland during the flight of the Nationalist Party in 1949.

Mandarin   A northern Chinese dialect chosen by the Chinese Communist Party to be the official language of China. It is also the official language of Taiwan.

Mao Thought   In the post-1949 period, originally described as "the thoughts of Mao Zedong." Mao's "thoughts" were considered important because he took the theory of Marxism-Leninism and applied it to the concrete conditions existing in China. But since Mao's death in 1976 and the subsequent reevaluation of his policies, Mao Thought is no longer conceived of as the thoughts of Mao alone but as the "collective wisdom" of the party leadership.

May Fourth Period   A period of intellectual ferment in China, which officially began on May 4, 1919, and concerned the Versailles Peace Conference. On that day, the Chinese protested what was considered an unfair secret settlement regarding German-held territory in China. The result was what was termed a "new cultural movement," which lasted into the mid-1920s.

Nationalists   The KMT (Kuomintang) Party. The ruling party of the Republic of China, now in "exile" on Taiwan.

Newly Industrialized Country (NIC)   A term used to refer to those developing countries of the Third World that have enjoyed rapid economic growth. Most commonly applied to the East Asian economies of South Korea, Taiwan, Hong Kong, and Singapore.

Offshore Islands   The small islands in the Formosa Strait that are just a few miles off the Chinese mainland but are controlled by Taiwan, nearly 90 miles away.

Opium   A bitter, addictive drug made from the dried juice of the opium poppy.

Opium War   The 1839–1842 conflict between Britain and China, sparked by the British import of opium into China. After the British victory, Europeans were allowed into China and trading posts were established on the mainland. The Treaty of Nanking, which ended the Opium War, also gave Britain its first control over part of Hong Kong.

People's Procuracy   The investigative branch of China's legal system. It determines whether an accused person is guilty and should be brought to trial.

People's Republic of China (P.R.C.)   Established in 1949 by the Chinese Communists under the leadership of Mao Zedong after defeating Chiang Kai-shek and his Nationalist supporters.

Pinyin   A new system of spelling Chinese words and names, using the Latin alphabet of 26 letters, created by the Chinese Communist leadership.

Proletariat   The industrial working class, which for Marx was the political force that would overthrow capitalism and lead the way in the building of socialism.

Republic of China (R.O.C.)   The government established as a result of the 1911 Revolution. It was ousted by the Chinese Communist Party in 1949, when its leaders fled to Taiwan.

Second Convention of Peking   The 1898 agreement leasing the New Territories of Hong Kong to the British until 1997.

Shanghai Communique   A joint statement of the Chinese and American viewpoints on a range of issues in which each has an interest. It was signed during U.S. president Richard Nixon's historic visit to China in 1971.

Socialism   A transitional period between the fall of capitalism and the establishment of "true" communism. Socialism is characterized by the public ownership of the major means of production. Some private economic activity and private property are still allowed, but increased attention is given to a more equal distribution of wealth and income.

Special Administrative Region (SAR)   A political subdivision of the People's Republic of China that is used to describe Hong Kong's status following Chinese sovereignty in 1997. The SAR has much greater political, economic, and cultural autonomy from the central government in Beijing than do the provinces of the P.R.C.

Special Economic Zone (SEZ)   An area within China that has been allowed a great deal of freedom to experiment with different economic policies, especially efforts to attract foreign investment. Shenzhen, near Hong Kong, is the largest of China's Special Economic Zones.

Taiwanese Independence Movement   An organization of native Taiwanese who want to overthrow the Mainlander KMT government and establish an independent state of Taiwan.

Taoism   A Chinese mystical philosophy founded in the sixth century B.C. Its followers renounce the secular world and lead lives characterized by unassertiveness and simplicity.

United Nations (UN)   An international organization established on June 26, 1945, through official approval of the charter by delegates of 50 nations at a conference in San Francisco. The charter went into effect on October 24, 1945.

Yuan   Literally, "branch"; the different departments of the government of Taiwan, including the Executive, Legislative, Judicial, Control, and Examination Yuans.

Bibliography

PEOPLE'S REPUBLIC OF CHINA

Periodicals and Newspapers

The following periodicals and newspapers are excellent sources for coverage of Chinese affairs:

Asian Survey
Australian Journal of Chinese Affairs
Beijing Review
China Business Review
China Daily
China Quarterly
Far Eastern Economic Review
Foreign Broadcasts Information Service (FBIS)
The Free China Journal
Free China Review
Joint Publications Research Service (JPRS)
Journal of Asian Studies
Modern China
Pacific Affairs
South China Morning Post

General

Jung Chang, *Wild Swans: Three Daughters of China* (New York: Simon and Shuster, 1992).
A superb autobiographical/biographical account that illuminates what China was like for one family for three generations.

Kwang-chih Chang, *The Archeology of China,* 4th ed. (New Haven: Yale University Press, 1986).

_____, *Shang Civilization* (New Haven: Yale University Press, 1980).
Two works by an eminent archaeologist on the origins of Chinese civilization.

History

Patricia Buckley Ebrey, *The Cambridge Illustrated History of China* (New York: Cambridge University Press, 1996).
Beautifully illustrated book on Chinese history from the Neolithic Period through to the People's Republic of China.

John King Fairbank, *China: A New History* (Cambridge: Harvard University Press, 1992).
Examines forces in China's history that define it as a coherent culture from its earliest recorded history to the present. Examines why China, whose advanced 11th and 12th century civilization, had fallen behind other areas by the 19th century. The Chinese Communist revolution and its aftermath are reviewed.

William Hinton, *Fanshen: A Documentary of Revolution in a Chinese Village* (New York: Random House, 1968).
Based on the author's eyewitness account of the process of land reform carried out by the CCP in the north China village of Long Bow from 1947 to 1949.

Tony Saich and Hans Van de Ven, eds., *New Perspectives on the Chinese Communist Revolution* (Armonk, NY: M. E. Sharpe, Inc., 1995).
Articles provide new perspectives on the CCP's rise to power from its founding in 1921 to its victory in the civil war in 1949. Looks at how the CCP operated, the role of intellectuals and women in the Communist movement, the peasants' responses to the CCP's efforts at mobilization, and other topics related to the ultimate success of the CCP.

Edgar Snow, *Red Star over China* (New York: Grove Press, 1973).
This book, which first appeared in 1938, is a journalist's account of the months he spent with the Communists' Red Army in Yan'an in 1936, in the midst of the Chinese civil war. It is a thrilling story about the Chinese revolution in action, and includes Mao's own story (as told to Snow) of his early life and his decision to become a Communist.

Jonathan D. Spence, *The Search for Modern China* (New York: W. W. Norton & Co., 1990).
A lively and comprehensive history of China from the seventeenth century to 1989. Looks at the cyclical patterns of collapse and regeneration, revolution and consolidation, and growth and decay.

Politics, Economics, Society, and Culture

Julia F. Andrews, *Painters and Politics in the People's Republic of China, 1949–1979* (Berkeley: University of California Press, 1994).
A fascinating presentation of the relationship between politics and art from the beginning of the Communist period until the eve of major liberalization in 1979.

Ma Bo, *Blood Red Sunset* (New York: Viking, 1995).
Perhaps the most compelling autobiographical account by a Red Guard during the Cultural Revolution. Responding to Mao Zedong's call to youth to "make revolution," the author captures the intense emotions of exhilaration, fear, despair, and loneliness. Takes place in the wilds of Inner Mongolia.

Nien Cheng, *Life and Death in Shanghai* (New York: Grove Press, 1987).
A gripping autobiographical account of a woman persecuted during the Cultural Revolution because of her earlier connections with a Western company, her elitist attitudes, and her luxurious lifestyle in a period when the Chinese people thought the rich had been dispossessed.

Qing Dai, *Yangtze! Yangtze!* (Toronto: Probe International, 1994).
Collection of documents concerning the debate over building the Three Gorges Dam on the upper Yangtze River in order to harness energy for China. Among opponents are many scientists, committed Communists who argue the dam will lead to environmental disaster. The book itself was banned in China in 1989.

William Theodore De Bary, ed., *Sources of Chinese Tradition,* Vols. I and II (New York: Columbia University Press, 1960).

A compilation of the major writings (translated) of key Chinese figures, from Confucius through Mao Zedong. Gives readers an excellent understanding of intellectual roots of development of Chinese history.

William Theodore De Bary and Weiming Tu, eds., *Confucianism and Human Rights* (New York: Colombia University Press, 1998).

Articles debate whether the writings of Confucius and Mencius (a Confucian scholar) are relevant to today's human rights doctrine (as defined by the United Nations). Looks for ideas about "rights," social justice, individual autonomy, and religious freedom in Confucian doctrine, and for the roots of constitutionalism and the rule of law in China and the West.

Michael S. Duke, ed., *World of Modern Chinese Fiction: Short Stories & Novellas from the People's Republic, Taiwan & Hong Kong* (Armonk, NY: M. E. Sharpe, Inc., 1991).

Collection of short stories written by Chinese authors from China, Taiwan, and Hong Kong during the 1980s. The 25 stories are grouped by subject matter and narrative style.

B. Michael Frolic, *Mao's People: Sixteen Portraits of Life in Revolutionary China* (Cambridge: Harvard University Press, 1980).

A must read. Through composite biographies of 16 different types of people in China, the author offers a humorous but penetrating view of "unofficial" Chinese society and politics. Biographical sketches reflect political life during the Maoist era, but the book has enduring value for understanding China.

Bruce Gilley, *Tiger on the Brink: Jiang Zemin and China's New Elite* (Berkeley: University of California Press, 1998).

A lively account of the life of China's president. Reveals much about China's elite struggles and the issues with which the leadership wrestles.

David S. G. Goodman, *Beijing Street Voices: The Poetry and Politics of China's Democracy Movement* (London: Marion Boyars, 1981).

An analysis of the 1978–1979 "democracy movement" and its participants. Includes translations from wall posters posted on "democracy wall" in Beijing, the first prodemocracy movement to occur in the P.R.C.

David S. G. Goodman and Beverly Hooper, eds., *China's Quiet Revolution: New Interactions between State and Society* (New York: St. Martin's Press, 1994).

Articles examine the impact of economic reforms since early 1980s on the social structure and society generally, with focus on changes in wealth, status, power, and newly emerging social forces.

Ruth Hayhoe, ed., *Education and Modernization: The Chinese Experience* (New York: Pergamon Press, 1992).

Examines the role that education has played in China's modernization, from Confucian education in imperial China to Marxist education in the Communist period. Looks at pedagogical issues and how women and minority groups are treated in the educational system.

Liang Heng and Judith Shapiro, *Son of the Revolution* (New York: Vintage, 1984).

A gripping first-person account of the Cultural Revolution by a Red Guard. Offers insights into the madness that gripped China during the period from 1966–1976 and how the politics of the Maoist era affected individuals and families.

Alan Hunter and Kim-kwong Chan, *Protestantism in Contemporary China* (New York: Cambridge University Press, 1993).

Examines historical and political conditions that have affected the development of Protestantism in China. Chinese cultural beliefs and religious practices, which are an eclectic mix of Shamanism, Buddhism, Daoism, animism, and ancestral worship, have shaped Protestantism, as have the government's policies toward religion. Includes comparative chapter on Buddhism and Catholicism.

Linda Jakobson, *A Million Truths: A Decade in China* (New York: M. Evans & Co., 1998).

Reveals the many contradictions and complexities of Chinese society from 1987 to 1997. Covers such topics on the urban scene as journalists, the work unit, the middle class, the Tiananmen tragedy, the rise of individualism and the entrepreneurial outlook, and the demise of Confucian values.

William R. Jankowiak, *Sex, Death, and Hierarchy in a Chinese City* (New York: Columbia University Press, 1993).

Written by an anthropologist with a discerning eye, this is one of the most fascinating accounts of daily life in China. Particularly strong on rituals of death, romantic life, and the on-site mediation of disputes by strangers (e.g., with bicycle accidents).

Maria Jaschok and Suzanne Miers, eds., *Women and Chinese Patriarchy: Submission, Servitude and Escape* (New York: Zen Books, 1994).

Examines Chinese women's roles, the sale of children, prostitution, Chinese patriarchy, Christianity, and feminism, as well as social remedies and avenues of escape for women. Based on interviews with Chinese women who grew up in China, Hong Kong, Singapore, and San Francisco.

Lane Kelley and Yadong Luo, *China 2000: Emerging Business Issues* (Thousand Oaks, CA: Sage Publications, 1998).

Looks to the 21st century's emerging business issues for Chinese domestic firms and foreign firms. Examines China's emerging capital markets, foreign exchange system, taxation, and accounting issues.

Conghua Li, *China: The Consumer Revolution* (New York: Wiley, 1998).

An impressive account of China's rapidly growing consumer society. Looks at the forces that are shaping consumption, China's cultural attitudes toward consumerism, consumer preferences of various age groups, and the rapid polarization of consumer purchasing power.

Zhisui Li, *The Private Life of Chairman Mao* (New York: Random House, 1994).

A credible biography of the Chinese Communist Party's leader Mao Zedong, written by his physician, from the mid-1950s to his death in 1976. Wonderful details about Mao's daily life and his relationship to those around him.

Michael B. McElroy, Christopher P. Nielsen, and Peter Lydon, eds., *Energizing China: Reconciling Environmental Protection and Economic Growth* (Cambridge: Harvard University Press, 1998).

Research reports address the dilemmas, successes, and problems in China's efforts to reconcile environmental protection with economic development. Addresses issues such as energy and emissions, the environment and public health, the domestic context for making policy on energy, and the international dimensions of China's environmental policy.

Suzanne Ogden, *China's Unresolved Issues: Politics, Development, and Culture,* 3rd ed. (Englewood Cliffs, NJ: Prentice Hall, 1995).

A thematic and issue-oriented approach to Chinese politics. Presents the ongoing issues in Chinese politics in terms of the interaction between Chinese culture, politics/ideology, and development.

Suzanne Ogden, Kathleen Hartford, Lawrence Sullivan, and David Zweig, eds., *China's Search for Democracy: The Student and Mass Movement of 1989* (Armonk, NY: M. E. Sharpe, 1992).

A collection of wall posters, handbills, and speeches of the prodemocracy movement of 1989. These documents capture the passionate feelings of the student, intellectual, and worker participants.

James Seymour and Richard Anderson, *New Ghosts, Old Ghosts: Prisons and Labor Reform Camps in China* (Armonk, NY: M. E. Sharpe, 1998).

A look inside labor camps in China's northwestern provinces, including details about prison conditions and management, the nature of the prison population, excesses perpetrated in prisons, and the fate of released prisoners.

David Shambaugh and Richard H. Yang, *China's Military in Transition* (Oxford: Clarendon Press, 1997).

Collection of articles on China's military covers such topics as party–military relations, troop reduction, the financing of defense, military doctrine, training, and nuclear force modernization.

James and Ann Tyson, *Chinese Awakening: Life Stories from Unofficial China* (Boulder, CO: Westview Press, 1995).

Lively verbal portraits of the lives of Chinese people from diverse backgrounds (for example, "Muddy Legs: The Peasant Migrant"; "Turning Iron to Gold: The Entrepreneur"; "Bad Element: The Shanghai Cosmopolite").

Ezra F. Vogel, *One Step Ahead in China: Guangdong under Reform* (Cambridge: Harvard University Press, 1989).

A case study of Guangdong Province, which abuts the "Special Economic Zones" and Hong Kong. Demonstrates how Guangdong has raced ahead of the rest of China through economic liberalization and the problems and opportunities created by a mixed (planned and free market) economy.

United Nations Development Program, *China: Human Development Report* (New York: UNDP China Country Office, 1997).

Provides measurements of the effect of China's economic development on human capabilities to lead a decent life. Areas examined include health care, education, housing, treatment and status of women, and the environment.

Chihua Wen, *The Red Mirror: Children of China's Cultural Revolution* (Boulder, CO: Westview Press, 1995).

A former editor and reporter for New China News Agency in Beijing presents the heartrending stories of a dozen individuals who were children at the time the Cultural Revolution started. It shows how rapidly changing policies of the period shattered the lives of its participants and left them cynical adults 20 years later.

Jianying Zha, *China Pop: How Soap Operas, Tabloids, and Bestsellers Are Transforming a Culture* (New York: W. W. Norton, 1995).

A Chinese Mainlander examines the impact of television, film, weekend tabloids, and best-selling novels on today's culture. Some of the material is based on remarkably revealing interviews with some of China's leading film directors, singers, novelists, artists, and cultural moguls.

Yuezhi Zhao, *Media, Market, and Democracy in China: Between the Party Line and the Bottom Line* (Urbana: University of Illinois Press, 1998).

Raises basic question of whether the expected value of a "free press" will be realized in China if the party-controlled press is replaced by private entrepreneurs and a state-managed press is required to make a profit. Argues that a democratic press and a heavily commercialized press are not the same thing. Examines the growing autonomy of China's media.

Tibet

Robert Barnett, ed., *Resistance and Reform in Tibet* (Bloomington: Indiana University Press), 1994.

An informative and quite balanced collection of articles on the highly emotional and politicized topic of Tibet.

Melvyn C. Goldstein, *The Snow Lion and the Dragon: China, Tibet, and the Dalai Lama* (Berkeley: University of California Press, 1997).

The single best book on issues surrounding a "free" Tibet and the role of the Dalai Lama. Objective presentation of both Tibetan and Chinese viewpoints.

Melvyn C. Goldstein and Matthew T. Kapstein, eds., *Buddhism in Contemporary Tibet: Religious Revival and Cul-*

tural Identity (Hong Kong: Hong Kong University Press, 1997).

Excellent, nonpolemical collection of articles by cultural anthropologists on Buddhism in Tibet today. Studies of revival of monastic life and new Buddhist practices in the last 20 years are included.

Foreign Policy

Elizabeth Economy and Michel Oksenberg, *China Joins the World: Progress and Prospects* (New York: Council on Foreign Relations, 1999).

An outstanding collection of essays on where China fits into the international institutional structure in such matters as arms control, human rights, trade and investment, energy, environmental protection, and the information revolution.

Harry Harding, *A Fragile Relationship: The United States and China since 1972* (Washington, DC: The Brookings Institution, 1992).

Traces U.S.–China relations from President Richard Nixon's historic visit to China in 1972 to the 1990s. Takes a U.S. perspective to interweave commentary on issues of U.S.–China relations with the corollary issue of U.S.–Taiwan relations.

Samuel S. Kim, ed., *China and the World*, 4th ed., (Boulder, CO: Westview, 1998).

Examines theory and practice of Chinese foreign policy with the United States, Russia, Japan, Europe, and the developing world. Looks at such issues as the use of force, China's growing interdependence with other countries, human rights, the environment, and China's relationship with multilateral economic institutions.

Richard Madsen, *China and the American Dream: A Moral Inquiry* (Berkeley: University of California Press, 1995).

Looks at the emotional and unpredictable relationship that the United States has had with China from the nineteenth century to the present.

James Mann, *About Face: A History of America's Curious Relationship with China, from Nixon to Clinton* (New York: Alfred A. Knopf, 1999).

A journalist's account of the history of U.S.–China relations since Nixon. Through examination of newly uncovered government documents and interviews, gives account of development of the relationship, with all its problems and promises.

Thomas Robinson and David Shambaugh, eds., *Chinese Foreign Policy: Theory and Practice* (New York: Oxford University Press, 1994).

Provides the most comprehensive study of China's foreign policy since 1949. Carefully documents the historical, cultural, domestic, perceptual, economic, ideological, geopolitical, and strategic issues influencing China's formulation of foreign policy.

Robert S. Ross, ed., *After the Cold War: Domestic Factors and U.S.–China Relations* (Armonk, NY: M. E. Sharpe, 1998).

Examines how domestic factors, such as public opinion and interest groups, affect the development of U.S.–China policy.

Robert S. Ross, *Negotiating Cooperation: The United States and China, 1969–1989* (Stanford: Stanford University Press, 1995).

The difficulties of engineering a cooperative relationship between the United Sates and China are presented from a "realist" framework that assumes that the primary concern of both sides is with national security and the "strategic balance." The Soviet threat is considered critical to Sino–American efforts to cooperate.

TAIWAN

Politics, Economics, Society, and Culture

Joel Aberbach, et al., eds., *The Role of the State in Taiwan's Development* (Armonk, NY: M. E. Sharpe, 1994).

Articles address technology, international trade, state policy toward the development of local industries, and the effect of economic development on society, including women and farmers.

Stevan Harrell and Chun-chieh Huang, eds., *Cultural Change in Postwar Taiwan* (Boulder, CO: Westview Press, 1994).

A collection of essays that analyzes the tensions in Taiwan's society as modernization erodes many of its old values and traditions.

David K. Jordan, *Gods, Ghosts, and Ancestors: The Folk Religion of a Taiwanese Village* (Berkeley: University of California Press, 1972).

A fascinating analysis of folk religion in Taiwan by an anthropologist, based on field study. Essential work for understanding how folk religion affects the everyday life of people in Taiwan.

Tse-kang Leng, *The Taiwan–China Connection: Democracy and Development across the Taiwan Straits* (Boulder: Westview Press, 1996).

A case study of Taiwan's policies toward the Chinese mainland. Includes analysis of institutional conflicts and power struggles in Taiwan over policies toward China as well as the role of the business community in developing these relations.

Robert M. Marsh, *The Great Transformation: Social Change in Taipei, Taiwan, since the 1960s* (Armonk, NY: M. E. Sharpe, 1996).

An investigation of how Taiwan's society has changed since the 1960s when its economic transformation began.

Murray Rubinstein, ed., *The Other Taiwan: 1945 to the Present* (Armonk, NY: M. E. Sharpe, 1994).

Articles focus on those groups within Taiwan whose views of Taiwan differ from those of the establishment. Critical perspectives on the "Taiwan miracle."

David Shambaug, ed., *Contemporary Taiwan* (Oxford-Clarendon Press, 1998).

Broad coverage of society, the economy, and politics in Taiwan today, including the impact of globalization and regionalization on Taiwan's technology, the impact of economic development on the environment, and Taiwan's policy toward reunification with mainland China.

Mayside H. Yang, ed., *Taiwan's Expanding Role in the International Arena* (Armonk, NY: M. E. Sharpe, 1997).

This book, edited by the director of Taiwan's main opposition party, presents the perspectives of a number of governments (including Taiwan, Australia, the United States, Hong Kong, China, and the governments of Germany and divided Korea) on Taiwan's role in the international arena.

Foreign Policy

Dennis Hickey, *United States–Taiwan Security Ties: From Cold War to Beyond Containment* (Westport, CT: Praeger, 1994).

Examines U.S.–Taiwan security ties from the cold war to the present and what Taiwan is doing to ensure its own military preparedness. Also assesses the P.R.C.'s security threat to Taiwan and under what conditions P.R.C. might use force to resolve the unification issue.

Robert G. Sutter and William R. Johnson, *Taiwan in World Affairs* (Boulder, CO: Westview Press, 1994).

Articles give comprehensive coverage of Taiwan's involvement in foreign affairs. Topics covered include Taiwan's role in the economic development of East Asia, Taiwan in the international arms market, Taiwan's efforts to gain legitimacy as an international actor, Taiwan's relations with the P.R.C., and the implications of Taiwan's international role for U.S. foreign policy.

HONG KONG

Periodicals and Newspapers

The following periodicals and newspapers are excellent sources for coverage in Hong Kong:

Hong Kong Commercial Daily
Hong Kong News Online
Hong Kong Standard
Ta Kung Pao

Politics, Economics, Society, and Culture

Ming K. Chan, ed., *Precarious Balance: Hong Kong between China and Britain, 1842–1992* (Armonk, NY: M. E. Sharpe, 1994).

Collection of essays concerning Hong Kong's efforts to balance its relations with China and Great Britain from the time it became a British colony in 1842 to 1992. Includes topics such as Chinese nationalism in Hong Kong, Hong Kong as a point of contention between China and Britain, and race-based discriminatory legislation in Hong Kong.

Ming K. Chan and Gerard A. Postiglione, *The Hong Kong Reader: Passage to Chinese Sovereignty* (Armonk, NY: M. E. Sharpe, 1996).

A first-rate collection of articles about the issues facing Hong Kong during the transition to Chinese rule. Also examines how the issues may be addressed after July 1, 1997, as well.

Joseph Y. L. Cheng, ed., *The Other Hong Kong Report, 1997* (Hong Kong: Hong Kong University Press, 1997).

An annual publication that takes a different perspective from the official governmental annual report on Hong Kong. Timely articles on Hong Kong's legal system, human rights, the new middle class, the environment, housing policy, and so on.

Robert Cottrell, *The End of Hong Kong: The Secret Diplomacy of Imperial Retreat* (London: John Murray, 1993).

Exposes the secret diplomacy that led to the signing of the "Joint Declaration on Question of Hong Kong" in 1984, the agreement which ended 150 years of British colonial rule over Hong Kong. Thesis is that Britain was reluctant to introduce democracy into Hong Kong before this point because it thought it would ruin Hong Kong's economy and lead to social and political instability. Notes support of this position by many members of Hong Kong political elite.

Michael J. Enright, Edith E. Scott, and David Dodwell, *The Hong Kong Advantage* (Oxford: Oxford University Press, 1997).

Examines the special relationship between the growth of Hong Kong's and mainland China's economies, such topics as the role of the overseas Chinese community in Hong Kong and the competition Hong Kong faces from Taipei, Singapore, Seoul, and Sydney as well as from such up-and-coming Chinese cities as Shanghai.

C. K. Lau, *Hong Kong's Colonial Legacy: A Hong Kong Chinese's View of the British Heritage* (Hong Kong: Chinese University Press, 1997).

Engaging overview of the British roots of today's Hong Kong. Special attention to such problems as the "identity" of Hong Kong people as British or Chinese, the problems in speaking English, English common law in a Chinese setting, and the "strictly controlled" but rowdy Hong Kong "free press."

Benjamin K. P. Leung, ed., *Social Issues in Hong Kong* (New York: Oxford University Press, 1990).

Collection of essays on select issues in Hong Kong such as aging, poverty, women, pornography, and mental illness.

Jan Morris, *Hong Kong: Epilogue to an Empire* (New York: Vintage, 1997).

Witty and detailed first-hand portrait of Hong Kong by one of its long-term residents. Gives the reader the sense of actually being on the scene in a vibrant Hong Kong.

Christopher Patten, *East and West: China, Power, and the Future of Asia* (New York: Random House), 1998.

The controversial last governor of Hong Kong gives a lively insider's view of the British colony in the last 5 years before it was returned to China's sovereignty. Focuses on

China's refusal to radically change Hong Kong's political processes on the eve of the British exit. Argues against the idea that "Asian values" are opposed to democratic governance, and suggests that "Western values" have already been realized in Hong Kong.

Mark Roberti, *The Fall of Hong Kong: China's Triumph and Britain's Betrayal* (New York: John Wiley & Sons, Inc., 1994).

A fast-paced, drama-filled account of the decisions Britain and China made about Hong Kong's fate since the early 1980s. Based on interviews with 150 key players in the secret negotiations between China and Great Britain. Raises questions as to whether Britain betrayed its colonial subjects in these agreements in order to advance its own diplomatic and commercial relations with China.

Gungwu Wang and Siu-lun Wong, eds., *Hong Kong in the Asia-Pacific Region: Rising to the New Challenge* (Hong Kong: University of Hong Kong), 1997.

Articles address issues that Hong Kong has had to tackle since it was returned to China's sovereignty in 1997, including how being part of China will affect Hong Kong's role as an international financial center, and other topics related to Hong Kong's role in the Asia-Pacific region.

Foreign Policy

Ming K. Chan, ed., *Precarious Balance: Hong Kong between China and Britain, 1842–1942* (Armonk, NY: M. E. Sharpe, 1994).

Collection of essays concerning Hong Kong's efforts to balance its relations with China and Great Britain from the time it became a British colony in 1842 to 1942.

Frank Welsh, *A Borrowed Place: The History of Hong Kong* (New York: Kodansha International, 1996).

Best single book on Hong Kong's history from the time of the British East India Company in the eighteenth century through the Opium Wars of the nineteenth century to the present.

MISCELLANEOUS

Johan Bjorksten, *Learn to Write Chinese Characters* (New Haven: Yale University Press, 1994).

A delightful introductory book for writing Chinese characters, with many anecdotes about calligraphy.

Index